ISRAEL and the
UNITED STATES

ISRAEL and the UNITED STATES

SIX DECADES OF US–ISRAELI RELATIONS

edited by

Robert O. Freedman

Routledge
Taylor & Francis Group
New York London

First published 2012 by Westview Press

Published 2018 by Routledge
605 Third Avenue, New York, NY 10017
2 Park Square, Milton Park, Abingdon, Oxon OX14 4RN

Routledge is an imprint of the Taylor & Francis Group, an informa business

Every effort has been made to secure required permissions for all text, images, maps, and other art reprinted in this volume.

Library of Congress Cataloging-in-Publication Data

Israel and the United States : six decades of US-Israeli relations / edited by Robert O. Freedman.

p.   cm.
Includes bibliographical references and index.
ISBN 978-0-8133-4494-2 (hardcover : alk. paper)—ISBN 978-0-8133-4497-3 (e-book)
1. United States—Foreign relations—Israel. 2. Israel—Foreign relations—United States. I. Freedman, Robert Owen.
E183.8.I7I83 2012
327.7305694—dc23

2011047237

ISBN 13: 978-0-8133-4494-2 (pbk)

This book is dedicated to my wife,
Sharon, a true partner for life.

Contents

Preface   *ix*

Acknowledgments   *xi*

List of Abbreviations   *xiii*

Maps   *xiv*

1 Introduction   1

   Robert O. Freedman

2 The United States and the Arab-Israeli Conflict
   from 1945 to 2000: Why the Arabists Are Wrong   22

   David Makovsky

3 George W. Bush, Barack Obama, and the Arab-Israeli
   Conflict from 2001 to 2011   36

   Robert O. Freedman

4 The Pro-Israel Lobby in the United States:
   Past, Present, and Future   79

   Dov Waxman

5 Six Decades of Public Affection: Trends in
   American Public Attitudes Toward Israel   100

   Amnon Cavari

6 Aid and Trade: Economic Relations Between
   the United States and Israel, 1948–2010   124

   Roby Nathanson and *Ron Mandelbaum*

7 Light and Shadows in US-Israeli Military Ties, 1948–2010   143

   Stuart A. Cohen

8 Apocalypse Now? The Iranian Nuclear Threat Against Israel   165

   Steven R. David

 9 American Influence on Israeli Law: Freedom of Expression   187
    Pnina Lahav

10 American Orthodox Jews and the State of Israel   215
    Steven Bayme

11 The Relationship Between American Evangelical
    Christians and the State of Israel   ✓   232
    Neil Rubin

12 The Quest for Impact: Lessons Learned from
    the American Jewish Peace Camp   257
    Mark Rosenblum and *Dan Fleshler*

Bibliography   283
Index   289
About the Contributors   303

Preface

I have been studying the Middle East, and the American role in the region, for more than forty-four years. My study of the Middle East began in February 1967 when, as a young US Army officer, I was appointed to teach in the Department of Social Sciences of the US Military Academy at West Point. There I met a number of officers who shared with me their experiences of military service in the region, which included equal doses of fascination and frustration. Several months later came the June 1967 Six-Day War, and discussion among the West Point faculty intensified as to what the proper role for the United States should be in the rapidly escalating Arab-Israeli conflict. Following completion of my army service, I participated in the Scholar-Diplomat Program of the US Department of State, where I had the opportunity not only to interact with high-ranking State Department officials, such as then US Deputy Secretary of State for Near Eastern and South Asian Affairs Alfred (Roy) Atherton, but also to read the cables coming into the Near Eastern and South Asian Bureau from diplomats in the Middle East. In subsequent years I had the opportunity to get to know and learn from a number of US State Department and National Security Council officials, such as L. Dean Brown, Hermann Eilts, Philip Habib, Hal Saunders, Richard Murphy, Robert Pelletreau, Dan Kurtzer, Dennis Ross, Bill Quandt, Sam Lewis, and Aaron David Miller. I also met and interviewed a number of Arab and Israeli leaders, such as Yasser Arafat, Mahmoud Abbas, Yitzhak Rabin, Ariel Sharon, Tsippy Livni, and Jordanian King Hussein Ibn Talal, as well as numerous Israeli, Egyptian, Jordanian, Kuwaiti, Iraqi, Syrian, Palestinian, Turkish, Saudi, and Tunisian diplomats. One issue became very clear from all of my discussions with State Department officials, Arab and Israeli leaders, and Middle Eastern diplomats: the centrality of the US-Israeli relationship as a major factor in US policy in the region.

Given this situation, I decided to organize a conference at Johns Hopkins University in October 2010 on the nature of the US-Israeli relationship. My goal was to achieve a more comprehensive understanding of the nature of the relationship. Thus, although one chapter of this book is devoted to the history of the diplomatic relationship between the United States and Israel, and another to the Iranian nuclear threat against Israel, other chapters cover areas not usually discussed in analyses of US-Israeli relations. These include the influence of the US legal system on Israel, the impact of US strategic thinking on the Israeli military, the interrelationship of the American Orthodox Jewish community and the State of Israel, evangelical Christian attitudes toward Israel, changing US public attitudes toward Israel, US-Israeli economic interactions, the nature of the pro-Israeli lobby in the United States, and the American Jewish peace movement's relationship with Israel. In addition, I have selected scholars from both the United States and Israel to contribute chapters to this book to ensure a balance of perspectives.

In sum, it is my hope that readers of this volume will come away with a fuller understanding of the dynamics of what is both a very intense and a very extensive US-Israeli relationship.

ROBERT O. FREEDMAN
Baltimore, Maryland
May 2011

Acknowledgments

There are many individuals whom I would like to thank for making this book possible. First, my thanks go to Rabbi Debbie Pine, the executive director, and Monica Davis, the office manager, of the Hillel Foundation of Johns Hopkins University, who made available the facilities of Hillel for the October 2010 conference, "Six Decades of US-Israeli Relations," on which this book is based. Second, I would like to thank Dr. Kenneth B. Moss, associate professor of modern Jewish history and director of the Leonard and Helen R. Stulman Jewish Studies Program of Johns Hopkins University, and Dr. Steven R. David, professor of political science and vice dean for undergraduate education at Johns Hopkins University, for their strong support from the beginning of this project. Third, I would like to thank the late Dr. Norman Lavy, along with Mrs. Marion Lavy, and the Leonard and Helen R. Stulman Jewish Studies Program of Johns Hopkins University for providing the funding both for the conference and for the book. Fourth, I would like to thank both the *Baltimore Jewish Times* and the Baltimore Jewish Council for their support in publicizing the conference. Fifth, I was fortunate to have two quality editors at Westview Press working with me on the project, Karl Yambert and Lindsey Zahuranec, and I would like to acknowledge their help. Sixth, the whole project would not have been possible without the outstanding assistance of Ms. Mary Otterbein, who serves as both academic coordinator of the Department of Political Science and administrator of the Leonard and Helen R. Stulman Jewish Studies Program of Johns Hopkins University. Seventh, I would like to thank Mrs. Diane Kempler for her untiring efforts in typing the book manuscript. Finally, I would like to thank my wife, Sharon, for her support for my academic efforts over forty-six years.

Abbreviations

ABM	antiballistic missile
AIPAC	American Israel Public Affairs Committee
AJC	American Jewish Committee
APN	Americans for Peace Now
APSA	American Political Science Association
AWACS	airborne warning and control system
AZEC	American Zionist Emergency Council
BARD	Binational Agricultural Research and Development Fund
BDS	boycott, divestment, and sanctions
CAMERA	Committee for Accuracy in Middle East Reporting in America
CBS	Central Bureau of Statistics
CUFI	Christians United for Israel
ESF	Economic Support Funds
FAZ	Federation of American Zionists
FMF	Foreign Military Financing
FTA	Free Trade Agreement
GATT	General Agreement on Tariffs and Trade
GDP	gross domestic product
IAEA	International Atomic Energy Agency
ICEJ	International Christian Embassy Jerusalem
IFCJ	International Fellowship of Christians and Jews
IRCG	Islamic Revolutionary Guard Corps
IDF	Israel Defense Forces
NATO	North Atlantic Treaty Organization
OECD	Organisation for Economic Co-operation and Development
PA	Palestinian Authority
PAC	political action committee
PLC	Palestinian Legislative Council
PLO	Palestinian Liberation Organization
QME	qualitative military edge
RCA	Rabbinical Council of America
RMA	revolution in military affairs
TRADOC	Training and Doctrine Command
UAV	unmanned aerial vehicle
USTR	US Trade Representative
ZOA	Zionist Organization of America

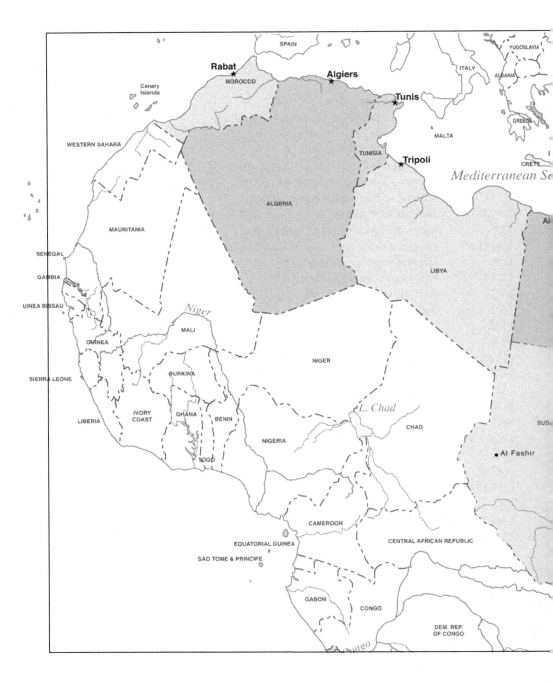

The Middle East and North Africa

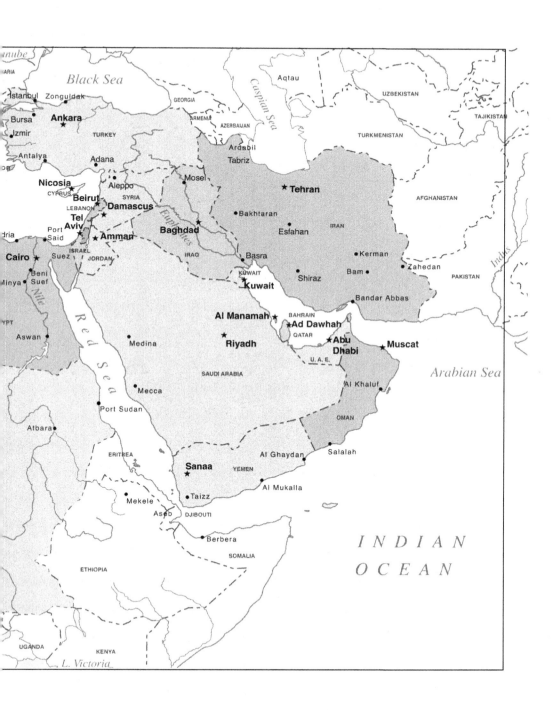

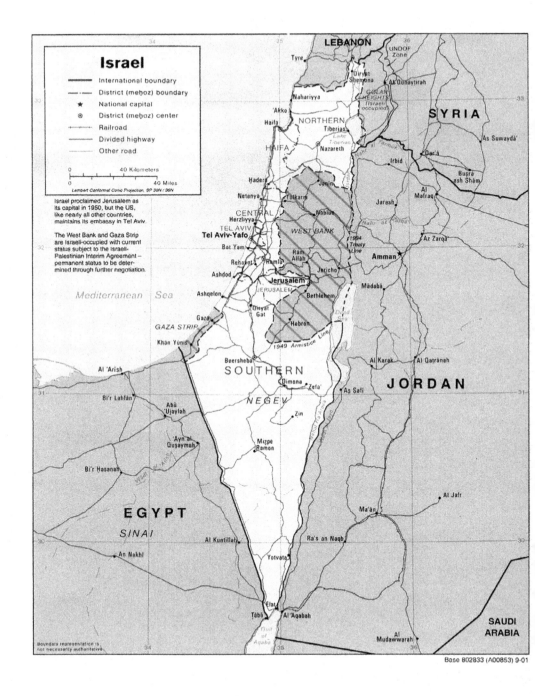

Israel

- ━━━ International boundary
- ─·─ District (meḥoz) boundary
- ★ National capital
- ◉ District (meḥoz) center
- ┼┼┼ Railroad
- ━━━ Divided highway
- ─── Other road

0   40 Kilometers

0   40 Miles

Lambert Conformal Conic Projection, SP 30N / 36N

Israel proclaimed Jerusalem as
its capital in 1950, but the US,
like nearly all other countries,
maintains its embassy in Tel Aviv.

The West Bank and Gaza Strip
are Israeli-occupied with current
status subject to the Israeli-
Palestinian Interim Agreement –
permanent status to be determined through further negotiation.

LEBANON

UNDOF Zone

Tyre

Qiryat Shemona

Az Qunaytirah

Nahariyya

GOLAN HEIGHTS (Israeli-occupied)

SYRIA

'Akko

NORTHERN

As Suwaydā'

Haifa

Tiberias

Lake Tiberias

HAIFA

Nazareth

Irbid

Darʿā

Hadera

Jenin

Al Mafraq

Busrā ash Shām

Netanya

Tulkarm

Jarash

CENTRAL

Nāblus

Herzliyya

WEST BANK

Nahr az Zarqā

TEL AVIV

Tel Aviv-Yafo

1994 Treaty Line

Az Zarqā'

Bat Yam

Rām Allāh

Amman

Rehovot

Ramla

Ashdod

Jericho

Madābā

Jerusalem

JERUSALEM

Ashqelon

Bethlehem

Mediterranean Sea

Qiryat Gat

Dead Sea

Gaza

Hebron

GAZA STRIP

1949 Armistice Line

Khān Yūnis

Beersheba

Al Karak

Al Qaṭrānah

Al ʿArīsh

Dimona

Zefa'

As Safi

JORDAN

Bi'r Laḥfān

SOUTHERN

Abū Ujaylah

NEGEV

Zin

'Ayn al Quṣaymah

Mizpe Ramon

Bi'r Hasanah

Al Jafr

Maʿān

EGYPT

SINAI

Al Kuntillah

Ra's an Naqb

An Nakhl

Yotvata

Elat

SAUDI ARABIA

Ṭābā

Al ʿAqabah

Gulf of Aqaba

Al Mudawwarah

Base 802833 (A00853) 9-01

Introduction

Robert O. Freedman

US-ISRAELI RELATIONS DISPLAY one of the most complex set of bonds between any two countries in the post–World War II world, as they comprise not only diplomatic and economic ties, but also religious (both Jewish and evangelical Christian), legal, military, and strategic ties as well as a close commonality of values, particularly democracy. In addition, both Israeli and American leaders have not hesitated to intervene in the domestic politics of the other country. These close bonds did not emerge immediately after the establishment of the state of Israel in May 1948. Indeed, relations were both cool and relatively limited in both the Truman and Eisenhower administrations. Relations then improved during the presidencies of John F. Kennedy and Lyndon Johnson but did not begin to develop the extensive ties visible today until the Nixon administration. Particularly in the military/strategic sector, relations developed after Israel aided the United States in supporting American ally Jordan when Soviet ally Syria invaded Jordan in September 1970. Then, following 9/11, when both the United States and Israel were confronting Islamic-motivated terrorism (the United States from al-Qaeda and the Taliban, and Israel from Hamas and Hizbollah) relations deepened further. This chapter is divided into two sections. The first provides a background for the reader by presenting an overview of US-Israeli relations from 1948 to 2000, giving the basic dynamics of the relationship until the George W. Bush and Barack Obama administrations, which are discussed in detail in Chapter 3. The second section of this chapter summarizes the main arguments of the book's contributors. The central goal is to enable the reader to come away with a comprehensive understanding of the US-Israeli relationship, as it has evolved since 1948.

Part One: The US-Israeli Relationship from 1948 to 2000

Security issues have become increasingly important in the Israeli-American relationship since 1948, although they did not become significant until 1970. At the time of Israel's birth in 1948, US Secretary of State George Marshall and Secretary of Defense James Forrestal saw the Jewish state as a major political and security liability. While recognizing Israel de facto against the advice of his secretaries of state and defense, President Harry Truman (1945–1953) nonetheless imposed an arms embargo on Israel—and on the Arab world—during Israel's 1948–1949 War of Independence. But Britain was arming Jordan, Egypt, and Iraq, which were among Israel's adversaries in the war, thus making the US embargo very much a one-sided policy. With the Cold War in full swing, Marshall feared driving the Arabs into the arms of the Soviet Union, while Forrestal feared that US troops—of which he had too few—would be needed to rescue the Jews of Palestine, who he felt most likely would be defeated by the invading Arab armies if a Jewish state were proclaimed. In addition, heavily influenced by the anti-Israeli position of the British, both Marshall and Forrestal saw Israel, if it survived the Arab invasion, as a likely Soviet client state in the Middle East.[1] There was also resistance in the US State and Defense Departments to de jure recognition of Israel and to a loan from the Export-Import Bank, although following the Israeli elections of January 1949, Truman granted both. Nonetheless, Truman also pressured Israel to allow the return of hundreds of thousands of Palestinian refugees from Israel's War of Independence, which Israel won thanks in part to arms from Czechoslovakia (agreed to by Moscow, which also gave Israel diplomatic support during the war), central lines of communication, divisions among the invading Arab armies, and better soldiers and officers. The Truman administration also called on Israel to cede some of the land it had captured during the war. Israel refused both US demands.

Israeli security ties with the United States would remain cool during most of the 1950s under the Eisenhower administration (1953–1961), and personal ties between the American president and Israeli Prime Minister David Ben-Gurion were chilly as well. Thus, in the so-called Alpha Plan, US Secretary of State John Foster Dulles sought, albeit unsuccessfully, to pressure Israel to give up some of the territory in its south (in the Negev region) to create a land bridge between Egypt and Jordan and strongly criticized Israel for its retaliatory strikes against Egypt and Jordan, which harbored terrorists who were attacking Israel. In addition, the main security structure for the Middle East, the Baghdad Pact, which the United States and Britain constructed in the mid-1950s, had no place for Israel. Perhaps most serious of all, the Eisenhower administration refused to sell arms to Israel even after the major Soviet-Egyptian arms deal of 1955, which provided Israel's primary Arab enemy with heavy bombers and tanks that were a strategic threat to Israel. This refusal, in part, prompted Israel to join Britain and France in the tripartite attack on Egypt in 1956, known as the Suez War, for which the United States severely condemned all three countries. Eisenhower, who as the US military hero of World War II was relatively immune to domestic pressure on foreign policy issues, also compelled Ben-Gurion to return to Egypt both the Sinai Desert and the Gaza Strip, which had been captured during the 1956 war, although the US president did support placing UN soldiers along the Egyptian-Israeli border to serve as a buffer between the two countries, and at the Straits of Tiran to protect Israeli shipping. Following the Iraqi Revolution of 1958, however, relations between the United States and Israel began to improve, as Israel's value as a stable and democratic state in an increasingly volatile Middle East began to be more greatly appreciated in Washington.[2]

It was not until the presidency of John F. Kennedy (1961–1963), however, that the United States began to sell arms to Israel, in the form of Hawk antiaircraft missiles to counter the long-range bombers the Soviet Union had supplied to Egypt. Nonetheless, there was friction between the United States and Israel during the Kennedy administration, primarily over Israel's nuclear program.[3] The presidency of Lyndon Johnson (1963–1969) had a mixed record on meeting Israel's security needs. Because the United States was badly bogged down in Vietnam, it did not respond favorably to Israeli requests for help immediately before 1967's Six-Day War, when Egypt moved troops to Israel's border, joined in an anti-Israeli alliance with Syria and Jordan, and closed the Straits of Tiran to Israeli shipping. The most the United States would do was to suggest a Straits of Tiran Users Association, an idea that generated little diplomatic support. Similarly, when the war broke out, the United States proclaimed its neutrality as a nonbelligerent, although it did serve as a buffer to protect Israel against possible Soviet action. Nonetheless, there was friction between the United States and Israel during the war when Israeli jets mistakenly attacked the USS *Liberty*, an American intelligence ship that was sailing near the coast of the Sinai. Following the war, however, there was a sharp improvement in US-Israeli relations, as Israel, which had defeated Moscow's two major Arab clients, Egypt and Syria (as well as pro-US Jordan), demonstrated its security value to the United States. It was under Johnson that the United States began to supply Israel with sophisticated fighter-bombers. In addition, unlike the Eisenhower administration following the Suez War, the Johnson administration did not demand that Israel withdraw before a peace agreement with its Arab neighbors was signed. Indeed, along with Britain and the Soviet Union, it sponsored UN Security Council Resolution 242, which in the US (and British) view, did not require Israel to give back all the land it had conquered in 1967, even for a peace treaty.[4]

It was during the presidency of Richard Nixon (1969–1974) that security co-operation between the United States and Israel reached a new high. Initially, though, there were strains in the relationship, as Nixon administration officials talked about a more "evenhanded" role for the United States in the Arab-Israeli conflict and the new US secretary of state, William Rogers, put forth a plan, which ultimately proved a nonstarter, that would have minimized Israeli terri-torial gains from the 1967 war. Rogers was more successful in the summer of 1970, when he secured a cease-fire between Israel and Soviet-backed Egypt in their fighting along the Suez Canal, which had threatened to escalate after Israeli pilots shot down five Egyptian planes piloted by Soviet airmen. However, Rogers was severely criticized by Israel for not preventing Egypt from exploiting the cease-fire to complete its deployment of surface-to-air missiles along the Suez Canal, which had the potential of providing cover for an Egyptian attack into the Sinai Desert, as indeed would happen in 1973.

As the Cold War between the United States and the Soviet Union in the Mid-dle East intensified, Israel's assistance in protecting Washington's client, Jordan, against Moscow's client, Syria, during the Palestinian uprising against Jordan's King Hussein in September 1970 set the stage for significant security cooperation between the United States and Israel, including the provision of major arms systems to Israel. During the 1973 Yom Kippur War, large shipments of US arms helped Israel repulse the attacks of Syria and Egypt and then take the offensive against both Arab countries.

Following the war, Henry Kissinger, who had become secretary of state just before the conflict (the first American Jew to hold that position), embarked on a program of "shuttle diplomacy" between Israel and Egypt, which moved the two countries from conflict toward peace (a similar effort with Syria was less successful). Although there was some friction between the United States and Israel over Kissinger's diplomacy, especially following the resignation of Nixon and the onset of the Ford administration (1974–1977)—at one point Ford and Kissinger threatened an "agonizing reappraisal" of US policy toward Israel as a means of pressuring Israeli Prime Minister Yitzhak Rabin to make more concessions—the Egyptian-Israeli peace process continued. Indeed, the signing of the Sinai II agreement between Israel and Egypt in August 1975 demonstrated a strong US commitment to the peace process. Under the agreement, American troops would occupy the Gidi and Mitla Passes in the Sinai Desert between the Egyptian and Israeli armies. The stationing of US forces, equipped with sophis-ticated radar systems, in the two mountain passes served to build confidence for both Egypt and Israel, as the United States now had the ability to warn either side if the other was maneuvering its forces for an attack. In addition, as part of the Sinai II agreement, the United States promised Israel it would not deal with the Palestine Liberation Organization (PLO) until it renounced terrorism, recognized Israel, and accepted UN Security Council Resolution 242.

Jimmy Carter's presidency (1977–1981) marked a watershed in US-Israeli relations. The somewhat naive American President initially sought to settle the Arab-Israeli conflict through a major international conference at Geneva, with the help of the Soviet Union (whose Middle East position Kissinger had severely weakened) and with the presence of "representatives of the Palestinian people." Vehement opposition by Egyptian President Anwar Sadat, who had become strongly anti-Soviet, and by Israel, which feared that PLO members would be included among the Palestinian representatives, doomed the conference before it could begin. Indeed, following the episode, Sadat chose to travel to Israel, where he began to negotiate a peace treaty with Israeli Prime Minister Menachem Begin. Although this development caught US diplomats by surprise and Carter was somewhat discomfited, US help was needed when Israeli-Egyptian negotiations bogged down. In September 1978 Carter convened a three-way summit with Sadat and Begin at the presidential retreat at Camp David, Maryland. After thirteen days of often difficult negotiations and considerable friction between Carter and Begin, the principles of a peace agreement were worked out, setting the stage for the Egyptian-Israeli peace treaty of March 1979. As part of the peace agreement, the United States pledged to give Israel $3 billion and Egypt $2.2 billion, which became an annual allocation, and the United States promised to maintain its position in the Sinai passes as part of what would become a multinational force. Nonetheless, Carter remained highly critical of Begin's settlement-building policy in the Israeli-occupied Gaza Strip and West Bank, although the Iranian Revolution in 1979 and the subsequent hostage crisis diverted Carter's attention from the Arab-Israeli conflict in the last two years of his administration.

Security relations between the United States and Israel deepened further during the presidency of Ronald Reagan (1981–1989), although not without difficulties, as in the case of the American sale of AWACS (airborne warning and control system) to Saudi Arabia, which Israel strongly opposed, and during Israel's invasion and occupation of Lebanon in 1982. Soon after taking office, Reagan sought, albeit unsuccessfully, to create an alignment of Israel and Arab states such as Egypt, Jordan, and Saudi Arabia in response to the Soviet occupation of Afghanistan. Indeed, Reagan embraced Israel as a strategic partner in his struggle with the Soviet Union and supported a number of Israeli goals vis-à-vis the USSR, including the exodus of Soviet Jews to Israel and the neutralization of the USSR as a primary backer of the Arabs in their conflict with Israel. These goals would be fulfilled in the last two years of the Reagan administration after Mikhail Gorbachev came to power in Moscow.[5]

In addition, although Washington and Jerusalem were sometimes at odds during Israel's invasion of Lebanon, it appears likely that the United States gave Israel a yellow light, if not a green light, to mount the invasion to destroy the state-within-a-state that the PLO, a Soviet ally, had established in southern

Lebanon. Israel and the United States did clash, however, over Reagan's plan for solving the Arab-Israeli conflict, which he issued in the aftermath of the Lebanese invasion.[6] The plan included a freeze on Israeli settlement building, something Begin strongly opposed. Later in the Reagan administration, Israel and the United States cooperated in the clandestine so-called Iran-Contra affair, in which Israel served as a conduit of arms to Iran to help in its war with Iraq, in return for the freeing of US hostages in Lebanon, the proceeds of the arms sales being used to arm the Reagan-backed Contras in Nicaragua. In addition, in November 1988, responding primarily to American pressure, PLO leader Yasser Arafat agreed to accept UN Security Council Resolution 242, to renounce terrorism, and to recognize Israel.

US-Israeli relations chilled somewhat during the presidency of George H. W. Bush (1989–1993). Bush's secretary of state, James Baker, and Israeli Prime Minister Yitzhak Shamir clashed over Israel's building of settlements in the West Bank and over who should be invited to the post–Gulf War US-sponsored Madrid conference in October 1991, whose purpose was to promote the Arab-Israeli peace process. Bush himself clashed with Shamir by withholding loan guarantees Israel needed to resettle the hundreds of thousands of Soviet Jews, many with higher education and scientific and technological expertise, who were pouring into Israel in the late 1980s and early 1990s. Bush withheld these guarantees until the Israeli government stopped building the settlements. Relations improved, however, when Yitzhak Rabin became Israeli prime minister in July 1992 and announced that Israel would stop building new settlements in the West Bank and would construct housing only in existing settlements. Following the Rabin announcement, Bush authorized the loan guarantees.[7]

Despite the often poor personal chemistry between Shamir and Bush, the Israeli prime minister did agree to a US request to refrain from retaliating against Iraqi missile attacks during the Gulf War, so as to enable the United States to maintain its Arab coalition fighting Iraq. As a gesture of support for Israel, the United States placed Patriot missiles in Israel, manned by US troops, to engage the Iraqi Scud missiles fired against Israel during the war. Although the Patriot missiles proved to be ineffective, the symbolism of the US action—deploying its troops to help protect Israel—was the key factor.

US-Israeli Relations Under Bill Clinton

When Bill Clinton took office as US president in January 1993, the Madrid peace process, begun by his predecessor, George H. W. Bush, had already begun to stagnate, primarily over the Palestinian issue, although there had been some progress on multilateral issues, especially economic cooperation. The peace process, however, was to receive a major boost when Israeli Prime Minister

Rabin supported back-channel talks with the PLO, and the talks were crowned with success in September 1993 when the Oslo I agreement, called the Declaration of Principles, was signed on the White House lawn. Here it is important to note that the Oslo agreement was negotiated directly between the Israelis and the Palestinians, with the United States serving primarily as a cheerleader once the agreement had been signed. Following the Oslo agreement, the Arab-Israeli peace process continued to make progress as Jordan and Israel signed a peace treaty in October 1994, with Clinton again serving as a cheerleader when the treaty was signed on the Jordanian-Israeli border. There was also limited progress on the Syrian-Israeli front as the two countries negotiated under US auspices.[8]

The Israeli-Palestinian peace process made further progress, and the Oslo II agreement was signed in September 1995, despite a crescendo in terrorist attacks by Palestinian groups, such as Hamas and Islamic Jihad, seeking to sabotage the peace process, and the murder in February 1994 of Muslims praying at the Tomb of the Patriarchs in Hebron by an Israeli terrorist. Here again, the United States served to support the agreement rather than play a major role in its negotiation.[9]

The peace process, however, soon would receive a series of blows. First, Rabin was assassinated in early November 1995 by a Jewish religious fanatic opposed to the prime minister's territorial concessions to the Palestinians. Rabin's successor, Shimon Peres, quickly moved to implement the Oslo II agreement, which enabled the Palestinians to gain control of all the major Palestinian-populated cities in the West Bank except Hebron, and this control, in turn, facilitated Palestinian elections for the parliament and executive of the Palestinian Authority (PA); Arafat was elected as the PA's executive. Then, however, another round of Palestinian terrorist attacks struck a nearly mortal blow to the peace process. After Peres had arranged for Israeli elections to be held in May 1996, four Hamas and Islamic Jihad terrorist attacks, killing scores of civilians in Jerusalem and Tel Aviv, undermined Israeli public support for the peace process and enabled Likud Party hard-liner Benjamin Netanyahu to be elected prime minister, albeit by a narrow margin—despite Clinton's efforts to support Peres by holding an international antiterrorism conference on March 13, 1996. Compounding the problem was the support given by Syria's official radio station to the terrorist attacks and Syria's boycott of the antiterrorism conference—developments that effectively ended the bilateral Syrian-Israeli talks.[10]

The Netanyahu Period

Following the 1996 Israeli elections, the personal conflict between Netanyahu and Arafat all but froze the peace process, which, according to the Oslo I agreement, was to begin discussion of the final-status issues of boundaries, Jewish settlements, security, refugees, and Jerusalem by May 1996. Netanyahu exacerbated the problem later, in September 1996, by secretly opening the ancient Hasmonean tunnel, which was close to but not attached to the Temple Mount/Haram, the site of the two Jewish temples, and where the Dome of the Rock and the Al-Aqsa mosque are located, and therefore holy to both Jews and Muslims. This act sparked severe rioting by the Palestinians, leading to seventy deaths, fifty-five Palestinians and fifteen Israelis. It took the personal intervention of Bill Clinton, with the help of Jordan's King Hussein, to bring an end to the rioting. Perhaps more important, the deep suspicion that had developed between Netanyahu and Arafat forced the United States to take, for the first time, direct control of the Israeli-Palestinian peace process; the goal was to secure an agreement over the divided city of Hebron, where the massacre of Jews by Arabs in 1929 and of Arabs by a Jew in 1994 had embittered relations. Dennis Ross, the chief American negotiator, worked intensively between October 1996 and January 1997 to secure an agreement, which split the city of Hebron between Israelis (20 percent) and Palestinians (80 percent) and called for three additional Israeli withdrawals from the West Bank, although no stipulation on the size of the withdrawals was agreed to.[11] However, following the Hebron agreement the Palestinian-Israeli peace process again stagnated. In part this stagnation was due to Netanyahu's policy of continuing to build Jewish settlements in the West Bank and also his authorization of the construction of a Jewish housing development on a hill in disputed East Jerusalem called Har Homa. A second cause of the stagnation in the peace talks was yet another outburst of Palestinian terrorism, beginning with a bomb in a Tel Aviv café in March 1997 that killed three Israelis and additional bombs in Jerusalem on July 30 and September 4 that killed twenty-one Israelis and wounded hundreds more. Netanyahu reacted to the bombing by imposing a border closure that prevented Palestinians living in the West Bank and Gaza from working in Israel (a tactic that Rabin had also periodically used), by withholding tax payments collected from Palestinians working in Israel and owed to the Palestinian Authority (a tactic that would also be used by Ehud Barak, Netanyahu's successor, following the outbreak of the Al-Aqsa Intifada in September 2000), and by threatening to send Israeli forces into Palestinian areas to root out the terrorists (a tactic to be employed by Barak's successor, Ariel Sharon).

In September 1997, after having stepped back somewhat from the peace effort to concentrate on expanding NATO (the North Atlantic Treaty Organization), the United States again intervened, this time with the peace process on the verge of total collapse after the two Hamas bombings. The new US secretary of state, Madeleine Albright, who had been sworn in on January 23, 1997, but had not yet made an official visit to the Middle East, went to Israel to jump-start the stalled peace process. She appealed to Arafat to take unilateral action to root out the terrorist's infrastructure and called on Netanyahu for a time-out in settlement construction in the occupied territories, a plea Netanyahu rejected.[12] The peace process continued to stagnate until November, when the Israeli cabinet voted, in principle, in favor of another troop withdrawal but specified neither its extent nor its timing. Meanwhile, Clinton had grown exasperated by what his administration perceived as Netanyahu's stalling, and he publicly snubbed the Israeli prime minister during Netanyahu's November 1997 visit to the United States to talk to Jewish organizations. Netanyahu's ties to the Republicans in Congress and to their allies on the religious Right of the American political spectrum—such as Jerry Falwell, whose Liberty University students regularly make pilgrimages to Israel—helped insulate the Israeli leader from US pressure, protection that would continue into 1998 as a weakened Clinton got bogged down in the Monica Lewinsky scandal.[13]

Despite his growing weakness, Clinton, acting through Secretary of State Albright, again sought in May 1998 to salvage the peace process, whose apparent demise was badly damaging the US position in the Middle East. Arab friends of the United States, as well as the country's Arab enemies, increased their complaints about a double standard of pressuring Iraq while not pressuring Israel. In an effort to reverse this situation, Albright, following meetings with Netanyahu and Arafat in London, issued Israel an ultimatum to accept withdrawal from 13 percent of its occupied territory in the West Bank. This ultimatum, however, failed because of the support Netanyahu received from Republicans in the US Congress, the pro-Israel lobby in the United States led by the American Israel Public Affairs Committee (AIPAC), and the Christian religious Right.[14] Interestingly enough, American Jewry was badly split over Netanyahu's policy. Reform and Conservative Jews, already angry at Netanyahu for his favoritism toward Israel's Orthodox Jews, called for Netanyahu to engage more energetically in the peace process, while Orthodox Jews (a clear minority in the American Jewish community) tended to support the Israeli prime minister.[15]

During the summer of 1998, the US effort took on a new focus: seeking Israeli approval by linking an Israeli withdrawal in stages to Palestinian action to combat terrorism and ensure Israeli security. Meanwhile, a new element had been added to the Israeli-Palestinian conflict: Arafat's threat to unilaterally declare a Palestinian state when the Oslo I agreement expired on May 4, 1999. Although Netanyahu issued a counterthreat of a unilateral Israeli response, which many interpreted as annexation of large parts of the West Bank if Arafat actually declared a state, the Palestinian leader's threat may have been enough to get Netanyahu to agree to meet in late September 1998 in Washington when both leaders were in the United States to address the United Nations. At his first meeting with Arafat in a year, Netanyahu finally agreed, in Clinton's presence, to the 13 percent withdrawal figure stipulated by the United States, but only on condition that 3 percent of the area would be a nature preserve on which the Palestinians would be prohibited from building, a condition to which Arafat agreed.[16]

However, besides the security questions involved in a Palestinian-Israeli agreement, there were real concerns among both Israelis and Palestinians about whether Clinton was strong enough to broker an agreement, given the Lewinsky affair. Despite the skepticism and the illness of King Hussein, Clinton was able to move the peace process several steps forward in mid-October as Netanyahu, Arafat, and King Hussein (who left the Mayo Clinic to play an important mediating role) gathered with US officials at the conference center of the Wye Plantation on Maryland's eastern shore. After eight days of intense bargaining, including the threat of a walkout by Netanyahu, a modest agreement was achieved between Netanyahu and Arafat. The agreement involved Israeli withdrawal in three stages from 13.1 percent of West Bank land (3 percent of which would become a nature preserve as Netanyahu had demanded), the transfer of an additional 14.2 percent of land jointly controlled to sole Palestinian control, the release of 750 Palestinian prisoners, and a promise by Israel to open a Palestinian airport in Gaza and two corridors of safe passage between the West Bank and Gaza. In return, Arafat agreed to change the PLO charter to eliminate the twenty-six articles calling for Israel's destruction, although how the change would take place was vague (reference was made to an assembly of Palestinian notables). Clinton's promise to be present during the Palestinian action, however, would serve to dramatize the event. Arafat also agreed to issue a decree prohibiting all forms of incitement to violence, to cut the number of Palestinian police from 40,000 to 30,000, to arrest and confine thirty terrorism suspects wanted by Israel, and to collect illegal weapons and suppress terrorism, the US Central Intelligence Agency being charged with attesting to the Palestinian Authority's making every effort to crack down on terrorism. The two sides also agreed to resume negotiations on final-status issues.[17]

Initially the Wye agreement appeared to restore a modicum of confidence between Arafat and Netanyahu. In the first and what turned out to be the only stage of the agreement, Israeli troops withdrew from 2 percent of the occupied West Bank, and Israel released 250 Palestinian prisoners and allowed the opening of the Palestinian airport in Gaza. However, the momentum for peace was quickly reversed. Palestinians, complaining that the prisoners who had been released were only "car thieves," not the political detainees they wanted, carried out violent protest activities.[18] These protests led Netanyahu, under heavy pressure from right-wing elements in his governing coalition, to freeze additional troop withdrawals on December 2. The protests had been accompanied by a series of Palestinian terrorist attacks against Israelis, including an attempt to set off a bomb in the Mahane Yehudah market in Jerusalem and an attack on an Israeli soldier in Ramallah—actions that Arafat proved unwilling or unable to prevent. The Israeli prime minister conditioned the resumption of the withdrawals on Arafat's halting what Netanyahu called a campaign of incitement against Israel, forgoing his intention to declare a Palestinian state on May 4, 1999, and acceding to Israel's selection of the prisoners who were to be released.[19]

For its part, the Clinton administration, despite the ongoing impeachment hearings, was making major efforts to keep the peace process going. On November 29, 1998, speaking at a Palestinian donor conference he had assembled in Washington, Clinton pledged $400 million in aid to the Palestinians, on top of the $500 million he had pledged in 1993. All told, some $4 billion in aid was pledged to the Palestinians (the European Union had pledged 400 million euros),[20] an amount that would greatly help the beleaguered Palestinian economy, although questions were raised at the conference about corrupt Palestinian officials' siphoning off previous aid for their own personal use.[21] The United States also sought to downplay the conditions Netanyahu had placed on further Israeli troop withdrawals under the Wye agreement, and State Department spokesman James P. Rubin stated on December 2, 1998, "The agreement should be implemented as signed. We do not believe it is appropriate to add new conditions to implementation of the agreement."[22]

The most important effort to restore momentum to the Israeli-Palestinian peace process was taken by Clinton himself when he journeyed to Gaza in mid-December to witness the Palestinians formally abrogating the clauses in the PLO charter calling for Israel's destruction, an action the Netanyahu government had long demanded. Clinton's visit resulted in a warming of relations between the United States and the Palestinian Authority, which received increased international legitimacy as a result of the US president's visit—an outcome that Israeli critics of Netanyahu blamed on the prime minister.[23]

This was the final blow to the Netanyahu government, which, suffering a series of defections and threatened defections, soon was on the verge of collapse. Under these circumstances, Netanyahu moved to call for new elections before his government could fall on a no-confidence vote. With elections scheduled for May 17, 1999, the peace process was in effect frozen, leaving the United States somewhat nervously on the diplomatic sidelines, hoping that Arafat would not prematurely declare a Palestinian state and thus strengthen the chances of Netanyahu's reelection.

Fortunately for Clinton, Netanyahu would lose the election to the new Labor Party leader, Ehud Barak, a highly decorated soldier and a disciple of Yitzhak Rabin. Barak had run on a peace platform and won the vote 56 percent to 44 percent, a far larger margin than when Netanyahu had defeated Peres in 1996 (50.5 percent to 49.5 percent). Following his defeat, Netanyahu withdrew both from the Knesset and from the leadership of the Likud Party, to be replaced by

Ariel Sharon. And yet, while Barak began his period as prime minister amid great hope, less than two years later he ended it in political disgrace, defeated by Ariel Sharon in the election for prime minister by a two-to-one margin. The peace process had been all but destroyed by the Al-Aqsa Intifada, which had erupted in September 2000 while Barak was prime minister.

Clinton and Barak

When Barak took office, he switched the direction of Israel's peace policy from the Palestinian track to the Syrian track and received positive signals from Syria. Barak must also have thought that peace with Syria, which basically involved only territorial issues, could be achieved more easily than peace with the Palestinians, where negotiations had yet to deal with the highly sensitive issues of the sovereignty of Jerusalem and the plight of Palestinian refugees. Needless to say, the Palestinian leadership took a dim view of the shift in priorities, as well as of Barak's decision to allow the continued expansion of Jewish settlements in the West Bank, which Barak permitted to keep the National Religious Party, whose constituency included the West Bank settlers, in his coalition. The expansion took place primarily in areas near Jerusalem, in such cities as Maaleh Adumim, which Barak hoped to annex. For his part, Clinton went along with Barak's peace process priority and invested a great deal of his personal prestige—including at a meeting with Syria's president, Hafiz al-Assad, in Geneva in March 2000—to try to obtain a breakthrough in negotiations.[24] Despite Clinton's best efforts, however, an agreement with Syria was not achieved, in part because of a dispute over Syria's claim to territory on the northeast shore of the Sea of Galilee, and in part because of Assad's rapidly deteriorating health; he died a few months after meeting Clinton in Geneva.

Barak then sought to politically outflank the Syrians by arranging a unilateral pullout from southern Lebanon in May 2000. Assad had been manipulating Hizbollah attacks against Israeli forces in southern Lebanon, as well as occasional rocket attacks into Israel proper, as a means of pressuring Israel to be more flexible in its negotiations with Syria. Indeed, just such an escalation of fighting had occurred following the collapse of the Syrian-Israeli talks in February 1996. By unilaterally withdrawing from southern Lebanon without a peace treaty, Barak may have hoped to avoid repeating these events and to gain support from the international community, including the United States, which had long pressed for such a pullback. Unfortunately for Barak, regardless of the support he received from the international community, he set a precedent for withdrawing under fire—without an agreement—from territory occupied by Israeli troops. This lesson was not lost on a number of Palestinians, who felt that if Israel could be made to withdraw from Lebanon under fire, it could also be made to pull out of at least the West Bank and Gaza under similar pressure.[25]

Following the failure of the Syrian talks, Barak turned back to the Palestinian track. After initial discussions between the two sides in May 2000, Barak pushed for a summit in July in the United States. He hoped that at one stroke all the remaining final-status issues, including those that had not yet been seriously discussed, such as the status of Jerusalem and the refugee problem, could be settled and a peace agreement achieved. Clinton went along with Barak's plan and devoted two weeks of scarce presidential time to the summit, which became known as the Camp David II Summit. There have been many explanations for the failure of Camp David II, and even members of the same delegation disagree on its causes. Those sympathetic to Arafat blame Barak's negotiating style, his take-it-or-leave-it attitude, and his unwillingness to meet what they felt were even the minimal needs of the Palestinians. Those sympathetic to Barak note that he offered unheard-of Israeli concessions, including giving up all of Gaza and 92 percent of the West Bank and dividing Jerusalem. These offers threatened the viability of Barak's coalition government, especially on the issue of Jerusalem, which Israel thus far had contended was to remain united under Israeli control. Barak's sympathizers also felt that by rejecting the Israeli concessions, demanding the return of the more than three million Palestinian refugees to Israel proper (which would have destroyed Israel as a Jewish state), denying the existence of Jewish temples on Temple Mount/Haram, and making no counteroffers, Arafat had demonstrated that he was not a serious partner for peace.[26] Following the summit, Clinton took Barak's side in the debate over who was responsible for the failure, thereby alienating Arafat. Arafat also fared badly in the court of Western opinion, including in Western Europe, where the Palestinian leader was blamed for the failure to reach an agreement. In addition to shouldering international disapproval for this failure, Arafat was criticized by Palestinians for his heavy-handed authoritarian ways and the corrupt practices within the Palestinian Authority. Arafat counterattacked, claiming he had defended the interests of the world's Muslims at Camp David by not making concessions on the Temple Mount/Haram. He also stepped up the military training given to Palestinian youth in special military camps, perhaps assuming that in the aftermath of the failure to reach a peace agreement, the only alternative was renewed conflict.

And conflict did come in late September 2000, following the visit of the new Likud leader, Ariel Sharon, accompanied by hundreds of Israeli police, to the Temple Mount/Haram, a move linked to internal Israeli politics, as Netanyahu had begun to challenge Sharon's leadership of the Likud Party. Palestinian rioting broke out, for which the Israeli police were ill prepared. As Palestinian casualties rose, the Intifada ("uprising") spread, and soon both the West Bank and Gaza had erupted. The causes of the Intifada, often referred to as the second Intifada or the Al-Aqsa Intifada, named for the mosque at the site visited by Sharon, are as much in dispute as the causes of the failure of Camp David II, as Palestinians and Israelis have very different narratives on the issue. For the Palestinians, the uprising was the result of increasing frustration over continued Israeli settlement expansion and the failure of the Oslo process to give them what they demanded; Sharon's visit to the Temple Mount/Haram had simply been the straw that broke the camel's back. For Israelis, the Intifada was an attempt by Arafat to get by force what he could not get by negotiation, an effort to win back international public opinion by again becoming the Palestinian David to Israel's Goliath, as Palestinian casualties rose more quickly than Israel's. Many Israelis also believed Arafat was applying the lesson learned in Lebanon, forcing Israel to withdraw by using not only stones, as in the first Intifada (1987), but also gunfire and mortar attacks.[27] The Palestinians turned against their onetime peace partners the weapons the Israelis had given them under the Oslo agreement. Many Israelis also suspected that Arafat, regardless of whether he planned the Intifada, was exploiting it to divert attention from Palestinian criticism of his authoritarian and corrupt practices.

Whatever the cause of the Intifada, President Clinton sought to quell it, much as he had after the eruption of violence in 1996 following Netanyahu's opening of the Hasmonean tunnel. Consequently, he convened a summit with both Arafat and Barak at Sharm al-Shaykh on October 16, 2000, and proposed an investigatory commission to analyze the causes of the conflict. The commission was headed by former US senator George Mitchell, who had been Clinton's special envoy to the conflict between Protestants and Catholics in Northern Ireland, and who was the father of the "Good Friday" agreement.

Unfortunately for Clinton, despite Arafat's pledge at Sharm al-Shaykh to stop the violence,[28] the task proved either beyond his will or beyond his ability to achieve. Not only did the Intifada continue, but the violence escalated. Clinton tried again in December, preparing, with the help of Dennis Ross and his colleagues, an American plan called the Clinton Parameters to settle all the final-status issues, including the most heavily disputed issues: Jerusalem's sovereignty and the so-called right of return of Palestinian refugees. Essentially, Clinton proposed some major trade-offs: the withdrawal of Israel from 97 percent of the West Bank; the compensation of Palestinians with Israeli territory near Gaza; the establishment of East Jerusalem as the capital of the new Palestinian state; and the partitioning of the Temple Mount/Haram area. The Temple Mount/ Haram was to go to the Palestinians, the Jewish quarter of the Old City and the Western Wall would go to Israel, and a passage to both would be established through the Armenian quarter. On the issue of the Palestinian right of return, Clinton's plan called for the vast majority of refugees to go to the new Palestinian state.[29]

Barak was willing to accept the plan even though he knew that with Israeli elections looming on February 7 (which he would lose badly to Ariel Sharon), he would run into problems with the Israeli electorate. For his part, Arafat added so many conditions to his acceptance of the Clinton plan that Arafat in fact rejected it, once again confirming to most Israelis that the Palestinian leader was not really interested in peace.[30]

It is possible, of course, that Arafat turned down Clinton's plan because he was expecting a better deal from Clinton's successor, George W. Bush, whose father, President George H. W. Bush, had repeatedly clashed with the Israeli leadership. If this was indeed Arafat's thinking, he was in for a rude awakening, as will be discussed in Chapter 3, with the policies of the Bush and Obama administrations.

Part Two: Perspectives of the Contributors

The first section of this book describes the political ties between the United States and Israel as they have evolved since 1948. Included in this section are studies of US-Israeli diplomatic relations, an analysis of the growth of the pro-Israel lobby in the United States, and an examination of the evolution of US public attitudes toward Israel.

Diplomatic issues in the triangular relationship among the United States, Israel, and the Arab world are highlighted by David Makovsky of the Washington Institute for Near East Policy and the Johns Hopkins School of Advanced International Studies in Chapter 2. Strongly disagreeing with the thesis of John Mearsheimer and Stephen Walt that Israel has been a liability to the United States in the Middle East, Makovsky contends that Israel has instead been an asset, first in curbing the Nasserist and Soviet threats and then, after the collapse of the Soviet Union, as a barrier against Iran's growing threat to the Arab world. Makovsky also argues convincingly that the US relationship with Israel and the Arab world is not a zero-sum game, with American backing for Israel causing it to lose its position in the Arab world. Instead, he posits, the United States can maintain good ties with both sides, as the Arab states give priority to their own national security interests, which, despite lip service to the importance of the Arab-Israeli conflict, are of far greater importance to Arab leaders.

In Chapter 3, Robert O. Freedman of Johns Hopkins University compares the policies of George W. Bush and Barack Obama toward the Arab-Israeli conflict. He argues that although there have been clear similarities in their approaches— both supported Israel diplomatically and militarily, both endorsed the idea of Israel as a Jewish state and as the homeland for the Jewish people, and both opposed an Israeli strike on Iranian nuclear facilities—there were also important differences. Thus, although Bush sought to isolate both Syria and Iran, Obama initially tried to embrace them; however, by May 2011 he had returned to a critical stance toward both countries. In addition, Bush had an episodic approach to Middle East peacemaking and Obama's was continuous, though he has made a number of tactical changes to his policy, first concentrating on getting Israel to stop settlement expansion on the West Bank and in East Jerusalem, then shifting to a call for the Israelis and Palestinians to work out all of their final-status issues simultaneously, and then finally, in May 2011, urging the two sides to concentrate first on border and security issues, and only then to turn to what Obama called the "emotional" issues of Jerusalem and Palestinian refugees. Obama was also clearer than any other US president had been in calling for a settlement based on the 1967 borders with "mutually agreed land swaps" that would take Israeli security into consideration.

In Chapter 4, Dov Waxman, of the City University of New York, discusses the rise of the pro-Israel lobby in the United States from its humble origins in the nineteenth century. He notes that the high point of the lobby's influence and unity came between the Six-Day War in June 1967 and the signing of the Oslo agreement in 1993. Since that time, differences over whether Israel should withdraw from the West Bank and whether a Palestinian state should be established have divided the pro-Israel lobby into three parts: a left wing, led by J Street and Americans for Peace Now, urging concessions to the Palestinians; a centrist section, led by AIPAC (still the most powerful element in the pro-Israel lobby) searching for consensus and willing to support whatever Israeli government is in power; and a right wing, led by the Zionist Organization of America, that opposes territorial withdrawals and a Palestinian state. Waxman concludes by stating that because "no single organization can credibly claim to represent the overwhelming majority of American Jews," the lobby's leverage is likely to decline.

One of the questions frequently raised about US-Israeli relations is the degree to which American public opinion is supportive of Israel. In Chapter 5, Amnon Cavari of the Interdisciplinary Center in Herzliya in Israel analyzes this question, noting that not only have most Americans supported Israel's right to exist and have sympathized with the country far more than with its Arab opponents, but they have been willing to support extensive economic and military aid to the Jewish state as well. Citing a series of public opinion studies, Cavari examines the steady American support for Israel since its birth in 1948, noting that at least until 2000, this support cut across all groups in the United States, although there was less support from African Americans than from other Americans. By 2000, however, the trends changed, with support increasing among Republicans and evangelical Christians and decreasing among college-educated Americans and members of the Democratic Party, trends that Cavari warns could undermine bipartisan support for Israel.

The second section of this book analyzes economic, military, security, and legal ties between the United States and Israel. It includes studies on the evolution of the US-Israeli economic relationship, the influence of military aid and military doctrine, the nuclear threat posed by Iran, and the impact of American jurisprudence on Israeli law.

Roby Nathanson and Ron Mandelbaum of the Macro Center for Political Economics in Tel Aviv present a detailed analysis of the evolution of US-Israeli trade and aid since 1948 in Chapter 6. They note that although in the early decades of the relationship American aid, both military and economic, exceeded trade between the two countries, by 1990 trade had surpassed aid and by 2009, after US economic aid to Israel had been phased out, Israeli exports to the United States were more than seven times the amount of the military aid it received from the United States. Nathanson and Mandelbaum also analyze the program of US loan guarantees to Israel and discuss the significance of the Free Trade Agreement (FTA) between Israel and the United States in 1985. They contend that the FTA was a model for other free trade agreements the United States would subsequently sign with other countries, although they also note that the US-Israeli FTA needs to be modernized, particularly in the areas of technical standards and intellectual property rights. They also discuss the numerous bilateral agreements between the United States and Israel, from energy cooperation to research in agricultural problems, and conclude that the future of US-Israeli economic ties is likely to be bright.

If US-Israeli economic ties have become extensive since 1948, so too have the military ties. As Stuart A. Cohen of Bar-Ilan University says in Chapter 7, these ties consist not only of the military hardware the United States sends to Israel, but also of the military cooperation that has developed. Thus, not only has the American military establishment learned lessons from Israeli wars—the American development of the unmanned aerial vehicle (UAV) is a result of Israel's 1982 war with the PLO and Syria—but also, after initially studying in British, French, and even German military colleges, Israeli officers, following the 1967 war when the United States replaced France as Israel's primary foreign ally, began to attend US military institutions, such as the US Army War College at Carlisle, Pennsylvania, and the National Defense University in Washington, D.C. As the two military establishments got closer, however, Cohen points to a negative trend: Israeli military thinkers tended to unquestionably accept US military doctrine, and Cohen asserts that this may well have been one of the reasons for Israeli problems during the 2006 Israeli-Hizbollah war. Cohen concludes by urging the Israeli military establishment to regain its independence of military thought.

While Israel currently faces a number of military challenges, whether from substate actors, such as Hamas and Hizbollah, and states, such as Syria and possibly Egypt once again if the course of the current Egyptian revolution (October 2011) takes a wrong turn as far as Israel is concerned, its biggest threat is a nuclear-armed Iran. In Chapter 8, Steven David of Johns Hopkins University discusses the challenges facing Israel if Iran got the bomb and notes that because the United States is unlikely to attack Iran's nuclear facilities, Israel will have to attack if it so decides. David evaluates the conditions that might lead to a nuclear attack by Iran on Israel, and also the consequences were Israel to attack Iran to prevent it from obtaining nuclear weapons. He also raises the question as to whether Iran's religiously motivated leaders can be deterred once they acquire nuclear weapons, and suggests that if Israeli leaders think the answer to that question is in the negative, then given their memories of the Holocaust, they may decide to strike; an attack on Iran's nuclear facilities is within Israel's military capabilities, however problematic the consequences might be.

Although the United States has certainly influenced Israeli military doctrine, it has also influenced Israeli legal doctrine. In Chapter 9, Pnina Lahav of Boston University's School of Law notes that although Israel's legal origins were primarily British, the country soon became influenced by American jurisprudence. Lahav emphasizes the important role of American-born Israeli Supreme Court Chief Justice Simon Agranat in this process, and points out a number of Israeli Supreme Court decisions in which he played a leading role. She notes, however, that the concept of Israel as a Jewish and a democratic state is fundamentally different than the founding concept of the United States, which is a state of its citizens, and this has affected Israeli Supreme Court decision-making as well. She also notes that after 9/11, when the United States came face-to-face with terrorism for the first time, US jurists began to study the Israeli experience and specifically Israeli court decisions on the permissibility of using torture.

The final section of this book deals with religious and communal issues affecting the US-Israeli relationship. It explores the ties between America's Orthodox Jewish community and the state of Israel, what can be called a "special relationship" between American evangelical Christians and Israel, and the role of the American Jewish peace movement and Israel.

Since the founding of Israel in 1948, American Orthodox Jews have developed very close ties with it. This topic is discussed in Chapter 10 by Steven Bayme of the American Jewish Committee, who concentrates on Modern Orthodox Judaism in the United States, which is closely tied to Religious Zionism in Israel. Bayme notes the high percentage of American Modern Orthodox Jews who visit Israel, as compared to Conservative, Reform, and unaffiliated Jews, and he also points to the significant impact of one- or two-year post–secondary study programs at Orthodox Yeshivot in Israel on Modern Orthodox Jewish life in the United States. As far as politics is concerned, Bayme discusses the split in the American Orthodox community over the Oslo agreement, and the soul searching that took place in some parts of the Orthodox community after the assassination of Israeli Prime Minister Yitzhak Rabin. Indeed, he cites Yeshiva University President Norman Lamm, who stated that Orthodox rabbis had created the atmosphere that led to the assassination. Bayme concludes by raising a series of fundamental questions about the future course of Religious Zionism, asking, among other questions, whether Religious Zionists, who are closely tied to American Orthodox Jews, will articulate "a humanistic vision that all mankind is created in the image of God," or a dualistic worldview that divides the world between Jews and others.

If most Orthodox Jews in the United States are passionate about Israel, so too are most evangelical Christians. Neil R. Rubin of Towson University discusses the evolution of the evangelical Christian relationship to Israel in Chapter 11, noting the key roles of leaders such as Pat Robertson, Jerry Falwell, and John Hagee. Rubin cites the basis of evangelical support for Israel as arising from Genesis 12:3, which describes God's blessing to Abraham: "And I will bless them that bless thee, and him that curseth thee will I curse, and in thee shall all the families of the earth be blessed." Rubin also discusses the splits among evangelicals with regard to Israel as well as the often uncomfortable position of American Jews toward the evangelicals whose support of Israel they appreciate, but whose political and social program for the United States they often strongly disagree with. Rubin concludes by stating that the influence of evangelicals is likely to rise in the United States, and he foresees possible problems for the relationship between evangelical Christians and American Jews and also for continuing evangelical support for Israel.

In the final chapter of the book, Mark Rosenblum of Queens College and Dan Fleshler, a media consultant, discuss the role of the American Jewish peace movement. They compare four American Jewish groups that have advocated a peace settlement between Israel and its Arab neighbors: Breira, Americans for Peace Now, the Israeli Policy Forum, and J Street. They conclude that American Jewish peace movements are most successful when there is an Israeli government opposing the peace process, credible Israelis with strong security credentials advocating peace, legitimate Arab interlocutors who are also seeking peace, and an activist American president willing to prod both sides toward peace.

In sum, the contributors to this book present a comprehensive view of US-Israeli relations as they have developed since 1948. It is hoped that the reader will come away with a deeper understanding of the dynamics of the US-Israeli relationship.

Notes

1. The political perspectives of Marshall and Forrestal are discussed by Clark Clifford, a participant in the discussions on US policy toward the future Jewish state. See Clark Clifford, *Coun-sel to the President: A Memoir* (New York: Random House, 1991), pp. 3–25.

2. On these issues, see Peter L. Hahn, *Caught in the Middle East: U.S. Policy Toward the*

Arab-Israeli Conflict, 1945–1961 (Chapel Hill: University of North Carolina Press, 2004). See also Zach Levey, *Israel and the Western Powers* (Chapel Hill: University of North Carolina Press, 1997).

3. See Warren Bass, *Support Any Friend: Kennedy's Middle East Policy and the Making of the U.S.-Israel Alliance* (New York: Oxford University Press, 2003).

4. For studies of the Johnson, Nixon, Carter, and Reagan administrations' policies toward Israel, see William B. Quandt, *Peace Process: American Diplomacy and the Arab-Israeli Conflict Since 1967*, 3rd ed. (Los Angeles: University of California Press, 2005), and Steven Spiegel, *The Other Arab-Israeli Conflict: Making America's Middle East Policy from Truman to Reagan* (Chicago: University of Chicago Press, 1985).

5. On the Soviet impact on US policy toward the Middle East, see Robert O. Freedman, *Moscow and the Middle East: Soviet Policy Since the Invasion of Afghanistan* (Cambridge: Cambridge University Press, 1991).

6. See Quandt, *Peace Process*, pp. 250–257, and Spiegel, *The Other Arab-Israeli Conflict*, pp. 412–429.

7. On these issues, see Dennis Ross, *The Missing Peace: The Inside Story of the Fight for Middle East Peace* (New York: Farrar, Straus & Giroux, 2005).

8. For the Israeli view of the negotiations by a participant-observer, see Itamar Rabinovich, *The Brink of Peace: The Israeli-Syrian Negotiations* (Princeton, NJ: Princeton University Press, 1998).

9. See Quandt, *The Peace Process*, and Ross, *The Missing Peace*.

10. See Rabinovich, *The Brink of Peace*, and Ross, *The Missing Peace*.

11. For Ross's personal account of the negotiations, see Ross, *The Missing Peace*.

12. Albright discusses these events in her memoirs. See Madeleine Albright, *Madam Secretary: A Memoir* (New York: Miramax Books, 2003), Chapter 18.

13. David Coven, "Liberty U. to Send 3,000 Students on a Study Tour of Israel," *Chronicle of Higher Education*, September 25, 1997, p. 51. See also Chapter 11 in this volume.

14. For an analysis critical of US strategy at this time, see Robert Satloff, "Shifting Sands: The U.S.'s Disturbing New Israel Policy," *New Republic*, June 1, 1998.

15. These divisions are discussed in Robert O. Freedman, "The Religious-Secular Divide in Israeli Politics," *Middle East Policy* 6, no. 4 (June 1999). See also Chapter 10, by Steven Bayme, in this volume.

16. Martin Sief, "Arafat Accepts Israeli Land Deal for West Bank," *Washington Times*, September 30, 1998.

17. See Ross, *The Missing Peace*, Chapter 15. Interestingly enough, Ross titles this chapter "The 13 Percent Solution."

18. Lee Hockstadter, "Attacks Kill Arab; Injure 3 Israelis," *Washington Post*, December 3, 1998.

19. Ann LeLordo, "Israel Issues Ultimatum, Halts West Bank Pull-Out," *Baltimore Sun*, December 3, 1998.

20. See Joel Peters, "Europe and the Arab-Israeli Peace Process: The Declaration of the European Council of Berlin and Beyond," in *Bound to Cooperate: Europe and the Middle East*, ed. Sven Behrendt and Christian-Peter Hanelt (Gutersloh, Germany: Bertelsmann Foundation, 2001), p. 162.

21. Philip Shenon, "U.S. and Other Nations Plan More Aid for Palestinians," *New York Times*, December 1, 1998; Martin Sief, Palestinians Get More U.S. Aid," *Washington Times*, December 1, 1998.

22. Cited in Hockstadter, "Attacks Kill Arab."

23. See Judy Dempsey, "Palestinians Turn the Tables on Israelis: Arafat Poses as Clinton's Friend as Netanyahu Sulks," *Financial Times*, December 16, 1998.

24. For a view of Barak's "Syria's my priority" policy, see Ross, *The Missing Peace*, Chapter 20. See also Albright, *Madam Secretary*, pp. 474–482.

25. Author's interviews with Palestinians, June–July 2000. In addition, Arafat's national security adviser, Jibril Ragoub, later noted that Palestinian organizations should "learn from Hizbollah"; cited in Arnon Regular, "Militants Agree to End Civilian Attacks, No Mention of Settlers," *Ha'aretz*, December 7, 2003.

26. For analyses of the failure of Camp David II, see Ross, *The Missing Peace*, Chapter 24; Quandt, *The Peace Process*, Chapter 12; Albright, *Madam Secretary*, pp. 482–494; and Bill Clinton, *My Life* (New York: Knopf, 2004), pp.

911–916. See also the interview in English with former Israeli foreign minister Shlomo Ben-Ami, "End of a Journey," *Ha'aretz,* October 3, 2001; Robert Malley and Hussein Agha, "Camp David: The Tragedy of Errors," *New York Review of Books,* August 9, 2001, pp. 59–65; Ehud Barak, "It Seems Israel Has to Wait for New Palestinian Leadership," *International Herald Tribune,* July 31, 2001; Alain Gresh, "The Middle East: How the Peace Was Lost," *Le Monde Diplomatique,* September 2001, pp. 8–9; Barry Rubin, "The Region," June 25, 2001, www1.biu .ac.il; and Bassam Abu-Sharif, "A Call to Israel to Understand What the Palestinians Want," September 14, 2001, http://ipcri.org.

27. For a different view of the "Lessons of Lebanon," see Roula Khalaf, "Misleading Ghosts of Lebanese Resistance," *Financial Times,* August 16, 2001.

28. Cited in Ross, *The Missing Peace,* p. 741.

29. Ibid., pp. 752–753.

30. Ibid., pp. 753–755.

2

The United States and the Arab-Israeli Conflict from 1945 to 2000

WHY THE ARABISTS ARE WRONG

David Makovsky

THE HISTORY OF THE US-Israeli relationship since 1948 has not been linear, as bilateral relationships seldom are over the course of several decades. Yet it has largely been characterized by its vitality, and the strength of this relationship has been critical for advancing peace in the region. Not only has a Middle East peace process allowed the United States to expand its influence in the Middle East over the past few decades, but the growth of the US-Israeli relationship over time has effectively deterred conflict and contributed to regional stability. Because of the strength of the US-Israeli relationship, there has not been a regional war since 1973.

This outlook is at odds with the emergence in the post-9/11 period of a liability school, which views Israel as a strategic liability to the United States as the latter seeks to bridge ties with the Arab world. This school has won headlines in recent years, as it is championed by two noted academics, the University of Chicago's John Mearsheimer and Harvard's Stephen Walt.[1] They are champions of the realist school. For realists, interests matter most. Values, though desirable, have, well, less value. Although they concede that during the Cold War, Israel may have been an asset to the United States, they suggest that in the post–Cold War period, whatever value the relationship had has long since been replaced by its costs. Their argument is that securing oil and good relations with the Arab world should be the primary US goal in the Middle East and that American association with and strong support for Israel impedes this aim. Specifically, they write that Arab and Muslim antipathy toward the United States results from their identifying the United States with Israel. This comes at a heavy cost, they assert. If the United States could halt its support for Israel, US relations would improve with both leaders and citizens of the oil-rich region. Yet, are their assertions correct? Are they rooted in reality or paradoxically divorced from it?

Their argument can be judged historically, since in fact, the liability school is not new. During the Cold War, it was often championed by the traditionalist, Arabist school in the US State Department. This school was most prominent at the inception of Israel and in the decades that followed. Arabists viewed Israel as an impediment to the ability of the United States to establish close ties with the Arab world. According to their zero-sum thinking, every step toward Israel necessarily represented a step away from the Arabs.[2] In other words, ties to one side ensured distance from the other.

Yet, with few exceptions and their own rhetoric to the contrary, the Arab regimes do not in fact think this way. Their actions are driven by their own national interests, not an automatic (or even a reflexive) zero-sum outlook. If the Arabs do not limit themselves to this approach, why should the United States? The zero-sum mind-set reflects an inability to appreciate the complex dynamics of the Middle East.

The FDR Years

The idea of liability is rooted in the idea that the Arab states would "link" their relationship to the United States based on American policy toward the Middle East. This idea of linkage has a history and has gone through different permutations over the decades. In its essence, it was an effort by Arab states to help define US foreign policy options in the Middle East. Specifically, US actions with regard to the Arab-Israeli conflict would depend on, or be linked to, US-Arab relations. There have been times that the United States has been guided by this concern, one it would never acknowledge, realizing that the American public would find it very objectionable and view it as an effort on the part of the Arabs to manipulate US foreign policy. One can see how this idea evolved over the decades.

In the earliest form of the linkage argument, the Arab-Israeli conflict was viewed as a contest where the United States was being asked to be on one side against the other. The United States was supposed to choose whether to be on the side of the Arabs or on the side of the nascent Jewish homeland. This was made clear by Saudi King Abdul Aziz Ibn Saud, who wrote a series of letters to President Franklin Delano Roosevelt over a period of several years, beginning in the late 1930s. Their correspondence culminated in a meeting between the two on the battleship *Quincy* just two months before FDR's death. Ibn Saud made the case against Zionism, citing arguments ranging from historic enmity between Muslims and Jews to allegations of nefarious Zionist intent and implications for relations between the United States and Arabs in the future. For the most part, Ibn Saud made threats about how the Arabs would treat Western powers if they supported Zionism, adding that he blamed the Jews for inciting the problems and making it evident that ties would suffer if the United States chose the wrong side. Western powers, according to Ibn Saud, cannot befriend both Arabs and Zionists, but rather should be forced to choose sides. He declared in his November 1938 letter that the Jewish presence in the Middle East was brief, beset by tragedy and massacres, saying the Jews had been driven out. Ibn Saud concluded that the Jewish cause was unjust. He said if the Jews went forward, "the Heavens will split, the earth will be rent asunder, and the mountains will tremble at what the Jews claim in Palestine, both materially and spiritually." In his 1943 letter, Ibn Saud mentioned "the religious animosity between Moslems and Jews which dates back to the time when Islam appeared and which is due to the treacherous behavior of the Jews towards Moslems and their Prophet." He added, "for if—God Forbid!—the Jews were to be granted their desire, Palestine would forever remain a hotbed of troubles and disturbances as in the past. This will bring great difficulties for the Allies in general and for our friend Great Britain in particular. In view of their financial power and learning the Jews can stir up enmity between the Arabs and Allies at any moment. They have been the cause of many troubles in the past." He concluded by saying he hoped the injustice would not occur and relations between the Allied powers and the Arabs would be "best and strongest."[3]

On February 1, 1945, Ibn Saud told US diplomats, "If America should choose in favor of the Jews, who are accursed in the Koran as enemies of the Muslims until the end of the world, it will indicate to us that America has repudiated her friendship with us and this we should regret. The choice, however, is for America."[4] Soon thereafter, FDR made his famous journey from the Yalta World War II summit with Winston Churchill and Joseph Stalin on the US battleship *Quincy*, where FDR entered the Suez Canal. As the ship anchored in the Great Bitter Lake, the US president held a summit with Ibn Saud on February 14. During the meeting, FDR sought Ibn Saud's support for Zionism, citing the destruction of millions of Polish Jews during World War II. However, the Saudi leader was adamant. He insisted that Jewish refugees from the Holocaust be settled in Poland.

In short, in its earliest years, the Arabs wanted the United States to disassociate itself from the Zionist enterprise that became Israel. Arab leaders contended that the nation was illegitimate, so there was no need for Arab accommodation. They asked that the United States decide where its interests lie: with the Zionists or with the Arab world. If the United States moved toward the Zionists, the Arab world would link its relationship with the United States accordingly. In other words, the Arab nations would shape their relationship to the United States based on the latter's choice. The onus was on America, not the Arabs. Specifically, US failure to choose sides meant that Washington was responsible not only for its poor standing in the region, but also for all the festering problems of the Middle East—even for ensuing wars and the instability of Arab regimes.

This had an impact on FDR. After his famous meeting with Ibn Saud on the USS *Quincy* in early 1945, FDR clearly feared that US-Saudi relations and access to oil would be jeopardized as a consequence of US support for Zionism. David Niles, one of only two White House political advisers to FDR who were asked to remain in the Truman administration and who played a role in President Harry Truman's support of Zionism, later declared he had "serious doubts that Israel would have come into being, if Roosevelt had lived."[5]

The Truman Years

Indeed, in the Truman administration, the diplomatic and security establishment believed that the nascent Jewish state would be overwhelmed militarily.[6] On February 12, 1948, Secretary of State George Marshall said at a meeting of the National Security Council that any serious attempt to implement a partition in Palestine could set in motion events that would result in at least a partial mobilization of the US armed forces.[7] Moreover, Marshall, Secretary of Defense James Forrestal, and others feared that US support for a Jewish state would jeopardize access to Mideast oil. Forrestal famously explained US dependency on Arab oil as such: "Unless we have access to Middle East oil, American motorcar companies [will] have to design a four-cylinder motorcar sometime within the next five years."[8] The Joint Chiefs of Staff issued a memorandum titled "The Problem of Palestine," in which they also argued that partitioning Palestine into Jewish and Arab states would endanger US access to Middle East oil.[9] Indeed, these same points about access to Middle East oil and the specter of US military intervention (along with unsubstantiated fears that key Israeli socialists were more pro-Soviet than supportive of the United States) were made by senior State Department official Robert Lovett in a fateful meeting with Truman on May 12, 1948. It was at this very session that Marshall, who was a towering figure in the United States due to his wartime and postwar leadership, made the dramatic and perhaps unprecedented statement for a sitting secretary of state that he would not vote for his boss if Truman recognized Israel. Although Truman offered no reply to Marshall, Truman spurned these advisers. He recognized Israel two days later.

However, despite the fears of the Joint Chiefs, Marshall, and Lovett, the United States did not find itself embroiled in the Mideast war of 1948. It even maintained an arms embargo until 1961. Saudi Arabia and other Arab countries provided a steady oil supply to the United States. In fact, the supply has remained uninterrupted until today, with the exception of a brief oil embargo after the 1973 war. Indeed, most critically, the US-Saudi oil relationship was not imperiled by Israel's existence. Saudi Arabia provided a steady, uninterrupted oil supply to the United States, despite Ibn Saud's demand that the United States choose between the Jews and the Arabs. Not only was the US-Saudi relationship undamaged, but it also greatly improved over time.

Ibn Saud had a wider-angle view than some American policy makers, who feared being cut off from Saudi oil as a result of US support of Israel. First, the Saudis were aware that the United States would be the dominant power in the postwar period and, as a country run by one family, they needed US support to ensure the regime's existence. Second, Ibn Saud saw the United States as a check on the British. He feared that London supported the rival Hashemites in Jordan more than it did the House of Saud. As would occur many times, an inter-Arab rivalry trumped other considerations. Over time, the US-Saudi oil relationship flourished.

Ibn Saud's threat never materialized. American policy makers who opposed Truman in this regard had accepted Ibn Saud's threat, saying, in effect, that the United States could not be friendly with both Arabs and Israelis, but their fears proved unfounded. The United States was able to both recognize the existence of Israel and maintain access to Saudi oil. In practice, the Saudi regime did not pursue a region-based confrontation with America but rather acted in its own interests, which required close ties with the United States to survive and prosper.

The Eisenhower Years

A key event in Middle East policy during the Eisenhower administration was the Suez War of 1956. During the crisis, Eisenhower adopted the Arabist thesis more clearly than ever before or after. However, this approach failed to win over any leaders or to strengthen pro-Western moderates in the Arab world. To the contrary, it led to an increase of Soviet influence in the region and helped Arab radicals led by Egyptian leader Gamal Abdel Nasser. In short, the irony is that Nasser became more defiant against the United States at the very time the United States felt it had to adopt a more Arabist, zero-sum approach. Making no demands on the Arab side was disastrous. The central point is that the United

States did not receive an ounce of credit from Nasser for taking on Britain, France, and Israel. One can argue that Eisenhower was correct to publicly insist that Israel withdraw from the Sinai after the brief war, but there should have been reciprocal steps from Nasser. This would have been quite significant for US standing in the region. But there was no quid pro quo, and Nasser met America's goodwill gesture with defiance and determination to play a more anti-Western role in the Middle East. Although the United States did the heavy lifting in reversing the Suez crisis, Nasser rose to iconic status and became the indisputable leader of Arab nationalism.[10] He used the victory to destabilize a variety of Arab regimes in the aftermath. As analyst Peter Rodman wrote, "Instead of the last roar of colonialism, the issues posed by Suez were the first roar of a new era—the first case of a Third World radical taking Soviet arms and playing the anti-Western card."[11]

The United States suffered from Suez, but so did the Europeans and more moderate Arab regimes. The United States did not seem to realize how the aftermath would affect pro- and anti-Nasser forces. Rodman assessed the situation as follows: "Instead of helping Arab moderates, we had undermined or weakened them. Instead of restoring stability to the Middle East, we had unbalanced it, against us."[12] Indeed, inspired by Nasser's strength, a bevy of negative consequences for Arab politics occurred in the wake of the Suez crisis. Nasser's appeal was such that Syria joined a union with Egypt in 1958. In the same year, a civil war broke out in Lebanon, and pro-Western forces lost. The same thing happened in Iraq, as the pro-Western Prime Minister, Nuri Said, was deposed and hanged from a lamppost. Other pro-Nasser coups occurred in Sudan and in Yemen a few years later. Critically, Nasser did not fear US insistence that Egypt not repeat what it had done in 1956 in closing the Straits of Tiran to Israeli ships emanating from the southern port of Eilat. Indeed, in 1967, Israel would go to war over the same issues. While visiting Jerusalem in 1957, Secretary of State John Foster Dulles pledged to his Israeli counterpart, Golda Meir, that the United States would fight to keep Egypt from again closing the strategic Straits of Tiran to Israeli passage.[13] Israel was keen on an agreement that if the straits were closed, it would have the right to defend itself against such a flagrant action. Yet in the month leading up to the 1967 war, Nasser closed the straits after he expelled UN peacekeepers stationed in the Sinai desert, and the United States did not act to reverse either move but did pressure Israel not to use force.

The Johnson Years

The 1956 Suez crisis set the stage for the 1967 war, and the Eisenhower administration shaped the problems that Lyndon Johnson faced in the run-up to that war. For a variety of reasons, the Johnson administration vacillated when confronting these challenges. Among these reasons was Johnson's preoccupation with Vietnam, but also the fear of offending Arab states. It was this uncertainty that in the end guaranteed a war. Could the United States have prevented war by developing a viable policy? It is unknowable. However, it is clear that linkage brought war closer. The Arabists in the State Department asked America to allow aggression, especially as Nasser threatened to cut off shipping to Israel and moved his army into the Sinai to attack Israel. During the course of US vacillation, Nasser openly gave speeches about his desire to liquidate Israel, and he reached a defense pact with Jordan.[14] Due to Nasser's popularity, Jordan's King Hussein was afraid not to mobilize. US indecisiveness led surrounding Arab armies to believe there would be no political consequences for their action.

But there were indeed political consequences as Israel easily defeated Egypt, Jordan, and Syria during the June 1967 Six-Day War, and occupied the Sinai Peninsula, the West Bank (including East Jerusalem), and the Golan Heights. Israel's remarkable victory in the 1967 war created both problems and opportunities. The disposition of the territories Israel won remains a key focus of diplomacy. However, it also gave the United States leverage, as the Arabs would ultimately seek out Washington because of its enhanced relationship with Israel.

The 1967 war produced two sets of consequences. First, by serving as America's proxy after the Six-Day War, as even Walt and Mearsheimer agree, Israel helped contain Soviet expansion in the region and inflicted humiliating defeats on Soviet clients, such as Egypt and Syria. Israel occasionally helped protect other US allies (such as King Hussein in 1970), and its military prowess forced Moscow to spend more in backing its losing clients.[15] Israel also gave the United States useful intelligence about Soviet capabilities.

And yet there was a second set of consequences. Israel's victory in the 1967 war, followed by its victory in 1973 after a hard-fought war, was the lever that enabled rapprochement between the United States and Egypt. Johnson's policy shifted in the aftermath of the 1967 war, apparently as a reaction to Eisenhower's pressure on Israel after the Suez crisis. Eisenhower had forced Israel to relinquish the Sinai in 1957, but this did not prevent the next war in 1967. The lack of consequences for Nasser's closing of the Straits of Tiran would ensure that he saw no risks to such unilateral moves. In the wake of the 1967 war, Johnson reversed precedent. Israeli withdrawal would not come without reciprocal actions, as it had in 1956. Rather, the Arabs and Israel would have to reach a negotiated peace. And so, toward the end of 1967, UN Security Council Resolution 242 was born. Land became a bargaining chip in peace negotiations—known as "land for peace," an approach whose efficacy would be at least partially proved with the peace negotiated between Israel and Egypt over the next twelve years.

The war catalyzed a political earthquake that shook the Middle East. Despite a US arms embargo during the war and its immediate aftermath, Israel's size tripled from the land it had won in 1967, and Nasser's pan-Arabism was eclipsed.[16] The Six-Day War became the open wound from which the Arab world would never recover. In the aftermath of the 1967 war, the Arab leaders refused to take any diplomatic steps toward Israel. At the same time, Nasser actually led the other Arab leaders to reject calls by some radical elements to maintain, in the postwar period, the short-lived suspension in oil supplies during the war—an action Nasser said was self-defeating for the Arabs. Diplomatic measures by some Arabs again did occur, but contrary to the fears of the advocates of linkage, the war and its aftermath did not lead to a material loss for the United States. There would be no looming confrontation between America and the Arab world.

The concept of linkage underwent a change beginning in 1967. Before the 1967 war, it took the form of calling for the United States to break its commitments to Israel and to side with the Arabs instead, even when doing so produced no meaningful reciprocal actions. However, Israel's stunning victory on three fronts introduced a new variable to the situation. The Arab states could act reciprocally by making peace with Israel in return for Israeli land withdrawal. But this idea was not immediately accepted by the Arab world. In the 1967 postwar conference in Khartoum in Sudan, the Arab League issued its infamous resolution declaring "three no's": no negotiations, no peace, no recognition of Israel.

But the more basic question of linkage remained. There were two views in the United States regarding Arab goals. One was that the Arabs were focused on comprehensive steps to maximize their leverage to force Israeli concessions with minimal, if any, reciprocal moves. The other was that they were more focused on their own national interests and willing to engage in reciprocity. Arabists in the United States almost always assumed the former, but the reality became increasingly clear: key players in the Arab world focused more on the latter at key junctures.

1973 War and Its Lessons

The 1973 war was the last regional war between Arabs and Israelis. A surprise attack on Israel's holiest day, Yom Kippur, led to Egyptian military advances in the Sinai and to Syrian advances in the Golan. Expecting a replay of 1967 with an Israeli military rout, the United States thought getting Israel back to the status quo ante would be difficult. However, the idea of limited victory by Egypt began to appeal to the United States, but a key blunder by Egyptian leader Anwar Sadat to end the war with Egypt slightly ahead led the United States to reverse course and back Israel. However, for four key days while this strategy had hope, the United States denied an airlift of supplies to Israel despite desperate Israeli requests.

President Richard Nixon and Secretary of State Henry Kissinger wanted to end the war with a limited Egyptian victory that did not jeopardize Israel's existence. They thought this outcome would be favorable to the United States, believing it would obviate the need for a Soviet airlift and would break the post-1967 diplomatic stalemate. It would give the Israelis an incentive to negotiate while allowing Sadat to feel that his country had regained its pride. Egypt would then feel freer to take diplomatic steps toward the United States, preserving US relations with the Arab world. Overall, it was the anticipation of Soviet action that shaped US behavior and not the concern for mounting fatalities (Israel sustained close to 3,000 deaths during the war). Permitting the airlift, US policy makers reasoned, would prolong the war and raise Soviet stakes to match those of the United States. The United States did not want a total Israeli victory because, in its view, this would cement Israel's resolve not to make any territorial concessions in the Sinai. Moreover, the linkage mind-set, at least in part, also affected US strategy. There was concern within the administration that a major Israeli victory—even without US assistance—would jeopardize US relations with moderate Arabs and enhance Soviet influence in the region.[17] And yet on October 13, 1973, with a Soviet airlift thirty-six hours away, Sadat rejected a UN Security Council resolution that would freeze the battlefield conditions. He seemed to be intoxicated by Egypt's early success, he may have wanted to maximize Israeli casualties, and he felt strong knowing that a Soviet airlift was on the way. Sadat rejected the winning terms in favor of holding out for maximalist demands. It is hard to escape the view that it was the lack of military progress by Israel that emboldened Sadat, and this lack of progress was tied to the lack of US support. The Egyptians reached the wrong conclusion. For the United States, it became imperative to shift gears and help Israel, believing this would humble the intransigent duo of the Soviet Union and Egypt. The US airlift was considered the biggest US weapons supply since the Berlin blockade of 1948. The US sent 1,000 tons of weapons and materiel using C-5A and C-141 aircraft, as well as C-130s, in a matter of days. Over the next weeks, there were 550 US military flights to Israel. By the end of the first few days, the US effort had surpassed the Soviet airlift to Egypt and Syria combined. This turned the tide of the war in Israel's favor, as the Israel Defense Forces ended the war outside Cairo and Damascus.

As with other cases of linkages, the US arm-twisting tactics in dealing with Israel in 1973 succeeded in getting Israel's acquiescence but did not achieve the US objective, given Sadat's opposition. Once again, as in 1956 and other instances, when the Arabs felt the United States was doing their bidding without Arab reciprocal steps, the result proved counterproductive, convincing Arabs that their own actions were irrelevant.

In looking more closely at the period after the 1973 war, it is striking how wrong the Arabist arguments turned out to be. Rather than harming US relations with the Arabs—the essence of the Arabist assumption—supporting Israel benefited America. Ironically, it was precisely the close US-Israeli relationship after the war that enabled the United States to become a decisive diplomatic player in the Middle East. Despite its defeat, Egypt moved into the US orbit and signed two sets of disengagement agreements with Israel in 1974 and 1975. Then came Sadat's historic visit to Jerusalem in 1977, which led to Camp David and the 1979 Egyptian-Israeli peace treaty.

Egypt came to view its ties with the United States as indispensable. Only America had influence over Israel, a key lever to reclaim land lost in the 1967 war. The hope of restoring Egyptian land would create a rapprochement between Washington and Cairo, since Moscow had no such influence over Israel. The peace process has been a vehicle for American influence throughout the broad Middle Eastern region. It has provided a rationale for Arab relationship with the United States, even if Americans remain devoted to Israel. In other words, the peace process has eased potential opposite pulls of US Middle East policy.

Arab wars against Israel stopped after 1973, because in the eyes of Arabs they became too costly, both militarily and economically, and because the strong military ties between the United States and Israel have made such wars unthinkable. To be sure, there was a brief and painful oil embargo for five months in 1973 and 1974. It was the zenith for the linkage school, but it would quickly pass for a variety of reasons and would not come anywhere close to achieving its objective of having Israel yield its gains of the 1967 war. Among those reasons was that Egypt lost interest in the embargo once it achieved its first disengagement agreement with Israel and entered the US orbit. The Saudis also wanted to maintain their military ties with the United States and were more focused on regional dynamics whereby the chief Saudi rival, the shah of Iran, would use extra funds for weapons that could be used to threaten Riyadh.

Close US-Israeli ties prevented bloodshed, led both Egypt and Jordan (which fought in 1948 and 1967 but not in 1973) to peacefully solve their conflicts with Israel, and helped bring Syria to the peace table. This does not mean that there are no more local conflicts involving at different times Hamas and Hizbollah, but these have not spilled over into a regional conflict.

Former Egyptian President Hosni Mubarak explained the futility of wars between the Arabs and Israel:

> We fought for many years, but where did we get? We also spent 100 billions on wars, apart from thousands of martyrs until we reached the present situation for which we are now suffering. I am therefore not ready to take more risks. . . . Wars have generally not solved any problem. Regardless of the difficulties or obstacles surrounding the peace process, our real effort focuses on removing these obstacles and bringing viewpoints closer.[18]

Indeed, Mubarak's view had been that war is self-defeating for Egypt, which sacrificed a lot for the Palestinian cause. For this pragmatic cost-benefit approach, Mubarak's regime was rewarded more than $2 billion in annual US assistance since the early 1980s. Foreign aid greatly helped stabilize the Egyptian regime. It is true that the United States spent $100 billion to support Israel and Egypt, but relatively little American blood has been spilled in the Middle East in close to forty years in the Arab-Israeli conflict zone. Compare this to the $1 trillion the United States spent since 2003 just defending Iraq, where more than 4,000 Americans were killed.

A strong US-Israeli relationship was part of the broader regional picture that would evolve by the early 1990s: the end of the Cold War, and a victory over a pillar of Arab rejectionism, Saddam Hussein's Iraq after the United States ousted the dictator from Kuwait. This broader environment facilitated a historic Middle East peace conference in Madrid in October 1991 and enabled the landmark Israeli-Palestinian Oslo accords, capped by the famous handshake between Yasser Arafat and Yitzhak Rabin on the White House lawn on September 13, 1993. Movement on the Palestinian track plus a favorable regional environment also facilitated the Israeli-Jordanian peace treaty on October 26, 1994. Held on the Israeli-Jordanian border, this treaty ceremony, like the Oslo ceremony, was presided over by the same US president, Bill Clinton. The United States, which had worked to stabilize the region, received political credit for both events.

Taken together, strong US efforts to stabilize the region and the favorable regional environment engendered by the end of the Cold War and the first Gulf War yielded dividends. They helped the Israeli-Palestinian conflict move more toward its communal roots and away from the destructive interstate warfare that had characterized the region in the past.

Post–Cold War, Post-9/11

Although Mearsheimer and Walt concede that during the Cold War, Israel may have been an asset to the United States, they suggest that in the post–Cold War period and certainly after 9/11, whatever value Israel had has long since been replaced by costs. Their argument is that securing oil and good relations with the Arab world should be the primary US goal in the Middle East, and American association with and strong support for Israel impedes this aim.

Specifically, they write that Arab and Muslim antipathy toward the United States results from their identifying the United States with Israel.

But the Mideast is far more complex than they appreciate. Not only has the US-Israeli relationship not been a liability for either country, but also it has been, at least to some extent, an asset to the Arab regimes, as a strategic counterweight to radicalism.

Radicals, led by Iran, are enemies not only of the United States and Israel but also of key Arab regimes. The Saudis and the other members of the Gulf Cooperation Council believe that Iran has hegemonic designs on Arab oil. Senior officials in these states, as well as their counterparts in Egypt, Jordan, and Lebanon, also fear Iran for security, territorial, and ideological reasons. They see Iran as hostile to the Arabs for reasons relating to a mix of historical incursions by Persia into the Arab world, aspirations for regional dominance, and sectarian differences. They fear that Iran will funnel money to militant organizations, such as Hizbollah and Hamas, so that these proxies will destabilize the Arab regimes and gain Iran a foothold in a Sunni Arab world. Iran could, in their eyes, also foment social unrest among Shiite communities in the oil-sensitive areas of Saudi Arabia and Bahrain. And the Arab regimes fear that Iranian support from abroad could fuel local extremism.

After all, if Iran can fund a Sunni Hamas, why could it not fund the Muslim Brotherhood in Egypt or the Islamic Action Front in Jordan?

And yet the United States and Israel are often the most likely to act—or at least to serve as the strongest countervailing forces—against Hamas and Hizbollah and perhaps against Iran, leaving Arab regimes to benefit while still maintaining an arm's distance from Israel. Few Arab governments actually believe that a weak Israel would serve their national interests.

Converging Interests

In the post-9/11 world, there are numerous cases of converging interests between Israel and Arab regimes, shaped by a perception of common enemies. Four recent cases highlight this point.

First, after the 2007 Israeli bombing of the Syrian reactor, Israel remained silent and, tellingly, so did the Arab regimes, with none condemning the action, indicating their displeasure with Syria's growing ties to Iran.

Second, in 2006, Arab states led by Saudi Arabia were horrified that Hizbollah went to war against Israel without the vote of the Lebanese government;[19] it was a unilateral decision, facilitated by Iranian weapons. Many Arab regimes were distressed by Israel's lackluster military performance and the inconclusive outcome of this war: the Arabs wanted Hizbollah to be defeated, not to emerge stronger from the conflict, as they feared the emergence of Iran-backed Islamist militias used as instruments for upending the existing order in the region.

In an unprecedented fashion, Arab regimes publicly blamed Hizbollah for being reckless in launching the 2006 war against Israel—a dramatic stance in a region where regimes reflexively blame Israel for confrontations with Arabs and have historically justified resistance against Israeli occupation.

Third, Iran's support for Hamas has added to Arab regimes' fears of Iran. When this support is combined with Iran's emerging nuclear program, Arab leaders see an Iran that appears to be on the march, without hesitation to do all it can to put pressure on them. At the start of the Gaza conflict in December 2008, Egyptian[20] and Saudi foreign ministers[21] publicly blamed Hamas as being responsible for the crisis. Egypt, the only country to share a border with Gaza, refused—and still refuses—to fully open it to Gaza.

In the same context, there is also an unstated convergence of interests between Israel and the Palestinian Authority, since both regard Hamas as an enemy and work toward curtailing the group's economic and military efforts.

And fourth, Israel and the Arabs share a desire to curb Iran's sphere of influence. It is widely believed that an Iran with nuclear weapons will lead Egypt and Saudi Arabia (as well as the non-Arab Turkey) to go down that same path.

The Arab states also fear that if Tehran gains a bomb, it could even lead to Iran providing nuclear materials to nonstate actors, such as Hizbollah and Hamas. They also recognize that a nuclear Iran would have a shield behind which it could engage in much greater coercion of its neighbors with little fear of recourse.

Conclusion

The current liability school is not new. It was often championed by the traditionalist, Arabist school that dominated the US State Department during the Cold War. Although this school of thought was most prominent during Israel's early years, it has persisted into subsequent decades. Adherents to both the Arabist and the liability schools tend to conceptualize American Middle East policy through a zero-sum lens. Both maintain that any step the US takes toward Israel is necessarily a step away from the Arabs. In other words, these schools align with one side to ensure distance from the other.

And yet history has shown that Arab governments are driven more by their own national interests than by such reflexive zero-sum thinking. This is true in the post-9/11 period, no less than the Cold War era. These governments are more in fear of Iran and nonstate actors seeking to destabilize the region than concerned with countering Israeli influence. Hence, a zero-sum mind-set reflects an inability to appreciate the complex dynamics of the Middle East.

As Americans, we should learn from history and recognize this complexity. We should avert any zero-sum diplomatic straitjackets as we pursue our foreign policy. The United States can in fact be close to Israel and close to Arabs simultaneously. The historical record of how these countries pursue their own national interests suggests that this does not pose an inevitable contradiction, since Arab states are more focused on their domestic priorities or view the United States as trumping inter-Arab rivalries.

History has shown that a strong US-Israeli relationship has deterred interstate conflict since 1973. The US ability to maintain cordial ties with Arab states has given the United States a unique role as a peace mediator in the Middle East, certainly since the landmark Madrid peace conference of 1991. Of course, peace in the Middle East is important for its own purposes, but also to ease contrasting pulls on American foreign policy. At the same time, the American ability to play this role going forward will depend upon many factors, including not falling prey to the mistaken approach of the Arabists of the past and the liability school of the present—even in the context of the rapid changes in the Arab world engendered by the Arab Spring.[22]

Notes

1. John J. Mearsheimer and Stephen M. Walt, *The Israel Lobby and U.S. Foreign Policy* (New York: Farrar, Straus & Giroux, 2007).

2. Robert D. Kaplan, *The Romance of an American Elite* (New York: Free Press, 1993), pp. 7, 86.

3. Ibn Saud to FDR on May 11, 1943, Foreign Relations of the United States (FRUS), 1943, 4: 773–774, University of Wisconsin Digital Collections.

4. Telegram from William Eddy to the Secretary of State, FRUS, 1945, 8: 687.

5. Peter Grose, *Israel in the Mind of America* (New York: Knopf, 1983), p. 113.

6. Ibid., p. 287.

7. "The Recognition of the State of Israel," Harry S. Truman Library and Museum, last updated June 20, 2011, www.trumanlibrary.org /whistlestop/study_collections/israel/large /index.php.

8. James Forrestal, *The Forrestal Diaries* (New York: Viking Press, 1951), p. 357.

9. Ibid., p. 372.

10. P. J. Vatikiotis, *Nasser and His Generation* (New York: St. Martin's Press, 1978), p. 226.

11. Peter Rodman, *More Precious than Peace: Winning the Cold War in the Third World* (Farmington Hills, MI: Gale, 1994), p. 85.

12. Ibid., p. 84.

13. Memorandum of a Conversation, Department of State, FRUS, 1955–1957, 16: 1344.

14. Gamal Abdel Nasser, in *Record of Aggression: The Arab Design for Israel's Annihilation* (New York: Israel Information Services, 1967), p. 6.

15. Richard A. Mobley, "U.S. Joint Military Contributions to Countering Syria's 1970 Invasion of Jordan," *Joint Force Quarterly* 55 (2009): 160.

16. The Shiloah Center for Middle Eastern and African Studies, *Middle East Record* (Jerusalem: Israel Universities Press, 1973), p. 75.

17. Henry Kissinger, *Years of Upheaval* (Boston: Little, Brown, 1982), p. 469.

18. Interview, Middle East News Agency (January 24, 1989) in Foreign Broadcast Information Service Daily Report: Near East: South Asia (January 25, 1989), p. 15.

19. Hassan M. Fattah, "Arab League Criticizes Hezbollah for Attacks," *International Herald Tribune*, July 17, 2006, www.nytimes.com/2006 /07/17/world/africa/17iht-arabs.2224812.html.

20. Steven Erlanger, "Egyptians Blame Hamas, yet Are Angry at Cairo As Well," *International Herald Tribune*, January 2, 2008, www.iht.com /articles/2009/01/02/mideast/egypt.php.

21. Ian Black, "Saudis Blame Hamas amid Calls for Talks with Fatah," *The Guardian*, January 1, 2009, www.guardian.co.uk/world /2009/jan/01/saudi-arabia-hamas-gaza.

22. For an analysis of the early approach of the Obama administration toward the Arab Spring, see Chapter 3 in this volume.

3

George W. Bush, Barack Obama, and the Arab-Israeli Conflict from 2001 to 2011

Robert O. Freedman

IT HAS BEEN MORE THAN TWO YEARS since Barack Obama took office. During this period, there have been numerous media comparisons between the policies of the Obama administration and those of its predecessor, the George W. Bush administration. Particularly regarding the Middle East, the policies of the two administrations have diverged the most sharply, especially concerning the Arab-Israeli conflict. This essay will compare the two administrations and seek to draw a number of conclusions as to where the policies were similar and where they have differed.

I would like to thank Dr. P. R. Kumaraswamy and his students at the Middle East Institute of Jawa-harlal Nehru University in New Delhi for their insightful comments on an earlier version of this chapter.

George W. Bush and Israel

The policy of the Bush administration toward Israel and the Arab-Israeli conflict moved through six distinct stages. First, from his inauguration until 9/11, George W. Bush was generally supportive of Israel while distancing his administration from the Arab-Israeli conflict. Second, from 9/11 to June 2002, the administration actively sought to solve the Israeli-Palestinian conflict to build Muslim support for Bush's war against the Taliban in Afghanistan and the coming war against Iraq. The third stage, from June 2002 to Yasser Arafat's death in November 2004, witnessed periodic attempts by the United States to facilitate an Israeli-Palestinian settlement; the April 2003 Road Map to lead to a peace settlement was the best example. The administration also developed a policy that called for democratization of the Arab world as a means of preventing terrorism. The fourth period, from Arafat's death in November 2004 to the Hamas election victory of January 2006, witnessed an attempt to politically boost Arafat's successor, Mahmoud Abbas, while also coordinating with the Palestinians Israel's plan for a unilateral withdrawal from Gaza. The fifth stage, from January 2006 to June 2007, was marked by increasing difficulties for the United States in Iraq, which drew the administration's attention away from the Arab-Israeli conflict. At the same time, the US democratization program in the Arab world had foundered. To make matters worse, during this period the United States found itself confronted with increasing conflict between Israel and the Palestinians and, in the summer of 2006, a war between Israel and Hizbollah. The final stage, from July 2007 to January 2009, witnessed a final, albeit unsuccessful, effort by the Bush administration to achieve a Palestinian-Israeli peace agreement, highlighted by the November 2007 Annapolis conference.

From the Inauguration to 9/11

When the Bush administration took office in 2001, it had a number of reasons not to continue Clinton's activist policy toward the Arab-Israeli conflict. First, Bush had witnessed the major effort Clinton had made and the relatively meager results he had achieved. Bush, who sought to clearly distinguish himself from Clinton, chose not to follow the same path. Second, even if he had wanted to, Bush was unwilling to risk his limited political capital (he had won a very narrow—and questionable—victory in a hotly disputed election) and he wanted to save his political capital for more promising policy initiatives, such as tax cuts and an ABM (antiballistic missile) program. As a result, the administration distanced itself from the Arab-Israeli conflict, a move shown most clearly when Dennis Ross, who had been the special US mediator for the Arab-Israeli conflict, resigned in January 2001 and was not replaced.

However, distancing itself from the Arab-Israeli conflict—and the ongoing Al-Aqsa Intifada—did not mean the administration had distanced itself from Israel. On the contrary—and much to the discomfiture of Arafat and other Arab leaders—Bush quickly developed a close and warm relationship with Israeli Prime Minister Ariel Sharon, who was invited to visit the White House in mid-March 2001.

On the eve of the visit, the new American secretary of state, Colin Powell, gave a major speech supportive of Israel to the pro-Israeli AIPAC lobbying organization. In the speech he echoed Israel's position that the starting point for peace talks had to be the end of violence. In a clear slap at Arafat, Powell publicly stated that "leaders have the responsibility to denounce violence, strip it of legitimacy [and] stop it." Powell also asserted the Bush administration's position that the United States would assist in but not impose a peace agreement; "the US stands ready to assist, not insist. Peace arrived at voluntarily by the partners themselves is likely to prove more robust . . . than a peace widely viewed as developed by others, or worse yet, imposed."[1]

In a meeting several days later, Bush again reassured Sharon that the United States would facilitate, not force, the peace process. Bush also sought to enlist Sharon in his campaign to develop a national missile defense system, something the Israeli leader, whose country was a prime target of such "rogue" states as Iran and Iraq, was only too happy to agree to. Sharon, for his part, pressed Bush not to invite Arafat to the White House unless Arafat publicly called for an end to the violence, a request endorsed by nearly three hundred members of Congress (87 senators and 209 House members), who also called on Bush to close the Washington office of the PLO and to cut US aid to the Palestinian Authority if the violence did not cease.[2]

The one bit of American activism on the peace process during this period came following the publication of the Mitchell Report in mid-May. The report contained a series of recommendations for ending the rapidly escalating Israeli-Palestinian conflict, first and foremost "a 100 percent effort to stop the violence."[3] Although Israel accepted the recommendation, with Sharon ordering a cease-fire, a series of Palestinian terrorist attacks that Arafat either could not or would not stop undermined the cease-fire. Visits by the new assistant secretary of state for Near Eastern affairs, Nicholas Burns, CIA chief George Tenet, and Powell himself failed to resuscitate the cease-fire. [4] Indeed, the escalating violence was now punctuated by Palestinian suicide bombings against Israeli civilian targets, such as pizza parlors and discotheques, attacks that the United States strongly denounced. It is quite possible that the Bush administration, having witnessed the failure of its one major activist effort to resuscitate the Israeli-Palestinian peace process, concluded that its original hands-off policy toward the conflict was the correct one, and until 9/11, it distanced itself from the conflict. All of this, of course, would change after 9/11.

From 9/11 to June 2002

Immediately after the terrorist attacks on the World Trade Center and the Pentagon, the United States changed its hands-off policy toward the Israeli-Palestinian conflict and sought to build a coalition, including Muslim states, against Osama bin Laden and his al-Qaeda terrorist organization. In an effort to gain Arab support, the United States announced its backing of a Palestinian state and exercised a considerable amount of pressure on Sharon to agree to a meeting between Israeli Foreign Minister Shimon Peres and Arafat to establish yet another cease-fire, even though Palestinian violence had not stopped as Sharon had demanded as the price for talks. Frustrated by this US policy, Sharon called it the equivalent of British and French policy at the 1938 Munich Conference, where Czechoslovakia had been sold out to the Nazis. His comments drew a retort from the White House press secretary, Ari Fleischer, who called them "unacceptable."[5]

This, however, would be the low point in the US-Israeli relationship under Bush. Following its rapid military victory in Afghanistan, the United States embarked on a twofold strategy. The first part, trying to reinvigorate the Israeli-Palestinian peace process, was warmly greeted by US European allies and by pro-US governments in the Arab world. The second part of the strategy, threatening to carry the war from Afghanistan to other supporters of terrorism, especially Iraq, met with far less support.

The US effort to invigorate the Israeli-Palestinian peace process began with a speech by President Bush at the United Nations in November 2001, in which he said, "We are working for the day when two states—Israel and Palestine—live peacefully together within secure and recognized boundaries." However, in a clear warning to Arafat to crack down on terrorists, he added, "Peace will come when all have sworn off forever incitement, violence, and terror. There is no such thing as a good terrorist."[6] Bush also pointedly did not meet Arafat at the United Nations, as National Security Adviser Condoleezza Rice noted, "You cannot help us with al-Qaeda, and hug Hizbollah or Hamas. And so the President makes that clear to Mr. Arafat."[7] The United States backed up Rice's words by adding Hamas, Islamic Jihad, and Hizbollah to its post–September 11 terrorist list.

The next step in the peace effort came on November 19 with a major speech by Secretary of State Colin Powell on the US view of a solution to the Israeli-Palestinian conflict.[8] In his speech, Powell strongly condemned Palestinian terrorism, noting that the al-Aqsa Intifada was mired in "self-defeating violence." He also stated that although the United States believed that there should be a two-state solution to the conflict—with the states of Palestine and Israel living side by side within secure and recognized borders—"the Palestinians must make a 100 percent effort to stop terrorism, and . . . this effort required actions, not words: Terrorists must be arrested." Powell emphasized that "no wrong can ever justify the murder of the innocent," that terror and violence must stop now, and that the Palestinians must realize their goals through negotiations, not violence. He further asserted—possibly in response to Arafat's call for the return to Israel of more than 3 million Palestinian refugees, a development that would have upset Israel's demographic balance—that the Palestinians must accept the legitimacy of Israel as a Jewish state.

While emphasizing that the United States and Israel were closely "bound together by democratic tradition" and that the United States had an "enduring and iron-clad commitment to Israeli security," Powell indicated that Israel, too, had to make concessions for peace to be possible. These included a stop to settlement expansion and an end to the occupation of the West Bank and Gaza, which "causes humiliation and the killing of innocents." In conclusion, Powell stated that the United States would do everything it could to facilitate the peace process, "but at the end of the day the peoples have to make peace"—a position very similar to the one Powell had held when he joined the cabinet nearly a year earlier.

To implement the US vision of peace Powell had outlined, in addition to promises of economic aid, Assistant Secretary of State William Burns and former marine general Anthony Zinni were dispatched to meet with Israeli and Palestinian delegations to reach a cease-fire that would lay the basis for peace negotiations to resume. In an effort to facilitate the Zinni mission, President Bush put his personal prestige on the line by writing to five important Arab leaders—King Abdullah II of Jordan, Egyptian President Hosni Mubarak, King Mohammed VI of Morocco, Saudi Crown Prince Abdullah (who had publicly praised Powell's speech), and President Ben-Ali of Tunisia—asking for their help in persuading "the Palestinian leadership to take action to end violence and get the peace process back on track."[9]

On November 27, soon after Zinni's arrival in the Middle East, two Palestinian terrorists, one of whom was a member of Arafat's Fatah organization (the other was from Islamic Jihad), killed three Israelis and wounded thirty others in Afulah, a town in northern Israel. Zinni responded to the violence in a balanced way, stating, "This is why we need a cease-fire. Both sides have suffered too much."[10] Zinni then met with Arafat, asking him to end the violence, but even as they were meeting, Palestinian gunmen fired at the Israeli Jerusalem neighborhood of Gilo from the neighboring Palestinian suburb of Beit Jala—despite an explicit October promise by Palestinian leaders not to do so.[11] The next day three more Israelis were killed as a suicide bomber exploded a bomb on a public bus near the Israeli city of Hadera.[12] This time Zinni's response was much stronger: "The groups that do this are clearly trying to make my mission fail. There's no justification, no rationale, no sets of conditions that will ever make terrorist acts a right way to respond."[13] Zinni's words, however, did not stem the tide of terrorism. Two days later, suicide bombers killed ten Israeli teenagers who had gathered at the Ben Yehuda pedestrian mall in Jerusalem. This time Arafat condemned the attacks, stressing not the loss of life by Israel but the negative political effect the suicide bombers were having on the Palestinian world image.[14]

By now Zinni was furious, as he saw his mission literally going up in flames: "Those responsible for planning and carrying out these attacks must be found and brought to justice. This is an urgent task and there can be no delay or excuses for not acting decisively. The deepest evil one can imagine is to attack young people and children."[15] President Bush, whose prestige had been put on the line by the Zinni mission, also responded strongly: "Now more than ever Chairman Arafat and the Palestinian Authority must demonstrate through their actions, and not merely their words, their commitment to fight terror."[16]

Arafat seemed to get the message, if rather belatedly, from US political pressure and from Israeli military retaliation. On December 16, he called for an immediate cease-fire, condemning both suicide attacks and the launching of mortar attacks.[17] Nonetheless, the Palestinian leader did not root out the Hamas and Islamic Jihad organizations from Gaza and the West Bank; rather, he negotiated a tenuous truce with them (a tactic later repeated by Mahmoud Abbas in March 2005), an action that was clearly unsatisfactory to the Israeli government. Arafat was kept penned up in Ramallah by Israeli tanks, and in a further blow to his prestige, he was prohibited from leaving his compound to attend Christmas services in Bethlehem.

Three weeks after Arafat's call for a cease-fire, Israeli forces captured a ship in the Red Sea, the *Karine A,* which held fifty tons of concealed weapons, including C-4 explosives and Katyusha rockets—clearly weapons of terrorism. Arafat's initial denial that the Palestinian Authority had anything to do with the vessel further undermined his credibility, both in Israel and in the United States.[18] In response to heavy pressure by the United States, Arafat eventually arrested several of the Palestinian officials involved, including a major general in his own security forces and an officer in the Palestinian Authority's naval police.[19]

Meanwhile, Hamas broke the truce by attacking an Israeli military outpost in Gaza, killing four soldiers and claiming the attack was in retaliation for Israel's seizure of the *Karine A.*[20] Israel retaliated, destroying, among other things, the runway of the Palestinian airport in Gaza, and after a terrorist attack against an Israeli bar mitzvah party in Hadera, in which six Israelis were killed and thirty wounded, Israel blew up the main Palestinian radio transmitter.[21]

Thus ended the first year of the Bush administration's efforts to resolve the Israeli-Palestinian conflict. Despite two major US efforts, one in June and one in November–December 2001, Palestinian terrorism, which Arafat was unable or, more likely, unwilling to control (he had long used terrorism as a political weapon), had sabotaged US efforts to resolve the Palestinian-Israeli conflict. Nonetheless, both Arab states and the European Union (EU) continued to urge the United States to get more engaged in the search for Arab-Israeli peace. In response, in a remarkably frank interview with the *New York Times* on February 28, 2002, Colin Powell stated, "We have not put it [the search for an Arab-Israeli peace agreement] on the back burner. What that [US engagement] usually means is 'Go and force the Israelis to do something.' That's what many people think when they say 'Get more engaged' or 'You're standing on the sidelines. You haven't made Israel blink in the face of violence.'"[22]

Meanwhile, President Bush had sent his vice president, Dick Cheney, who often took a much harder line than Powell, to the Arab world to build Arab support for a planned US attack on Iraq. Cheney was met with strong Arab calls for the United States to work out a solution to the Israeli-Palestinian conflict before engaging in a war with Iraq. This position apparently convinced Bush to send Zinni back for another try at achieving a cease-fire. To facilitate the Zinni visit, Sharon made a major concession by lifting his demand for the passage of seven days without violence before talks could resume. The atmosphere of the Zinni visit was further improved by the announcement of an Arab-Israeli peace plan suggested by Saudi Arabia. This plan would be introduced at the Arab summit scheduled for the end of March in Beirut and involved Arab recognition of Israel in return for Israel's return to its 1967 boundaries and a fair solution to the Palestinian refugee problem. To help reinforce the momentum for peace, the United States pushed for the new UN Security Council Resolution 1397, on March 13, 2002, which called for a two-state solution to the Israeli-Palestinian conflict; the end of violence, incitement, and terrorism; and the resumption of negotiations based on the Tenet and Mitchell plans.[23]

Unfortunately, the diplomatic momentum was shattered by another series of Palestinian terrorist attacks just as Zinni was seeking to consolidate a cease-fire and the Arab summit was taking place in Beirut. On March 27, the first night of the Jewish holiday of Passover, twenty-nine Jews were murdered and more than one hundred wounded at a Passover seder in the coastal resort town of Netanya. This attack was followed by suicide bombings in Jerusalem, Tel Aviv, and Haifa over the next three days, resulting in the deaths of an additional seventeen people and the wounding of eighty-four. These events precipitated an Israeli attack on Arafat's compound in Ramallah, followed by a sweep into the major Palestinian cities of the West Bank, in what Sharon called Operation Defensive Shield.

As these events were unfolding, the United States at first strongly backed Israel, with Powell noting, "Sharon made concessions, while Arafat backed terrorism."[24] Then, when mass demonstrations broke out in the Arab world, which may have worried Bush as he stepped up his preparations for an attack on Iraq, the president decided to once again involve the United States. In a major speech on April 4, 2002, after first denouncing terrorism and pointedly noting that "the chairman of the Palestinian Authority has not consistently opposed or confronted terrorists nor has he renounced terror as he agreed to do at Oslo," Bush called for the Israelis to withdraw from the West Bank cities they were occupying.[25] Bush also announced that he was sending Powell to the Middle East to work out a cease-fire. Several days later, the president urged the Israelis to withdraw "without delay,"[26] but then he ran into a firestorm of domestic criticism for pressuring Israel. First, neoconservatives who were the intellectual lifeblood of the administration attacked Bush for urging Sharon to withdraw, claiming the Israeli leader was fighting terrorism just as the United States was doing after 9/11. Then evangelical Christians, a large and energetic base of Bush's core constituency, also attacked the president for pressuring Israel.[27] Third, on April 15, 250,000 people rallied for Israel on the Mall in Washington, a demonstration organized by the US Jewish community; the demonstration also included evangelical Christians among its speakers. The message of the rally was that the United States should support Israel's fight against Palestinian terrorism, which was similar to the US antiterrorism policy after 9/11. Finally, the administration was severely criticized by influential members of Congress, including Republican House Majority Leader Tom DeLay, a strong friend of Israel.[28]

Another factor prompting Bush to change his position was Arafat's continued sponsorship of terrorism. When Arafat's wife came out in support of suicide bombings as a legitimate form of resistance against Israeli occupation, and the Israelis gave the United States documents showing that Arafat had not only tolerated terrorism but also had helped finance it, Bush further turned against the Palestinian leader. On May 26, while on a state visit to Russia, Bush noted that Arafat "hasn't delivered. He had a chance to secure the peace as a result of the hard work of President Clinton and he didn't. He had a chance to fight terrorism and he hasn't."[29]

As Palestinian terrorist attacks continued to proliferate, Sharon, who had pulled Israeli forces out of the cities of the West Bank in May 2002, sent them back in June, this time with minimal criticism from the United States. Indeed, in a major speech on June 24, Bush called for a "new and different Palestinian leadership" so that a Palestinian state could be born. In the most anti-Arafat speech in his presidency, Bush stated:

> I call on the Palestinian people to elect new leaders, leaders not compromised by terror. I call upon them to build a practicing democracy, based on tolerance and liberty. If the Palestinian people actively pursue these goals, America and the world will actively support their efforts. If the Palestinian people meet these goals, they will be able to reach agreement with Israel and Egypt and Jordan on security and other arrangements for

independence. And when the Palestinian people have new leaders, new institutions, and new security arrangements with their neighbors, the United States of America will support the creating of a Palestinian state whose borders and certain aspects of its sovereignty will be provisional until resolved as part of a final settlement in the Middle East.

Today, Palestinian authorities are encouraging, not opposing, terrorism. This is unacceptable and the United States will not support the establishment of a Palestinian state until its leaders engage in a sustained fight against the terrorists and dismantle their infrastructure. This will require an externally supervised effort to rebuild and reform the Palestinian security services. The security system must have clear lines of authority and accountability and a unified chain of command.[30]

President Bush then called on Israel to respond to a new Palestinian leadership when it was formed:

As new Palestinian institutions and new leaders emerge, demonstrating real performance on reform, I expect Israel to respond and work toward a final status agreement. With intensive security and effort by all, this agreement could be reached within three years from now. And I and my country will actively lead toward that goal. . . . As we make progress toward security, Israeli forces need to withdraw fully to positions they held prior to September 28, 2000. And consistent with the recommendations of the Mitchell Committee, Israeli settlement activity in the occupied territories must stop.[31]

Although Bush chided the Israelis somewhat on settlement activity, the brunt of the president's ire was clearly on Arafat, and with this speech Bush formally joined Sharon in ruling out Arafat as a partner in the peace process.

US Policy from June 2002 to November 2004

Following the June 24 speech, US foreign policy in the Middle East had two main objectives. The first was to work with the European Union, Russia, and the United Nations as part of a "Diplomatic Quartet" to fashion a road map leading to a Palestinian-Israeli peace settlement. The second was to build a large coalition to prepare for war with Iraq.

In designing the road map with the EU, Russia, and the UN, the Bush administration faced a major problem. Although the United States had written off Arafat as a suitable partner for peace, as had Israel, the other three members of the Diplomatic Quartet had not, and this discrepancy caused problems in subsequent diplomacy. In addition, the presentation of the Road Map, which the Quartet began planning in July 2002, was delayed on numerous occasions and was not made public until the major combat phase of the Anglo-American invasion of Iraq was completed at the end of March 2003. As a result, many cynical, and not so cynical, Middle East observers felt that the Road Map was aimed at merely assuaging the Arabs while the Bush administration prepared to attack Iraq.[32] Indeed, in the run-up to the war in September 2002, when the Israelis laid siege to Arafat's compound in Ramallah following another series of brutal suicide bombings, the United States chose to abstain on, rather than veto, a UN Security Council resolution condemning the Israeli action, with Condoleezza Rice reportedly telling the Israeli government that the United States expected a speedy resolution of the siege because it "doesn't help" US efforts to galvanize support for the campaign against Iraq.[33]

In any case, following delays on account of the Israeli elections of January 2003 (in which Sharon's Likud Party scored an impressive victory) and the invasion of Iraq, which began in late March, the Road Map was finally published on April 30, 2003. At the time, it appeared that Bush, spurred on by his ally, British Prime Minister Tony Blair, wanted to prove his critics wrong by demonstrating that he was genuinely interested in an Israeli-Palestinian peace agreement. According to the Road Map, which the Bush administration announced with great fanfare, the Palestinians, in phase one of the three-phase plan leading to a Palestinian state, had to "declare an unequivocal end to violence and terrorism and end incitement against Israel and undertake visible efforts on the ground to arrest, disrupt, and restrain individuals and groups conducting and planning attacks on Israelis anywhere."[34] Second, the Palestinians had to appoint an "empowered" prime minister and establish a government based on a strong parliamentary democracy and cabinet and have only three security services, which would report to the empowered prime minister. By these measures, the United States had hoped to weaken, if not eliminate, Arafat's power base and in his place create a prime minister who would be a proper partner for peace. For its part, Israel, under phase one of the Road Map, had to refrain from deporting Palestinians, attacking Palestinian civilians, and confiscating or demolishing Palestinian homes and property, and as the "comprehensive security performance" of the Palestinians moved forward, the Israeli military had to "withdraw progressively" from areas occupied since September 28, 2000; dismantle settlement outposts erected since March 2001; and "freeze all settlement activity [including natural growth of settlements]."

With Bush at the peak of his international influence, as a result of the apparent military victory in Iraq, Arafat was compelled to accede to the Road Map's demands to create the post of prime minister, to which senior Palestinian leader Mahmoud Abbas, also known as Abu Mazen, was appointed. Yet this appointment appeared to be a ploy; it soon became evident that Abbas was not the "empowered" prime minister the United States had in mind, since Arafat retained control over most of the Palestinian security forces. Apparently the United States had overlooked this fact in the hope that Abbas, who unlike Arafat had never been demonized by either Sharon or the Israeli public, had sufficient power to be a credible negotiating partner for Israel. Although the Palestinian Authority accepted the Road Map, Hamas, Islamic Jihad, the al-Aqsa Martyrs Brigade, and the Tanzim (young militants tied to Arafat's Fatah organization) did not. Israel also accepted it, albeit with a number of reservations. When the Road Map was published, it was attacked by eighty-eight US senators, who asserted that its position against Palestinian terrorism was not as strong as that in Bush's statement of June 24, 2002.[35]

Initially the Road Map was greeted with optimism, especially when on June 29, 2003, Abbas succeeded in eliciting a ninety-day *hudna,* or truce, from the leaders of Hamas, the Tanzim, and Islamic Jihad, though not from the al-Aqsa Martyrs Brigade.

Although Israeli military leaders worried that the terrorist group would use the ninety days to rebuild their forces and armaments (especially the Qassam rockets that had been fired into Israel from Gaza), Sharon proved willing to take a chance on the *hudna.* He called for the withdrawal of Israeli forces from northern Gaza and Bethlehem; the closing of some checkpoints hindering traffic between Palestinian villages and cities; the shutdown of some illegal outposts on the West Bank (although other outposts were set up); the release of some Palestinian prisoners (though far fewer than the Palestinians wanted), including an elderly terrorist who had killed fourteen Israelis in 1975; and the loosening of work restrictions on Palestinians.

President Bush sought to move the peace process forward by meeting with both Abbas and Sharon in Washington in July 2003, although differences over Israel's construction of its security wall proved to be problematic during Bush's talks with the two leaders.[36] Meanwhile, during the *hudna,* attacks on Israel continued, including the murder of Israeli civilians, although the number of attacks decreased significantly from the period preceding the *hudna.* In addition, Abbas worked to lessen anti-Israeli incitement, painting over some of the anti-Israel slogans displayed on walls in Gaza. However, the key demand of both Bush and the Israelis—that Abbas crack down on the terrorists—was not met, primarily because Arafat refused to allow it. Nonetheless, Abbas tried to convince the United States that he could negotiate a permanent truce with the terrorist groups. Although some in the US State Department seemed to be willing to go along with Abbas, Sharon was not, and as attacks on Israelis continued during the *hudna,* Sharon decided to retaliate by attacking the Hamas and Islamic Jihad terrorists who were seen as responsible. Then, on August 19, less than two months into the *hudna,* a terrorist attack in Jerusalem killed twenty-one Israelis, including a number of children. In response, Sharon stepped up his attacks on the terrorists, which led Hamas to declare an end to the *hudna.* Soon afterward, blaming both Arafat and Israel for a lack of support, Abbas resigned and the peace process again came to a halt.

In the aftermath of Abbas's resignation, with the peace process stalled, the United States again distanced itself from the Israeli-Palestinian peace process, as the Bush administration increasingly concentrated on the deteriorating situation in Iraq. Bush did, however, begin to push a policy of democratization for the Middle East. Influenced by Israeli politician Natan Sharansky's book *The Case for Democracy,* Bush came to argue that there were two major reasons the US should push to democratize the Middle East.[37] First, if young men had a chance to participate politically in their societies by joining political parties, demonstrating in the streets for their political positions, enjoying freedom of the press, and playing a role in choosing their nation's leaders through fair elections, they would be less likely to become terrorists. Second, democracies were less likely to fight each other than autocratic or totalitarian states. Thus, the administration's reasoning went, if the Middle East became more democratic, it would be less likely to spawn terrorists and would be a more peaceful region of the world. Bush's democratization policy also benefited Israel. As the only genuine democracy in the region (with the partial exception of Turkey), Israel was not only an antiterrorism ally of the United States, but a democratic one as well.

While Bush was formulating his democratization policy, Sharon was developing a new strategy of his own, the unilateral withdrawal from Gaza. This was conceived in part as an initiative to prevent other diplomatic efforts being imposed on Israel (such as the Geneva initiative of Yossi Beilin),[38] and in part to preserve Israel as both a Jewish and a democratic state by ending Israeli control over the approximately 1.4 million Palestinian Arabs living in the Gaza Strip.[39] At the same time, Sharon decided to make a major effort to speed up the building of the Israeli security fence between Israel and the West Bank to prevent Palestinian terrorist attacks on Israel. The fence, however, did not run along the old 1967 border but took in a swath of land on the West Bank.

By early 2004 the United States and Israel began detailed bargaining on the unilateral withdrawal and the security fence, and under US pressure (and that of the Israeli Supreme Court), Sharon agreed to move the security fence closer to the 1949 armistice line. According to then Israeli ambassador to the United States Daniel Ayalon, Sharon also agreed to add four settlements in the northern part of the West Bank to his disengagement plan.[40]

The result of the bargaining was a meeting between Sharon and Bush in Washington in mid-April 2004 that was structured not only to reinforce the Sharon disengagement initiative but also to help each leader politically. Thus Bush went a long way toward supporting Sharon's policies. Not only did he welcome Sharon's disengagement plan as "real progress" and assert that the United States was "strongly committed" to Israel's well-being as a Jewish state within "secure and defensible borders," but he also went on to reject any Palestinian "right of return" to Israel, stating, "It seems clear that an agreed, just, fair, and realistic framework for a solution to the Palestinian refugee issue as part of any final status agreement will need to be found through the establishment of a Palestinian state, and the settling of Palestinian refugees there, rather than in Israel."[41]

Bush also reinforced Israel's position that it would not fully return to the 1949 armistice lines and that any final agreement would have to reflect the settlements Israel had built since 1967, stating, "In light of new realities on the ground, including already existing population centers, it is unrealistic to expect that the outcome of final status negotiations will be a full and complete return to the armistice lines of 1949."

Finally, Bush reaffirmed Israel's "right to defend itself against terrorism including taking action against terrorist organizations." This statement not only endorsed Israel's right to go back into Gaza to fight terrorism but also implicitly endorsed Israel's strategy of assassinating the leaders of Hamas, a process that continued during the spring and summer of 2004.

In his meeting with Sharon, Bush also made a number of gestures toward the Palestinians. Not only did he reaffirm his commitment to a two-state solution to the Israeli-Palestinian conflict and call for Israel to freeze settlement activity and remove unauthorized outposts, but he also put limits on Israel's security wall, asserting, "As the government of Israel has stated, the barrier being erected by Israel should be a security rather than a political barrier, should be temporary, and therefore not prejudice any final status issues including final borders, and its route should take into account, consistent with security needs, its impact on Palestinians not engaged in terrorist activities." Nonetheless, returning to the theme he had emphasized since 9/11, Bush demanded that the Palestinians "act decisively against terror, including sustained, targeted, and effective operations to stop terrorism and dismantle terrorist capabilities and infrastructure."

Sharon clearly had scored a great diplomatic success with his visit, and he heaped lavish praise on President Bush. After noting that the disengagement plan "can be an important contribution" to the president's Road Map for peace, he went on to state, "You have proven, Mr. President, your ongoing, deep, and sincere friendship to the State of Israel and to the Jewish people. . . . In all these years, I have never met a leader as committed as you are, Mr. President, to the struggle for freedom and the need to confront terrorism wherever it exists."

Needless to say, for a president then deeply engaged in an election campaign against John Kerry, a liberal senator from Massachusetts, who normally could expect to get the vast majority of Jewish votes, Sharon's words were extremely helpful, especially in such pivotal states as Florida, with its large Jewish population. Indeed, not only did Bush strongly support Sharon on the disengagement plan, but the Bush administration also sent a twenty-six-page booklet, titled "President George W. Bush—A Friend of the American Jewish Community" to American Jewish organizations, stressing Bush's commitment to the state of Israel and to the world Jewish community. Prominent themes in the booklet were Bush's opposition to terrorism aimed at Israel and his opposition to PLO leader Yasser Arafat. The booklet stated, "For Yasser Arafat the message has been clear. While he was a frequent White House guest during the last administration, he has never been granted a meeting with President Bush."[42] In another effort to court Jewish support, Bush reportedly overrode opposition to create an office at the State Department to monitor the rising tide of anti-Semitism around the world. Perhaps reflecting on the political nature of the proposed office, an unnamed State Department official told the *Washington Times*, "It's more of a bureaucratic nuisance than a real problem. We are not going to fight a bill that has gained such political momentum."[43] Finally, on the eve of the US presidential election, Bush sent National Security Adviser Condoleezza Rice to address the AIPAC meeting in Florida. The very fact of her presence, despite an ongoing FBI probe of a Pentagon analyst who had allegedly passed secrets to the pro-Israeli lobbying organization, underlined the great importance the Bush administration placed on getting Jewish support in the election.[44]

Bush won the 2004 election by 3.5 million votes, and soon thereafter Arafat, seen by both the United States and Israel as the main obstacle to an Israeli-Palestinian settlement, died. Arafat's death set the stage for another US attempt to revive the Arab-Israeli peace process.

From Arafat's Death to the Hamas Victory in the Palestinian Elections

In the aftermath of Arafat's death and Bush's reelection victory, the situation initially appeared to improve, as far as US policy in the Middle East was concerned. First, the replacement of Colin Powell by Condoleezza Rice as secretary of state added a great deal of coherence to US policy, as the old rifts between the Department of State on the one hand and the White House and the Defense Department on the other were minimized. In addition, as Defense Secretary Donald Rumsfeld's influence declined because of the increased problems the United States was encountering in Iraq, Rice became the unquestioned administration spokesperson on foreign policy, especially on the Middle East. Second, the US plan for democratizing the Middle East appeared to score major triumphs with democratic elections being successfully held in Iraq, Lebanon, and the Palestinian Authority. In the PA, an election was held to choose Arafat's successor, and in what international observers considered a fair and democratic election, Mahmoud Abbas, a Fatah leader who had earlier served a brief term as Palestinian prime minister under the Road Map, was elected with 60 percent of the votes. What made Abbas such an appealing candidate for the United States was his regular denunciation of terrorism as inimical to Palestinian interests. Thus, with Abbas's election, the two main strands of US post-9/11 Middle

East policy—the fight against terrorism and support for democratization—came together, and it was not long before Abbas was welcomed to the White House with full pomp and ceremony, a privilege that had been denied to Arafat, whom the Bush administration saw as closely linked to terrorism. Sharon, for his part, made a series of gestures to Abbas in February 2005, including the release of seven hundred Palestinian detainees and agreement to a cease-fire. And to help Abbas strengthen his position in the PA, the United States dispatched Lieutenant General William Ward to reorganize the Palestinian armed forces and James Wolfensohn, former head of the World Bank, to help develop the Palestinian economy. Unfortunately, neither proved to be very effective. Ward was never able to transform the disparate Palestinian military groupings into an effective fighting force, and he was replaced by Major General Keith Dayton. As far as Wolfensohn was concerned, despite his heroic efforts—including the use of his personal funds to facilitate the purchase by the Palestinians of Israeli greenhouses in Gaza—the Palestinian economy remained problematic.

Although US-Palestinian relations got off to a good start after Abbas's election, the new Palestinian leader took a risky gamble in March 2005, when, in an effort to achieve harmony among the contending Palestinian forces, he signed an agreement with Hamas and several other Palestinian organizations (but not Islamic Jihad) providing that, in return for a cease-fire with Israel, the only mode of interaction among the Palestinians would be "dialogue."[45] This agreement ran counter to Israeli and American calls for Abbas to crack down on Hamas and the other Palestinian terrorist organizations. This issue became particularly pressing as Israel prepared to disengage from Palestinian territories during the summer of 2005, an action involving the pullout of Israeli settlements and military forces from Gaza and of Israeli settlements from the northern West Bank. Though Hamas had signed the cease-fire agreement, Islamic Jihad had not, and there were concerns that the Iranian-supported organization might disrupt the Israeli disengagement. This disruption never materialized, but Islamic Jihad did undertake a number of terrorist attacks against Israel in 2005, and the Israeli government responded with "targeted killings" (assassinations) of Islamic Jihad operatives.

The main problem for Israel, however, was Hamas, and unless Abbas moved against the Islamic organization, it appeared unlikely that Israel would take him seriously as a peace partner. Abbas, however, appeared more interested in creating Palestinian solidarity than in satisfying Israel. Indeed, in responding to my question in late June 2005 in Ramallah about why he had chosen not to crack down on Hamas after his strong victory in the Palestinian presidential elections, Abbas replied, "What, and have a Palestinian civil war?"[46] Unfortunately for Abbas, two years later the Palestinian civil war between Fatah and Hamas did occur, at a time when Abbas was much weaker and Hamas much stronger than in June 2005.

Despite Abbas's failure to crack down on Hamas, Secretary of State Rice sought to facilitate cooperation between Israel and the Abbas-led Palestinian Authority as the disengagement took place. Thus, she helped to negotiate a number of agreements between Israel and the PA, including one to haul away debris from the destroyed Jewish settlements (the PA had demanded their destruction), another on the modus operandi of the crossing points between Gaza and Egypt and between Gaza and Israel, and a third agreement on travel between Gaza and the West Bank. Although the disengagement went relatively smoothly, despite the protests of Jewish settlers in Gaza, the next issue to arise was the election for the Palestinian Legislative Council (PLC). Abbas had postponed the elections from their original July 2004 date to January 2006, in part to get political credit for the Israeli withdrawal, and in part because he could not settle the rifts between the old and young guards of his Fatah organization. A key issue in the elections was whether Hamas would run and, if so, under what conditions. Israeli Prime Minister Ariel Sharon initially opposed Hamas's participation in the elections, citing the Oslo Accords requirement that no "racist" party could run in the elections; because Hamas continued to call for the destruction of Israel, it was clearly "racist." Only if Hamas renounced terrorism and recognized Israel's right to exist should it be allowed to run, Sharon asserted. The United States, however, took a contrary position. In part because forbidding Hamas to participate would hurt the US plan to democratize the Middle East, and in part because Abbas had promised to finally crack down on Hamas after the PLC elections, Rice exerted heavy pressure on Sharon to allow Hamas participation. The Israeli leader, perhaps preoccupied with Israeli domestic politics (he had broken away from his Likud Party and formed the new Kadima Party in November 2005, four months before the Israeli parliamentary elections), gave in to the US pressure. It was a decision that both the United States and Israel would come to regret.[47]

From the Hamas Electoral Victory to Its Seizure of Gaza

Capitalizing on Fatah's corruption, the PA's inability to provide law and order in the West Bank, and the continued divisions between Fatah's old and young guards, Hamas swept to a massive victory in the January 25, 2006, PLC elections. Hamas representatives were quick to claim that their victory was due to their policy of "resistance" against Israel.[48] The Hamas victory created a major dilemma for the United States, as its two main policies in the Middle East—the war against terrorism and support for democratization—had come into direct conflict with each other: a terrorist organization, Hamas, utilizing democratic means, had taken control of the Palestinian legislature, and a Hamas leader, Ismail Haniyeh, had become the new Palestinian prime minister. Meanwhile,

Israel faced another challenge. By the time of the Hamas election victory, Sharon, who had suffered a massive stroke in early January 2006, was no longer Israel's prime minister. His replacement, as acting prime minister, was his Kadima colleague Ehud Olmert, who now not only had to prepare his new party for the March 28 Israeli elections but also had to deal with the Hamas election victory. Olmert quickly decided Israel would have nothing to do with Hamas unless the group changed its policies toward Israel, a position embraced by most of the Israeli political spectrum. For her part, Rice quickly convened the Diplomatic Quartet (the United States, the EU, the UN, and Russia), which agreed not to have any dealings with the Hamas-led Palestinian government until Hamas renounced terrorism, agreed to recognize Israel, and acceded to the agreements signed between Israel and the PLO, including Oslo I, Oslo II, and the Road Map. Russia, however, soon broke with the Quartet consensus by inviting a Hamas delegation for an official visit to Moscow. In April 2006, after the United States and the EU, seeing no change in Hamas policy, had decided to cut all aid to the PA (except humanitarian assistance), Russia again broke ranks with its Quartet colleagues by offering the PA economic assistance.

The newly elected Israeli government led by Olmert refused to have anything to do either with Abbas (who they claimed was ineffectual) or with the Hamas-led Palestinian government. For its part, the new Hamas government repeated its refusal to recognize Israel or make peace with it, and supported, as "legitimate resistance," continued attacks on Israel whether in the form of Qassam rockets fired from Gaza into Israel or in the form of suicide bombings, such as the one on April 17, 2006, that claimed ten Israeli lives.[49] Meanwhile, as Israel was confronting a Hamas-led government in the Palestinian territories, it also had to face a rising threat from Iran.

After two years of on-again, off-again negotiations with the European Union over its secret nuclear program, in August 2005 Iran broke off negotiations and announced it was moving ahead with nuclear enrichment. Making matters worse for Israel, which along with the United States feared that Iran was on the path to developing nuclear weapons, the newly elected Iranian president, Mahmoud Ahmadinejad, called for Israel to be "wiped off the map" and declared that the Holocaust was a myth.[50] While the United States was highly supportive of Israel in the face of the Iranian leader's provocative statements (on February 1, 2006, Bush had stated, "Israel is a solid ally of the United States; we will rise to Israel's defense if need be"),[51] the Israeli leadership had to question whether the United States, increasingly bogged down in both Iraq and Afghanistan (where the Taliban had revived), would act to eliminate the nuclear threat from Iran, or whether Israel would have to do the job itself.

Meanwhile, Israel's relations with the Hamas-led Palestinian government continued to deteriorate, with stepped-up shelling of Israeli territory from Gaza and

Israeli retaliation. Then, in the summer of 2006, full-scale war broke out, first with Hamas and then with Hizbollah following the kidnapping of Israeli soldiers. In looking at US-Israeli relations during both conflicts, there are a number of similarities. The Bush administration saw both Hamas and Hizbollah as terrorist organizations linked to Syria and to Iran and, as such, enemies of the United States. Consequently, when Israel was fighting both terrorist organizations, it was on the same side of the barricades as the United States, and the United States adopted a strongly pro-Israeli position in both conflicts. Thus it vetoed a UN Security Council resolution condemning Israel for bombarding the Gaza town of Beit Hanoun, from which rockets were being launched into Israel, and condemned both Iran and Syria for their aid to Hizbollah in its war against Israel. Indeed, in an "open-mike" incident at the G-8 summit in Saint Petersburg, Russia, Bush told British Prime Minister Tony Blair that the global powers had to "get Syria to get Hizbollah to stop doing this s___ and then it's over." Bush sought, without success, to get the G-8 to condemn both Iran and Syria for their role in the violence.[52]

In the Second Lebanon War, however, there was one additional factor that influenced US policy. The anti-Syrian Fouad Siniora government, which had come into office in Lebanon following the departure of Syrian forces in 2005, was seen as a US ally, and as one of the few remaining successes of the US democratization program. Consequently, the United States sought to ensure that if the Israeli-Hizbollah fighting did not enhance Siniora's position, by weakening Hizbollah, at least it would not hurt it. Thus, for the first two weeks of the war, the United States gave full diplomatic backing to Israel, hoping it would destroy Hizbollah, the Siniora government's main opposition. However, in late July, after an Israeli attack in Qana aimed at a Hizbollah bunker accidentally killed sixty Lebanese civilians,[53] it became clear that Israeli dependence on its air force to deal with Hizbollah was not working and that Siniora's position was being threatened by the growing popularity of Hizbollah, which was successfully "standing up to Israel."[54] This situation also negatively affected the governments of US allies Jordan, Egypt, and Saudi Arabia. Consequently, the United States began to work for a cease-fire, and the result was UN Security Council Resolution 1701, which called for the Lebanese army to move to the Israeli border and for the expansion of the UN troops in southern Lebanon to 15,000. Israel was less than happy with the cease-fire because it did not lead to the disarming of Hizbollah or to a cessation of Syria's transfer of weapons to Hizbollah.

In the aftermath of the Israeli-Hizbollah war, US Secretary of State Rice, who had originally spoken of a "new Middle East" emerging from the conflict, sought to build on the fears of rising Iranian influence in the region following the political victory of its ally Hizbollah. She tried to construct an anti-Iranian Sunni Arab bloc of Jordan, Egypt, Saudi Arabia, and the United Arab Emirates and to align it with Israel against Iran and its allies, Hizbollah and Hamas. Helping

Rice in this project was Saudi Arabia's decision to revive the 2002 Arab peace plan, which offered Arab-state recognition of Israel if it withdrew to its pre–1967 war boundaries and agreed to a "fair" settlement of the Palestinian refugee problem. Unfortunately for Rice, the Democratic victory in the November 2006 US congressional elections weakened the Bush administration, which had already been damaged by the failures in its Iraq policy and in the Hurricane Katrina recovery effort. This Democratic victory gave rise to a feeling, especially in the Middle East, that Bush had become a lame-duck president and that any serious discussion of peace should wait until his successor took office in January 2009. Nonetheless, Rice urged Olmert to negotiate with Abbas, while the United States continued to try to strengthen him militarily and clashes between Hamas and Abbas's Fatah increased in intensity. Saudi Arabia succeeded in temporarily stopping the fighting through an agreement in Mecca in February 2007 that established a Palestinian national unity government, but neither the United States nor Israel was pleased with the platform of the new government, which was dominated by Hamas and took positions closer to those of Hamas than to those of Fatah.[55]

Despite the new Palestinian government, Rice pressed on with her efforts to resuscitate the Israeli-Palestinian peace process, which she saw as necessary to facilitate the alignment between the Sunni Arab states and Israel. Thus, she agreed to speak with non-Hamas members of the Palestinian national unity government, an action Israel feared would "sanitize" Hamas.[56] Rice also announced that at some point the United States, in order to create a "political horizon," might suggest its own solutions to the conflict, thus appearing to bring US policy back to where it had been in the Clinton administration, with the Clinton Parameters.[57]

As part of her strategy, Rice suggested the speedy implementation of the November 2005 agreement between Israel and the Palestinian Authority, under which Israel would permit bus travel between Gaza and the West Bank (Israel had suspended implementation of the agreement following the Hamas victory in the January 2006 PLC elections), as well as lift Israeli checkpoints in the West Bank, if the Palestinians stopped firing Qassam rockets from Gaza into Israel and stopped smuggling arms into Gaza from Egypt. Both Hamas and Israel rejected the plan, Israeli officials complaining that bomb makers and engineers with the knowledge to build Qassams would travel from Gaza into the West Bank, and that the checkpoints were necessary to prevent the movement of terrorists.[58]

As Rice pursued her strategy, Olmert appeared to go over her head by ingratiating himself with Bush and Vice President Cheney. Thus, speaking to an AIPAC meeting in April 2007, he publicly opposed an American withdrawal from Iraq, and in May he condemned US Speaker of the House Nancy Pelosi's "mishandling" of the Israeli conditions for peace in her discussions with Syrian leader Bashar Assad—comments that echoed Cheney's criticism of the Pelosi visit. Needless to say, leaders of the US Democratic Party took a dim view of Olmert's comments and his apparent close identification with the Bush administration.[59] Olmert also followed the US lead in refusing to negotiate with Syria despite Assad's offer to resume peace negotiations with Israel; Rice, seeking (albeit with limited success) to isolate Syria, had reportedly told Olmert, "It is best you avoid even exploring this possibility."[60]

From the Hamas Seizure of Power to the End of the Bush Administration

Rice's efforts to expedite the Israeli-Palestinian talks got an unexpected boost in June 2007, when the escalating fighting between Hamas and Fatah led to the seizure of Gaza by Hamas and the crackdown on Hamas by Fatah in the West Bank. Though the Hamas seizure of Gaza was a blow to Palestinian unity, it did provide the Bush administration with the opportunity to try to make the West Bank a showcase while Gaza, under a tightening Israeli blockade because of Hamas rocket fire and the continued imprisonment of Israeli soldier Gilad Shalit, who had been captured in 2006, would stagnate. Thus, the United States began a major program of economic aid to the West Bank and stepped up its efforts to train Fatah's West Bank security forces, a policy continued by Bush's successor, Barack Obama. At the same time, the Bush administration moved to further assist Israel in the security field, pledging $30 billion in military assistance over the next decade and promising to maintain Israeli's qualitative military edge over its Middle Eastern enemies.[61] However, the Bush administration not only refused to attack Iran's nuclear installations, but it also opposed an Israeli attack on Iran, despite Iranian leaders' rejection of International Atomic Energy Agency (IAEA) requests for information about the possible weaponization of Iran's nuclear fuel, which the country continued to enrich despite opposition from the United States, the EU, and the IAEA.[62]

As President Bush sought to strengthen Abbas's Fatah-led West Bank economically and militarily, it also attempted to build an anti-Iranian coalition of forces, primarily made up of Sunni Arabs, to support a renewed effort to achieve an Israeli-Palestinian peace settlement. By holding a major international conference at Annapolis, Maryland, bringing together the leading Arab states, the Diplomatic Quartet, and representatives of the World Bank and the Islamic Conference, along with Israeli leader Ehud Olmert and Palestinian leader Mahmoud Abbas, the Bush administration sought to give an Arab and international imprimatur for the renewed peace talks, thereby giving Abbas additional political cover against Hamas. That the Arab League in 2007 had again come out with its peace plan, first introduced in 2002 at the height of the al-Aqsa Intifada, was seen as also helping Abbas. Nonetheless, the difficulties the two sides had in even agreeing to an opening joint statement foreshadowed some of the negotiating problems that lay ahead. But with the help of Condoleezza Rice, a joint statement was worked out—at the last minute—that stated the meeting's goal: "We agree to immediately launch good faith bilateral negotiations in order to conclude a peace treaty, resolving outstanding issues, including all core issues, without exception . . . and shall make every effort to conclude an agreement before the end of 2008."[63]

A number of committees were set up to deal with the major issues dividing Palestinians and Israelis, although the principle that "nothing is agreed until everything is agreed" made it difficult to monitor the day-to-day success. To expedite the negotiations, Rice made numerous trips to the Middle East, and according to Bush in his memoirs, *Decision Points,* Olmert made a significant offer to Abbas covering the central issues in the conflict under which (1) Israel would return the "vast majority" of the West Bank to the Palestinians, (2) a tunnel would be built linking the West Bank and Gaza, (3) a limited number of refugees would return to Israel, with the rest going to the new Palestinian state, (4) Jerusalem would be the joint capital of both Israel and the new Palestinian state, and (5) control of the holy places would be given to a panel of "nonpolitical elders." According to Bush, Olmert would travel to Washington and "deposit" the offer with the US president, Abbas would announce that the plan was in line with Palestinian interests, and Bush would then convene the two leaders to finalize the deal.[64]

Unfortunately for all concerned, the deal was not consummated. Bush gives the reason as the fact that Olmert was under investigation on a series of corruption charges, and Abbas did not want an agreement with an Israeli prime minister who soon would leave office.[65] Although there is truth to the Bush assertion (Olmert was forced to step down and was replaced by Israeli Foreign Minister Tsippy Livni as acting prime minister, and new Israeli elections were set for February 2009 when Livni proved unable to put together a ruling coalition), there would appear to be more to the story than Olmert's weakness. After the defeat of his forces in Gaza, Abbas himself was also seen as a weak leader, while by the time of the Annapolis conference, with the US Congress now controlled by the Democrats and facing continued difficulties in Iraq and a renewed insurgency in Afghanistan, Bush was very much a lame-duck president.

In any case, while Olmert and Abbas and their teams had been negotiating, the border between Israel and Gaza had been heating up. A Hamas-Israeli ceasefire had become increasingly shaky, and by the end of November 2008 Hamas forces had begun to fire volleys of rockets into Israel, making life in Israeli regions north and east of Gaza increasingly difficult for Israeli civilians. By the end of December 2008, Israel had decided on a policy of massive retaliation for the

Hamas rocket attacks and mounted a major invasion of Gaza under the code name Operation Cast Lead. Unlike the Israeli-Hizbollah conflict of 2006, in which after the first two weeks of that conflict the United States had pressured Israel to stop fighting in order to preserve the pro-Western Siniora government (see above), this time Israel was fighting Hamas, an organization on the US terrorist list, and the United States gave full backing to Israel. However, this would be the last Middle East policy decision taken by the Bush administration, which was replaced on January 20, 2009, by the administration of Barack Obama.

The Obama Administration: A Preliminary Appraisal

One of Obama's first acts after taking office was to appoint former US senator George Mitchell, who had served as mediator of the Northern Ireland peace agreement and played a role in the Israeli-Palestinian conflict (see above), as special envoy to the Arab-Israeli peace process. This demonstrated the president's serious interest in achieving an Arab-Israeli peace settlement. A major challenge to Obama's peace-process efforts, however, would come less than a month after his inauguration, with the Israeli elections of February 10, 2010. At the end of March, a right-of-center Israeli government took office, under the leadership of Benjamin Netanyahu—the same Netanyahu who had clashed with Obama's Democratic predecessor, President Bill Clinton, between 1996 and 1999. It wasn't long before there were also clashes between Netanyahu and Obama, in part because of their different worldviews and in part because of their different Middle East priorities.

Obama's Approach to World Affairs

In all US presidential transitions, especially when one party replaces another that has been in office for two terms, the new incumbent seeks to demonstrate that his policies are different from his predecessor's. This was the case when George W. Bush replaced Bill Clinton, and it was also the case when Barack Obama replaced Bush. Thus, when Obama took office, he made a major effort to show that in foreign policy he would replace the unilateralism of the Bush era with a policy of outreach to countries that had come into sharp conflict with United States during the Bush administration. These included Iran, Syria, Cuba, Venezuela, Russia, China, North Korea, and Myanmar. The operative assumption of the Obama administration appeared to be that if one met an opponent halfway, he would reciprocate. Though to many of Obama's critics, including those in Israel, such an assumption appeared to be dangerously naive, the administration held fast to this policy during its first year. A second aspect of the administration's approach involved outreach to the Muslim world. In speeches in both Turkey and Egypt, Obama sought to portray the United States as a friend of the Muslim world, not an enemy, despite the US wars in the Muslim countries of Iraq and Afghanistan. To emphasize this point, he played down the Islamic nature of the terrorism the United States faced, much to the displeasure of conservatives in the United States who condemned him for giving a free ride to Islamic terrorism.[66] A third aspect of the new policy was a cooling of ties with Israel, after the warm, if not cozy relationship of the Bush years. Obama appeared to feel that such a distancing would help the United States appear more even-handed in the Arab-Israeli conflict and thus facilitate US peacemaking efforts. Thus, early in the administration Obama called for a halt in settlement construction, including in Jerusalem, despite the understanding Bush and Sharon reached in April 2004. In addition, despite trips to Egypt, Turkey, and Saudi Arabia, Obama failed to visit Israel, despite being urged to do so by a number of American Jewish organizations, including those affiliated with the liberal J Street movement. Reinforcing the chill in relations was the fact that although Obama was a left-of-center liberal, Netanyahu was a right-of-center conservative. Gone were the days when the conservatives Bush and Sharon could easily relate because they saw the world in the same focus. Indeed, in the very first public meeting between Obama and Netanyahu in May 2009, the tension between the two leaders was clearly visible in their body language as they issued statements following the meeting.

In addition to their different political perspectives, Obama and Netanyahu differed on Middle East priorities. To Netanyahu, Iran was the primary issue. With Iranian President Mahmoud Ahmadinejad continuing to call for Israel to be wiped off the face of the earth and strengthening Iran's ability to do so by rapidly developing Iran's nuclear capability, Netanyahu pressed Obama to take action against Iran. For Obama, however, the priority was to try to get the Iranians to change their policies by dialogue, not force. During his first year in office, Obama made numerous appeals to the Iranian regime for improved relations, only to be continually rebuffed. For his part, Obama saw a solution to the Arab-Israeli conflict as a priority in the Middle East, seeing such a solution both as a means of weakening Iran's proxies, Hizbollah and Hamas, of pulling Syria away from Iran, and of rallying the Sunni Arab world against Iran, should it not respond to his outreach policy.[67] Here again the settlement issue was key, as Obama felt that getting Israel to stop building settlements in Jerusalem and the West Bank would facilitate the resumption of Palestinian-Israeli negotiations and bring closer an overall settlement of the conflict.[68] Unfortunately for Obama, as he would later ruefully admit, he did not understand the changes in Israeli politics that had been caused by the Israeli-Hizbollah war of 2006 and the Israeli-Hamas war of December 2008 to January 2009.

Israel's Move to the Right

The 2009 Israeli elections reflected a clear move to the right by the Israeli body politic. Netanyahu's right-wing Likud Party jumped from twelve to twenty-seven seats and the right-of-center Yisrael Beiteinu party of Avigdor Lieberman rose from eleven to fifteen seats. At the same time, the left-wing Meretz Party dropped from five to three seats and the left-of-center Labor Party fell from nineteen to thirteen seats. In explaining the shift to the right, one factor is clear: the policy of unilateral withdrawals to win peace had not worked. Thus, although Ehud Barak had unilaterally withdrawn from southern Lebanon in 2000, instead of attaining peace with Lebanon, Israel had to endure repeated rocket attacks leading up to a major war with Hizbollah in 2006 that the centrist Kadimah Party did not wage effectively. Similarly, instead of facilitating the peace process, Israel's withdrawal of both settlements and military bases from Gaza in 2005 brought increased rocket fire from Gaza, which Hamas had seized in 2007, leading to the major Israeli invasion of Gaza in December 2008. Given these events, the majority of Israelis were not only wary of any further withdrawals, which, as Netanyahu pointed out in the campaign, would bring Tel Aviv and Ben-Gurion Airport into rocket range, but also highly suspicious of the Palestinians, whose Hamas-Fatah split made any final Israeli-Palestinian peace agreement a far-off possibility, at best. Making matters worse was a general feeling that Palestinian Authority leader Mahmoud Abbas was well-meaning but weak and that his prime minister, Salam Fayyad, was honest but lacked a political base. In addition, the stance of Israel's Arab community (20 percent of the Israeli population) had become problematic to the country's Jewish majority, as the leaders of the Arab community increasingly sided with Israel's Arab enemies while at the same time demanding the replacement of Israel as a Jewish state, with Israel "as a state of its peoples."[69] Given this turn to the right, Obama's pressure on Israel was received coldly, and Obama's popularity, as measured in Israeli polls, fell to the single digits.[70]

Consequently, Netanyahu initially took a hard line on the Middle East peace process, refusing to agree to a two-state solution and promoting an active Jewish settlement program on the West Bank. Under heavy US pressure, however, he modified his position. Thus, in June 2009, in a speech at Bar-Ilan University in Israel, Netanyahu agreed to a two-state solution, albeit with the important qualification that Jerusalem remain united under Israeli control. Then in November 2009 Netanyahu also agreed to a ten-month partial settlement construction ban, although the ban did not include Jerusalem. In making these concessions, Netanyahu actually went further than the Arabs, whom Obama had also pressured. Thus, Abbas had refused to enter into negotiations with the Netanyahu government until all settlement activities, including in East Jerusalem, ceased; Syria did not break with Iran, as Obama had hoped, or even stop assisting Hamas and Hizbollah (Syria continued to provide arms to Hizbollah, in violation of UN Security Resolution 1701), and Saudi Arabia refused to provide the confidence-building measures to Israel, such as providing flyover rights for Israeli civilian airliners, which Obama had requested.

However, by the beginning of 2010, it initially looked as though the split between Obama and Israel might be overcome. Obama had begun to take a tougher stand on Iran after the Iranian government, now beset by increasing domestic dissent, continued to rebuff Obama's call for improved ties and rejected international efforts to deal with Iran's nuclear enrichment efforts. In addition, a tougher tone had begun to enter the Obama administration's diplomatic efforts, after the apparent failure of outreach efforts toward Venezuela, Cuba, Myanmar, and North Korea. As far as Israel was concerned, Obama had publicly stated in a *Time* magazine interview on February 1, 2010, that he had "overestimated" the US ability to get the Israelis and Palestinians to engage in a "meaningful conversation" because of the domestic political problems both sides faced.[71] Consequently, the United States had backed off from its calls for a full settlement freeze and had accepted the partial freeze Netanyahu had proposed. Nonetheless, despite this apparently improving situation in US-Israeli relations, a crisis erupted in mid-March 2010, during the visit of US Vice President Joe Biden to Israel.

There were several aspects of the crisis. First, after a great deal of effort, the United States had gotten Abbas to agree to resume peace talks with Israel, albeit at the low level of indirect or proximity talks under which the US Middle East special envoy, George Mitchell, would shuttle between the two sides. Biden's trip to Israel was aimed, in part, at adding the US imprimatur to the start of the talks, which had been endorsed by the Arab League, thus giving Abbas a modicum of legitimization. However, as the date of Biden's visit approached, the situation in East Jerusalem became more explosive. The Israeli government, with either Netanyahu's active support or his toleration, had begun to accelerate the construction of Jewish housing in Arab-populated neighborhoods of East Jerusalem, such as Silwan and Sheikh Jarrah, while at the same time destroying Arab-owned housing in these neighborhoods and elsewhere in East Jerusalem, because they had been "illegally" constructed, that is, built without the municipal permit that, under an Israeli catch-22 policy, was almost impossible for East Jerusalem Arabs to obtain. This had inflamed Arab opinion. In addition, in February the Israeli government had added both the Cave of Machpelah in Hebron and Rachel's Tomb (a Jewish religious enclave near Arab Bethlehem, just south of Jerusalem, surrounded by high walls and watchtowers) to the list of Jewish heritage sites across Israel and the West Bank slated for millions of dollars of renovation work.[72] The Palestinians saw these actions as further attempts by Israel to unilaterally extend its control over areas they wanted for their future Palestinian state. For the Palestinians, control over Arab East Jerusalem is vital because, for both political and religious reasons, they want it as the capital of their long-hoped-for Palestinian state, and with the Jewish construction in Arab East Jerusalem, it appeared that this hope was rapidly slipping away. Thus the announcement, in the midst of Biden's visit, that Israel would construct an additional 1,600 homes in East Jerusalem, even though the construction would take place in the all-Jewish neighborhood of Ramat Shlomo, was the straw that broke the camel's back as far as the Palestinians were concerned, and they refused to enter into the indirect negotiations to which they had committed. This in turn undermined not only the Biden mission but also the months-long diplomacy the Obama administration had been actively pursuing to get the Israeli-Palestinian talks under way. Netanyahu's response that he had been unaware of the announcement before it had been made was seen as specious by the Obama administration, which appeared to lose trust in the Israeli leader. Following the fiasco of the Biden visit, where heated words were exchanged between Netanyahu and high-ranking members of the Obama administration, and a failed Netanyahu visit to Washington ten days later, a debate appeared to break out in the administration as to what to do.[73] One group argued that it was time for the United States to come up with its own plan for an Israeli-Palestinian peace settlement, and in well-placed leaks in the *New York Times* and the *Washington Post* in early April, the administration was portrayed as actively considering coming up with its own peace plan.[74] Advocates of this position cited then Central Command commander David Petraeus's argument in a mid-March 2010 policy paper that the Arab-Israeli conflict was damaging the US position in the Middle East, although in the thirty-five-page paper, the conflict was actually mentioned only twice,[75] and Petraeus later would claim that his position had been misunderstood.[76] However, others in the Obama administration argued that the United States could not want a solution more than the parties themselves. In a news conference at the end of April, Obama appeared to come down midway between the two positions, thereby enabling the United States to keep both options open. Thus, on the one hand Obama stated:

> Even if we are applying all of our political capital to that issue [solving the Israeli-Palestinian conflict], the Israeli people through their government, and the Palestinian people through the Palestinian Authority, as well as other Arab States, may say to themselves— we are not prepared to resolve this—these issues—no matter how much pressure the United States brings to bear—and the truth is, in some of these conflicts the United States can't impose solutions unless the participants in these conflicts are willing to break out of old patterns of antagonism. I think it was former Secretary of State James Baker who said, in the context of Middle East peace, we can't want it more than they do.

But on the other hand, Obama also noted that an Israeli-Palestinian peace was a "vital national security interest of the United States" and that "what we can make sure of is that we are constantly present, constantly engaged." He also said, "I'm going to keep at it."[77]

Meanwhile, as discord between the Obama administration and Netanyahu continued, nearly three hundred members of the US Congress who were sympathetic to Israel made their position clear in a letter to Secretary of State Hillary Clinton in late March, in which they expressed "deep concern" over the US-Israeli crisis:

> The US and Israel are close allies whose people share a deep and abiding friendship based on a shared commitment to core values including democracy, human rights, and freedom of the press and religion. Our two countries are partners in the fight against terrorism and share an important strategic relationship. A strong Israel is an asset to the national security of the United States and brings stability to the Middle East. We are concerned that the highly publicized tensions in the relationship will not advance the interests the US and Israel share. Above all, we must remain focused on the threat posed by the Iranian nuclear weapons program to Middle East peace and stability.
>
> We recognize that, despite the extraordinary closeness between our country and Israel, there will be differences over issues both large and small. Our view is that such differences are best resolved quietly, in trust and confidence, as befits long-standing strategic allies. We hope and expect that with mutual effort and good faith, the United States and Israel will move beyond the disruption quickly, to the lasting benefit of both nations.[78]

Perhaps heeding the call of Congress, or realizing that without a good working relationship with Israel, the United States could not move the peace process forward, in early May Obama resumed efforts to convene the indirect talks between Israel and the Palestinians and to improve relations with Israel. The indirect talks were in fact resumed, and the United States made a major gesture to Israel by granting it an additional $205 million in military aid, over and above the $3 billion per year Israel was getting, to help it expand its Iron Dome antimissile system to help protect Israel against rocket attacks from Gaza and Lebanon.[79] For his part, Netanyahu appeared to have reciprocated by putting a de facto freeze on construction in East Jerusalem. At the same time, however, Obama's attempt to eliminate nuclear weapons from the world, an effort that appeared partially aimed at putting additional pressure on Iran to scrap its nuclear enrichment program, came into conflict with Israel's need for nuclear weapons as a deterrent against a possible attack by its enemies, principally Iran and the Arab countries with whom it had not yet made peace. Consequently, Israel was unhappy with the US decision during a review session for the Nuclear Non-Proliferation Treaty in late May 2010 to support a call for Israel to join the treaty, a development that would force the country to disclose and then give up its nuclear weapons. Israel was further concerned that the conference's final document did not mention Iran's failure to comply with IAEA demands to stop enriching uranium. The US support for the document contrasted sharply with that of the Bush administration during the 2005 treaty review conference, when the US refused to sign a similar declaration calling for Israel to join the treaty.[80]

Despite this disagreement, by July US-Israeli relations appeared to be on the upswing. The United States had refused to join Turkey in condemning Israel over an incident on May 31, 2010, in which Israel intercepted a Gaza-bound flotilla and killed nine Turkish Islamists who were resisting the Israeli capture of one of the ships in the flotilla (the others surrendered peacefully). In July, Netanyahu again visited Washington and this time his reception was much more cordial than during his previous visit in March, at the height of the East Jerusalem settlement construction crisis. After meeting Netanyahu, Obama stated, "The US will never ask Israel to do anything that undermines its security," and emphasized that the bond between Israel and the United States was "unbreakable."[81]

By early September, US diplomacy had scored a minor breakthrough when Abbas, with the backing of the Arab League, finally agreed to enter into direct negotiations with Israel. The timing was, however, problematic. The end of Israel's partial settlement freeze was set for September 26—just three weeks after the formal start of the direct negotiations. Despite a great deal of pomp and ceremony in Washington, little was actually accomplished in the three weeks of direct talks, and when the partial settlement construction freeze ended, Israel resumed construction in the settlements—and East Jerusalem—actions that Obama called "unhelpful" and that prompted Abbas to break off negotiations.[82]

At this point the United States floated an offer to Netanyahu to extend the settlement building moratorium for an additional ninety days, in the hope that a general border delineation could be worked out by that time so that future Israeli settlement construction would take place only in areas that Abbas and Netanyahu would agree would remain part of Israel under a land-swap arrangement. Reportedly the offer included providing Israel with an additional twenty F-35 stealth fighter planes (Israeli had already planned to buy twenty), negotiating a security treaty between the United States and Israel, and the United States pledging to protect Israel against Palestinian Authority efforts to get the UN Security Council to vote to establish a Palestinian state, even without an agreement with Israel.[83] Despite this generous offer, which would have enhanced Israeli security considerably, Netanyahu refused to accept the US initiative, which was subsequently taken off the bargaining table. Meanwhile, the United States and Israel continued to differ over policy toward Iran. In the face of strong urging by Israel—and as the WikiLeaks (the publication of secret talks between US and foreign diplomats and other foreigners visiting US officials abroad) revelations have shown, also by a number of Arab states for military action against Iran[84]—the United States continued to resist calls to attack Iran, arguing that the sanctions the United States, the EU, and the UN Security Council enacted against Iran were the proper path. As Secretary of Defense Robert Gates noted,

> We even have some evidence that [the Supreme Religious Leader, the Ayatollah] Khameini now [is] beginning to wonder if [Iranian President] Akhmadinejad is lying to him about the impact of the sanctions on the economy. And whether he is getting the straight scoop in terms of how much trouble the economy really is in. . . . A military solution as far as I am concerned . . . will bring together a divided nation. It will make them absolutely committed to obtaining nuclear weapons . . . and they will just go deeper and more covert.[85]

As US-Israeli relations remained tense because of differences over policy toward Iran and over the Israeli-Palestinian peace process, Secretary of State Hillary Clinton made a major address on US policy on the Israeli-Palestinian conflict on December 9, 2010, at the Brookings Institution in Washington, D.C. After noting that the US commitment to Israel's security and to its future remained "rock solid," Clinton asserted that solving the Israeli-Palestinian conflict was a national interest of the United States and could not be postponed, because the continuing conflict strengthened "the hands of extremists and rejectionists across the region while sapping the support of those open to coexistence and cooperation." Clinton then announced a change in the US strategy to achieve such a peace agreement. Instead of concentrating on the settlement issue, which had been the Obama administration's policy during its first two years, Clinton said, it was now time to "grapple with (all) the core issues of the conflict, on borders and security, settlements, water, refugees, and on Jerusalem itself." She also stated that "no matter how much the United States and other nations around the region and the world work to see a resolution to this conflict, only the parties to the conflict will be able to achieve one, and that the United States and the International Community cannot impose a solution." She concluded by chiding both the Palestinians and the Israelis, advising them to downplay the past and work toward a settlement, asserting "the people of the region have to move beyond a past that they cannot change and embrace a future they can shape together."[86]

As 2011 began, one of the issues that had bedeviled US-Israeli relations—that of an attack on Iran's nuclear facilities—appeared to be removed, at least temporarily, from the agenda. The primary reason was a computer virus, called Stuxnet, reportedly jointly developed by the United States and Israel, that had seriously infected Iran's Natanz nuclear centrifuge facility.[87] Because of Stuxnet, as well as an increasingly effective US-led sanctions effort against Iran and the assassination of key Iranian nuclear scientists, the outgoing Israeli chief of Mossad, the Israeli intelligence agency, Meir Dagan, asserted that Iran would not be able to produce nuclear weapons until 2015.[88] Although some Israelis, including Prime Minister Netanyahu, and some Americans thought Dagan's estimate was overly optimistic, at least for the time being the issue of Iran, which had become divisive in US-Israeli relations, receded in importance.[89]

Although the delay in Iran's nuclear program benefited both the United States and Israel, another development in early 2011 raised serious questions for the leaders of both countries. The outbreak of popular uprisings throughout the Arab world, called by some commentators the "Arab Spring," began in Tunisia and quickly spread to Egypt, Jordan, Yemen, Bahrain, Syria, and Morocco. For the United States, there was concern that longtime US allies, such as Presidents Zine el-Abidine Ben Ali of Tunisia and Hosni Mubarak of Egypt, who, as noted above, had helped the United States try to facilitate an Israeli-Palestinian peace agreement, as well as the Khalifa family of Bahrain, which had hosted the US Fifth Fleet; President Saleh of Yemen, who was an ally, if a troublesome one, in the fight against al-Qaeda; and King Abdullah II of Jordan, would be overthrown. Adding to these fears was the concern that Islamists might come to power if the existing regimes fell. It was an almost classic case of the clash between national interests—keeping US allies in power—and national values—supporting the democratic aspirations of the leaders of the popular uprisings. Indeed, President Obama would discuss this dilemma in his speech on the Arab uprisings on May 19, 2011 (see below). Given this conflict, the United States was slow to support the leaders of the popular movements in Tunisia and Egypt, although in mid-January 2011, as street battles in Tunisia were escalating, Secretary of State Clinton, speaking at a conference on democracy in Doha, Qatar, strongly criticized Arab governments for stalled political change and warned that extremists could exploit a lack of democracy to promote their political agendas.[90] Clinton's emphasis on the need for democracy appeared to be a reversal of the previous Obama policy, which, in another departure from the Bush administration, initially had appeared to downplay the issue of democratization. Indeed, as Obama had noted in his Cairo speech in June 2009, "no system of government can or should be imposed on one nation by any other."[91] By contrast, Clinton asserted in Doha:

> While some countries have made great strides in governance, in many others people have grown tired of corrupt institutions and a stagnant political order. Those who cling to the status quo may be able to hold back the full impact of their countries' problems for a little while, but not forever. If leaders don't offer a positive vision and give young people meaningful ways to contribute, others (extremist elements and terrorist groups) will fill the vacuum.[92]

One month later, following the ouster of Egyptian President Mubarak from power, Obama seemed to echo Clinton, as he stated that the uprising in Egypt had "changed the world" and he pledged US support for a "genuine transition to democracy."[93] Thus, by February 2011 it appeared that the United States had in many ways returned to the old George W. Bush democratization policy.

From the Israeli perspective, the Arab Spring of popular uprisings was also problematic. Especially in the case of Egypt, there was the fear that anti-Israeli Islamists of the Muslim Brotherhood could take power, despite the fact that they were latecomers to the demonstrations in Cairo's Tahrir Square that brought down Mubarak in mid-February 2011. Although, following Mubarak, the Egyptian military took control of the country, formed an interim government, and stated it would honor the Israeli-Egyptian peace agreement of 1979, the actions of the new government were worrisome to Israel. These actions included scheduling early parliamentary elections, which the Israelis feared would enable the well-organized Muslim Brotherhood to dominate Egypt's Parliament, warming Egypt's ties with Iran, announcing the opening of Egypt's blockade of Gaza, and calling for a renegotiation for the Israeli-Egyptian natural gas agreement (Israel currently depends on Egypt for 40 percent of its natural gas needs).

In any case, it was not long before Israel had problems closer to home. In mid-March there was a sharp increase in the number of rockets and mortar rounds fired from Gaza into civilian areas of Israel (some fired by Islamic Jihad and some by Hamas), and many Israelis feared that the deterrence benefits that Israel had achieved as a result of Operation Cast Lead in late 2008 and early 2009 had evaporated. At the height of the escalating conflict, a Hamas-fired rocket hit an Israeli school bus, killing a sixteen-year-old Israeli student. The Israelis retaliated forcefully, hitting a number of targets in Gaza including weapon-smuggling tunnels and Hamas and Islamic Jihad rocket teams, and by the end of April a cease-fire of sorts had been worked out. US Secretary of Defense Robert Gates visited Israel in the midst of the fighting and condemned both the rocket attacks from Gaza and a terrorist attack in Jerusalem that took place in March.[94]

Meanwhile, negotiations between Israel and Abbas's Palestinian Authority remained frozen. In part because Abbas had been embarrassed by the "Palileaks" exposé by Al Jazeera, which described the concessions he had been willing to make to former Israeli Prime Minister Ehud Olmert,[95] in part to gain popular support at a time of protest movements throughout the Arab world, and in part because Israeli Prime Minister Netanyahu had refused to stop housing construction in West Bank settlements (the United States had vetoed a UN Security Council denunciation of the housing construction in February 2011), Abbas had begun to push the idea of a UN resolution proclaiming a Palestinian state and had sent emissaries around the world to garner support for a projected UN General Assembly action in September 2011. In addition, after years of futile negotiations with Hamas, by May 2011 Abbas had reached a preliminary agreement with the Gaza-based organization to form an interim national unity government to prepare for elections in the West Bank and Gaza.[96] In making this interim agreement, not only was Abbas responding to popular calls in both the West Bank and Gaza for a reconciliation, but he was also able to exploit Hamas's weakening position in Syria, where its leadership was based, because of the escalating anti-Assad rioting there, as well as Hamas's greater willingness to cooperate with Egypt, whose new government was far more sympathetic to the organization than Mubarak's had been, and which helped to mediate the agreement. Netanyahu reacted angrily to the Hamas-Fatah agreement and said he would have nothing to do with that government so long as Hamas, which remained dedicated to destroying Israel, did not change its program.

As the Israeli-Palestinian relationship worsened, and as the popular uprisings in the Arab world grew in intensity, President Obama was faced with yet another dilemma: what to do about Libya. When a group of Libyans sought to oust Libyan dictator Muammar Gadhafi, and Gadhafi vowed to murder all those opposing him, the Arab League and a number of European leaders led by French President Nicolas Sarkozy called for a no-fly zone to protect Libyan civilians from Gadhafi. Obama somewhat belatedly agreed to join in a military effort to establish the no-fly zone (after the UN Security Council voted in favor of it), although the US president called on his partners in NATO to take the lead in the operation, despite the fact that the United States was by far the leading military power in NATO, albeit one bogged down by wars in Iraq and Afghanistan. Obama justified US military action in a speech to the National Defense University on March 28, 2011, in which he stated that if he had failed to act, the Libyan city of Benghazi, held by Gadhafi's opponents, would suffer a massacre that "would have reverberated across the region and stained the conscience of the world."[97] Nonetheless, some commentators, evaluating Obama's speech and the limited role the president had projected for the US military in Libya, called Obama's position a case of "leading from behind."[98]

In addition to having to confront a series of major changes in the Arab world, a stalled Israeli-Palestinian peace process, and a war in Libya—to go along with a continuing, albeit declining US military effort in Iraq and an escalating war in Afghanistan—Obama also faced a difficult domestic situation with a high unemployment rate (9 percent in May 2011) that hampered his reelection effort, and, following the fall 2010 elections, Republican control of the US House of Representatives, which led to a bitter budget battle over the growing US deficit. The one bit of good news for Obama during late spring 2011 was a successful raid by a US Navy SEAL commando group on the home of Osama bin Laden in Pakistan that resulted in the death of the terrorist leader responsible for a series of attacks, the most important of which was 9/11. Given Obama's close personal involvement in the mission, which in many ways resembled the targeted assassinations carried out by Israel, the success of the mission at least temporarily strengthened his domestic position.

By May 2011, with the Israeli-Palestinian peace process stalled, Obama was coming under increasing pressure, both domestically and from America's NATO allies, to present a US plan to solve the conflict.[99] In mid-April, Secretary of State Clinton had already articulated the US frustration with the stalemate in the peace process in a speech to the US-Islamic World Forum, in which she stated, "The status-quo between Palestinians and Israelis is no more sustainable than the political systems that have crumbled in recent months."[100] In addition, Obama's Republican opponents in the US House of Representatives, trying to exploit for their political benefit the ongoing chill between the president and Netanyahu, had invited the Israeli prime minister to address a joint session of Congress in late May.[101] Adding to the pressure on Obama was the resignation of the chief US Middle East peace mediator, George Mitchell, on May 13, 2011, given that in an effort to demonstrate his administration's interest in solving the conflict, Obama had appointed Mitchell to his position on his second day in office, in January 2009.[102] As a result of all these pressures, Obama apparently decided on the eve of Netanyahu's speech to the US Congress to outflank the Israeli prime minister by adding a section on US strategy for achieving an Israeli-Palestinian peace settlement to his speech on the response to the Arab Spring that had already been scheduled for May 19, 2011, at the US State Department.

The bulk of Obama's speech dealt with US support for the democratic movements in the Arab world.[103] After noting the tension between American interests and American values, Obama appeared to give priority to values, noting that "after decades of accepting the world as it is in the region, we have a chance to pursue the world as it should be." Obama went on to assert,

> The United States supports a set of universal rights. And these rights include free speech, the freedom of peaceful assembly, the freedom of religion, equality for men and women, under the rule of law, and the right to choose your own leaders—whether you live in Baghdad or Damascus, Sanaa or Tehran. . . . Our support for these principles is not a secondary interest. Today I want to make it clear that it is a top priority that must be translated into concrete actions, and supported by all of the diplomatic, economic and strategic tools at our disposal.

In addition, Obama emphasized the need for proper treatment of religious minorities in the Arab world, noting that "Coptic Christians must have the right to worship freely in Cairo, just as Shia must never have their mosques destroyed in Bahrain." He also strongly argued for women's rights in the Arab world, asserting that "the region will never reach its full potential when more than half of its population is prevented from achieving their full potential."

In his section on the Israeli-Palestinian conflict, Obama made a number of major gestures to Israel. Thus he displayed his empathy with Israelis "living in fear that their children could be blown up in a bus, or by rockets fired at their homes" and "knowing that other children in the region are taught to hate them." Obama also stated his strong opposition to Arab efforts to delegitimize Israel, called for two states for two peoples—Israel as a Jewish state and the homeland for the Jewish people (a clear repudiation of the mass return of Palestinian refugees to Israel)—asserted that the proposed Palestinian state had to be non-militarized, demanded that the Palestinian leadership deal with Hamas's unwillingness to recognize Israel's right to exist, and put strong emphasis on Israel's security needs, noting that in any Israeli-Palestinian agreement, security arrangements had to be robust enough to (1) prevent a resurgence of terrorism, (2) stop the infiltration of weapons, and (3) provide border security.

Obama also reiterated the position that the United States would not seek to impose a peace agreement. Nonetheless, he emphasized, as Secretary of State Clinton had done in her speech to the US-Islamic World Forum in April, that the status quo was unsustainable. In addition, he stated that Israeli settlement activity on the West Bank was "an obstacle to peace," called on Israel to "act boldly" to advance a lasting peace, and noted that the dream of a Jewish and democratic state could not be fulfilled with permanent occupation. In his most controversial statement, Obama put into words what had been the practice not only of US presidents but also of Israeli and Palestinian negotiators over the past decade since the Camp David II Summit in July 2000 when he stated that "the borders of Israel and Palestine should be based on the 1967 lines with mutually agreed swaps, so secure and recognized borders are established for both states." Obama also came out with a third iteration of the US strategy to achieve an Israeli-Palestinian agreement. After having tried first in 2009–2010 to kick-start the peace process by trying to stop Jewish settlement expansion in East Jerusalem and the West Bank, and from December 2010 to April 2011 to deal with all the core issues simultaneously—and succeeding in neither strategy—Obama now suggested beginning with border and security issues first and only then turning to the "wrenching and emotional issues" of Jerusalem and the fate of Palestinian refugees.

Despite Obama's emphasis on the need to ensure Israeli security in a Palestinian-Israeli settlement, which he repeated in his speech to an AIPAC conference several days later, his comments about the 1967 border set off a firestorm of criticism among right-wing circles in Israel—Netanyahu openly criticized Obama's plan—as well as among Israel's supporters in the US Congress, led by Republican representatives and senators. Nonetheless, Obama's speech did serve to, at least in part, outmaneuver Netanyahu, whose speeches both to AIPAC and to a joint session of Congress were in large part a reaction to Obama's

May 19 speech. In any case, the Obama speech of May 19, 2011, serves as a useful point of departure for evaluating US policy toward Israel under George W. Bush and Barack Obama.

Conclusion

In comparing the Bush administration's policy toward Israel and the Arab-Israeli conflict with that of the Obama administration, there are both similarities and differences. In the area of similarities, both administrations have committed themselves to Israel's security. Of the $5 billion in annual US foreign aid, Israel receives $3 billion, 60 percent of the total. In a 2007 memorandum of understanding with Israel, under the Bush administration, the United States committed itself to supply Israel with $30 billion in security assistance over the next decade, and not only has the Obama administration agreed to continue funding security assistance to Israel at that level, but it also has added $205 million to support Israel's Iron Dome antirocket system. A second similarity is that neither the Bush administration nor the Obama administration has supported Israel's calls for an American attack on Iran's nuclear installations, and both were hesitant to support an Israeli attack on Iran as well, although by early 2011, the issue of Iran had receded in importance as a factor in US-Israeli relations. Third, both the Bush and Obama administrations supported Israel as a Jewish state.

Despite these similarities, there have been a number of differences, and in the mind of the Israeli public, at least, they tend to outweigh the similarities. First and foremost have been the differences over Israeli settlement building. Though no US administration has formally supported the building of Israeli settlements in the West Bank and East Jerusalem, and the administration of George W. Bush's father, George H. W. Bush, actually came into sharp conflict with Israel over this issue in the early 1990s, in April 2004 George W. Bush tacitly supported Israel's continued building when he stated "in light of new realities on the ground, including already existing population centers, it is unrealistic to expect that the outcome of the final status negotiations will be a full and complete return to the armistice lines of 1949." In contrast, early in his administration Obama came out strongly against settlements in the West Bank not only outside but also inside the settlement blocs and in Jerusalem as well. Although Netanyahu agreed to a partial settlement freeze, one not including East Jerusalem, the settlement issue has been a major cause of conflict between Israel and the Obama administration, reaching its peak during the visit of US Vice President Joe Biden to Israel in March 2010.

A second difference can be seen in the different worldviews of the two administrations. George W. Bush was a conservative with a black-and-white understanding of terrorism, one that was reinforced by 9/11. In this, both Israeli Prime Minister Ariel Sharon, a conservative, and Prime Minister Ehud Olmert, a moderate conservative, were very much on the same wavelength as Bush, and this reinforced their relationship. In contrast, Obama is a liberal, and his view of the world has clashed with that of Netanyahu, also a conservative. A third difference can be seen in the different approaches to Iran. Bush, in his first term, sought to isolate Iran, and although in his second term he proved willing to co-operate with key European Union states in getting Iran to stop enriching uranium, relations between the United States and Iran remained hostile during his entire term of office. In contrast, Obama's outreach policy toward Iran—one that so far at least has proven as unsuccessful as Bush's in getting Iran to stop enriching uranium—was seen as the height of naïveté by Netanyahu, who saw the time Obama spent trying to win over the Iranian leadership as more time for Iran to develop its nuclear weapons.

A related outreach program by Obama involved Syria—a country the Bush administration sought to isolate following the assassination of Lebanese Sunni leader Rafik Hariri in 2005. Obama apparently hoped that by warming up relations with Syria, his administration could not only get the Syrians to stop the infiltration of anti-US fighters into Iraq, but also get Syria to break its ties with Iran and stop aiding Hamas and Hizbollah. So far that policy has not worked very well either, as Syrian-Iranian ties appear as strong as ever and there is no evidence that Syria has cut off support for Hamas or Hizbollah. Indeed, by May 2011 Obama had begun to openly criticize Syria as well as sanction the Assad regime for its brutal crackdown on demonstrators. Yet another difference between Netanyahu and Obama lies in the latter's pursuit of a nuclear-free world. Obama appeared to the Israelis to be sacrificing their interests by not insisting, at a minimum, that no pressure be put on Israel to give up its nuclear weapons until after a comprehensive Middle East peace agreement had been achieved.

Another major difference between the two administrations has been their approaches to the Arab-Israeli peace process. After 9/11, Bush sought to end the Al-Aqsa Intifada and support a Palestinian state existing peacefully alongside Israel. Though the Obama administration has had the same goal, Bush's post-9/11 efforts, unlike Obama's, tended to be episodic, and all but ceased after both the Zinni mission to the Middle East and the 2003 Road Map were sabotaged by Palestinian terrorism. It was not until Arafat's death and the subsequent election of Mahmoud Abbas as the Palestinian Authority's president that the United States could move ahead with its peace plan, given that unlike Arafat, Abbas was a strong opponent of terrorism. Unfortunately for Bush, however, Abbas proved to be a weak leader, and the US Middle East democratization program, which had become a centerpiece of his administration's policy in the Middle East, foundered when Hamas won the Palestinian Legislative Council elections in

January 2006. Bush's strategy experienced another blow after Israeli Prime Minister Ariel Sharon suffered a stroke in January 2006 soon after his unilateral withdrawal from Gaza. Then the Palestinian government collapsed when Hamas seized power in Gaza in June 2007, signaling a major split in the Palestinian movement. By that time, with the war in Iraq going badly and with the Democrats having won control of both houses of the US Congress in the 2006 midterm election, Bush was very much a lame-duck president. His subsequent efforts at peacemaking—the Annapolis conference in November 2007 did not prove successful, though if one is to believe Bush's memoirs, the two sides did come close. However, that the Bush administration came to an end as war was raging between Israel and Hamas illustrates the failure of the administration's peacemaking strategy.

Obama, by contrast, has had a very different approach. Unlike Bush's episodic approach to Middle East peacemaking, Obama's was continuous, although he has had to revise his strategy on several occasions. In part this was because of a desire to show he was different from Bush—a pattern typical when the president of one political party replaces a two-term president of the other party. We saw this in George W. Bush when he replaced Bill Clinton. Thus, whereas Clinton had been personally involved in the Arab-Israeli peace process, particularly in his second term, convening summits at the Wye Plantation and Camp David, and personally negotiating with Syrian leader Hafiz al-Assad, the failure of his efforts convinced Bush to take a hands-off approach to the conflict until 9/11. Similarly, Obama also made a major effort to distance himself from his predecessor's policies. Thus, although Bush was inactive in pursuing the Arab-Israeli peace process at the start of his presidency, Obama on his second day in office appointed George Mitchell as his special Middle East mediator. In addition, although mention has already been made of Obama's outreach policies toward Iran and Syria, Obama also undertook a major outreach effort to the Muslim and Arab worlds with speeches in Turkey and Egypt in an effort to show that even though the United States was involved in wars in two Muslim countries, Iraq and Afghanistan, the United States was not at war with Islam. To emphasize this point, Obama downplayed the Islamic nature of the terrorism the United States faced—much to the displeasure of conservatives in the United States who claimed he was whitewashing Islamic terrorism. At the same time, however, he appeared to deliberately cool ties with Israel. Thus, despite the advice of members of the J Street lobby, his American Jewish allies in the peace process, who told him in July 2009 that he should visit Israel, by May 2011 he had not done so. Sending Vice President Biden to Jerusalem, as he did in March 2010, was seen by most Israelis as a poor substitute—and a belated one at that.

Essentially Obama's peacemaking strategy has gone through six periods up through May 2011 (the time of writing). During the first, lasting through most of 2009, he sought to get Israel to agree to a two-state solution to the conflict and stop building settlements, to get the PA under Abbas to return to direct negotiations with Israel, to get Syria to cut its ties to Hamas, Hizbollah, and Iran, and to get Saudi Arabia and the Gulf emirates to make confidence-building gestures to Israel, such as allowing Israeli civilian flyovers of their countries and visits by Israeli businessmen. This ambitious plan, however, did not prove successful. Although Netanyahu did accept a two-state solution, albeit with conditions, and adopted a ten-month partial settlement freeze (not including East Jerusalem), Abbas did not agree to direct negotiations, Syria did not cut ties with Hamas, Hizbollah, or Iran, and Saudi Arabia and the Gulf emirates refused to make confidence-building gestures to Israel. This led the Obama administration to undertake a reappraisal of its policy at the end of 2009, and by February the administration had decided on a more modest policy. Obama himself acknowledged in a *Time* magazine interview in February 2010 that the United States had overestimated its ability to bring about a settlement, and the United States now sought to get indirect or proximity talks under way between Israel and the Palestinians. Joe Biden's visit to Israel in mid-March 2010 was supposed to kick off the talks but instead precipitated a crisis in US-Israeli relations as the Israeli government embarked on plans to add 1,600 housing units in East Jerusalem. The crisis led to another reappraisal of US policy and there were well-placed leaks in the *New York Times* and *Washington Post* that the United States was about to issue its own peace plan.

Obama, however, did not endorse the suggestion to issue his own peace plan and went back to trying to get the indirect talks started, which he succeeded in doing in May, and a July 2010 Netanyahu visit to Washington was much more cordial than his March visit had been. Nonetheless, the indirect talks did not bear fruit other than to finally get Abbas's agreement to enter into direct talks with Israel in early September 2010, with Obama and Secretary of State Hillary Clinton looking on. This third stage of US peacemaking appeared to be too little and too late as Netanyahu's partial settlement freeze ended on September 26, and the Netanyahu government then reverted to its old policy of settlement building, leading Abbas to break off negotiations. The United States then made a major offer of security assistance to Israel, including the provision of twenty F-35 fighter aircraft to Israel in return for a ninety-day extension of the settlement freeze, an offer Israel did not accept, thus ending the fourth phase of the US effort.

Following Netanyahu's rejection of Obama's offer, the United States changed its policy. In a speech to the Brookings Institution on December 9, 2010, Secretary of State Clinton downplayed the settlement issue in favor of dealing with all of the core issues: Jerusalem, refugees, water, borders, security, and settlements. This strategy did not prove successful either, as the Palestinian-Israeli peace process remained frozen, and in May 2011 Obama announced still another strategy: to deal with the issues of borders and security first and then deal with what he called the more "emotional issues" of Jerusalem and Palestinian refugees. It remains to be seen whether this strategy will be any more successful than the previous two were.

However, by the spring of 2011, the policies of the Bush and Obama administrations began to draw closer in one area: Middle East democratization. After Obama downplayed the issue of democratization during his first two years in office, the emergence of the Arab Spring in 2011 appeared to shift Obama's position and by May, in a major policy speech at the US State Department, he strongly endorsed the emerging democratic trends in the Arab world.

In sum, although there have been important similarities between the George W. Bush and Obama administrations in their policies toward Israel, particularly in providing military aid to help ensure Israeli security, there have also been major differences, particularly over Israel's settlement-building policy and the Arab-Israeli peace process. Given the differences that have become noticeable over the first two and a half years of the Obama administration, one may well expect more differences until the end of his presidency.

Notes

1. Cited in Roula Khalaf, "Powell Sets Out Bush Line on Middle East," *Financial Times,* March 20, 2001.

2. Alan Sipress, "Lawmakers Criticize Palestinians," *Washington Post,* April 6, 2001.

3. For the text of the Mitchell Report, see *Ha'aretz,* May 6, 2001, English edition online.

4. For Tenet's effort to help work out an Israeli-Palestinian peace agreement, see his memoirs: George Tenet, *At the Heart of the Storm: My Years at the CIA* (New York: Harper-Collins, 2007), Chapters 4, 5, and 6.

5. Cited in Aluf Benn, "Sharon Calls Powell After White House Blasts PM Comments," *Ha'aretz,* October 5, 2001.

6. For the text of Bush's speech, see *New York Times,* November 12, 2001. See also Serge Schmemann, "Arafat Thankful for Bush Remark About 'Palestine,'" *New York Times,* November 12, 2001.

7. Cited in Bill Sammon, "Bush Will Not Meet with Arafat," *Washington Times,* November 9, 2001.

8. For the text of Powell's speech, see "United States Position on Terrorists and Peace in the Middle East," November 19, 2001, State Department website.

9. Janine Zacharia, "Bush Asking Arab Nations to Pitch in for a Secure Peace," *Jerusalem Post,* November 25, 2001.

10. Cited in *New York Times,* November 28, 2001.

11. See James Bennet, "U.S. Envoy Meets Arafat and Asks for End of Violence," *New York Times,* November 29, 2001.

12. Avi Machlis, "Israeli Bus Blast Casts Shadow on Peace Process," *Financial Times,* November 30, 2001.

13. Joel Greenberg, "Envoy to Middle East Assails Palestinian Militants," *New York Times,* December 1, 2001.

14. Cited in Lee Hockstadter, "Bomber in Bus Kills 15 in Israel," *Washington Post,* December 3, 2001.

15. Ibid.

16. Cited in Peter Herman, "Terrorists Kill at Least 15 in Israel," *Baltimore Sun,* December 2, 2001.

17. Clyde Haberman, "Arafat Demands Halt in Attacks Against Israelis," *New York Times,* December 7, 2001.

18. For a discussion of this point, see David Frum, *The Right Man: The Surprise Presidency*

of George W. Bush (New York: Random House, 2003), p. 256. Frum was a speechwriter for Bush from January 2001 to February 2002. See also Bob Woodward, *Bush at War* (New York: Simon & Schuster, 2002), p. 297. In his memoirs, *Decision Points* (New York: Crown, 2010), p. 401, Bush also indicates his anger with Arafat.

19. Lee Hockstadter, "Arafat Arrests Three in Arms Incident," *Washington Post,* January 12, 2002.

20. Mary Curtius, "Hamas Takes Responsibility for Attack," *Los Angeles Times,* January 10, 2002.

21. Amos Harel, "IDF Plans to Hit More PA Targets, Voice of Palestine Radio Torched in Ramallah, Police Bombed in Tulkarm," *Ha'aretz,* January 20, 2002.

22. Todd S. Purdum, "Powell Says U.S. Will Grab Chances at Middle East Peace," *New York Times,* February 28, 2002.

23. The text of UN Security Council Resolution 1397 is on the United Nations website.

24. For Powell's comments, see "Excerpts from Powell's News Conference of March 29, 2002," *New York Times,* March 30, 2002. See also Tracy Wilkinson, "Israel Corners a Defiant Arafat," *Los Angeles Times,* March 30, 2002.

25. Woodward, *Bush at War,* p. 34.

26. Ibid.

27. Israel has been carefully cultivating the support of evangelical Christians. The Israeli ambassador to the United States, Ayalon, regularly visited evangelical churches to thank them for their support, which he has called "so important in this day and age"; cited in James Morrison, "Israel Gives Thanks," *Washington Times,* Embassy Row Section, November 27, 2003. See also James Morrison, "Praying for Israel," *Washington Times,* Embassy Row Section, October 28, 2003, citing Ayalon speaking in an evangelical church in Tampa, Florida, where he stated, "The American Christian community is a bedrock of support for the State of Israel and its people."

28. Howard Kohr, executive director of AIPAC, called DeLay "one of the more important, resolute, and outspoken supporters of Israel"; cited in Juliet Eilperin, "Mideast Rises on DeLay's Agenda," *Washington Post,* October 16, 2003.

29. Cited in "Bush Slams Arafat but Sees 'New Attitude' in Some PA Leaders," *Ha'aretz,* May 26, 2002.

30. For the text of the Bush speech, see *Washington Post,* June 25, 2002.

31. Ibid.

32. The skepticism was reinforced in December 2002 when neoconservative Elliott Abrams was made Condoleezza Rice's deputy for Arab-Israeli affairs on the National Security Council. For a view of the evolving thinking of Abrams and his relationship with other neoconservatives, see Connie Bruck, "Back Roads: How Serious Is the Bush Administration About Creating a Palestinian State?" *New Yorker,* December 15, 2003.

33. Cited in Aluf Benn, "U.S. Telling PM that the Muqata Siege Undermining Plans for Iraq," *Ha'aretz,* September 29, 2002.

34. The text of the Road Map is found on the US Department of State website, April 30, 2002.

35. For the text of the letter of the eighty-eight senators, see *Journal of Palestine Studies* 32, no 4 (Summer 2003): 185.

36. See Elaine Monaghan, "Bush Praises Palestinian Leader's Courage," *Times* (London), July 26, 2003; Guy Dunmore, "Bush Attacks Israelis for Building of West Bank Wall," *Financial Times,* July 26, 2003; and Brian Knowlton, "Sharon Meets with Bush but Says Security Fence Will Still Go Up," *International Herald Tribune,* July 30, 2003.

37. Natan Sharansky, *The Case for Democracy: The Power of Freedom to Overcome Tyranny and Terror* (New York: PublicAffairs Press, 2004). See also Joel Rosenberg, "Two Great Dissidents: Natan Sharansky's Vision and President Bush's," *National Review,* online (November 19, 2004). For an early critique of the democratization program, see Thomas Carothers and Marina Ottoway, eds., *Uncharted Journey: Promoting Democracy in the Middle East* (Washington DC: Carnegie Endowment, 2005).

38. See Yossi Beilin, *The Path to Geneva: The Quest for a Permanent Agreement, 1996–2004* (New York: RDV Books, 2004).

39. For an analysis of Sharon's disengagement strategy, see David Makovsky, *Engagement Through Disengagement: Gaza and the Potential*

for Renewed Israeli-Palestinian Peacemaking (Washington, DC: Washington Institute for Near East Policy, 2005). See also "Sharon: The Evolution of a Security Hawk," *Midstream* 48, nos. 6–7 (May–June 2004).

40. Cited in Nicholas Kralev, "White House Urged West Bank Action," *Washington Times,* August 13, 2004.

41. All quotations from Bush's and Sharon's speeches are taken from *Ha'aretz,* April 15, 2004.

42. Cited in Nathan Guttman, "President Bush Woos the Jewish Vote," *Ha'aretz,* August 12, 2004.

43. Cited in Nicholas Kralev, "Anti-Semitism Office Planned at State Department," *Washington Times,* October 14, 2004. See also "State Department Opposes Anti-Semitism Bill," *Washington Post,* October 14, 2004.

44. Cited in Nathan Guttman, "Kerry and Bush Send in Top Guns to Woo AIPAC," *Ha'aretz,* October 26, 2004.

45. The agreement was published on the Associated Press website March 17, 2005.

46. Author's interview with Mahmoud Abbas, Ramallah, June 26, 2005.

47. In a *Financial Times* interview on April 20, 2007, Rice clung to the democratization policy, stating, "I'll choose elections and democracy, even if it brings to power people that we don't like. . . . Without reform and democratization you're going to have a false stability in the Middle East which will continue to give rise to extremism"; interview, "What the Secretary Has Been Saying," on the US State Department website.

48. Hamas leader Mahmoud Zahar said Hamas would not renounce the right to armed resistance against Israel to keep the money flowing from Europe and the United States and stated, "I'm sure Israel will disappear as the Crusaders and other empires disappeared. All of Palestine will become part of the Arab and Islamic land—as the Koran promised"; cited in Paul Martin, "Leader Likely to Cut Ties with Israel," *Washington Times,* January 27, 2006.

49. Cited in Greg Meyer, "Suicide Bombing in Israel Kills 9; Hamas Approves," *New York Times,* April 18, 2006.

50. Iran's policy toward Israel is discussed in Robert O. Freedman, *Russia, Iran, and the Nu-*

clear Question: The Putin Record (Carlisle, PA: Strategic Studies Institute of the US Army War College, 2006), pp. 32–36.

51. Cited in Bernard Reich, "The United States and Israel: A Special Relationship," in *The Middle East and the United States,* ed. David W. Lesch, 4th ed. (Boulder, CO: Westview Press, 2007), p. 221.

52. Cited in Yochi Drazin, "Battle in Middle East Widens U.S.-Russia Rift," *Wall Street Journal,* July 16, 2006.

53. Cited in Marina Grishina and Yelena Suponina, "Qana Tragedy—Russia and UN Urge Immediate Cease-Fire in Lebanon," *Vremya Novostei,* July 31, 2006. For Bush's view of the war, see Bush, *Decision Points,* pp. 413–415.

54. See Elli Lieberman, "Israel's 2006 War with Hizbollah: The Failure of Deterrence," in *Contemporary Israel,* ed. Robert O. Freedman (Boulder, CO: Westview Press, 2009), pp. 317–358.

55. See Hassan M. Fattah, "Accord Is Signed by Palestinians to Stop Feuding," *New York Times,* February 9, 2007.

56. See Harvey Morris, "Israel Pleads for Hamas to Remain in Isolation," *Financial Times,* March 19, 2007.

57. See the report by Glenn Kessler, "Secretary Rice to Try New ME Formula," *Washington Post,* March 23, 2007.

58. Cited in Avi Issacharoff, "Hamas, PRC Say Will Act to Torpedo New U.S. Benchmarks for Israel," *Ha'aretz,* May 5, 2007.

59. These statements by Olmert are analyzed in Shmuel Rosner, "Is the Democratic-Israeli Disengagement Getting Out of Hand?" *Ha'aretz,* April 20, 2007, and Nathan Guttman, "Dems Warn Olmert about Playing Politics," *Forward,* April 20, 2007.

60. Cited in Ze'ev Schiff, "U.S. Envoy Denies Pressure on Israel Not to Engage in Talks with Syria," *Ha'aretz,* May 21, 2007.

61. For an analysis of the US efforts to bolster Israeli security, see the report by Andrew J. Shapiro, assistant secretary of state for political-military affairs, delivered to the Brookings Institution, July 16, 2010; www.brookings.edu.

62. The leading US opponent to an American attack on Iran was Secretary of Defense Robert

Gates, who was appointed to his post by George W. Bush in 2006 and retained by Barack Obama. For Bush's view of a possible US attack on Iran, see Bush, *Decision Points,* pp. 417–420.

63. For the text of the joint statement, which Bush read at the opening of the Annapolis conference, see Walter Laqueur and Barry Rubin, eds., *The Israel-Arab Reader* (New York: Penguin Books, 2008), pp. 625–626.

64. Bush, *Decision Points,* pp. 408–409.

65. Ibid., p. 410.

66. A leading critic of the Obama administration's policy on Islam has been the conservative *Washington Times,* whose editorials and op-eds regularly condemn him for being weak on Islam. Former US Defense Secretary Donald Rumsfeld has also been critical. See Donald Rumsfeld, *Known and Unknown: A Memoir* (New York: Sentinel, 2011).

67. According to the revelations of WikiLeaks, by 2006 most of the Sunni Arab leaders were already vehemently anti-Iranian and some, such as those of Saudi Arabia, were urging a US attack on Iran's nuclear installations, a development that by 2009 Obama was undoubtedly aware of. Nonetheless, Obama seems to have thought that an Israeli-Palestinian peace agreement would have made it easier for these Arab leaders to have rallied their people against Iran. See David E. Sanger, "Around the World, Distress over Iran," *New York Times,* November 28, 2010.

68. In his June 2009 Cairo speech, Obama said, "The US does not accept the legitimacy of continued Israeli settlements"; cited in Ethan Bronner, "New Focus on Settlements: Obama Pressures Israelis over West Bank, but Effort to Stop Growth Faces Hurdles," *New York Times,* June 6, 2009.

69. See As'ad Ghanem and Mohamad Mustafa, "Coping with the Nakba: The Palestinians in Israel and the 'Future Vision' as a Collective Agenda," *Israel Studies Forum* 24, no. 2 (2009): 52–66.

70. Cited in Gil Hoffman, "Only 6% of Israelis See US Government as Pro-Israeli," *Jerusalem Post Online,* June 19, 2009.

71. See Obama interview with Joe Klein, *Time,* February 1, 2010.

72. Joshua Mitnik, "Holy Sites Stir Anger in Israel," *Wall Street Journal,* March 1, 2010.

73. See Yossi Alpher, "Too Many Constraints on the Administration," in *The US-Israel Crisis and the Peace Process,*www.bitterlemons.org, March 22, 2010.

74. See, for example, Helene Cooper, "Weighing an Obama Plan to End a Middle East Logjam," *New York Times,* April 8, 2010.

75. See the statement of General David H. Petraeus before the Senate Foreign Relations Committee on the future of the US Central Command, Washington, D.C., March 16, 2010.

76. See Natasha Mozgovaya, "Petraeus to Ashkenazi: I Never Said Israeli Policy Endangers US," *Ha'aretz Online,* March 27, 2010.

77. Cited in Hilary Leila Krieger, "Forcing the Peace," *Jerusalem Post,* April 30, 2010.

78. Cited in Natasha Mozgovaya, "Nearly 300 Congress Members Declare Commitment to US-Israeli Bond," *Ha'aretz Online,* March 27, 2010.

79. See AFP report, "Obama Seeks Funds to Boost Israeli Rocket Defenses," *Turkish Daily News Online,* www.hurriyetdailynews.com, May 16, 2010.

80. See Janine Zacharia and Mary Beth Sheridan, "Israel Angry at Being Singled Out in Action Plan on Nuclear Weapons," *Washington Post,* May 30, 2010.

81. Cited in Sheryl Stolberg, "Easing Tension with Obama, Israeli Leader Will Push Talks," *New York Times,* July 6, 2010.

82. Cited in Barak Ravid, "Obama: East Jerusalem Building Plans Unhelpful to Peace Efforts," *Ha'aretz Online,* November 9, 2010.

83. For descriptions of the proposed US-Israeli deal, see Charles Levinson, "Netanyahu Supports US Plan for Freeze," *Wall Street Journal,* November 15, 2010; and Joel Greenberg, "Netanyahu Moves on US Incentives for Construction Freeze in West Bank," *Washington Post,* November 15, 2010.

84. See Sanger, "Around the World."

85. Cited in Reuters report, "US Defense Chief Says Iran Sanctions Working, Argues Against Military Strike," *Ha'aretz Online,* November 16, 2010.

86. Clinton's speech can be found at www .state.gov/secretary/rm/2010/12/152664.htm, December 11, 2010.

87. See William Broad et al., "Israel Tests on Worm Called Crucial in Iran Nuclear Delay," *New York Times,* January 16, 2011.

88. See Herb Keinon, "As Nuke Talks with Iran Resume, Israel Urges Forceful Action," *Jerusalem Post,* January 21, 2011, and Roula Khalaf et al., "The Sabotaging of Iran," *Financial Times,* February 12, 2011.

89. See Robert O. Freedman, "Stuxnet's Impact," *Baltimore Jewish Times,* January 28, 2011.

90. Cited in Jay Solomon, "Clinton Raps Arabs for Lack of Reform," *Wall Street Journal,* January 14, 2011.

91. Cited in Ryan Lizza, "The Consequentialist: How the Arab Spring Remade Obama's Foreign Policy," *New Yorker,* May 2, 2011, p. 70.

92. Cited in Matthew Lee, "Without Reform, Arabs Face Disaster," *Jerusalem Post,* January 14, 2011.

93. Cited in Domberg, "Obama Vows Help Towards Democracy," *Financial Times,* February 12, 2011.

94. Cited in Isabel Kirshner, "In Israel, Gates Condemns Recent Attacks from Gaza," *New York Times,* March 25, 2011.

95. See Tobias Buck, "Ramallah Accuses Al-Jazeera of Plot to Weaken Abbas," *Financial Times,* January 25, 2011. For an anti-Abbas (and anti-US) view of the documents, see "The Palestine Papers: Chronicling the US Abandon-ment of the Road Map," *Journal of Palestine Studies* 40, no. 3 (Spring 2011): 84–114.

96. See Isabel Kirshner, "UN Praises Palestinians' Progress Toward State," *New York Times,* April 23, 2011; and David Miller, "A Palestinian Plan That's Doomed to Fail," *Washington Post,* April 15, 2011.

97. Cited in remarks by the president in address to the nation on Libya, White House Office of the Press Secretary, www.whitehouse.gov, March 28, 2011.

98. Cited in Lizza, "The Consequentialist," p. 55.

99. Cited in Helene Cooper, "Diplomatic Race over Peace Plan for Middle East," *New York Times,* April 21, 2011.

100. Cited in Edmund Sanders, "Israel Pressed to Offer Peace Initiative," *Los Angeles Times,* April 19, 2011.

101. See Cooper, "Diplomatic Race over Peace Plan for Middle East."

102. See Steven Lee Myers, "Amid Impasse in Peace Negotiations, America's Chief Middle East Envoy Resigns," *New York Times,* May 14, 2011.

103. For the text of Obama's speech, see *Washington Post,* May 20, 2011.

4

The Pro-Israel Lobby in the United States

PAST, PRESENT, AND FUTURE

Dov Waxman

NOWADAYS, DISCUSSIONS OF US-ISRAELI relations rarely take place without some mention of the pro-Israel lobby in the United States (also sometimes referred to as the Zionist lobby or the Jewish lobby). Frequently the pro-Israel lobby is invoked to help explain the policy toward Israel of whatever American presidential administration is in power. It is widely believed that the pro-Israel lobby is somehow behind this policy, influencing it, if not directly shaping it. Such a view has gained a great deal of popularity in recent years, especially as American Middle East policy in general has come under greater public scrutiny and discussion as a result of the terrorist attacks of 9/11 and the war in Iraq.

How much influence the pro-Israel lobby really wields is a subject of much debate and controversy.[1] Some attribute awesome powers to the pro-Israel lobby, holding it responsible not just for US policy toward Israel, but also for US foreign policy toward the Middle East as a whole.[2] Others argue that the power of the pro-Israel lobby is grossly exaggerated and that at most it has only a marginal effect on US policy-making.[3] Both of these perspectives are oversimplified. The pro-Israel lobby in the United States is neither all-powerful nor insignificant.

Although it is only one factor among many influencing US policy toward Israel, the Palestinians, and the Middle East, it can be an important one at times, especially on certain issues (most notably, US foreign aid to Israel). Indeed, if domestic lobbying were irrelevant to the formation of US policy-making toward Israel and the Middle East, the pro-Israel lobby would have no reason to exist and probably would have disappeared long ago. The continued vitality of pro-Israel lobby groups offers clear evidence of their utility. They do not control American foreign policy, but they sometimes make a difference.

The purpose of this chapter, however, is not to take sides in the continuing debate over the power of the pro-Israel lobby. Rather than assess the lobby's power, this chapter will review the history of the pro-Israel lobby and examine its current composition. It will explain what the pro-Israel lobby is, what it does, and how it came into being. Finally, the chapter will end by briefly considering the lobby's future. The chapter will focus primarily on the Jewish element of the pro-Israel lobby, although the growing role of evangelical Christians will also be discussed. The central thesis of this chapter is that after a century of lobbying on behalf of the Zionist movement and subsequently the State of Israel, the pro-Israel lobby in the United States has become more organizationally fragmented and ideologically divided than ever before. The heterogeneous nature of the pro-Israel lobby today reflects the diverse attitudes of the American Jewish community toward Israel, and the Israeli-Palestinian conflict in particular. Just as the American Jewish consensus over Israel has eroded, so too has the unity of the pro-Israel lobby.[4] Ultimately, this may well weaken its future political influence.

Defining the Pro-Israel Lobby

What, then, is the pro-Israel lobby? The pro-Israel lobby in the United States is composed of an assortment of advocacy groups, political action committees (PACs), think tanks, and media watchdog groups that seek to influence US government policy toward Israel in a direction that they believe is in Israel's interests.[5] The members of these organizations are mostly American Jews, but a large number of evangelical Christian Zionists also are involved in pro-Israel activities—which is why the term "pro-Israel lobby" should be used rather than "Jewish lobby."[6] The pro-Israel lobby is defined by its political agenda, not by religion or ethnicity. The groups that make up the pro-Israel lobby do not necessarily represent the views of American Jews, Israelis, or whatever Israeli government is in power, although some may try to do so with varying degrees of success. And although they all define themselves as "pro-Israel," they can have widely different interpretations of what this actually means in practice. What defines pro-Israel groups is not their stance on specific policies, but their attitude toward the State of Israel itself. An unwavering commitment to the survival of Israel as a Jewish state is fundamentally what distinguishes pro-Israel groups from other organizations involved in lobbying the US government on Middle East issues. Every pro-Israel group is motivated by a bedrock concern for securing Israel's existence as a Jewish state (that they want Israel to exist as a Jewish state is what differentiates pro-Israel groups from non-Zionist or even anti-Zionist groups that are outside the pro-Israel tent).

It is important to stress that the pro-Israel lobby does not officially represent the State of Israel. Although some pro-Israel groups may have close relations with Israeli governments and in practice follow their lead, the pro-Israel lobby is not completely beholden to Israel, and pro-Israel groups do not simply follow the orders of Israeli governments. Pro-Israel groups are independent actors whose views can differ, sometimes significantly, from those of Israeli governments, and they can take actions that Israeli policy makers may oppose. During the early years of the Oslo peace process, for example, the Rabin government in Israel complained that some pro-Israel organizations in the United States were acting against its policies and attempting to undermine the peace process.[7] More recently, a number of right-wing Jewish groups in the United States publicly insisted before and after the US-sponsored Annapolis summit meeting between Israel's government and the Palestinian Authority in November 2007 that Jerusalem remain Israel's undivided capital, opposing Prime Minister Ehud Olmert's willingness to make territorial concessions on Jerusalem.[8]

In trying to influence US policy concerning Israel, the pro-Israel lobby engages in a wide variety of activities. As its name suggests, lobbying lawmakers in Congress as well as policy makers and officials in the executive branch is a major part of the work of the pro-Israel lobby. This lobbying is done regularly rather than intermittently and involves not only promoting or opposing particular policy initiatives or pieces of legislation (at times even drafting the legislation itself), but also just maintaining good relationships with elected politicians and government bureaucrats and keeping them informed about issues concerning Israel (one way this is done is by taking politicians on free "study missions" to Israel). In addition to lobbying the US government, pro-Israel groups also engage in regular outreach to religious groups, ethnic groups, trade unions, students, and journalists. In doing so, they seek to gain domestic allies, build coalitions, and influence the opinion of certain segments of the American public, as well as the public opinion of Americans in general. Pro-Israel think tanks (e.g., the Washington Institute for Near East Policy and the Jewish Institute for National Security Affairs) conduct research and analysis that is then disseminated to policy makers and other members of the policy community in Washington, D.C., and beyond; and pro-Israel media watchdogs (such as Honest Reporting and the Committee for Accuracy in Middle East Reporting in America, or CAMERA) try to combat what they perceive as anti-Israeli bias in the news media. Last (but by no means least), pro-Israel PACs monitor congressional races around the country, raise money, pool it, and then donate it to their preferred candidates for their election campaigns (this way, they can contribute more money to political campaigns than individual donors). Campaign contributions from pro-Israel PACs (which amounted to more than $2.5 million in the 2008 election)[9] can help ensure support for Israel from politicians and help defeat politicians considered unsympathetic to Israel.

The Rise of the Pro-Israel Lobby: A Brief History

Today the pro-Israel lobby commands a lot of respect and fear. It is widely regarded as one of the most effective lobbies in Washington, D.C., and its supporters and critics alike consider it to be a major player in American politics and foreign policy-making. The pro-Israel lobby's current reputation is particularly impressive considering its humble beginnings. What is now a large, diverse, well-financed, and highly sophisticated lobby began as a single, small, and weak organization, with minimal support among American Jews, let alone from American policy makers. The first group formed by American Jews to lobby for the Zionist movement was established in July 1898 (a year after the first Zionist Congress in Basel, Switzerland) when the Federation of American Zionists (FAZ) held its founding convention in New York. In its early years, the group attracted little support from American Jews, for whom Zionism and its appeal for mass Jewish emigration and settlement in Palestine seemed at best irrelevant, if not potentially troublesome insofar as it challenged their attempt to Americanize and assimilate into American society (socialist and ultra-Orthodox Jews had other reasons to reject Zionism). Moreover, the leadership of the American Jewish community at the time, mostly wealthy German-born Jews, such as the banker and philanthropist Jacob Schiff (who founded the non-Zionist American Jewish Committee, or AJC, in 1906), initially opposed Zionism, fearing that it might jeopardize the position of American Jews by calling their national allegiance into question.

It was not until Louis Brandeis (then a Boston attorney and later a Supreme Court judge) took the leadership of the FAZ in 1914 that the organization began to grow in size and importance. Under Brandeis's leadership, FAZ membership greatly increased (from just 12,000 in 1914 to over 176,000 in 1919), and other prominent Jewish leaders, such as Rabbi Stephen Wise and Henrietta Szold (founder of Hadassah, the women's Zionist organization), joined it. It was at this time that American Zionist leaders really began lobbying the US government on behalf of the Zionist movement. Their first major success came during WWI, when Brandeis and Wise used their personal connections with President Woodrow Wilson to lobby for the Zionist cause. In 1917, their efforts helped convince Wilson and Secretary of State Edward House to endorse Britain's plan to issue a statement of support for establishing a Jewish national home in Palestine. When the British government then issued its famous Balfour Declaration, Wilson's administration publicly declared its support, against the advice of its own State Department. Subsequent Zionist lobbying on Capitol Hill resulted in a joint congressional resolution supporting the Balfour Declaration (the resolution passed unanimously in September 1922).

In 1918, the FAZ became the Zionist Organization of America (ZOA). After Brandeis lost the leadership of the ZOA in 1921, the organization was beset with internal divisions and leadership rivalries. Over the next two decades, it mainly focused on providing philanthropic support to the Zionist enterprise in British mandatory Palestine, but in the mid- to late 1930s it also lobbied American policy makers to oppose British plans to limit Jewish immigration into Palestine. In 1936, for instance, Wise (who became head of the ZOA in 1935) appealed to President Franklin Roosevelt to urge the British not to suspend all Jewish immigration to Palestine, a policy change they were considering in order to appease mounting Arab opposition to the Zionist movement. Roosevelt did so, and Britain continued to allow Jewish immigration to Palestine until British Prime Minister Neville Chamberlain sharply curtailed it with the White Paper of 1939.

Wise's appeal to Roosevelt and Brandeis's earlier lobbying of Wilson typified the approach of the pro-Zionist/pro-Israel lobby during its first half-century of existence (1898–1948). Unable to mobilize much grassroots support, and lacking resources, the pro-Zionist lobby largely relied upon the high-level personal connections of its most prominent leaders to achieve its goals. In this respect, it operated much as Jewish politics traditionally had in the Diaspora, using *shtadlanim* (court Jews) to intercede with rulers on behalf of the Jewish community's interest. Only in 1939 did the ZOA actually set up a formal lobbying organization in Washington run by a full-time lobbyist. Headed by Rabbi Isadore Breslau, the American Zionist Bureau, as it was called, existed for only two years before it was closed due to lack of funds.

The outbreak of WWII and the desperate plight of European Jews trying to flee Nazi-occupied Europe led to the formation of the American Emergency Committee for Zionist Affairs (later renamed the American Zionist Emergency Council, or AZEC), an umbrella group that represented all the major American Zionist organizations of the time (the ZOA, Hadassah, and two smaller groups, Mizrahi, the religious Zionist organization, and Poalei Zion, the Labor Zionist organization). During the war, under the leadership of Rabbi Abba Hillel Silver, AZEC lobbied Congress to encourage Britain to change its policy on Palestine and allow Jewish immigration. As part of this effort, AZEC's lobbying office in Washington recruited and trained Jewish activists around the country to lobby their representatives and senators. By the end of the war, AZEC had established a national network of activists to engage in grassroots activism to supplement its efforts on Capitol Hill. These activists later made an important contribution to the pro-Zionist lobby's success in winning congressional and presidential backing for the cause of Jewish statehood.

The most significant achievement of American Zionist groups during WWII occurred in New York City, rather than in Washington, D.C., when a conference was held in the Biltmore Hotel in May 1942 that included Zionist and non-Zionist organizations and was attended by the leaders of the world Zionist movement, Chaim Weizmann (president of the World Zionist Organization) and David Ben-Gurion (then chair of the Jewish Agency in Palestine). The Biltmore conference resulted in the announcement of a declaration of support for the establishment of a Jewish commonwealth in Palestine (known as the Biltmore Program). For the first time, Jewish statehood was now the open and unequivocal goal of the Zionist movement. It was also clear that achieving this goal depended upon the United States and that American Jewish Zionists therefore had a key role to play in the coming struggle for Jewish statehood. The United States had replaced Europe as the central political arena for the Zionist movement outside Palestine, and American Jews were now at the forefront of the movement.

By the end of WWII, the long debate over Zionism within the American Jewish community had finally come to an end. More than anything else, it was the destruction of much of European Jewry in the Holocaust that convinced the vast majority of American Jews of the need for Jewish statehood. After the war, therefore, with widespread support for Jewish statehood within the American Jewish community, the pro-Zionist lobby actively worked to build American political support for Jewish statehood. AZEC played an important role in convincing Congress to support Jewish statehood (in the 1944 election, support for Jewish statehood became part of the platforms of both the Democratic and Republican Parties—in large part as a result of Zionist lobbying and both parties' attempts to win the support of Jewish voters). AZEC activists also reached out to governors, state legislatures, mayors, churches, and trade unions to get them to voice support for Jewish statehood. They even set up two front groups to attract non-Jewish supporters to the Zionist cause: the Christian Council on Palestine (for clergymen) and the American Palestine Committee (which had seventy-five regional chapters and 15,000 members nationwide).

AZEC's public campaign in support of Jewish statehood played an important role in helping the State of Israel come into existence. By rallying Jewish and non-Jewish supporters to the cause of Jewish statehood, AZEC succeeded in making it a domestic political issue within the United States. This undoubtedly influenced the stance of the Truman administration toward the future of Palestine. By winning support for the Zionist cause in Congress, among Jewish voters, and within American public opinion in general, AZEC increased the political pressure on the Truman administration to support the partition of Palestine and the establishment of an independent Jewish state. This partly accounts for President Harry Truman's immediate recognition of the State of Israel in May 1948 (like President Wilson before him, Truman went against the State Department's advice). Thus, the pro-Zionist lobby was instrumental in securing American support for Israel's establishment (though other factors, personal, political, and strategic, were also responsible).

Israel's creation in 1948 marks the end of what can be identified as the first phase of American Jewish advocacy on behalf of Zionism and Israel. During a fifty-year period from 1898 to 1948, Zionism emerged and gradually spread within the American Jewish community, and many pro-Zionist Jewish organizations that later became part of the pro-Israel lobby were established (such as the Anti-Defamation League in 1913, and the American Jewish Congress in 1918). During this time as well, support for Zionism and Jewish statehood became part of American domestic politics, thereby influencing American foreign policy, most notably under Presidents Wilson and Truman.

The second period in the history of pro-Israel lobbying in the United States lasted from 1948 to 1967. The most important development for the pro-Israel lobby that took place during this time was the formation in the 1950s of its two flagship organizations, the American Israel Public Affairs Committee (AIPAC) and the Conference of Presidents of Major American Jewish Organizations. Both organizations were set up to influence US policy on Israel and the Middle East, with AIPAC intended to focus on Congress and the Conference of Presidents on the executive branch (this division of labor, however, has become less clear-cut over time as AIPAC has also come to focus its attention on the White House and the federal bureaucracy). To this day, AIPAC and the Conference of Presidents remain the most prominent and most powerful pro-Israel organizations in the United States.

The Conference of Presidents was formed when Henry Byroade, an aide to then secretary of state John Foster Dulles, suggested to Dr. Nahum Goldmann, head of the World Jewish Congress, that the American Jewish community speak with one voice to the White House and State Department. Following this suggestion, Goldmann, together with Abba Eban (Israel's ambassador to the United States) and Philip Klutznick (head of B'nai B'rith, the oldest Jewish organization in the United States), organized a gathering of the leaders of all the major American Jewish organizations in March 1954. This led to the formation of the Conference of Presidents, which was to serve as the voice of the American Jewish community to the US administration on issues concerning Israel.

Now a multimillion-dollar operation with hundreds of employees and 100,000 members, AIPAC began as a one-man operation. In 1951, Isaiah "Si" Kenen, an American Jew who had been working for the Israeli embassy in Washington, became the Washington representative of the American Zionist Council (the successor organization to AZEC). The main purpose of pro-Israel lobbying was now to secure American aid for the fledgling Jewish state. Working quietly behind the scenes, Kenen cultivated relationships with members of Congress and succeeded in getting modest amounts of aid for Israel ($65 million in US economic assistance to Israel in 1951 and $73 million in 1952). In 1954, worried that the American Zionist Council was about to be investigated by the Eisenhower administration for carrying out lobbying activities that violated its tax-exempt status, Kenen set up the American Zionist Committee for Public Affairs as an independent domestic lobbying group (thereby allowing it to engage in an unlimited amount of congressional lobbying). In 1959, he changed the organization's name to the American Israel Public Affairs Committee (AIPAC) to attract the support of non-Zionist American Jewish leaders.

AIPAC's primary mission was, and is, to strengthen the relationship between the United States and Israel. In the 1950s, this was no easy task, as the Eisenhower administration was more concerned with gaining Arab allies in the Cold War than helping Israel. Thus, AIPAC could not stop US aid to Arab states (such as Iraq and Egypt), nor could it prevent the Eisenhower administration from pressuring Israel to completely withdraw from the Sinai, which it seized in the 1956 Suez War. In its early years, therefore, AIPAC had little success in winning US support for Israel. Israel was simply not a US ally; it was at most a humanitarian cause.

The 1967 war (the Six-Day War) dramatically changed both the relationship between Israel and the United States and between American Jews and Israel. Israel's stunning victory against the armies of Egypt, Syria, and Jordan demonstrated to American policy makers Israel's strategic value to the United States. To American Jews, the victory was a source of great relief and pride, and for many, identification with Israel subsequently became a major component of their Jewish identity. Largely as a result of the 1967 war and then the 1973 war (the Yom Kippur War or October War), Israel became the top item on the American Jewish public agenda and pro-Israel lobbying dominated the political activities of the organized American Jewish community.[10]

The period from 1967 to 1993 marks the high point of pro-Israel advocacy by American Jews. Pro-Israel lobbying was no longer limited to a few well-connected Jewish leaders; instead it became a popular mass activity channeled through large membership-based organizations. As one scholar writes, "Israel and Zionist advocacy [in the United States] prior to 1967 in many ways is a story of how prominent individual Jewish and non-Jewish leaders utilized their personal influence with decision-makers in Washington. Following the Six-Day and Yom Kippur Wars, the national and grassroots organizations themselves became the instruments through which American Jews, who felt increasingly at home in America, sought to achieve their policy objectives."[11] This change meant that AIPAC's funding massively increased following the 1967 war and that other Jewish organizations increasingly focused their activities on Israel (in 1968, for example, the Anti-Defamation League, set up to counter anti-Semitism, established its own Middle East Affairs department, headed by Abraham Foxman, who later became the organization's national director).

Nevertheless, the pro-Israel lobby was not the driving force behind the warming relationship between the United States and Israel. Although AIPAC did help convince the Johnson administration in 1968 to sell Israel F-4 Phantom jet fighters (which was important in terms of legitimizing the sale of advanced US weaponry to Israel), pressure from the pro-Israel lobby had little if anything to do with the major increase in US arms sales to Israel that occurred in the 1970s under the Nixon administration. It was the belief of both President Richard Nixon and Secretary of State Henry Kissinger that US military assistance to Israel served American strategic interests in the Cold War that was responsible for their decision to substantially increase US arms sales to Israel and upgrade the US-Israeli relationship.

It was in the 1980s that the pro-Israel lobby, and AIPAC in particular, really came to national attention and began to acquire the fearsome reputation it has today. Ironically, it was a defeat that, in the words of J. J. Goldberg, "created the myth of AIPAC."[12] In 1981 AIPAC, together with the Conference of Presidents and the National Community Relations Advisory Council (now known as the Jewish Council for Public Affairs), tried to prevent the Reagan administration's proposed sale of AWACS (airborne warning and command system) reconnaissance planes to Saudi Arabia. Although the pro-Israel lobby succeeded in getting the House of Representatives to oppose the sale, the Senate approved it and the sale went ahead. Despite failing to achieve its goal, the pro-Israel lobby's AWACS campaign demonstrated its abilities, especially AIPAC's influence in Congress. Henceforth, AIPAC was considered a force to be reckoned with.

Over the next decade, AIPAC went from a small lobbying group to a large national organization with a mass membership. Under the leadership of Thomas Dine (its director from 1980 to 1993), AIPAC's staff grew from several dozen to 150, its annual budget increased from $1.2 million to $15 million, and its membership expanded to more than 55,000.[13] Dine also expanded AIPAC's lobbying activities, so that it dealt not just with Congress but also with the federal bureaucracy, especially the Departments of State, Defense, and Commerce. It was not just Dine's leadership, however, that was responsible for AIPAC's transformation into the preeminent pro-Israel lobby organization. Policy makers in the United States and Israel also played a part. The Reagan administration preferred dealing with AIPAC over other American Jewish pro-Israel groups because it was a single-issue organization, unlike the liberal and left-of-center American Jewish groups that opposed the Republican and conservative administration on a host of domestic issues.[14] Similarly, Israel's Likud Party under Yitzhak Shamir preferred AIPAC (and the Conference of Presidents) to other more democratic and hence unpredictable and uncontrollable American Jewish organizations (the National Community Relations Advisory Council in particular).[15]

Augmenting AIPAC's growing power in the 1980s were pro-Israel PACs (AIPAC itself is not a political action committee and cannot legally raise money for election candidates). They first appeared in the 1980 congressional elections, and in 1982, Nat PAC, a national pro-Israel PAC based in Washington, D.C., was established. In that year, pro-Israel PAC money helped to defeat Representative Paul Findley, a prominent critic of Israel, and in the next election in 1984, pro-Israel PACs claimed an even bigger victory with the defeat of Senator Charles Percy, chair of the Senate's Foreign Relations Committee.[16] Pro-Israel PACs quickly became a highly effective (and discreet) means of rewarding or punishing elected politicians for their track record on issues concerning Israel.

Just when some commentators were beginning to decry the outsize influence of the pro-Israel lobby in Washington,[17] it lost its biggest battle ever. In 1991, the pro-Israel lobby went up against the George H. W. Bush administration over $10 billion in US loan guarantees to Israel. To pressure the Shamir government in Israel to stop settlement building in the occupied territories (the West Bank and Gaza Strip), the administration wanted to delay congressional approval of Israel's request to help it pay for absorbing immigrants from the Soviet Union. Opposed to linking the loan guarantees to the issue of settlements, the pro-Israel lobby (led by the Conference of Presidents) organized a national advocacy day on September 12, 1991, when over 1,000 Jewish leaders came to Washington, D.C., to lobby Congress for the loan guarantees. In response, during a press conference that day, Bush described himself as "one lonely little guy" who was "up against some powerful political forces."[18] With this single statement, the president galvanized American public opinion behind him (although he offended and angered many American Jews) and turned Congress against immediately approving the loan guarantees (which it had been poised to do). The administration ultimately succeeded in delaying the loan guarantees until the left-of-center Rabin government came to power in Israel. The pro-Israel lobby's defeat in this battle underscores that a determined US administration can withstand pressure from the lobby and carry out its own agenda in its relations with Israel (although Bush undoubtedly paid a domestic political price for doing so).

The fourth and most recent period in the history of pro-Israel advocacy in the United States began in 1993 with the signing of the Oslo Accords between

Israel's Rabin government and the Palestinian Liberation Organization (PLO), led by Yasser Arafat. The ensuing peace process generated deep divisions within both the pro-Israel lobby and the American Jewish community at large.[19] Just as Israeli Jews acrimoniously argued over the peace process and the Israeli territorial withdrawals that accompanied it, so too did American Jews. In Israel and the United States, the debate over the Oslo peace process was bitter and divisive, exposing the lack of political consensus among Jews in both Israel and the United States. For American Jews, the consensus over Israel that once united them was now clearly a thing of the past. The first cracks in this consensus, which prevailed after 1967, had already appeared in the mid-1970s when criticism of Israeli government policies, especially its settlement building in the West Bank and Gaza Strip, first began to be publicly voiced by some Jewish organizations (such as the left-wing group Breira)[20] and individual Jewish leaders. This public criticism greatly increased after Menachem Begin's Likud Party came to power in Israel in 1977, and especially during Israel's war in Lebanon from 1982 to 1985. By the time the first Palestinian Intifada broke out in 1987, criticism of Israel and dissent from the positions of the pro-Israel lobby in the United States had become increasingly common among American Jews. Yet this criticism and dissent were largely sporadic and unorganized until the Oslo peace process, when they became ongoing and organized.

During the Oslo peace process (1993–2000), left-wing and right-wing American Jewish groups mobilized both for and against it. On the right, a reinvigorated ZOA led by Morton Klein was a vocal critic. The organization tried to block US financial assistance to the newly created Palestinian Authority, successfully lobbying Congress in 1994 to pass the Specter-Shelby Amendment, which linked Palestinian aid to presidential certification that the PA was complying with the Oslo Accords (the Rabin government opposed the amendment). On the Left, Americans for Peace Now and Israel Policy Forum enthusiastically supported the peace process, and between 1996 and 1999 they called for the United States to pressure Israel's right-wing, Likud-led government under Benjamin Netanyahu to continue it.

For AIPAC, the Oslo peace process was a major challenge. Not only did the organization face new criticism from pro-Israel groups on the Right and the Left, but also it had to contend with internal discontent, as many of its supporters and donors were uncomfortable with the sea change in AIPAC's positions. After years spent staunchly defending Israel's refusal to negotiate with and make territorial concessions to the PLO, AIPAC suddenly had to shift to supporting these things. The organization now had to lobby Congress for American aid to the Palestinians and to the PLO, headed by longtime nemesis Yasser Arafat, in particular. This abrupt reversal of position was very difficult for AIPAC to make. It was caught between supporting the policies of the Clinton administration and the Rabin government and the views of its more hawkish and right-wing membership (leading some discontented AIPAC members who opposed the Oslo Accords to join the revived ZOA).[21]

Growing internal divisions within the pro-Israel lobby and the increasingly open expression of them were not the only problems the pro-Israel lobby had to contend with during the Oslo peace process. An equally significant problem was a decline in pro-Israel activism at the grassroots level. The era of mass Jewish mobilization on behalf of Israel that was ushered in by the 1967 war came to an end in the 1990s. It became harder to mobilize American Jews around Israel because Israel simply didn't seem to need American Jewish support the way it had in the past. Israel no longer appeared to be endangered or impoverished. Instead the country was now widely perceived as more secure and economically prosperous and as moving toward peace. This perception undercut the efforts of the pro-Israel lobby to recruit and rally American Jews to support Israel. As Martin Raffel notes, "It was easier to mobilize the community to defend an embattled Israel, or an Israel facing international condemnation. The challenge of assisting Israel in its peacemaking efforts simply did not seem to motivate the grassroots the way the 'survival agenda' did in earlier eras."[22] Consequently, contributions to pro-Israel PACs declined, and multi-issue American Jewish national organizations, such as the American Jewish Committee and the Jewish Council for Public Affairs, shifted their attention and resources away from Israel advocacy toward other issues,[23] particularly what became known as Jewish continuity (an issue sparked by the publication of the National Jewish Population Survey in 1990, which revealed an alarmingly high rate of 52 percent intermarriage by American Jews). The focus of the organized American Jewish community, therefore, switched from an external one—defending Israel—to an internal one—responding to the challenges of Jewish assimilation and intermarriage. Israel had lost its unrivaled place at the top of the American Jewish communal agenda.

Thus, the decade of the 1990s saw the biggest crisis the pro-Israel lobby had faced so far. The lobby was deeply and publicly divided, and seemed in danger of becoming obsolete, as Israel was less in need of it and American Jews less supportive of it. This all changed in 2000 with the collapse of the peace process and the outbreak of the second Intifada (2000–2004). The wave of suicide terrorist attacks unleashed against Israeli civilians in the early years of the second Intifada turned back the clock on pro-Israel activism in the United States. Once again, support for Israel became the top priority of the organized American Jewish community, pro-Israel activism increased, and a new sense of unity and consensus prevailed among American Jews.[24] Now that Israel was under attack again, the American Jewish community overwhelmingly rallied behind it. Pro-Israel groups found a new/old sense of purpose and means of mobilizing the grassroots, and their fund raising benefited accordingly (contributions to AIPAC, for example, soared after the second Intifada erupted).[25]

However, the consensus and unity that American Jews and the pro-Israel lobby enjoyed during the second Intifada were short-lived. The support (both real and imagined) of the pro-Israel lobby for the US invasion of Iraq in 2003 (which was very unpopular among American Jews) and for other highly controversial policies and actions by the George W. Bush administration in its "War on Terror," as well as the lobby's steadfast backing of Israel's aggressive response to the second Intifada (involving, among other things, the military reoccupation of large parts of the West Bank and the "targeted killing" of Palestinian terrorists) aroused growing dissatisfaction on the Left of the American Jewish community.[26] Opposed to what they regarded as the pro-Israel lobby's "tilt to the Right" during the George W. Bush and Ariel Sharon governments and the perceived suppression of debate within the organized Jewish community over Israel's actions toward the Palestinians, left-wing and liberal Jews began speaking out and organizing in greater numbers.[27] The left-wing American Jewish group Brit Tzedek v'Shalom (the Alliance for Peace and Justice, founded in 2002), for example, collected over 10,000 signatures in support of the Geneva Accord (a model Israeli-Palestinian permanent-status agreement negotiated by Yossi Beilin and Yasser Abed Rabbo and released in December 2003, which the Sharon government strongly opposed).[28]

The clearest and most significant manifestation of a resurgence of left-wing Jewish activism after the second Intifada was the formation of J Street, the self-described "pro-peace, pro-Israel movement," in April 2008. J Street presented itself as the voice of American Jews who support Israel's existence as a Jewish and democratic state, but not necessarily the policies of Israeli governments. As its founder and director, Jeremy Ben-Ami, stated, "You don't have to be non-critical. You don't have to adopt the party line. It's not, 'Israel, right or wrong.'"[29] In line with this attitude, J Street openly criticized Israel's war in Gaza (December 2008–January 2009) and later supported the Obama administration's pressure on the Netanyahu government over the expansion of Jewish settlements in the West Bank and East Jerusalem. Although these public stances earned J Street angry denunciations from right-wing Jewish groups and individuals who labeled the organization "anti-Israel"[30] (and initially led it to be cold shouldered by Michael Oren, Israel's ambassador to the United States),[31] they did not stop the organization from quickly becoming a major player in pro-Israel advocacy, with almost 110,000 online supporters and a budget of $3 million in 2010. It also established its own political action committee, JStreetPAC, which contributed almost $400,000 to congressional candidates in the 2008 election.[32] Its first national conference, held in Washington, D.C., in October 2009 drew more than 1,500 supporters from across the country and featured a keynote speech by US National Security Adviser James L. Jones and a gala dinner attended by forty-four members of Congress. Although J Street was certainly no match for AIPAC, which remained the giant of pro-Israel groups, it emerged as the most prominent left-wing alternative within the pro-Israel lobby.[33]

The Pro-Israel Lobby Today

The pro-Israel lobby today is more fragmented and fractious than ever before. It is internally divided by disagreements over what is in Israel's best interests and what is the proper role that Americans Jews should play in supporting Israel. Indeed, as a result of these divisions, the pro-Israel lobby is really not a single lobby at all but is in fact composed of different lobbies, each of which advocates different policies for Israel and for the United States vis-à-vis Israel. It is now more accurate to speak of three pro-Israel lobbies: a centrist lobby, a left-wing lobby, and a right-wing lobby. The centrist lobby is composed of many of the most established and well-known organizations: most notably, AIPAC,[34] the Conference of Presidents, the Jewish Council for Public Affairs, the American Jewish Committee, and the Anti-Defamation League. The centrist lobby is fundamentally oriented toward what may be termed "consensus politics." Consensus politics is based on the conviction that the best way to be influential is to present a united front before Congress and the White House. Hence, it seeks to represent the consensus of the American Jewish community (more precisely, the organized American Jewish community),[35] when such a consensus exists. When there are differences of opinion, it attempts to resolve these differences internally, behind closed doors, then in public supports a common position. As a result of this political orientation, the centrist lobby tries to avoid taking clear, strong stances on controversial and polarizing issues.

Hence, although groups in the centrist lobby support the principle of territorial compromise and favor a two-state solution to the Israeli-Palestinian conflict, they do not loudly and energetically promote establishing a Palestinian state, nor do they actively and openly oppose Israel's occupation of the West Bank. In fact, they tend to defend the expansion of Israeli settlements there. In the past, the centrist lobby supported the Oslo peace process and Israel's 2005 disengagement from Gaza, but in both cases its support was widely regarded as unenthusiastic, if not wary. The centrist lobby is more concerned with addressing the threats to Israel's security than with promoting peace processes that will necessarily involve Israeli concessions. Writing about groups in the centrist lobby, Dan Fleshler notes that "their organizational cultures are most comfortable when they can take forceful stances against Israel's 'enemies'—e.g., Iran, Hamas, Hezbollah, and far-left critics of Israel. They tend to be less comfortable about enthusiastically supporting peace initiatives that require a certain amount of trust in Arab intentions or bold territorial compromises."[36]

For the centrist lobby, being "pro-Israel" generally means supporting the Israeli government of the day. Whatever the political makeup of the Israeli government, the centrist lobby tries to promote the policies of that government. But the nature of this support may vary, from half-hearted to full-throated.

Though the centrist lobby will almost never publicly criticize or challenge the Israeli government's policy positions, it will not necessarily lend its full support. What matters to the centrist lobby more than anything else is ensuring American support for Israel. The informal alliance between the United States and Israel is considered the cornerstone of Israeli security. Hence, maintaining this alliance is the central mission of the centrist lobby, which means that the centrist lobby opposes any kind of American pressure on Israel. Moreover, the centrist lobby is generally hostile to public criticism of Israel in the United States or elsewhere. In recent years, the centrist lobby has become increasingly concerned with combating what it perceives to be a global campaign to delegitimize Israel, spearheaded by Arab and anti-Zionist groups on the Left.

The single biggest difference between the centrist lobby and the left-wing and right-wing lobbies is that the latter two lobbies, unlike the former, are much more willing to challenge and oppose the policies of Israeli governments. Both left-wing and right-wing lobbies have strong views that they forcefully advocate, even if they are at odds with Israeli government policy or the consensus of the organized American Jewish community. The left-wing and right-wing lobbies are thus based on ideological politics, rather than the consensus politics of the centrist lobby. It is more important to them to express their beliefs and opinions than to echo the views of Israeli governments or the prevailing American Jewish consensus. Fundamentally, they believe they are entitled to save Israel from itself and are not willing to muzzle themselves for the sake of Jewish unity.

The left-wing lobby is currently made up of such groups as J Street, Americans for Peace Now, and Meretz USA. These groups are dovish and favor diplomacy, engagement, negotiations, and concessions over the use of diplomatic isolation and/or military force. The left-wing lobby opposes Israel's occupation of the West Bank, favors a division of Jerusalem, and strongly supports establishing a Palestinian state. They want the United States to take a lead role in bringing this about, even if doing so means pressuring Israel. Strong US-Israeli relations are, therefore, of secondary importance to the left-wing lobby. Peace between Israel and the Palestinians, and Israeli-Arab peace more generally, is their chief concern.

The right-wing lobby (which includes the ZOA, the Orthodox Union, American Friends of Likud, and the Jewish Institute for National Security Affairs), in stark contrast, is very hawkish, skeptical of the value of diplomacy and negotiations, suspicious of engagement, and opposed to Israeli concessions to its enemies. It embraces the use of military force and believes that it should be applied ruthlessly and devastatingly when necessary. Above all, it supports Israel's control of the West Bank (i.e., "Greater Israel") and opposes a division of Jerusalem and the establishment of a Palestinian state. The right-wing lobby tends to regard the Palestinians not as potential partners for peace, but as implacable foes of Israel. As such, according to the right-wing lobby, Israeli-Palestinian peace is simply not possible for the foreseeable future. For them, the greatest challenge Israel faces is from the forces of radical Islamism, represented by Hamas, Hizbollah, and above all Iran, whose leaders have called for Israel's destruction.

Pro-Israel groups today, therefore, seldom agree among themselves. Though they try to promote Israel's interests, they differ greatly in their views on what those interests actually are (just as Israelis themselves do). Some groups oppose Israel's continued occupation of territories gained in the 1967 war; others staunchly support Israel's control over these territories, for either security, historical, or religious reasons (or a combination of them). Some support the establishment of a Palestinian state in the West Bank and Gaza Strip; others are adamantly opposed. Some fiercely resist any American pressure on Israel; others oppose unconditional American support for Israeli policies and favor a more even-handed US role in Arab-Israeli peacemaking. Thus, the designation "pro-Israel" tells us very little about the specific policies that different organizations actually lobby for.

As a result of the disagreements within the pro-Israel community in the United States, pro-Israel advocacy groups rarely act in unison; more frequently they oppose one another. Though at times groups in the left-wing and right-wing lobbies can find enough common ground with groups in the centrist lobby to enable them to work together, the left-wing and right-wing lobbies, given their radically different political orientations and views, do not cooperate with each other. Hence, more often than not, American policy makers hear from many different voices, each of which claims to be "pro-Israel" and to represent the views of American Jews. In the words of former US secretary of state George Shultz, "Anyone who thinks that Jewish groups constitute a homogeneous 'lobby' ought to spend some time dealing with them."[37]

The different pro-Israel groups, however, are by no means equal. They vary greatly in size (membership and staff), finances, and political influence. Some are merely "one-man shows" led by a single individual; many others are just shoestring-budget operations run out of a single office and reliant upon volunteers. Only a few are well staffed, with fancy offices and large sums of money at their disposal. AIPAC is still the biggest,[38] wealthiest,[39] and most powerful.[40] It continues to exert a lot of influence in Congress—the bills supporting Israel that it drafts and/or promotes often receive almost unanimous support in both the House of Representatives and the Senate—and although it has less influence within the White House, it can nonetheless effectively limit the room for maneuver of any US administration on issues related to Israel and the Israeli-Palestinian conflict because American presidents are generally reluctant to carry out a particular policy or launch a foreign policy initiative without congressional backing.[41] Every year, AIPAC flexes its political muscle at its policy conference in Washington, D.C., a huge event that draws thousands of activists (over 7,000 people attended the 2010 conference) and over half the members of Congress to its gala dinner. The event is a dramatic display of the continuing vitality of the pro-Israel lobby and its importance in American domestic politics.

Conclusion: The Future of the Pro-Israel Lobby

This chapter has charted the rise of the pro-Israel lobby from its humble origins over a century ago to its current composition of many different groups competing to shape US foreign policy toward Israel and define the meaning of being "pro-Israel." The tremendous success over the past century of the pro-Israel lobby (and its earlier incarnation, the pro-Zionist lobby) is undeniable. Pro-Zionist lobbying helped ensure American political and diplomatic support for the Zionist movement and was instrumental in bringing about the vital support of the United States for Israel's establishment. Since then, pro-Israel advocacy has played a major role in winning American economic and military aid to Israel. The massive amount of US aid that Israel has received, totaling more than $100 billion, and the roughly $3 billion in US military aid it continues to receive each year (making Israel the largest annual recipient of US aid), is due in no small part to the work of the pro-Israel lobby in Congress. Though it is not the only factor at work, direct lobbying and campaign contributions by pro-Israel groups have undoubtedly helped convince many politicians in Congress to always vote in favor of American aid to Israel, as well as other kinds of largesse.[42]

The pro-Israel lobby is also at least partly responsible for the fact that successive US administrations have not applied much leverage to stop Israeli settlement construction in the occupied territories, even though this building goes against American wishes and policy goals. The pro-Israel lobby, and AIPAC in particular, has helped forestall pressure, threats, and even sanctions that American administrations, frustrated by the continued expansion of Israeli settlements in the West Bank, might otherwise have applied on Israeli governments. More broadly, although many forces, domestic and international, have shaped US-Israeli relations over time, the pro-Israel lobby in the United States has certainly been one of them. Simply put, the de facto alliance that now exists between the two countries is partly a result of the sustained efforts of the pro-Israel lobby.[43] This is not to say that the pro-Israel lobby is all-powerful, as some perceive it to be, or that it controls US policy toward Israel, let alone toward the Middle East in general. The pro-Israel lobby has suffered setbacks and defeats, most famously over the sale of AWACS aircraft to Saudi Arabia and US loan guarantees to Israel. But its successes have been more numerous than its failures, and over the years its power has increased, not diminished.

What, then, does the future hold for the pro-Israel lobby? In the short term, it looks set to remain influential, especially in Congress. In the long term, however, the pro-Israel lobby faces three major challenges. First is the challenge posed by its internal diversity. The pro-Israel lobby is not nearly as united as it once was. Instead, it is deeply divided between left-wing, right-wing, and centrist groups, and as such, it can no longer speak to the US government with a single voice (as it did in earlier eras). This threatens to reduce the lobby's political influence. In the past this influence was based in part on the belief that pro-Israel organizations, in particular AIPAC and the Conference of Presidents, spoke for the American Jewish community as a whole. Today no single organization can credibly claim to represent the overwhelming majority of American Jews. Consequently, American policy makers and legislators may well become less inclined to listen to these organizations, let alone follow their advice. Thus, the pro-Israel lobby's internal diversity could ultimately undermine its political leverage.

A second future challenge facing the pro-Israel lobby concerns its relationship with American Jewry. The pro-Israel lobby has always consisted mostly of American Jews. Their commitment to Israel—a commitment that grew stronger after 1967—has traditionally been the driving force behind pro-Israel activism in the United States. Nowadays, this commitment is in serious doubt. Although American Jews for the most part continue to be committed to Israel, the strength of this commitment and its ability to mobilize political action, especially among the younger generation of American Jews, is much less certain than it once was. There is an ongoing debate over whether a generational decline in emotional attachment to Israel is occurring, with younger Jews becoming more alienated from Israel.[44] Regardless of whether this is the case, it is clear that young Jews are now less willing to unite behind Israel, and more are embracing causes other than Israel (such as domestic social justice issues). If this continues, the pro-Israel lobby will find it more difficult to recruit and mobilize American Jews, and it will have to increasingly rely upon support from religiously Orthodox American Jews.[45]

Although Jewish support for the pro-Israel lobby may be declining, evangelical Christian support for it is undoubtedly increasing. In fact, the largest pro-Israel organization in the United States today is made up of evangelical Christians, Christians United for Israel. The organization was founded in 2006 by Pastor John Hagee and already claims to have 426,000 members.[46] The group's phenomenal growth points to the growing role that evangelical Christians are likely to play in the pro-Israel lobby in the future. As this occurs, the pro-Israel lobby will be gradually transformed from a predominantly Jewish movement to one that includes a substantial and growing segment of evangelical Christians (a development that some American Jews welcome but many others are decidedly uneasy about). This too could weaken its political influence because the evangelical community is largely Republican, not Democratic, and a highly partisan pro-Israel lobby will therefore enjoy less American political support.

Given these future challenges, the power of the pro-Israel lobby looks set to eventually decline. For now, though, it remains a political force to be reckoned with.

Notes

1. Michael Massing, "The Storm over the Israel Lobby," *New York Review of Books* 53, no. 10 (June 8, 2006).

2. John J. Mearsheimer and Stephen M. Walt, *The Israel Lobby and U.S. Foreign Policy* (New York: Farrar, Straus & Giroux, 2007).

3. Michelle Goldberg, "Is the 'Israel Lobby' Distorting America's Mideast Policies?" *Salon,* April 18, 2006; Christopher Hitchens, "Overstating Jewish Power," *Slate,* March 27, 2006; Joseph Massad, "Blaming the Lobby," *Al-Ahram Weekly,* March 23–29, 2006; David Gergen, "An Unfair Attack," *US News & World Report,* April 3, 2006; Max Boot, "Policy Analysis—Paranoid Style," *Los Angeles Times,* March 29, 2006.

4. On the dissolution of the American Jewish community's consensus concerning Israel, see Steven T. Rosenthal, *Irreconcilable Differences? The Waning of the American Jewish Love Affair with Israel* (Hanover, NH: Brandeis University Press, 2001).

5. This definition excludes individuals, typically very wealthy and well-connected, who personally engage in pro-Israel advocacy without any formal organizational support.

6. On Christian Zionism in the United States, see Paul Charles Merkley, "American Christian Support for Israel," in *U.S.-Israeli Relations in a New Era,* ed. Eytan Gilboa and Efraim Inbar (New York: Routledge, 2009), pp. 108–122, and Chapter 11 in this volume.

7. AIPAC, for instance, lobbied the US Congress to pass a bill requiring the United States to move its embassy from Tel Aviv to Jerusalem, despite the behind-the-scenes objections from the Rabin government.

8. Ami Eden, "Criticism of Olmert Foreshadows Jewish Showdown," *Jewish Telegraphic Agency,* November 27, 2007.

9. Eric Fingerhut, "Will J Street Money Translate into Influence?" *Jewish Telegraphic Agency,* November 10, 2008.

10. Steven M. Cohen and Charles S. Liebman, "Israel and American Jewry in the Twenty-First Century," in *Beyond Survival and Philanthropy,* ed. Allon Gal and Alfred Gottschalk (Cincinnati, OH: Hebrew Union College Press, 2000).

11. Martin J. Raffel, "History of Israel Advocacy," in *Jewish Polity and American Civil Society,* ed. Alan Mittleman, Jonathan Sarna, and Robert Licht (Lanham, MD: Rowman & Littlefield, 2002), pp. 118–119.

12. J. J. Goldberg, *Jewish Power: Inside the American Jewish Establishment* (Reading, MA: Addison-Wesley, 1996), p. 199.

13. Ibid., pp. 202–203.

14. Ibid., pp. 213–215.

15. Ibid., pp. 217–218.

16. Ibid., pp. 136–137.

17. See, for example, Paul Findley, *They Dare to Speak Out: People and Institutions Confront Israel's Lobby* (Westport, CT: Lawrence Hill, 1985); Edward Tivan, *The Lobby: Jewish Political Power and American Foreign Policy* (New York: Simon & Schuster, 1987); Noam Chomsky, *The Fateful Triangle: The United States, Israel, and the Palestinians* (Boston, MA: South End Press, 1983); and Richard Curtiss, *Stealth PACs: How Israel's American Lobby Took Control of U.S. Middle East Policy* (Washington, DC: American Educational Trust, 1990).

18. Quoted in Goldberg, *Jewish Power,* pp. xv–xvi.

19. Ofira Seliktar, *Divided We Stand: American Jews, Israel, and the Peace Process* (New York: Praeger, 2002).

20. Breira (meaning "alternative" in Hebrew) was formed in 1973 in the aftermath of the Yom

Kippur War. It was a small organization composed mostly of rabbis and intellectuals. What made Breira significant was not its size but the fact that it claimed to be driven by a concern for Israel's interests, and the interests of Jews more generally. That is, Breira presented itself as essentially "pro-Israel," although it openly opposed Israeli policies toward the Palestinians in the occupied territories (it also opposed the mainstream American Jewish establishment). Its many Jewish detractors, however, denounced Breira as an anti-Israeli organization that risked undermining US support for Israel, and the organized Jewish community effectively boycotted it and ostracized its members. Rapidly losing its support, Breira was forced to dissolve in 1977. For a history of Breira, see Michael E. Staub, *Torn at the Roots: The Crisis of Jewish Liberalism in Postwar America* (New York: Columbia University Press, 2002), pp. 280–308.

21. Rafael Medoff, *Jewish Americans and Political Participation* (Santa Barbara, CA: ABC-CLIO, 2002), p. 250.

22. Raffel, "History of Israel Advocacy," p. 156.

23. Ibid., p. 167.

24. The second Intifada had a similarly unifying effect on Israeli Jews; see Dov Waxman, "From Controversy to Consensus: Cultural Conflict and the Israeli Debate over Territorial Withdrawal," *Israel Studies* 13, no. 2 (2008): 73–96.

25. "AIPAC Doubles Earnings," *Jewish Telegraphic Agency,* February 12, 2009.

26. For a rebuttal of the claim that the pro-Israel lobby was a major influence behind the Bush administration's decision to invade Iraq, see Dov Waxman, "From Jerusalem to Baghdad? Israel and the War in Iraq," *International Studies Perspectives* 10, no. 1 (February 2009): 1–17.

27. See Philip Weiss, "AIPAC Alternative?" *The Nation,* April 23, 2007; and Gary Kamiya, "Can American Jews Unplug the Israel Lobby?" *Salon,* March 20, 2007.

28. Jonathan Rynhold, "Israel's Foreign and Defence Policy and Diaspora Jewish Identity," in *Israel and Diaspora Jewish Identity,* ed. Danny Ben-Moshe and Zohar Segev (Brighton, UK: Sussex Academic Press, 2007), p. 150.

29. Quoted in Traub, "The New Israel Lobby."

30. See, for instance, Morton Klein, "J Street Should Rescind Its Invitation to Al-Marayati," *Jewish Telegraphic Agency,* September 9, 2009; Lenny Ben-David, "Protecting the Quarterback in the White House," *Jerusalem Post,* September 13, 2009; Isi Leibler, "J Street's 'Pro-Israel' Stance Is Phoney," *The Guardian,* October 26, 2009; Natasha Mozgovaya, "Dershowitz Lays into J Street in AIPAC Conference Dust-Up," *Ha'aretz,* March 22, 2010.

31. Hilary Leila Krieger, "Michael Oren Rejects J Street Conference Invite," *Jerusalem Post,* October 20, 2009.

32. This amount was more than any other pro-Israel PAC in the country, leading the *Washington Post* to describe J Street's PAC as "Washington's leading pro-Israel PAC"; Dan Eggen, "New Liberal Jewish Lobby Quickly Makes Its Mark," *Washington Post,* April 17, 2009. But this was still a relatively small amount compared with the total pro-Israel contributions to congressional candidates in the 2008 election ($11.5 million, according to figures compiled by the Center for Responsive Politics, www.opensecrets.org). Fingerhut, "Will J Street Money Translate into Influence?"

33. See, for example, Traub, "The New Israel Lobby"; Jonathan Broder, "New Pro-Israel Lobby, New Point of View," *Congressional Quarterly,* August 15, 2009; Robert Dreyfuss, "Is AIPAC Still the Chosen One?" *Mother Jones,* September 9, 2009; Adam Horowitz and Philip Weiss, "American Jews Rethink Israel," *The Nation,* October 14, 2009.

34. AIPAC is often depicted in the media as a hawkish right-wing organization. This popular image, however, is largely erroneous (it is true that some of the group's leadership and major donors have been supporters of Israel's Likud Party). Although AIPAC has frequently supported the policies of Likud governments in Israel, it does so less out of strong ideological convictions than because of its policy of backing all Israeli governments (albeit some more energetically and enthusiastically than others). Moreover, AIPAC has on occasion supported Israeli government initiatives that were deeply unpopular with right-wing hawks, most notably

Israel's 2005 disengagement from Gaza. By and large, its activists are politically centrist American Jews (mostly Democrats) who are primarily concerned for Israel's security and survival.

35. Many American Jews are not at all involved in the organized Jewish community. According to the National Jewish Population Survey of 2001, 44 percent of American Jews are "unaffiliated"—they don't belong to a synagogue, Jewish community center, or any other Jewish organization. United Jewish Communities, *The National Jewish Population Survey 2000–01,* 2003; available online at www.jewishfederations.org/page.aspx?id=33650.

36. Dan Fleshler, *Transforming America's Israel Lobby* (Dulles, VA: Potomac Books, 2009), p. 64.

37. George P. Shultz, "The 'Israel Lobby' Myth," *US News & World Report,* September 9, 2007.

38. As of 2010, AIPAC had eighteen offices around the US, three hundred employees, and 100,000 dues-paying members.

39. AIPAC spent almost $2.5 million on lobbying in 2008, and it has a huge $140 million endowment. Alan Fram, "The Influence Game: Pro-Israel Doves Seek DC Clout," Associated Press, May 25, 2009.

40. Although it is still very prominent, the power of the Conference of Presidents is more limited than AIPAC's because of its need for consensus among its fifty-one member organizations.

41. American presidents are particularly wary of trying to exert strong pressure on Israeli governments in the face of congressional opposition. This was one of the reasons President Barack Obama backed down in his conflict with Israel's Netanyahu government over his demand for a complete freeze on settlement building. See Chapter 3, by Robert O. Freedman, in this volume.

42. American strategic considerations have also played an important role in motivating US aid to Israel, as A. F. K. Organski has persuasively argued in his book *The $36 Billion Bargain: Strategy and Politics in U.S. Assistance to Israel* (New York: Columbia University Press, 1990).

43. Many other factors are also behind the US informal alliance with Israel, most notably the belief that Israel can help serve US strategic interests in the Middle East and beyond; the perception of Israel as the only democratic state in the region; the identification of Israel and the United States as similar nations; Christian religious devotion to the Jewish state and homeland; and a widespread public sympathy for Jewish suffering in the Holocaust and, more recently, Israeli suffering from Palestinian terrorist attacks, especially after the United States also suffered from terrorism on 9/11.

44. Numerous surveys have noted a declining emotional attachment to Israel among younger American Jews; see, for instance, Steven M. Cohen and Ari Kelman, *Beyond Distancing: Young Adult American Jews and Their Alienation from Israel* (New York: Bronfman Philanthropies, 2008). Some scholars have argued, however, that this does not necessarily indicate a future decline in American Jewish attachment to Israel, as Jews tend to feel emotionally closer to Israel as they get older. For this argument, see Theodore Sasson, Charles Kadushin, and Leonard Saxe, *American Jewish Attachment to Israel: An Assessment of the "Distancing" Hypothesis* (Waltham, MA: Steinhardt Social Research Institute, Brandeis University, February 2008). See also Theodore Sasson, "Mass Mobilization to Direct Engagement: American Jews' Changing Relationship to Israel," *Israel Studies* 15, no. 2 (Summer 2010): 173–195.

45. Lower levels of emotional attachment to Israel are especially apparent among the younger generation of nonorthodox American Jews, particularly among the children of intermarried Jews who are growing within the ranks of the nonorthodox Jewish population. Those American Jews who care most about Israel are increasingly Orthodox. See Chapter 10 in this volume.

46. Jennifer Rubin, "Onward, Christian Zionists," *Weekly Standard,* August 2, 2010.

5

Six Decades of Public Affection

TRENDS IN AMERICAN PUBLIC ATTITUDES TOWARD ISRAEL

Amnon Cavari

MOST AMERICANS POSSESS LITTLE KNOWLEDGE about foreign countries and events, but they are highly informed about Israel and are generally supportive of it. The support dates back to Israel's independence. Americans supported Israel's right to exist, have viewed the country in favorable terms since then, and have sympathized more with Israel than with Arab countries or Palestinians. Americans have continuously viewed Israel as an ally of the United States and have been willing to follow up on their support for Israel with economic and military aid, making Israel the largest cumulative recipient of US foreign assistance since World War II.

The strength of American public support for Israel is illustrated in Figure 5.1, which compares public attitudes toward Israel in forty-five countries in 2007.[1] Respondents were asked which side in the Middle East conflict they sympathized with more: Israel or the Palestinians. The bars represent the difference between the percentage of people sympathizing with Israel and the percentage of people sympathizing with the Palestinians, thus indicating the overall (aggregate) direction and strength of public sympathies in each country. The longer the bar, the more homogenous public views are. On aggregate, citizens from fewer than half of the forty-five countries sympathize with Israel than with the Palestinians. The nation that sympathizes with Israel the most is the United States, where 60 percent of the population sympathizes with Israel compared to only 13 percent sympathizing with the Palestinians. As the bars show, the strength of support is much smaller in most of the other favorable countries. For example, only 45 percent of citizens in the third–most supportive nation, the Czech Republic, sympathize with Israel, compared to 17 percent who sympathize with the Palestinians. In Japan, only 17 percent sympathize with Israel compared to 9 percent sympathizing with the Palestinians. Only seven of the twenty countries that have, on balance, a sympathetic view of Israel are members of the Organisation for Economic Co-operation and Development (OECD). Most European countries have an overall neutral balance, exhibiting a slightly more sympathetic view toward the Palestinians. Of the five largest countries in Europe—Britain, France, Germany, Italy, and Spain—only Germany has a public balance that is supportive of Israel. As can be expected, the least favorable countries are Muslim countries in the Middle East, such as Egypt, Kuwait, Pakistan, and Jordan. In sum, the support among Americans is outstanding internally and comparably.

The strong support for Israel among Americans dates back to Israel's struggle for independence. In November 1947 the UN General Assembly passed Resolution 181 to end the British Mandate for Palestine and partition the territory into two independent states: one Jewish and one Arab. Following the decision, the National Opinion Research Center asked Americans whether they sympathized more with the Jewish or with the Arab position. Only half of all respondents had an opinion about this issue. Among this half, 69 percent supported Israel. Following the Israeli declaration of independence and the invasion of Arab countries in May 1948, this support climbed to 75 percent. Support for Israel has mostly remained high since then.[2] As the data reveal, Americans respond to events by adjusting their support for Israel, but overall, when asked to choose between Israel and Arab nations or Palestinians, they have consistently favored Israel.

The support Americans have for Israel has important consequences. Most Americans have a limited knowledge of foreign events, yet they possess meaningful attitudes about foreign policies. This is partly explained by Americans' ability to turn to their values and beliefs, their political attitudes and predispositions, as well as their perceptions about countries and leaders when they form attitudes about foreign policies.[3] The fact that Americans have a favorable view of Israel, therefore, may affect their attitudes about foreign policy. These attitudes, in turn, influence American foreign policy. Studies reveal that administrations take into account public opinion when they choose which policy to pursue. In sum, although Americans' favorable view of Israel has no direct policy outcome, its importance cannot be exaggerated.

From this standpoint, the support for Israel is an important factor in understanding the strong relationship between the United States and Israel. Israel is

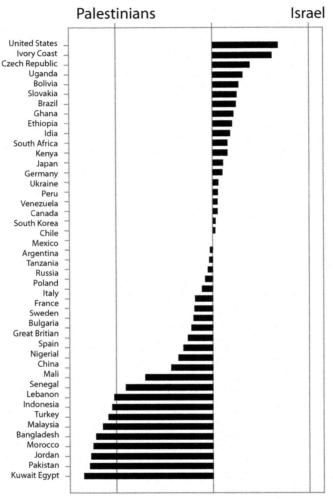

Palestinians   **Israel**

United States
Ivory Coast
Czech Republic
Uganda
Bolivia
Slovakia
Brazil
Ghana
Ethiopia
Idia
South Africa
Kenya
Japan
Germany
Ukraine
Peru
Venezuela
Canada
South Korea
Chile
Mexico
Argentina
Tanzania
Russia
Poland
Italy
France
Sweden
Bulgaria
Great Britian
Spain
Nigerial
China
Mali
Senegal
Lebanon
Indonesia
Turkey
Malaysia
Bangladesh
Morocco
Jordan
Pakistan
Kuwait Egypt

Sympathies in the Middle East Conflict
In the dispute between Israel and the Palestinians, which side do you sympathize with more?

FIGURE 5.1 Global Views of the Israeli-Palestinian Conflict
Source: Pew Global Attitudes Survey, May 2007

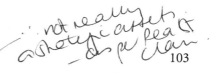

an extremely small country in both population and territory. It lacks natural resources and has been entangled in myriad economic, military, and social problems. In contrast, the Arab world is large in population and territory and is rich in natural resources, markets, and political power. Despite the significant commercial and strategic interests in the Arab world, the United States has continued to support Israel politically, economically, and militarily. This is commonly attributed to various factors, including a dominant Jewish population, a strong pro-Israel lobby, cultural and religious values, media attention, and mutual strategic interests in the Middle East. Yet, as Eytan Gilboa correctly argued more than twenty years ago, the special relationship would be untenable were it not for a highly favorable American public opinion.[4]

To assess the trends in public support for Israel, this chapter examines survey data since the establishment of Israel. During this period, hundreds of surveys from different polling agencies have asked Americans for their views on events in the Middle East, their support for US policies in the region, their attitudes toward Arab and Israeli leaders, and so forth. Most of these surveys asked a specific question about an event or policy. A more limited set of questions ask for broad views about the Middle East and are asked in surveys every year. Although these questions are not specific, they offer an invaluable opportunity to track changes over time. This chapter mostly relies on these latter "time-series" questions and occasionally refers to specific questions of interest.

The chapter is divided into four parts: the support of Americans for Israel, their views of Israel as a friendly country, their preferred side in the Middle East conflict, and group differences among the American public. The evidence reveals that American public support for Israel has been consistently strong, yet that recent transformations in the structure of public opinion toward Israel raise important concerns about the future of this historical bond between the American public and the state of Israel.

Public Support

In a postwar survey conducted in December 1944, 36 percent of Americans reported that they support the establishment of a Jewish state, compared to only 22 percent who said that a Jewish state should not be established.[5] Two years later, when President Harry Truman was considering his policy toward the establishment of an independent Jewish state, he ignored the strong recommendations of his top secretaries and publicly announced that the United States would support such a state. In explaining his decision, he made a clear connection to the public view shared by most Americans.

The Jewish Agency proposed a solution of the Palestine problem by means of the creation of a viable Jewish state in control of its own immigration and economic policies
in an adequate area of Palestine instead of in the whole of Palestine. . . . This proposal
received widespread attention in the United States, both in the press and in public forums. From the discussion which has ensued it is my belief that a solution along these
lines would command the support of public opinion in the United States. . . . To such
a solution our Government could give its support.[6]

As the issue of Israel's independence further progressed in international tri-
bunals and events in Palestine, Truman continued to voice a position that was
in tandem with the views of the majority of Americans. In November 1947, the
United Nations voted in favor of the partition plan for Palestine with a key
vote of support from the United States. This support was strongly approved by
the majority of Americans. Asked in February 1948, soon after the UN resolution
and three months before the Israeli war for independence, three-quarters of
Americans had heard about the partition plan, most of whom supported the
plan.[7] A month later, when fighting was already under way, a Foreign Affairs
Survey asked, "What should be the policy of our government toward the new
Jewish state" if "the Jews in Palestine go ahead on their own and set up a Jewish
state anyhow?" Americans were clearly supportive: 51 percent thought the US
government should encourage Jews to establish an independent state, 10 percent
thought the US government should discourage them, and 21 percent said the
United States should stay away from this issue (an additional 18 percent had no
opinion).[8] Soon after, on May 14, 1948, the provisional government of Israel
proclaimed the new state of Israel. On that same day, without discussing the
matter with US delegates to the UN or State Department officials (to their dismay), Truman recognized the provisional Jewish government as the de facto
authority of the new Jewish state.

Despite his enthusiastic support, President Truman refused to supply arms
to the Jewish people in Israel. Although the arms embargo was imposed also
on Arab countries, that Jordan, Egypt, and Iraq were armed and trained by
Britain made this embargo very much a one-sided policy.[9] This policy was supported by Americans who strongly rejected selling arms to any side in the war,
so in his support of the establishment of Israel and in refusing to sell arms to
Israel, Truman was in tune with the views of the majority of Americans.

Following its establishment, Israel was seen by some American leaders as a
liability that was likely to turn into a Soviet client state in the Middle East. The
cold relations between the United States and Israel extended through most of
the Eisenhower administration, which was focused on Arab countries in the hope
that they would adopt pro-Western positions. Despite these efforts, the Soviet
Union strengthened its hold in a number of Arab countries such as Egypt, Syria,

and Iraq by providing them with weapons and political support.[10] By contrast, Israel by the early 1950s had distanced itself from Moscow and found France as its new ally. The rise to power of Gamal Nasser, his increasingly pro-Soviet position, and the revolution in Iraq in 1958 led to a change in the Eisenhower administration's view of the Middle East. The administration now saw Israel as a stable democracy and as an outpost of Western influence in an increasingly volatile Middle East.[11]

After Israel's independence, the American public, however, continuously viewed Israel in favorable terms. In 1950, 61 percent of Americans said they believed it was important for the United States to cooperate closely with Israel, a rate that increased during the rest of that decade.[12] Although Americans strongly opposed Israel's actions in war against Egypt in 1956 and assigned most of the blame for the escalation on Israel's aggression, they remained supportive of Israel. Asked in March 1957, during Israel's retreat from Sinai, 55 percent of Americans reported that they had a positive opinion of Israel compared to only 19 percent who said they had a negative view.[13]

A significant increase in the support of Americans for the state of Israel was evident during the 1960s. At that time, the situation in the Middle East was already fully aligned with the Cold War divisions: Israel with the Western world and Arab countries with the Soviet bloc. The increased support among Americans can be illustrated by comparing a thermometer poll from the 1950s and 1960s that asked respondents to rank their views of Israel on a scale from −5 (least favorable) to 5 (most favorable). In 1956, 49 percent of Americans had a favorable view of Israel, compared to 26 percent having a negative view. By 1966, American opinion was significantly more favorable toward Israel: 63 percent had a favorable view of Israel, compared to only 19 percent who had an unfavorable view.[14]

This support further increased following the 1967 war. In contrast to the blame Americans assigned to Israel during the 1956 war, most Americans thought after the 1967 war that Israel had "more right on their side," and 71 percent thought Israel should keep all or some of the territories conquered in the war.[15] In 1970, three-quarters of Americans agreed to the statement that "Israel is a small, courageous democratic nation which is trying to preserve its independence."[16]

Starting from the 1970s, pollsters routinely collected data on general favorability of Israel. Figure 5.2 plots the aggregate favorability of Americans for the state of Israel. In this question, Americans were simply asked to report whether their view of Israel was favorable. As the figure reveals, most Americans have had a favorable view of Israel. A brief decline in public support is evident during the late 1980s. This can be attributed to Americans' view of the Israeli actions to suppress the first Intifada and the pressure on Israel to attend the Madrid Conference in 1991.

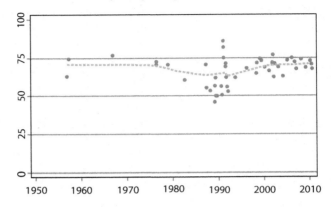

FIGURE 5.2 Israel Favorability
Key: The dots represent each available data point (survey), and the dashed line represents
a weighted average.
Source: Roper iPoll Survey Archive

Americans' favorable view of Israel also is exceptional when we compare it
to American feelings toward other countries. Figure 5.3 compares the favorability
of fourteen countries around the world. In most years, the favorability of Israel
is matched only by neighboring countries—Canada and Mexico—and by countries that have strong military and economic relations with the United States—
Britain, Germany, France, and Japan. During the 1990s, a large number of
Americans viewed Egypt and Jordan favorably. By then these two countries,
however, had ended their military conflict with Israel and strengthened their
ties with the United States.

Views of Israel as a
Friendly Country or as a US Ally

Following its establishment, Israel seemed to be moving toward the Soviet Union.
Its political elite had close ties with Moscow and, during the War of Independence,
Israel enjoyed Moscow's diplomatic support and purchased arms from Soviet-
controlled Czechoslovakia. This, however, soon changed as the political elite in
Israel distanced themselves from Moscow and strengthened their connections
with the Western world. In 1955 and 1956, Russia began to arm Egypt and Syria
from its surplus stocks and, later, with up-to-date MIG fighter aircraft, missiles

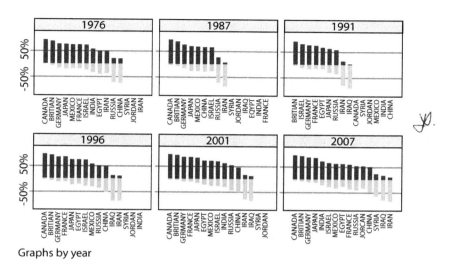

Graphs by year

FIGURE 5.3 American Favorability of Selected Countries
Source: Roper iPoll Survey Archive

and tanks. This set the stage for turning the Middle East into another theater of the Cold War in which Israel served as the only country associated with the Western world. Starting from the early 1960s, the United States began to provide Israel with arms to balance the Soviet military aid to Arab countries in the Middle East. As the Cold War ended, Israel maintained its important role as the only democracy in the Middle East and as an ally in protecting American interests in the Middle East, and later in the US fight against fundamentalist Islam.

During most of the period since its establishment, Americans have viewed Israel as an ally and supported a strong relationship between the two countries. Although in 1952 a plurality of Americans (42 percent) did not know whether the government of Israel was more on the side of Russia or on the side of the United States, 35 percent believed that Israel was "more on the American side," compared to only 4 percent believing that Israel was "on the Russian side." In 1971, a plurality of Americans viewed the conflict between Israel and Egypt in terms of war between Russia and Israel.[17]

More focused and consistent data on the relationship between the two countries have been available only since 1977, when pollsters began routinely to ask Americans whether they saw Israel as a US ally, a friendly country, an unfriendly country, or a US enemy. Figure 5.4 shows that since that time, Israel mostly has been viewed as a friendly country. This view of Israel gradually dropped to nearly 60 percent support at the end of the 1980s but increased once again in

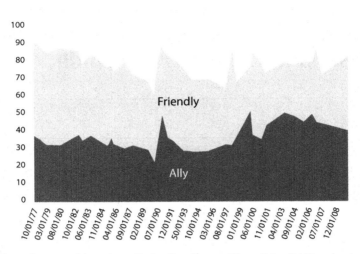

FIGURE 5.4 Percent of Americans Seeing Israel as an Ally or Friendly Country

1991 in response to Operation Desert Storm. Starting in the late 1990s the relative share of people feeling that Israel was a US ally increased significantly,
reaching nearly 50 percent of the entire population. This reveals the strength
of American attitudes toward Israel—a bond that has always been strong and
was further strengthened as the United States began to face terrorism and increased its involvement in the Middle East.

Attitudes toward military aid further indicate the close relationship between
the United States and Israel. Over time, Israel has received substantial military
and economic aid from the United States, making it the largest cumulative recipient of US foreign assistance since World War II. From 1976 to 2004, Israel
was the largest annual recipient of US foreign assistance, having since been
supplanted by Iraq. Since 1985, the United States has provided nearly $3 billion
in grants annually to Israel. Aid has been given primarily to maintain the military balance in the Middle East, deter aggression, and induce negotiations
and peace agreements.[18]

Although Americans usually have strong reservations about foreign aid,
they have shown strong support for military aid to Israel. As mentioned above,
in 1948, an overwhelming majority of Americans did not support any sale of
arms to either side in the war in Palestine. Even following the Soviet-Egyptian
arms deal in 1955, 50 percent of Americans believed that the US should not
supply arms to Israel, compared to only 24 percent who believed the United
States should supply arms to Israel. Three-quarters of those who sided with supplying arms to Israel noted the danger of communism as their reason to support
arms supply.[19]

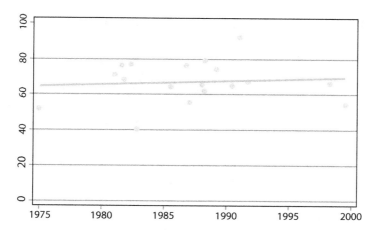

FIGURE 5.5 Percent of Americans Thinking Military Aid Should Stay the Same or Increase (at existing level or more)
Key: The dots represent each survey. The solid line represents the overall trend, showing high levels of public support for military aid.
Source: Roper iPoll Survey Archive

But this view soon changed. Following the 1967 war and in response to the war of attrition and the massive Soviet buildup of the Egyptian and Syrian armies, Americans began to acknowledge the need to assist Israel to maintain a balance in the Middle East and protect Israel from Arab aggression and Soviet expansion. This public support was further strengthened during and after the Yom Kippur War of 1973.

In 1975, pollsters routinely began asking whether respondents thought military aid to Israel should stay the same, increase, be reduced, or be eliminated altogether. Figure 5.5 plots the percentage of people who reported that military aid should stay the same or increase. As a whole, nearly three in every four Americans supported the current level of aid and agreed to expand it.

Sympathies in the Middle East Conflict

Since its establishment, Israel has been bogged down in a conflict with other Arab nations and with an Arab population within its borders. This conflict has defined Israel's actions: fighting wars, controlling occupied territories and its population, and negotiating peace. The conflict has also defined the relationship of the international community with Israel. During the Cold War,

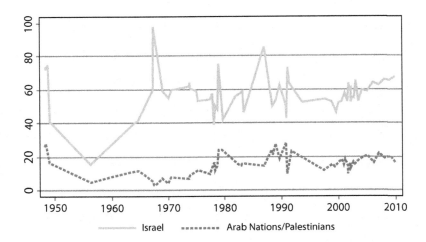

FIGURE 5.6 Percent Sympathizing with Israel and Arab Nations/Palestinians
including both or neither (not graphed)
Source: Roper iPoll Survey Archive

the conflict was aligned with the world divisions of East and West; with the
rise of the Palestinian nationalist movement, Israel was viewed in terms of
the internal conflict with the Palestinians; and since the rise of fundamentalist
Islam, Israel has been associated with the fight against terrorism. Although
the data above reveal the strength of Americans' favorable view of Israel, they
do not directly relate to this conflict because they do not juxtapose Americans'
attitudes about Israel with their attitudes about Arab countries or the Palestinian people. One way to evaluate American attitudes toward Israel within
this context is by examining a question asking respondents to identify which
side in the conflict they sympathize with more: Israel, Arab nations or Palestinians, both, or neither.[20] This question has been asked repeatedly by numerous pollsters since Israel's independence.

Figure 5.6 plots the time-series of Americans' sympathies with Israel and with
the Palestinians or Arab nations since Israel's independence. Throughout the
entire period, Americans have sympathized more with Israel than with Arab
nations or the Palestinians. During the 1950s and 1960s, the majority of Americans showed little knowledge or preferences about the region. And yet, among
those who had an opinion, a clear majority was in favor of Israel. Starting from
the 1967 war, the majority of Americans have had knowledge about the region
and voiced clear preferences that, on balance, have been in favor of Israel. Although there have been significant fluctuations in sympathies toward Israel, be-

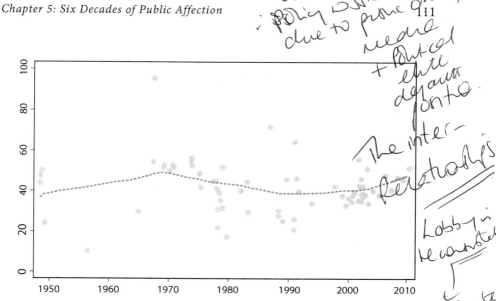

FIGURE 5.7 Sympathies with Israel: Difference Between Sympathies with Israel and with Arabs
Source: Roper iPoll Survey Archive

tween 1970 and 2000 these fluctuations reverted to a stable mean. Starting from 2000, Americans have on aggregate steadily increased their sympathies for Israel.

Given the differences in polling methods and the effect of immediate events on each poll, we should be cautious in trying to make any conclusions about the public opinion in one or a few polls. Instead, we should examine overall trends in American attitudes toward Israel. This is well illustrated in Figure 5.7, which plots the *difference* in support for Israel and for Arab nations or Palestinians. During the entire period, the Israeli "advantage" was between 20 and 60 percentage points. The dashed line represents the moving average, indicating that public support has consistently averaged at approximately 40 percentage points' advantage for Israel over Arab nations or Palestinians. In other words, on average, during more than sixty years of independence, of every five Americans, three sympathize more with Israel, one with Arab nations or Palestinians, and one with both or neither. The trend in the past decade indicates that Americans have been gradually increasing their support for Israel.

Group Differences

The aggregate data reveal that Americans, as a whole, have viewed Israel favorably, as a US ally, and sympathized with Israel in the Arab-Israeli conflict. Yet, treating the American public as a homogenous whole may be misleading. At a given point in time, the makeup of public support for Israel may be markedly different than the makeup of American support at other times. For example, although Americans have been supportive of Israel throughout the entire period, the aggregate support may have been mostly due to the support of Democrats in the early years and Republicans more recently. Similarly, one can suggest that Americans' views about Israel are influenced by several demographics such as age, education, race, gender, or religious differences and that the level of support of these groups has not been constant over time. Group preferences can vary because of differing interests; different social, economic, political, and cultural environments; diverse experiences; or different positions in society.[21] These preferences may independently change in each group in response to exogenous events or internal transformations within each group.

Studies of American public attitudes on foreign policy find modest associations between demographic factors—such as gender, age, region, education, and race—and public attitudes about foreign policy. Partisan and ideological cleavages and religious affiliations, on the other hand, are strongly correlated with policy positions and have been more so since the end of the Cold War.[22] Eytan Gilboa notes the importance of group differences, yet finds that although specific groups have been more pro-Israel than others, the pro-Israeli views are consistent among each stratum of American society.[23] Gilboa's data, however, extend only to 1985 and thus fail to examine the possible effect of the end of the Cold War and significant changes in American politics since the 1980s.

The following figures plot the time-series of sympathies with Israel from 1967 to 2010 of six dominant demographic and political divisions: education, age, race, sex, religion, and party identification.[24] Taken together, the figures indicate that public opinion has moved in the same direction among different social strata. There are, however, noticeable differences among several subgroups at specific points in time.

Figure 5.8 breaks down the percentage of people sympathizing with Israel by education groups: people who did not finish school, people who have a high school diploma, people who completed some college or technical education but did not earn a college degree, and people who have a college degree or more. In most years, there was no significant difference between people with different education levels. Starting in the past decade, however, we see a clear divergence of the more educated group that is becoming significantly less supportive of Israel.

Figure 5.9 plots the sympathies of different age groups: under thirty, between thirty and forty-nine, between fifty and sixty-four, and over sixty-five years of age. Although there are significant fluctuations for each age group, the trends are very similar. The only groups that can be identified for holding outstanding views are the youngest age group, which is usually less supportive of Israel, and the oldest age group, which generally has been more supportive of Israel.

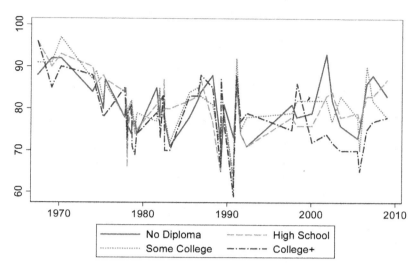

Percentage sympathizing with Israel among respondents
choosing Israel or Arab nations/Palestinians.

FIGURE 5.8 Sympathies with Israel: by Education

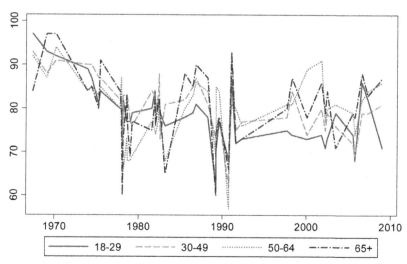

Percentage sympathizing with Israel among respondents choosing Israel or Arab nations/Palestinians.

FIGURE 5.9 Sympathies with Israel: by Age Groups

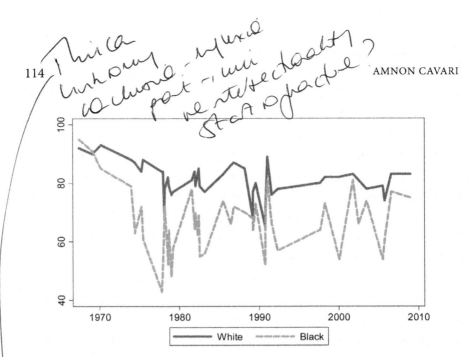

Percentage sympathizing with Israel among respondents choosing Israel or Arab nations/Palestinians.

FIGURE 5.10 Sympathies with Israel: by Race

We find clear racial divisions. Figure 5.10 illustrates that from 1970 to the present, blacks have been less supportive of Israel than whites. This is commonly attributed to the fact that African Americans view the Palestinian campaign for national rights as analogous to their campaign for civil rights.[25] As rhetoric about the Israeli occupation of Palestinian territory has taken the form of comparison to apartheid in South Africa, African Americans have further distanced themselves from Israel.

Figure 5.11 plots the attitudes of men and women. More often than not, men are less supportive of Israel. Yet overall there are very minimal differences between these two groups and no clear pattern of higher support among women.

More substantial divisions are evident among religious groups. Naturally, American Jews have been highly supportive of Israel, yet the relatively small Jewish population in the United States contributes very little to overall American public opinion. A more influential source of support for Israel is Christianity. Although Christian clergy and congregations around the world have been suspicious of Israel and often are critical of its actions, Christianity in the United States is commonly viewed as a source of strong support for Israel. Studies indicate that Christian commitments stand at the root of presidents' actions toward Israel and that the strength of one's Christian beliefs in the United States is positively associated with his or her support for Israel.[26] Most interesting is the uniquely American phenomenon of Christian Zionists, who have been more

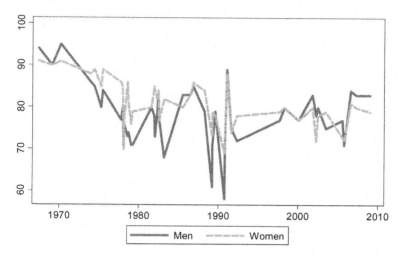

Percentage sympathizing with Israel among respondents choosing Israel or Arab nations/Palestinians.

FIGURE 5.11 Sympathies with Israel: by Gender

consistent supporters of Israel than any other group in the United States, including American Jewry.

As discussed by Neil Rubin in Chapter 11 of this volume, Christian Zionism reflects a basically pro-Israeli disposition rooted in the belief, mostly among Protestants, that the state of Israel came into the world in fulfillment of biblical prophecy. The well-being of the United States therefore requires that it display a preference for Israel's cause in all the challenges Israel faces.[27] More fundamentalist views are influenced by dispensationalist eschatology, or the belief about the nearness of Armageddon, commonly associated with evangelical Christians. From this standpoint, the return of the Jews to their land, the emergence of the Jewish state, and Israel's capture of Jerusalem are chronologically successive dispensations, or periods in history that mark the end of the "times of Gentiles." That brings history to the end of the age and to a new phase that will culminate in the "coming of the Son of Man." The existence of Israel, in the words of one of the most dominant Christian Zionists in America, Jerry Falwell, is "the single greatest sign indicating the imminent return of Jesus Christ."[28] Any change in the current state of Israel would only interfere with this historical process.

Most surveys of American attitudes toward Israel identify two main Christian denominations—Protestant and Catholic—and consistent religious minorities such as Jews, Buddhists, Mormons, and recently, Muslims. Yet, the largest religious

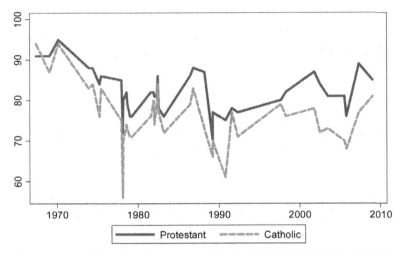

Percentage sympathizing with Israel among respondents choosing Israel or Arab nations/Palestinians.

FIGURE 5.12 Sympathies with Israel: by Religion

minority is the Jewish population, which is less than 2 percent of the general population. Therefore, unless we conduct a specific survey that examines these populations, we cannot rely on the general surveys to provide accurate information about the attitudes of these groups toward Israel. Given their small share in the general public, their effect on the aggregate attitudes toward Israel—in contrast to their possible effect on representation and policy-making or their effect on public opinion in specific states where they are a larger minority—is also almost insignificant.

Existing work reveals that until the 1967 war, Protestants and Catholics held similar positive views of Israel. Starting from 1967, the two religious groups diverged, mainly due to the strengthening support among Protestants (see Figure 5.12).[29] This trend dovetails with demographic changes among Protestants in the United States. During the last half century, the number of Protestants in the United States has remained steady, yet the balance among the different Protestant churches has significantly changed. Membership in mainline Protestant churches has decreased whereas evangelical and fundamentalist churches have grown significantly, thus turning the Protestant group in America into a more conservative one.[30]

In addition to these demographic changes, conservative Protestant groups have gradually increased their support for Israel. In 1981, 52 percent of mainline Protestants supported Israel, compared to 67 percent support among born-again evangelical Christians. Starting from 1997, the gap between these two Protestant groups increased from 15 points to more than 20 points. The increase in support among Protestants, illustrated in Figure 5.12, is therefore a result of both the growing population of Christian evangelicals among American Protestants and their increasing support of Israel.

The growth of Christian conservatism and its support of Israel have had significant effects on partisan attitudes toward Israel. During the 1960s and 1970s, an increasing number of religious leaders began to preach for political activism. This culminated into political power during the 1980s when the "Christian Right" aligned with the Republican Party.[31] Jerry Falwell and Pat Robertson, two outspoken figures in the Christian Zionist movement, were among the most vocal leaders of this process. By the mid-1990s, and especially following the 1994 election, a significant number of GOP leaders associated with the Christian Right secured influential positions in government. Some leaders who mark this change include powerful congressional leaders such as Dick Armey (R-TX), the House majority leader between 1995 and 2003 who on several occasions voiced a staunch position against any negotiations over territory in Israel; Tom DeLay (R-TX), Republican whip between 1995 and 2003 and House majority leader from 2003 to 2005, who, while serving as majority leader, delivered to the Israeli Knesset a speech urging Israel not to make land concessions; and Jim Inhofe (R-OK), US representative through 1994 and senator since 1994, who delivered a speech on the Senate floor on March 4, 2002, as the Al-Aqsa Intifada reached a new intensity, making the case for why Israel should not compromise over the land it now holds, raising several reasons, including a biblical right. These leaders and others have taken an important role in identifying attitudes toward Israel with partisan politics.

The election of George W. Bush, a self-described born-again Christian, as well as the 9/11 terrorist attacks and their consequential wars in Afghanistan and Iraq, deepened the commitment of Republican leadership to Israel. Bush's relationship with Israel was strengthened by the presence of senior figures within the administration that reflected a neoconservative agenda and sharply defined the administration's views on foreign policy. This agenda was wedded to an almost missionary sense that American power should be used to spread American values of democracy and freedom. For these neocons, power, not diplomacy, would resolve international conflicts and therefore the United States would do better by backing the strongest party—Israel—than by working as a mediator.[32]

Once the war in Iraq was under way, the relationship with Israel was significantly strengthened. The shared fears against the rise of fundamentalist Islamic movements, the growing power of Iran, and the fear of terrorism made it difficult for the Bush administration to critique Israeli actions in the region. This position was aptly summarized by Secretary of State Colin Powell in a speech delivered at Princeton University in February 2004: "It is difficult for us . . . to put this kind of pressure on the Israeli side as long as terrorism is seen as a legitimate political act on the part of the Palestinians. It is not—it can't be, not in this post 9/11 age."[33] Similarly, Republican leaders in Congress also connected the US involvement in Iraq and Israel's struggle with terrorism, arguing that Israel was fighting terrorism just as the United States was doing in Afghanistan and Iraq.

The change in partisan leadership has inevitably affected the attitudes of rank-and-file Republicans to take a more positive view of Israel. Studies indicate that when forming their political attitudes, people tend to rely on leadership cues that offer important shortcuts to reach a meaningful attitude.[34] With regards to foreign countries and events, where the public possesses limited knowledge, the effect of leadership cues on mass opinion is paramount. Opinion leaders frame the issues on the foreign agenda, help organize information about events, and generate coherent public attitudes.[35] Therefore, starting in the 1990s, Republicans who were tuned to their leaders were exposed to a strong, favorable view of Israel, regardless of their religious views.

This is illustrated in Figure 5.13, which plots public attitudes of different partisan groups. From 1967 until the early 1990s, Democrats, Republicans, and independents all maintained similar attitudes. Yet, starting from the 1990s we see a clear divergence of opinion in which Republicans have become more supportive of Israel compared to both Democrats and independents.

The polarization of the issue along partisan lines may have important consequences for the relationship between Israel and the United States. Prompted

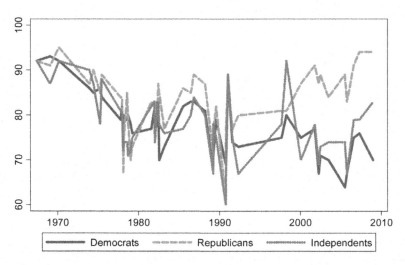

Percentage sympathizing with Israel among respondents choosing Israel or Arab nations/Palestinians.

FIGURE 5.13 Sympathies with Israel: by Party Identification

by an increase in Republican support for Israel, the issue may further polarize as the Democratic Party responds to Republican leadership by taking a more critical view of Israel. The inevitable consequence is a divergence of public views of the parties on this issue, where one party—ostensibly the Republicans— would be viewed in terms that are more supportive of Israel, and the other party—the Democrats—would be viewed in terms critical of Israel's actions.

The Republican critique of Barack Obama's increased pressure on the Israeli government in 2010 illustrates how these views affect public opinion. In April 2010, a Quinnipiac poll asked Americans whether they thought "the President of the United States *should* be a strong supporter of Israel or not." Sixty-six percent of Americans thought he should. Nineteen percent thought he should not. When asked specifically whether President Obama *was* a strong supporter of Israel, only 34 percent thought he was, and 42 percent thought he was not.[36]

Another consequence of this process of party polarization is the change in the partisan makeup of the supportive, pro-Israeli group in America. Figure 5.14 plots a time-series of the partisan makeup of the pro-Israel lobby in American public opinion—that is, partisan divisions of Americans who sympathize with Israel. As the figure clearly shows, until the mid-1980s most of the support came from Democrats (who also were a much larger constituency). Starting from the early 1980s, Republicans have increased their share in this lobby, and by 2000 they had become the more dominant partisan group supporting Israel. In other words, among people who support Israel today, more are Republicans than are Democrats or independents.

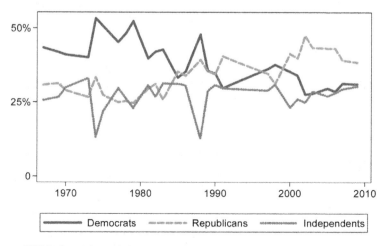

100% is the total population sympathizing more with Israel.

FIGURE 5.14 The "Israel Lobby" of American Public Opinion: the partisan makeup of the supportive group (in percentages)

Conclusion

A recent series of surveys asked Americans whether they thought the United States should support Israel. In all of these surveys, the majority of Americans thought it should, but the rate of support was not constant. In June 2010, 58 percent of Americans thought the United States should support Israel, a decline of 5 points from a year ago. A month later this support dropped to 51 percent but went up to 58 percent in September.[37] The trend suggests that public support for Israel is declining. Yet, as the analysis above indicates, we should be cautious in making any strong conclusions from one or only a few surveys.

Over time public support for Israel has been strong, yet it was not without fluctuations. At times, Israel enjoyed overwhelming public support among the majority of Americans, but in others, the support was limited. Comparing these surveys with several others during the past year, we can conclude that public support for Israel is still strong in America. For example, a CNN survey from March 2010 indicates that 80 percent of Americans think of Israel as an ally or a friendly country.[38] In another survey discussed above, 66 percent of respondents thought that the American president should be a strong supporter of Israel.

Nonetheless, for people interested in the special relationship between the United States and Israel, the trends in public opinion indicate an important change in the structure of public opinion toward Israel. In the past, the underlying factors of public opinion toward Israel have been consistent and shared by the majority of Americans. Public attitudes toward Israel were not associated with any social demographic group in America—Americans from all dominant religions, of different ages and levels of education, men and women, and Americans identifying with every partisan and ideological group have been supportive of Israel. This broad support was crucial to maintain the high public support that was not dependent upon the party in office or on major social and political changes in the United States. It was taken for granted that Americans as a whole supported Israel.

This, however, has changed. Starting in the 1990s, public opinion toward Israel has taken a partisan dimension that did not exist before. Today Americans who identify with one party—the Republican Party—share increasingly favorable views of Israel, and Americans associated with the other party—the Democratic Party—are increasingly critical of Israel.

American foreign policy toward Israel has always been influenced by global and regional processes as well as opportunities and restrictions imposed by internal domestic politics, greatly determined by public opinion.[39] For a country that depends on American support, this polarization of partisan attitudes may be destructive. Since its independence, Israel's relationship with the United States was influenced by the policy priorities of each administration. But these priorities were based on the administration's understanding of world events and the role of the United States in relation to them—not on a different view of and support for Israel itself. The polarization of support for Israel at the mass level may result in a party-based policy toward Israel, a process that will significantly alter the special relationship between the United States and Israel.

Notes

1. Pew Global Attitudes Project Poll, April 2007. Princeton Survey Research Associates International.

Question: "Now thinking about the dispute between Israel and the Palestinians, which side do you sympathize with more, Israel or the Palestinians?"

The survey results reported here were obtained from searches of the iPOLL Databank and other resources provided by the Roper Center for Public Opinion Research, University of Connecticut.

2. Foreign Affairs Survey, February 1948, National Opinion Research Center, University of Chicago; based on 1,265 personal interviews of national adults.

Question: "(The United Nations has recommended that Palestine be divided between the Jews and the Arabs.) The Arabs say they will not agree to have Palestine divided, and fighting has broken out between the Jews and Arabs. Do you sympathize with the Arabs or with the Jews in this matter?"

Foreign Affairs Survey, October 1948, National Opinion Research Center, University of Chicago; based on 1,258 personal interviews of national adult.

Question: "In the conflict in Palestine, do you sympathize with the Arabs or with the Jews?"

3. Benjamin I. Page and Marshall M. Bouton, *The Foreign Policy Disconnect: What Americans Want from Our Leaders but Don't Get* (Chicago: University of Chicago Press, 2006).

4. Eytan Gilboa, *American Public Opinion Toward Israel and the Arab-Israeli Conflict* (Lanham, MD: Lexington Books, 1987), p. 2.

5. Postwar Problems, Income Tax, December 1944, National Opinion Research Center, University of Chicago; based on 2,471 personal interviews of national adults.

Question: "There are over a million Arabs and over a half million Jews in Palestine. Do you

think the British, who control Palestine, should do what some Jews ask and set up a Jewish state there, or should they do what some Arabs ask and not set up a Jewish state?"

6. In October 1946, President Truman publicly rejected the British proposal of provincial autonomy and adopted the proposal of the Jewish Agency to establish an independent state.

7. Foreign Affairs Survey, February 1948, National Opinion Research Center, University of Chicago; based on 1,265 personal interviews of national adults.

Question: "Under the circumstances, do you approve or disapprove of dividing Palestine into these two countries (one for the Jews and one for the Arabs)?"

8. Foreign Affairs Survey, March 1948, National Opinion Research Center, University of Chicago; based on 1,289 personal interviews of national adults.

9. Robert O. Freedman, "Israel and the United States," in *Contemporary Israel,* ed. Robert O. Freedman (Boulder, CO: Westview Press, 2009), pp. 253–295.

10. Michael B. Oren, *Power, Faith, and Fantasy: America in the Middle East, 1776 to the Present* (New York: W. W. Norton and Company, 2007).

11. Peter L. Hahn, *Caught in the Middle East: US Policy Toward the Arab-Israeli Conflict, 1945–1961* (Chapel Hill: University of North Carolina Press, 1997).

12. Foreign Affairs Survey, January 1950, National Opinion Research Center, University of Chicago; based on 1,284 personal interviews of national adults.

Question: "How important do you think it is for the United States to cooperate closely with . . . Israel—very important, only fairly important, or not important at all?"

13. Roper Commercial Survey, March 1957, Roper Organization. Based on 1,508 personal interviews. Sample: national adult.

Question: "The State of Israel has been in the news a lot lately. Which of these statements comes closest to expressing your attitudes toward Israel at the present time . . . I have a high opinion of the State of Israel, although Israel has done some things I don't approve of, in general I think well of her, although I can understand Israel's difficult position, in general I don't think well of her, or I have a low opinion of the State of Israel?"

14. Gallup poll, December 1956 (1,543 personal interviews of national adults) and 1966 (1,469 personal interviews of national adults).

Question: "Here's an interesting experiment. You notice that the 10 boxes on this card go from the highest position of plus 5 or something you like very much—all the way down to the lowest position of minus 5—or something you dislike very much. Please tell me how far up the scale or how far down the scale you would rate . . . Israel?"

15. Gallup poll, June 22–27, 1967; based on 1,549 personal interviews of national adults.

Question: "As you know, the Israelis conquered a lot of land in the recent war with the Arab nations. What do you think should be done—should Israel be required to give back all this conquered land, keep it all, or keep some of it?"

16. Harris survey, August 1970, Louis Harris & Associates; based on 1,600 personal interviews of national adults.

Question: "Now let me read you some statements about the Middle East situation. For each, tell me if you tend to agree or disagree. . . . Israel is a small, courageous democratic nation which is trying to preserve its independence."

17. Roper commercial survey, January 1952, Roper Organization; based on 2,495 personal interviews of national adults.

Question: "Would you say that the government of . . . Israel is more on the side of Russia, more on our side, or not on one side or the other?"

Harris survey, July 1971, Louis Harris & Associates; based on 1,600 personal interviews of national adults.

Question: "(Now let me read you some statements that have been made about the Middle East situation. For each, tell me if you tend to agree or disagree.) . . . The situation in the Middle East has now changed, so it is no longer Egypt against Israel but is Russia and Egypt against Israel."

18. Jeremy M. Sharp, "U.S. Foreign Aid to Israel," Congressional Research Service, 2010, p. 2, www.fas.org/sgp/crs/mideast/RL33222.pdf.

19. Foreign Affairs Survey, January 1950, National Opinion Research Center, University of Chicago; based on 1,284 personal interviews of national adults.

Question: "How important do you think it is for the United States to cooperate closely with . . . Israel—very important, only fairly important, or not important at all?"

20. During this time, multiple pollsters asked various questions about Israel, including opinion about specific events, people, and policies as well as general questions. To allow for comparison over time, I collected all surveys that asked respondents to state whom they sympathized with more in the dispute between Israel and the Palestinians or with Arab nations. There were forty-five surveys totaling nearly 70,000 respondents.

21. Benjamin I. Page and Robert Y. Shapiro, *The Rational Public: Fifty Years of Trend in America's Public Preferences* (Chicago: University of Chicago Press, 1992).

22. Ole R. Holsti, *Public Opinion and American Foreign Policy*, rev. ed. (Ann Arbor: University of Michigan Press, 1996); Page and Bouton, *The Foreign Policy Disconnect*.

23. Gilboa, *American Public Opinion*, p. 301. Among the more supportive groups are whites, people of higher socioeconomic status, men and young adults, Protestants, and Republicans.

24. To better illustrate the differences within each group, these figures plot the percentages of people who sympathize more with Israel among people who sympathize with Israel and those who sympathize with Arab nations or Palestinians. This elevates the overall support.

25. C. Miller Jack, "Black Viewpoints on the Middle East Conflict," *Journal of Palestinian Studies* 10, no. 1 (Winter 1981): 37–49.

26. Paul Charles Merkley, *American Presidents, Religion, and Israel: The Heirs of Cyrus* (New York: Praeger, 2004).

27. Ibid.; Stephen Spector, *Evangelicals and Israel: The Story of American Christian Zionism* (New York: Oxford University Press, 2009). For a more expansive view of Christian Zionism that goes beyond the American experience, see Victoria Clark, *Allies for Armageddon: The Rise of Christian Zionism* (New Haven, CT: Yale University Press, 2007).

28. Quoted in Spector, *Evangelicals and Israel*, p. 28.

29. Gilboa, *American Public Opinion*.

30. On the evangelical mosaic and its relation to fundamentalist views, see Spector, *Evangelicals and Israel*.

31. Duane Murray Oldfield, *The Right and the Righteous: The Christian Right Confronts the Republican Party* (Lanham, MD: Rowman & Littlefield, 1996).

32. William B. Quandt, *Peace Process: American Diplomacy and the Arab-Israeli Conflict Since 1967*, 3rd ed. (Washington, DC: Brookings Institution Press, 2005).

33. Cited in Ron Kampus, "Election Year Aberration: White House Presses Israel and Gaza Withdrawal Plan," *Washington Jewish Week*, February 26, 2004. See also Robert O. Freedman, "The Bush Administration and the Arab-Israeli Conflict: The First Term and Beyond," in *The Middle East and the United States*, 4th ed., ed. David W. Lesch (Boulder, CO: Westview Press, 2007), pp. 275–311.

34. John R. Zaller, *The Nature and Origins of Mass Opinion* (New York: Cambridge University Press, 1992).

35. Holsti, *Public Opinion and American Foreign Policy*.

36. Quinnipiac University poll, April 14–19, 2010, Quinnipiac University Polling Institute; based on 1,930 telephone interviews of national registered voters.

Question: "Do you think the President of the United States should be a strong supporter of Israel or not?" "Do you think President (Barack) Obama is a strong supporter of Israel or not?"

37. Public Opinion Strategies and Greenberg Quinlan Rosner Research Foundation, August 2009, June 2010, July 2010, September 2010.

Question: "Does the US need to support Israel?"

38. CNN/Opinion Research Corporation poll, March 19–21, 2010, Opinion Research Corporation; based on 1,030 telephone interviews of national adults.

Question: "Do you consider Israel an ally of the United States, friendly but not an ally, unfriendly toward the US, or an enemy of the United States?"

39. Sobel, *The Impact of Public Opinion on U.S. Foreign Policy*.

6

Aid and Trade

ECONOMIC RELATIONS BETWEEN THE UNITED STATES AND ISRAEL, 1948–2010

Roby Nathanson and Ron Mandelbaum

ON MAY 14, 1948, the United States became the first country to extend de facto recognition to Israel. Over the years, the United States and Israel have developed a close relationship based on common democratic values, religious affinities, and security interests. These relations have grown through legislation, memorandums of understanding, and diplomatic agreements regarding a variety of economic, scientific, and military issues.[1]

The relationship, however, evolved slowly. For years after Israel's independence in 1948, the United States provided minimal military or economic aid.[2] This changed with a major increase in aid in the early 1970s and a one-time grant following the signing of the Camp David peace treaty in 1979. Since the 1980s, US aid to Israel has averaged $3 billion per year.[3]

Ever since the signing of the US-Israeli Free Trade Agreement (FTA) in 1985, trade has supplanted aid, becoming the central feature of the US-Israeli economic relationship. In 1985, for example, Israel's exports to the United States, which totaled $2.7 billion, equaled almost three-quarters of the $3.7 billion it received in economic and military aid. By 1990, trade had surpassed aid. In 2009, Israel's exports to the United States were seven times the amount of military aid it re-

We wish to thank Natalia Simanovsky for her editing remarks and comments.

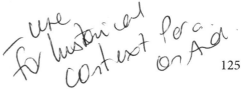

ceived. Israel has also become an export market for US-produced goods and services worth $10 billion.[4]

US Aid to Israel

Israel has been the largest aggregate recipient of US foreign aid since World War II. From 1976 to 2004, Israel was the leading annual recipient of US foreign aid, only to be replaced by Iraq in 2005. Since 1985, average US aid to Israel has leveled out at nearly $3 billion annually.[5]

Throughout the years, US Economic Support Funds (ESF) and Foreign Military Financing (FMF) to Israel have been major components in cementing and reinforcing the two countries' strong bilateral relations. At one point, specifically in 1979, cumulative aid reached 20 percent of Israel's GDP (see Figure 6.1).

In the past, a large portion of US aid sent to Israel was in the form of economic assistance (see Figure 6.2).[6] More recently, however, nearly all the assistance Israel received from the United States is in the form of military aid (see Figure 6.3). US military aid has helped make the Israeli Defense Force one of the most technologically sophisticated armies in the world. It has also helped Israel build a strong domestic defense industry, ranked among the top ten arms exporters in the world. As a consequence of the rapid expansion of Israel's high-tech sector in the 1990s, Israel is considered a fully industrialized country, which led the

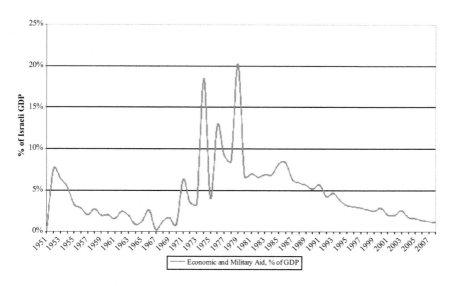

FIGURE 6.1 U.S. Aid to Israel, As Percentage of Israel GDP.
Source: US Aid—US Overseas Loans and Grants; Central Bureau of Statistics Israel.

United States and Israel to agree to gradually phase out economic aid to Israel. In FY 2008, Israel stopped receiving ESF grants altogether.[7]

Since Israel's independence, there have been four stages of increased US aid both to Israel (see Figure 6.4) and to the region in general. Between 1948 and 1967, US aid to Israel was relatively quite small. The first increase occurred between 1967 and 1972, the second in 1973–1974, the third in 1980–1981, and the fourth in 1984–1985. Since then, aid levels have remained stable, although the composition of aid—military versus economic—has changed.

Following World War II, annual US aid to the Middle East was a small fraction of current flows to the region. After the war, US policy focused on supporting the development of oil-producing countries while trying to manage a neutral stance in the Arab-Israeli conflict. Although the United States supported Israel's security, it also tried to prevent Soviet influence from gaining hold in Iran and Turkey.[8] Prior to 1968, US aid to Israel came mainly from private, tax-exempt Jewish contributions, while the transfer of arms to Israel came in the form of sales.[9]

From 1949 to 1965, US aid to Israel averaged $63 million per year and more than 95 percent was given for economic development and food. In 1959, a limited military loan program began that increased annual aid to approximately

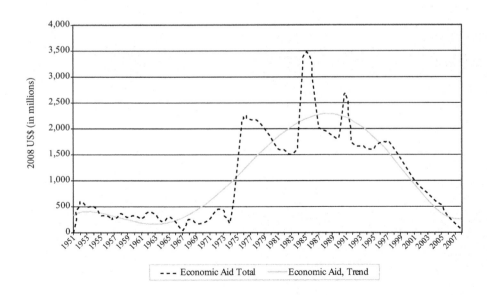

FIGURE 6.2 US Economic Aid (ESF) to Israel, in 2008 Dollars (millions).
Source: US Aid—US Overseas Loans and Grants; Central Bureau of Statistics Israel.

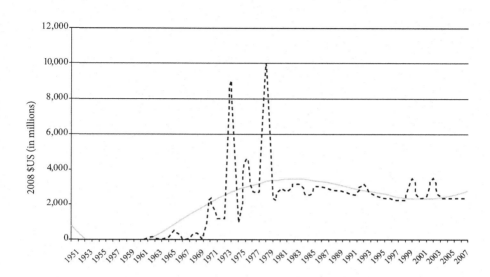

FIGURE 6.3 US Military Aid (FMF) to Israel, in 2008 Dollars (millions).
Source: US Aid—US Overseas Loans and Grants; Central Bureau of Statistics Israel.

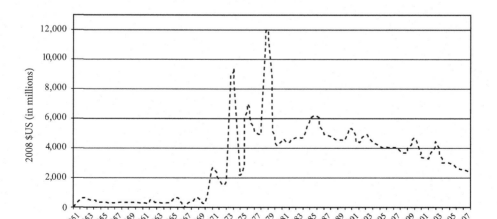

FIGURE 6.4 Total US Aid to Israel, in 2008 Dollars (millions).
Source: US Aid—US Overseas Loans and Grants; Central Bureau of Statistics Israel.

$100 million, with military loans increasing to almost half of the total.[10] Although Israel received US loans for economic aid, the country's main supplier of advanced military equipment and technology at the time was France.[11] It was only in 1962 that Israel purchased its first advanced weapons system from the United States (Hawk antiaircraft missiles). That sale, in essence, was the beginning of US support for Israel's qualitative military edge (QME) over its neighbors.[12]

With the Six-Day War in 1967, the United States saw Israel—a democracy—defeat the combined forces of multiple Soviet-backed countries. At the time, the perception in Washington was that many Arab states had permanently drifted toward the Soviet Union, for which they received approximately $11.2 billion (in 1982 dollars) in military aid. Following the Six-Day War, however, Israel's QME compelled future Egyptian president Anwar Sadat to conclude that Israel could not be defeated easily. This conclusion helped prepare the way for the future Egyptian-Israeli peace settlement and reinforced the argument within the Israeli government that the Israeli QME serves as both a political and a military deterrent. In 1968, President Lyndon Johnson, backed by Congress, approved the sale of F-4 Phantom fighters to Israel. Following the Yom Kippur War in 1973, the United States tacitly adopted the doctrine of actively maintaining Israel's QME.[13]

The first half of the 1970s brought with it a substantial decline of 80 percent in US economic aid to the Middle East for various reasons, the main one being the rising cost of the Vietnam War. Following the US withdrawal from Vietnam, US foreign aid to the region dramatically increased; the Middle East became the main battlefield during the Cold War, with Israel receiving $2.7 billion (in 1982 dollars) in military aid. Thus, the middle of the decade marked the beginning of large-scale aid delivered to the Middle East—a trend that continues today.[14]

Through the 1970s, the US Congress committed itself to strengthening Israel's military and economy through increases in foreign aid. For example, Israel received $30 million in aid in 1970. In 1971, the amount increased to $545 million, and the first US military grant was given to Israel in 1974.[15] The United States stepped in to fill the void left by France, as President Charles de Gaulle refused to supply equipment to Israel in protest of Israel's preemptive launch of the Six-Day War.[16]

What factors led the United States to increase aid to Israel in 1971? The first answer is straightforward in terms of US foreign policy: the Soviet Union was arming Israel's opponents. The second reason has to do with the fact that the sale of arms was and continues to be a US foreign policy tool. The United States simultaneously provides both Israel and Arab states with large quantities of arms in exchange for accommodation of its interests. Israeli objections to the sale of American weapons to the Arab states were met with assurances that the weapons sales would not change the balance of power in the region, and the United States asserted that the Israeli QME would be maintained.[17]

One consequence of the increase in aid to Israel in the early 1970s was that it was used by the United States to persuade Israel to back certain policies that Israel arguably would not have supported had it not been promised aid. This practice began after the Yom Kippur War, when after being defeated by the Israelis, some Arab countries turned to the United States for help. The United States then used its influence with Israel to convince the Israelis to return territories they had won in the war. Indeed, each Israeli withdrawal was rewarded with large increments in aid.[18]

The second increase came after the Yom Kippur War. The year 1973–1974 marks the shift that saw American aid change from being solely reactive to active in that the United States utilized foreign aid to achieve its strategic goals in the region. The enormous cost in both men and equipment in the Yom Kippur War made both the Soviet Union and the United States dispense equipment to the region so the two sides could continue fighting. During this period, and contrary to previous years, US aid outmatched Soviet aid overwhelmingly. President Richard Nixon and Secretary of State Henry Kissinger claimed that the United States could not afford to have Soviet allies armed with Soviet weapons beat a US ally armed with US weapons.[19]

The 1979 Camp David peace treaty between Israel and Egypt ushered in the current era of US financial support for peace between Israel and its Arab neighbors.[20] At the time, the United States believed that the only successful long-term strategy in the Middle East was to obtain an Arab commitment to reduce Soviet influence in their countries and to seek some sort of compromise between the Arab world and Israel. To reach an agreement, the United States had to convince Israel that even though its security concerns were legitimate, *real* security could be found only in its neighbors' willingness to accept the conditions of the agreement to live in peace. The means of achieving this end was the return of conquered territory; this has become the main formula in attempting to solve the Arab-Israeli dispute ever since.[21]

To facilitate the Egyptian-Israeli peace treaty, the United States provided $7.3 billion to both Israel and Egypt in 1979. The aid was in the form of military and economic grants and was received by Israel and Egypt at a ratio of 3 to 2, respectively.[22]

In 1981, economic aid to Israel was sent as a grant cash transfer, and military aid became a grant in 1985.[23] Official cooperation between the United States and Israel on security issues also began in 1981. Ariel Sharon, then Israel's defense minister, and Caspar Weinberger, then US secretary of defense, signed a memorandum of understanding that recognized "the common bonds of friendship between the U.S. and Israel and builds on the mutual security relationship that exists between the two nations."[24] That memorandum of understanding marked the beginning of close security cooperation and coordination between the two governments, and afterward, joint military exercises began. Cooperation in defense trade and access to maintenance facilities were also facilitated.[25]

The fourth and final increase of US aid to Israel was made between 1984 and 1985. The reasons for the fourth increase were mainly economic. Throughout 1985, Israel suffered from a severe economic crisis characterized by hyper-inflation of more than 400 percent, high public debts, and budget deficits. To tackle the situation, the national unity government, led by Shimon Peres, introduced the Economic Stabilization Plan in 1985. The plan was a joint effort by the government, the Histadrut (trade unions), and the Manufacturers Association. The program involved a number of radical measures, including but not limited to cuts in subsidies and the freeze of exchange rates, prices, and private-sector wages. The program was deemed successful by the US government, which then agreed to give Israel a grant worth $1.5 billion on top of the annual foreign aid it had given already. Additionally, the fourth increase was driven by Israel's military need to purchase arms to keep up with what the Soviet Union had given Arab nations.

Although the United States has not canceled any of Israel's debts, it has waived repayment of aid to Israel that was originally classified as loans. After the Yom Kippur War, President Nixon petitioned Congress for emergency aid for Israel, including loans for which repayment would be waived. Israel's preference was that the aid be in the form of loans, as opposed to grants, to avoid having a US military presence in Israel to oversee the spending. Thus, although the aid is technically called a loan, the military aid is in fact a grant.[26]

Additionally, the Cranston Amendment, which was added to American foreign aid legislation in 1984, maintained that it was both the policy and intention of the US government to supply Israel with economic aid "not less than" the amount Israel owed the United States in annual debt service payments (principal and interest). In 1998, Israel received $1.2 billion in ESF and owed the US government approximately $328 million in debt service for direct loans. The Cranston Amendment was supported each year in the annual aid appropriation bill until FY 1998, when it was no longer needed.[27]

Current Aid

In 1998, Israel received $1.8 billion in FMF and $1.2 billion in ESF. Beginning in 1999, an agreement was made to reduce ESF to zero within ten years. In August 2007, the Bush administration announced that it would increase military aid by $6 billion over the next decade through incremental annual increases in FMF. The increments stand at $150 million per annum.[28] According to former undersecretary of state for political affairs Nicholas Burns, who signed the memorandum of understanding:

We consider this 30 billion dollars in aid to Israel to be an investment in peace—in long-term peace. Peace will not be made without strength. Peace will not be made without Israel being strong in the future. Of course, our objective as a country and our specific objective as a government is to contribute to that peace, a peace between Israel and the Palestinian people, the creation of an independent Palestinian state willing to live side by side in peace with Israel, and a general peace in the region that has eluded the Israeli people for 59 years but which is, we hope, the destiny of the Israeli people as well as the Arab peoples of the region. Our policy in this entire region is dedicated to that final objective.[29]

In 2009, Israel received nearly $2.8 billion and in 2010, it received nearly $3.8 billion. Despite the recent economic crisis, Andrew Shapiro, US deputy secretary of state, said Israel would receive $3.2 billion in FMF in 2011. Furthermore, for 2011, the US government requested $3 billion and an additional $205 million for the continued development of Iron Dome, a short-/medium-range system designed to counter long-range rockets and slower flying cruise missiles, such as those possessed by Hizbollah and Hamas. The Iron Dome project is being jointly developed by Israel's Rafael Advanced Defense Systems and the US company Raytheon.[30]

Special Benefits for Israel

Israel enjoys a number of special benefits from the US government. For example, Israel is allowed to spend 26 percent of its aid on Israeli-manufactured military equipment. No other recipient of US aid has been granted such a benefit, and this benefit has helped develop the Israeli defense industry. Some experts claim that high annual amounts of US aid force private and semiprivate Israeli defense companies to place greater emphasis on exports, since a large portion of the Israeli weapons procurement is spent on American equipment. In any event, Israel has become a global leader in arms sales and is one of the ten biggest arms exporters in the world.[31]

Israel also is allowed to set aside FMF funds for current-year payments only, as opposed to setting aside the full cost of multi-year purchases. This is because the US General Accounting Office deems that cash-flow financing generates a commitment to continue aid in future years at a sufficient level.[32]

Another benefit Israel enjoys stems from its 1982 request that ESFs be transferred in one lump sum at the beginning of the fiscal year rather than in four quarterly installments, as is done with other countries.[33] Once it is received, the aid is transferred to an interest-bearing account at the Federal Reserve Bank. Israel utilizes the interest to pay down its debt to the United States. It cannot, however, use the accrued interest for defense procurement in Israel.[34]

A final benefit is related to arms purchases. Usually countries wishing to purchase arms from the United States must deal with the Department of Defense. Israel, however, may bypass the Department of Defense entirely and deal directly with US companies. Furthermore, other countries are constrained to a minimum purchase price of $100,000, yet Israel is allowed to purchase arms for less.[35]

US-Israeli Economic Relations: FTA

From 1948 to 1983, bilateral trade between the United States and Israel did not exceed $1 billion. The foundation for the current US-Israeli economic relationship is the FTA, signed in 1985, which has enabled US-Israeli trade to increase sevenfold.[36]

The FTA was signed while the United States was trying to develop a platform for eliminating trade tariffs between countries in the context of General Agreement on Tariffs and Trade (GATT).[37] At the time, most countries were not willing to drop their trade barriers. Former US senator William Brock approached President Ronald Reagan with a suggestion to develop a bilateral free trade agreement with Israel that would serve as a model for the rest of the world. The hope was that the program, once ratified, would be so successful that other countries would want to follow suit. Israel was a perfect candidate for such an experiment for several reasons: it was small; it had a good business community; and it had the ability to ratify the deal quickly. After a two-year negotiation, the FTA was signed between the two countries. Today Israel ranks among the top twenty US trading partners, and the FTA model has multiplied worldwide.[38] Attesting to the importance of the agreement, at the time, Reagan said, "I believe this new economic relationship with our friends in Israel will further our historic friendship, strengthen both of our economies, and provide for new opportunities between our peoples for communication and commerce. Nothing better demonstrates the shared community of aspirations between our nations than our promotion of free and harmonious trade for our mutual benefit."[39]

The conditions of the FTA called for zero tariffs by 1995, banned new import limits after 1990, tentatively suggested work programs on services trade and intellectual property, and outlined the beef trade implications of kashruth dietary laws.[40] In addition, the FTA has afforded US products the opportunity to compete equally with European goods, which have free access to Israel's domestic markets. In essence, the FTA eliminated all duties and virtually all other restrictions on trade between the two countries.[41]

Even though the FTA looks quite limited compared to today's agreements, at the time it was radical for both countries. For the United States, it was the first real attempt at a bilateral free trade agreement. For Israel, it signified a shift from the country's traditional commitment to agrarian socialism and self-reliant development and its early orientation toward Europe.[42]

The agreement has also been the foundation of a unique experiment in integrating Israel with its neighbors. For instance, in the 1990s Israel and Jordan agreed to a series of qualifying industrial zones in Jordan. Some housed factories, which were sometimes partially owned by Israeli businesses and used Israeli inputs to make such products as clothing, luggage, and other light goods for export. Today the zones supply over $500 million a year in Jordanian textile exports to the United States. In 2005, fifteen similar zones opened in Egypt, and they account for $900 million (out of $2.5 billion) in annual Egyptian exports to the United States. Recent studies estimate that the zones employ 15,000 Jordanians and 100,000 Egyptians.[43]

But the FTA's main achievement was to eliminate tariffs and quota limits on trade in physical goods. However, the agreement today is only of minor relevance to the US-Israeli relationship, because trade agreements in the 1990s eliminated most rich-country tariffs on high-tech goods and sophisticated manufactured products. With tariffs eliminated or minimal, US importers of such goods (and probably Israeli importers as well) no longer register them under the agreement.[44] For that very reason, the FTA's importance has declined, as only 14 percent of US imports from Israel now are carried out under the agreement. No information is available about a similar percentage regarding Israeli imports.[45]

More recent trade agreements between the United States and Singapore, for example, have added chapters to enhance the trade in services, facilitate electronic commerce, ease cooperative standards for newly emerging technologies, and address sophisticated intellectual property issues. The US-Israeli FTA, however, fails to mention Internet commerce, which did not exist at the time. Furthermore, it has no "technical barriers to trade" chapter to address setting standards and obtaining regulatory approval for new technologies, such as nanotechnology and biotechnology. A limited chapter on services trades exists, yet it barely covers intellectual property rights. Thus, the US-Israeli FTA is already obsolete—ignored in the majority of manufacturing-trade sectors important to bilateral trade, and irrelevant to trade in services, standards setting, and other modern issues.[46]

Since the 1980s, trade has replaced aid in US-Israeli economic relations. Currently, Israel exports roughly $20 billion to the United States, nearly seven times the amount of military aid it receives, and accounts for two-thirds of US manufacturing imports from the Middle East. Israel has also become a global export market worth approximately $10 billion in US-produced goods and services.[47]

By 2007, bilateral trade between the United States and Israel surpassed $30 billion. However, US companies have been losing market share in Israel, partly because the FTA does not provide the necessary level of regulation that more recent agreements do in areas such as technical standards and intellectual property rights protection. Standards procedures have become nontariff barriers limiting US exporters' access to the Israeli market. Imported products may be held to rigorous testing that is not imposed on local products. Israeli legislation permits adoption of multiple international standards, and the United States has asked Israel to consider international standards when it considers developing its regulations.[48]

Another substantial feature of the US-Israeli economic relationship came after the United States implemented a policy of opening trade and investment offices worldwide. In the beginning of the 1990s, Massachusetts was the first state to open an office for these purposes in Israel, followed by California and later by eighteen other states that either established an office or retained Israel-based representation. Most of the offices covered the entire Middle East, from Turkey to the United Arab Emirates. During the 2000–2001 economic downturn, several states were forced to rescind overseas operations, and currently ten states maintain offices in Israel.[49]

Tariff and nontariff barriers continue to affect a portion of US agricultural exports. In 1996, to address the disparities on how the FTA applies to agriculture, the United States and Israel signed the Agreement on Trade in Agricultural Products, which established a program of market access liberalization for food and agricultural products through December 31, 2001.[50] Negotiation and implementation of a successor agreement was completed in 2004 and was effective through December 31, 2008. Grants improved access for select US agricultural products, resulting in a succeeding agreement extended through December 31, 2010.[51] However, many technical barriers still remain for the US agricultural products' entry into the Israeli market.

R&D Cooperation

Several foundations foster research and development cooperation between the United States and Israel, such as the Binational Agricultural Research and Development Fund (BARD), the Binational Industrial Research and Development Foundation (BIRD), and the Binational Science Foundation (BSF). These foundations generate cooperation in industrial R&D, technological innovation, and agricultural and scientific research.[52]

BARD is a competitive funding program for mutually beneficial research of agricultural problems, jointly conducted by US and Israeli scientists. Most projects focus on increasing agricultural productivity, specifically in hot and dry climates. BARD's research areas include animal health, food quality and safety, and environmental issues. Postdoctoral fellowships and international workshops are also supported. To date, BARD has funded over 850 projects throughout most of the fifty states.[53]

BIRD supports approximately fifteen projects annually with a total investment of about $11 million per year. One of the initiatives is called Trilateral Industrial Development, a program developed by the US, Israeli, and Jordanian governments that aims to promote joint research between companies from the three countries.[54]

The BSF was established in 1972 by the US and Israeli governments. Since then it has supported and promoted cooperative scientific and technological research for peaceful purposes whose merit is decided upon by peer review. Nearly 4,000 projects have been supported by the BSF, and several grantees have won prestigious awards, including the Nobel Prize.[55]

Another form of cooperation was brought about by the US-Israeli Energy Cooperation Act, part of the Energy Independence and Security Act of 2007. The law establishes a grant program for cooperative R&D between US and Israeli businesses, government agencies, academic institutions, and nonprofit entities toward developing alternative sources of energy. Specifically, the grant aims to promote the following forms of energy: solar, wind, biomass, geothermal, wave and tidal, advanced battery and energy efficiency.[56] The act also establishes an advisory board consisting of one representative each from the US government, BIRD, and the BSF.[57]

In early 2009, the United States–Israel Energy Cooperation Act received funding for the first time. In FY 2009 and FY 2010, Congress allocated $4 million, and in November 2009 the US Department of Energy and the Israeli Ministry of National Infrastructure announced that they each would contribute $3.3 million for clean energy initiatives. The BIRD Foundation was awarded the funding as part of the act, and the joint programs are currently researching the conversion of solar energy into electricity, Smart Grid technology, building materials that can capture solar energy, and biodiesel production.[58]

Intellectual Property Rights

The Special 301 provisions of the Trade Act of 1974, as amended, require the Office of the US Trade Representative (USTR) to identify countries that deny adequate and effective protection of intellectual property rights. In 2005, the US Trade Representative moved Israel from its watch list to its priority watch list because the country had an "inadequate data protection regime" and because Israel intended to pass legislation to reduce patent term extensions. In 2006, Israel remained on the list due to continuing concern about copyright matters and because it passed legislation that weakened protection for American pharmaceutical companies. The United States was also concerned about software, music, and DVD piracy. In 2007 and 2008, the US Trade Representative once again placed Israel on the list because Israel had done little to remedy its intellectual property policies.[59]

In 2009, however, based on the Special 301 Out-of-Cycle Review that was extended to Israel, the United States and Israel reached an understanding on several long-standing issues concerning Israel's intellectual property rights policies for pharmaceutical products. As part of the understanding with the United States, Israel has committed itself to strengthen its laws protecting pharmaceutical test data and patent term extension, and to publish patent applications before they are granted. Additionally, Israel confirmed that it would expedite approvals of new pharmaceutical drugs by the Ministry of Health.[60]

Once appropriate legislation is submitted to the Knesset, Israel will be moved back from the Special 301 priority watch list to the watch list. When legislation is fully implemented, Israel will be moved off the list altogether. Lately Israel has signaled its willingness to make progress on other intellectual property rights concerns. Specifically, the country announced plans to issue a draft copyright-related "exposure bill" (an early step in the legislative process) in a year's time, intended to solicit public comments on specific proposals relating to enacting requirements of the World Intellectual Property Organization Copyright Internet Treaties.[61]

Loan Guarantees

Loan guarantees are a form of indirect aid the United States gives to Israel.[62] Israel pays all fees and subsidies and the US president considers Israel's economic reforms when determining terms and conditions for the loan guarantees.[63] Israel has never defaulted on a US-backed loan guarantee, as it needs to maintain its credit rating to secure financing to offset its annual budget deficits. Congress directs that subsidies, a percentage of the total loan, be set aside in a US treasury account for possible default. In the 1990s the amount of subsidies for loan guarantees was 4.1 percent.[64]

Since 1973, Israel has also received grants from the State Department's migration and refugee aid fund. Funds are paid to the United Israel Appeal, a private philanthropic organization based in the United States, which then transfers the funds to the Jewish Agency. Annual amounts have varied from $12 million to $80 million, depending on the influx of Jewish immigrants from the former Soviet Union (and other areas) to Israel. Congress earmarks the funds, as the US administration usually does not request specific amounts of migration and refugee aid for Israel.[65]

During the early 1990s, Israel accepted a substantial number of immigrants, nearly 1 million, from the former Soviet Union. Their arrival generated enormous pressure on the government to construct homes and other infrastructure to ensure the successful integration of the newcomers into Israeli society. To achieve this goal, Israel required large amounts of funding from the US government. In 1991, Israel submitted a request for $10 billion in loan guarantees, which the United States agreed to issue. However, in an attempt to prevent a population increase in West Bank settlements, US President George H. W. Bush tied the guarantees to West Bank settlement expansion. This linkage created a major dispute between Bush and Israeli Prime Minister Yitzhak Shamir, which led to a crisis in Israeli-US relations. Although the guarantees were approved in 1992, the linkage remains valid today.[66]

In 2003, Israeli Prime Minister Ariel Sharon requested $8 billion in loan guarantees to help support Israel's troubled economy, as well as an additional $4 billion in military grants to help Israel prepare for possible attacks from the looming US war with Iraq and to help the Israeli government end the second Palestinian Intifada. The Emergency Wartime Supplemental Appropriations Act also authorized $9 billion in loan guarantees over three years for Israel's economic recovery and $1 billion in military grants. Proceeds from the loans, however, could be used only within Israel's pre-1967 borders, and the US Congress reduced the guarantee amount to counterbalance money Israel spent constructing new settlements in the occupied territories. The loan guarantees have been extended several times until 2011, though Israel has not borrowed any funds since 2005.[67]

That same year, the US Department of State announced that the $3 billion in loan guarantees for FY 2003 would be reduced by nearly $290 million due to Israel's continued construction in the settlements and the security barrier. In FY 2005, the American government reduced the guarantees by nearly $796 million. Since then, no deductions have been made.[68]

In 2002, to help Israel deal with a recession caused by the global economic downturn and by the second Palestinian Intifada, the United States provided a $9 billion package in loan guarantees, enabling Israel to sell bonds internationally with US backing. Such guarantees have been key to upgrading Israeli sovereign ratings. As of 2009, Israel still had $3.8 billion left, which was to be used by 2011, after issuing a further $4.1 billion in bonds backed by the United States and accounting for the $1.1 billion deduction for Israeli settlement construction in the West Bank. This means that in 2009, Israel was able to use up to $3.2 billion. An additional $333 million annually was released in both 2010 and 2011, provided that Israel adheres to its fiscal targets.[69]

Arab Boycott

In 1945, the Arab League initiated a boycott of Zionist goods and services in the British Mandate territory of Palestine. It was formalized after Israel's establishment and continues to be administered by the Damascus-based Central Boycott Office, a specialized bureau of the Arab League.[70]

There are two main tiers to the boycott. The primary boycott prohibits the imports of Israeli-origin goods and services into boycotting countries. The secondary boycott prohibits individuals, as well as private and public sector firms and organizations, from engaging in business with any entity that does business in Israel.[71]

In 1959, the US Senate adopted an amendment opposing foreign aid to countries that discriminate against the United States on religious grounds. The main motivation behind the adoption of the amendment was the Arab policy of refusing visas to US citizens, specifically Saudis' refusal to permit US Jews to be stationed in the US base at Dhahran. In 1965, Congress adopted broad regulation that held that US policy opposed boycotts or restrictive trade practices against other countries friendly to the United States.[72] In 1975, US Senator Frank Church made public a list of 1,500 American firms that were on the 1970 Saudi blacklist. This was the first time the American public was made aware of the scope of the Arab boycott.[73] Moreover, in 1977, the US Congress adopted legislation encouraging American companies to refuse to take action in support of the restrictive trade practices or boycotts fostered by any foreign government against a country friendly to the United States.[74]

Based on recent US Trade Representative reports, of the twenty-two members of the Arab League, only three countries—Iraq, Libya, and Syria—continue to enforce the secondary boycott, and only Syria actively pursues the boycott's implementation.[75] The changing nature of world trade has been responsible for the de facto demise of the boycott, with various bilateral investment treaties signed between Arab and non-Arab countries and WTO rules that prohibit discriminatory policies, thus reducing the effective capability of the boycott.

Conclusion

The US-Israeli economic relationship has developed throughout the years since 1948, changing in both nature and content as history has progressed. In the beginning, the United States was cautious in supplying aid to Israel. Only after the Yom Kippur War in 1973 did that change. Since the mid-1980s, the economic relationship has been based more on trade than on aid, although military support in the form of grants continues. Economic aid has been phased out as Israeli companies have become competitive at the highest levels of technology and industry.

The future is unknown. However, based on shared common values and on the development of the unique partnership, greater cooperation can be expected in the years to come.

Table 6.1 US Economic and Military Aid to Israel

Year	Economic aid, in total 2008 US$ (in millions)	Military aid, in total 2008 US$ (in millions)	Economic and military aid, in total 2008 US$ (in millions)	Economic and military aid, as % of Israel GDP
1951	0.71	—	0.71	0.01
1952	590.91	—	590.91	7.62
1953	494.28	—	494.28	6.47
1954	495.95	—	495.95	5.44
1955	346.88	—	346.88	3.34
1956	325.8	—	325.8	2.88
1957	252.78	—	252.78	2.05
1958	367.14	—	367.14	2.78
1959	294.73	2.36	297.1	1.99
1960	322.16	2.92	325.08	2.05
1961	276.77	0.01	276.77	1.57
1962	402.27	75.11	477.38	2.47
1963	356.27	74.74	431.01	2.01
1964	205.47	—	205.47	0.88
1965	266.41	70.42	336.84	1.32
1966	196.69	481.05	677.74	2.64
1967	31.58	36.25	67.83	0.25
1968	259.02	125.01	384.03	1.27
1969	175.5	406.46	581.96	1.70
1970	186.36	136.03	322.38	0.87
1971	240.97	2,353.6	2,594.58	6.35
1972	429.7	1,237.15	1,666.85	3.63
1973	433.68	1,184.92	1,618.6	3.36
1974	189.72	9,145.64	9,335.35	18.41
1975	1,178.22	1,001.03	2,179.25	4.13
1976	2,223.39	4,668.36	6,891.75	12.88
1977	2,148.35	2,895.35	5,043.69	9.24
1978	2,147.92	2,712.7	4,860.62	8.55
1979	1,983.5	10,041.79	12,025.29	20.21
1980	1,814.05	2,308.1	4,122.15	6.69
1981	1,606.1	2,943.12	4,549.23	7.05
1982	1,585.86	2,754.6	4,340.46	6.63
1983	1,479.24	3,203.44	4,682.68	6.97

(continues)

Table 6.1 US Economic and Military Aid to Israel (continued)

Year	Economic aid, in total 2008 US$ (in millions)	Military aid, in total 2008 US$ (in millions)	Economic and military aid, in total 2008 US$ (in millions)	Economic and military aid, as % of Israel GDP
1984	1,653.76	3,089.44	4,743.2	6.91
1985	3,432.4	2,464.23	5,896.63	8.22
1986	3,265.51	2,963.11	6,228.63	8.39
1987	2,011.65	3,017.48	5,029.13	6.38
1988	1,950.3	2,925.45	4,875.75	5.97
1989	1,877.36	2,816.03	4,693.39	5.67
1990	1,802.33	2,815.12	4,617.46	5.23
1991	2,689.63	2,679.77	5,369.4	5.73
1992	1,708.92	2,619.4	4,328.32	4.31
1993	1,664.09	3,241.18	4,905.26	4.71
1994	1,629.07	2,672.64	4,301.7	3.86
1995	1,598.81	2,506.29	4,105.1	3.23
1996	1,735.02	2,390.66	4,125.68	3.07
1997	1,756.54	2,312.33	4,068.87	2.95
1998	1,621.47	2,282.2	3,903.66	2.71
1999	1,437.91	2,352.44	3,790.35	2.55
2000	1,252.63	3,482.9	4,735.53	2.92
2001	1,018.27	2,381.51	3,399.78	2.09
2002	853.73	2,421.54	3,275.27	2.03
2003	737.08	3,556.65	4,293.73	2.62
2004	625.04	2,430.43	3,055.48	1.78
2005	524.34	2,426.57	2,950.91	1.63
2006	300.57	2,374.84	2,675.41	1.40
2007	172.03	2,395.74	2,567.77	1.28
2008	44.11	2,380.56	2,424.67	1.16

Source: US Aid—US Overseas Loans and Grants; Central Bureau of Statistics Israel.

Notes

1. Carol Migdalovitz, "Israel: Background and Relations with the United States," Congressional Research Service, CRS.RL33476, 2009, Summary, www.fas.org/sgp/crs/mideast/RL33476.pdf.

2. Robert J. Lieber, "U.S. Israeli Relations Since 1948," *Middle East Review of International Affairs* 2, no. 3 (1998): 12.

3. Jeremy M. Sharp, "U.S. Foreign Aid to Israel," CRS.RL33222, 2008, Summary, http://fpc .state.gov/documents/organization/100102.pdf.

4. US Census Bureau, Foreign Trade Statistics, www.census.gov/foreign-trade/balance /c5081.html#2010.

5. Sharp, "U.S. Foreign Aid to Israel," Summary.

6. Ibid.

7. Ibid.

8. Jeremy M. Sharp, "U.S. Foreign Aid to the Middle East: Historical Background, Recent Trends, and the FY2010 Request," CRS.R32260, 2010, Summary, www.fas.org/sgp/crs/mideast /RL32260.pdf.

9. A. F. K. Organski, *The $36 Billion Bargain: Strategy and Politics in U.S. Aid to Israel* (New York: Columbia University Press, 1990), p. 161.

10. Clyde R. Mark, "Israel: U.S. Foreign Aid," CRS.IB85056, 2005, p. 1.

11. Sharp, "U.S. Foreign Aid to the Middle East," p. 19.

12. Ibid.

13. William Wunderle and Andre Briere, "U.S. Foreign Policy and Israel's Qualitative Military Edge, the Need for a Common Vision," Washington Institute for Near East Policy, Policy Focus no. 80, 2008, p. 5. See also Chapter 7, by Stuart A. Cohen, in this volume.

14. Sharp, "U.S. Foreign Aid to the Middle East," pp. 19–20.

15. Sharp, "U.S. Foreign Aid to the Middle East," p. 15.

16. Ibid.

17. Organski, 1990, pp. 158–161.

18. Ibid., pp. 163–172.

19. Ibid., p. 163.

20. Sharp (b), 2009, p. 21.

21. Organski, *The $36 Billion Bargain*, p. 167.

22. Sharp, "U.S. Foreign Aid to the Middle East," p. 21.

23. Mark, "Israel: U.S. Foreign Aid," p. 1.

24. "Israel and the United States: The Special Bond Between Two Nations and Two Peoples," Israel Ministry of Foreign Affairs, 2008, p. 126.

25. Ibid.

26. Mark, "Israel: U.S. Foreign Aid," p. 6.

27. Ibid.

28. Sharp, "U.S. Foreign Aid to Israel," Summary.

29. Nicholas R. Burns, undersecretary of state for political affairs, "Remarks and Press Availability at Signing Ceremony for Memorandum of Understanding on U.S. Military Aid," American Embassy Tel Aviv–Press Section, August 16, 2007, p. 1.

30. Ora Koren, "Israel to Receive $3.2 Billion in 2011," *The Marker*, July 17, 2010 (in Hebrew).

31. Sharp, "U.S. Foreign Aid to Israel," Summary.

32. Mark, "Israel: U.S. Foreign Aid," p. 8.

33. Ibid.

34. Sharp, "U.S. Foreign Aid to Israel," p. 3.

35. Mark, "Israel: U.S. Foreign Aid," p. 9.

36. "Israel and the United States," p. 128.

37. The GATT, which covers international trade in goods, was formed in 1949 and lasted until 1993. It was replaced by the World Trade Organization in 1995.

38. Sherwin Pomerantz, in "Israel and the United States: The Special Bond Between Two Nations and Two Peoples," p. 130.

39. Reagan quoted in "Israel and the United States," p. 128.

40. Edward Gresser, "Update the Israel Free Trade Agreement," New Democratic Leadership Council, 2010, p. 2, www.dlc.org/documents /IsraelFTA.pdf.

41. Mitchell Bard, "Free Trade Agreement," 2010, Jewish Virtual Library, www.jewish virtuallibrary.org/jsource/US-Israel/Fighting _the_boycott.html .

42. Gresser, "Update the Israel Free Trade Agreement," p. 2.

43. Ibid., pp. 3–4.

44. Ibid., pp. 4–6.

45. Ibid.

46. Ibid.

47. Ibid. For comparative purposes, Israel's trade with the EU comprised roughly $16 billion in exports and $20 billion in imports in 2008. See "Delegation of the EU to Israel: Bilateral Trade," http://eeas.europa.eu/delegations /israel/eu_israel/trade_relation/bilateral_trade.

48. Pomerantz, in "Israel and the United States: The Special Bond Between Two Nations and Two Peoples," p. 131.

49. Ibid., pp. 130–131.

50. Office of the US Trade Representative, "Israel Free Trade Agreement," pp. 191–192.

51. Ibid.

52. "Israel and the United States," p. 128.

53. Ibid.

54. Ibid.

55. Ibid.

56. AIPAC, "U.S.-Israel Energy Cooperation: A Renewable Resource," 2010.

57. Ibid.

58. Ibid.

59. Migdalovitz, "Israel," p. 36.

60. Office of the US Trade Representative, "2010 Special 301 Report," pp. 40–41, www .ustr.gov/about-us/press-office/reports-and -publications/2010–3.

61. Ibid.

62. A loan guarantee is when a reliable financial entity promises to pay off the balance of a loan if the borrower cannot. Loan guarantees by the Federal Reserve enable Israel to borrow at much lower interest rates than if Israel sought the loan without backers. In loan guarantees it is not always clear how much money is "given." Congress has attached a series of stipulations to the packages, including one that reserves the right to reduce the guarantee amount to counterbalance any money Israel spends creating new settlements in contested territories.

63. Ibid.

64. Sharp, "U.S. Foreign Aid to Israel," pp. 13–15.

65. Ibid.

66. Donald Neff, "Israel Requests $10 Billion in U.S. Loan Guarantees for Soviet Immigrants," *Washington Report on Middle East Affairs*, April/May 1995, pp. 79–80.

67. Sharp, "U.S. Foreign Aid to Israel," pp. 17–18.

68. Neff, "Israel Requests $10 Billion in U.S. Loan Guarantees for Soviet Immigrants."

69. Reuters, "U.S. Reapproves Israel Loan Guarantees Program," *Ha'aretz*, June 30, 2009.

70. Martin A. Weiss, "Arab League Boycott of Israel," CRS.RS22424, 2006, pp. 1–2.

71. Ibid.

72. "Fighting the Arab Boycott," Jewish Virtual Library, www.jewishvirtuallibrary.org /jsource/US-Israel/Fighting_the_boycott.html.

73. Ibid.

74. Ibid.

75. Roger Alford, "The Death of the Secondary Boycott Against Israel," Northwestern Law, In the News, 2010, www.law.northwestern.edu /news/article_full.cfm?eventid=4803.

7

Light and Shadows in US-Israeli Military Ties, 1948–2010

Stuart A. Cohen

MILITARY TIES HAVE ALWAYS CONSTITUTED an essential ingredient in the overall strategic relationship between the United States and Israel. The alliance between the two countries, although rooted in a confluence of cultural affinities and geostrategic interests, has been cemented by the severely practical steps taken to ensure that their armed forces enjoy battlefield superiority over potential foes. In this reading, policy pronouncements and verbal guarantees, for all their symbolic importance, provide observers of the US-Israeli relationship with little more than a general framework for the analysis of its dynamics. The true barometer of its health has always been more mundane: in which fields, to what extent, and how frequently have Israeli and US armed forces cooperated to improve their war-fighting capabilities?

Answers to those questions are not easy to ascertain. One reason is that the story is far more complex than is often acknowledged. From time to time, the overall spirit of amity has been disturbed by moments of friction. For the most part, these have been derivative of general policy disputes between the US and Israeli governments, usually over the peace process in its various guises. On occasion, however, the relationship has been soured by incidents of specifically military

For comments on an earlier version of this chapter, I am grateful to Professor Robert Freedman and Dr. Eitan Shamir.

relevance. During the Yom Kippur War, for instance, some Israeli officials charged that members of the Nixon administration were delaying the replenishment of Israel Defense Force (IDF) stocks depleted by the fighting; in the mid-1980s, they likewise suspected the US government of deliberately grounding the Lavi jet fighter. Even more dramatic have been the military episodes that have generated American ire. Surely no other recipient of US largesse can match Israel's record of (inadvertently?) shooting up American military personnel (the USS *Liberty* in 1967); of paying (through a rogue intelligence outfit?) an American citizen, Jonathan Pollard, to commit high treason; and of (innocently?) selling advanced weapons systems to one of America's great power rivals in eastern Asia (the Israeli-Chinese Phalcon deal of 2000).

Analysis of the military dimension of the US-Israeli relationship is further hampered by its comparatively restricted confines. Some of the conventional indications of a strategic partnership simply are not at hand. True, since the mid-1980s Haifa has been the principal Mediterranean port of call for the American Sixth Fleet, US military supplies have been stockpiled on Israeli soil, and units of the two countries' armed forces have made use of each other's training facilities.[1] As will be seen below, the two sides also have a long history of sharing ideas and information, arrangements that are now institutionalized by, for instance, the exchange of permanent liaison officers by the US Army Training and Doctrine Command and the Israel Ground Forces Command. Nevertheless, unlike every other major American ally, Israel has never hosted a larger long-term US military presence. The Patriot missile crews deployed around Tel Aviv during the Iraq wars of 1991 and 2003 returned to their bases in Germany immediately when cease-fires came into effect.[2]

Other forms of practical military US-Israeli cooperation have also been intermittent, and usually limited to ad hoc arrangements with respect to developing high-tech battle systems, of which the best known are the Arrow antimissile system, the Tactical High-Energy Laser (Nautilus), and, most recently, the Iron Dome multilayer defensive umbrella against rocket attacks. Even the record of joint military exercises is patchy. Certainly Juniper Cobra, a biennial test of ballistic defense interoperability, has steadily grown in size since first instituted in 2001, so much so that by the fall of 2009, more than 1,000 US troops were reported to have been deployed for that purpose. Similarly impressive have been the additions to the list of IDF units sent to train with their counterparts in US European Command.[3] Both developments illustrate the US government's commitment to preserving Israel's qualitative military edge, which in fact was written into American law in the innocuous-sounding Naval Vessel Transfer Act of 2008.[4] Nevertheless, what remains important is that neither enterprise can compare in scope with the Bright Star exercises the United States has conducted with Egyptian forces since 1983, still less with the establishment of joint US-Egyptian (and even US-Syrian) command centers during Desert Storm.

In the absence of any such shared practical experience, surveys of the military dimension of the US-Israeli alliance invariably resort to what may be termed the "arms + cash" template. From this perspective, the balance of the relationship is necessarily unequal. Certainly, of late several Israeli products have begun to appear in inventories of US armaments. According to one senior official in the State Department:

> Israeli origin equipment deployed on Iraqi and Afghan battlefields are protecting troops every day. This includes armor-plating technology for U.S. military vehicles and unique medical solutions, such as the Israeli bandage, a specifically designed antibiotic-treated dressing that has been widely used by our men and women in uniform in Iraq and Afghanistan. It also includes sensors, surveillance equipment, unmanned aerial vehicle technology, and detection devices to seek out IEDs.[5]

Nevertheless, the principal flow of weapons and weapon platforms has clearly been in the opposite direction. Over the past five decades, the United States has become Israel's principal source for numerous items of military ordnance, providing supplies across a spectrum that ranges from the M-16 rifle, which in the late 1970s briefly became the personal weapon of almost every Israeli soldier, to supersonic jet fighters and from GPS systems to Patriot missiles. Even more unmistakably pronounced has been the direction of the cash flow. Overall, Israel has received from the US government almost $100 billion, much in the form of outright grants, to purchase whatever ordnance might be on offer.[6] In 2010 it was reported that under the terms of the Foreign Military Financing Program, Israel receives $3 billion a year for training and equipment—more than all other disbursements under that program put together.[7]

Useful though it may be, as a framework for analyzing US-Israeli military ties, the arms + cash template suffers from two major flaws.

- First, it telescopes history. Inevitably, attention focuses on the period that covered major advances in deliveries and credits. Hence, the story generally commences in December 1971, when Prime Minister Golda Meir first secured a public promise from President Richard Nixon that "the United States will continue to maintain its ongoing relationship of financial assistance and military supply to Israel."[8] What followed assumes quasi-teleological meaning; preceding years are relegated to the status of a prologue.
- Less blatant, but in many ways even more insidious, is the second drawback in the arms + cash perspective. By focusing almost exclusively on the "hard" dimensions of those ties, it downplays the role of "soft" elements, of which the most important are intellectual: the exchange of information and thoughts. This is not just a matter of intelligence sharing,

a field in which it is sometimes claimed, but almost impossible to verify, that the United States may have received even more than it has given.[9] More pertinently, the intellectual dimension of US-Israeli military ties finds expression in the ways, overt as much as covert, that the two sides share ideas about how military power might be exercised and the ways in which military organizations ought to behave.

This chapter seeks to present a review of US-Israeli military ties that compensates for both faults. That aim also dictates the chapter's structure. Although necessarily concentrating on the relationship as it developed during and after the 1970s, this chapter nevertheless commences with a survey of the preceding period. More substantially, this chapter deliberately avoids a blow-by-blow account of the various agreements that authorized Israel's access to American military resources, whose landmarks are in any case fully recorded in other studies.[10] Instead, it examines the ways in which, over time, the war-fighting experience accumulated by both sides, in low- as well as high-intensity combat, may have influenced each other's military thought and practice.

False Starts: 1948–1962

America's contribution to the IDF's earliest modes of action and organization was decidedly subsidiary. During the formative pre-state period, by far the most substantial foreign influences on Jewish military behavior were European, initially Russian and thereafter Polish and German, too. These were soon superseded by British traditions, not surprisingly since it was from British Mandate forces that many of the IDF's earliest commanders had received their military education. Some, such as Moshe Dayan and Haim Laskov (respectively, the fourth and fifth chiefs of the IDF General Staff), were graduates of the "Night Squads" formed in the late 1930s by Major Orde Charles Wingate, from whom, it has been said, "An entire generation of future IDF commanders would learn their tactics . . . , adopt his disregard for rank and protocol, and accept his demand that officers set an example by leading their men into battle."[11] Many more of the early IDF commanders had during World War II served in the British army proper, for the most part as members of the Jewish Brigade established in 1944.[12]

David Ben-Gurion highly valued the vast store of practical military know-how that had thus been placed at the Jews' disposal. As early as 1946, he was convinced that the existing militias fielded by the Yishuv (Jewish community in Mandate Palestine) had to be transformed from what were basically small guerrilla forces into full-fledged armies, capable of besting the conventional forces that the Arab states could feed into battle. That purpose required personnel who knew how an army was organized and functioned. How were orders composed, transmitted, and filed? Who was responsible for ensuring that logistic facilities were maintained? What were the basic field formations? These were subjects that to all World War II servicemen—whatever their rank—had become almost second nature. No wonder, therefore, that from the first, Ben-Gurion sought to ensure that veterans of the Jewish Brigade would constitute the backbone of the emergent IDF, rather than members of the less-disciplined principal militias, notably the Haganah and the Palmach (about whose political leanings he in any case harbored severe doubts).[13]

Nevertheless, even at this early stage, some American input was also in evidence. After all, and as Ben-Gurion and his closest cronies fully appreciated, the British legacy—although invaluable—nevertheless suffered from three major lacunae.

- The first, and most obvious, was financial. When departing, the British forces had taken with them almost all their light and heavy weapons. What they had left behind consisted largely of tools, office and communications equipment, and spare parts. Hence, the Jewish forces still suffered from severe deficiencies in major fighting platforms. These would have to be purchased from whichever foreign supplier was willing (or legally able) to sell, and for that what Ben-Gurion needed was cash.
- The second deficiency was more specific and reflected the fact that almost all the members of the Yishuv who had fought under British colors in World War II had done so in infantry formations. Very few (Ezer Weizman was one) had served in an air force. Given the enormity of the contribution that air power had made to Allied victory in World War II, this was potentially a very serious failing that would have to be repaired.
- And finally there was the absence of senior commanders. The vast majority of the Yishuv's military expertise was based on a record of command at the tactical level. Of all the veterans who had fought in the British army during World War II, only two had risen through the ranks to positions that required a wider perspective on operations. (One was Efraim Ben-Artzi, who had commanded a brigade in the Jewish Legion, and subsequently became Israel's first military attaché to the United States. The other was Yochanan Ratner, who had served on the British General Staff at Cairo, and who became the first commanding officer of the IDF's planning branch.) Prior to 1948, the largest combat formation commanded by any of the Palmach's leaders was a brigade. For the IDF to win its wars, it would have to obtain the services of more people with senior experience.

In different degrees, resources obtained from the United States would make some contributions in each of these spheres, most obviously in the material side of the military framework. True, the US government rigidly maintained the embargo it had imposed on arms supplies to the adversaries in Palestine as early as December 1947.[14] The small amounts of financial aid that it was prepared to grant were strictly earmarked for nonmilitary purposes. Nevertheless, Ben-Gurion was able to persuade a select group of wealthy American Jews to form the "Sonneborn Circle." Resorting to a variety of means—many on the wrong side of US law—these men made possible the purchase and transfer to the new Jewish state of armaments that were otherwise unobtainable.[15]

Different methods were employed to help make up Israel's deficiency in pilots, navigators, and aircraft engineers. Jewish ex-servicemen who had fulfilled such capacities in the US Air Force offered one obvious source that soon was tapped. In this case, Haganah representatives appealed to a mixture of incentives: the emotional pull of Jewish peoplehood, a chance to experience once again the thrill of war, and—not least—hard cash. Almost two hundred American citizens responded to this heady mix, with the result that, all told, roughly 30 percent of all IDF air crews in 1948–1949 and 111 of its 303 pilots consisted of American volunteers (not all of whom were Jews).[16]

Finally, there was the American contribution to senior command. At this level, by far the most famous figure is Mickey Marcus, the Brooklyn-born colonel in the US Army who in 1947 obtained the US War Department's permission to accept Ben-Gurion's plea to help the Yishuv's fighting forces, and went on to become the very first person in the IDF to hold the rank of *aluf* (major-general), and one of its first—and certainly most senior—victims of "friendly fire."[17] Far less limelight, by contrast, has been shed on Fred Gronich, a young administrative officer in the US Army, whom Ben-Gurion recruited in 1948 to be his adviser on command and control structures. Gronich, who had served on the staff that General Albert Wedemeyer set up to plan for D-Day and who during his extended stay in Israel adopted the bland nom de guerre of "Fred Harris," performed the task to perfection. Indeed, according to his recollection, the IDF's unique early command structure, which was a curious hybrid of American and British elements, owed its origins to a sketch that Gronich had made for Ben-Gurion on the back of an envelope stretched out on the hood of a car while they were reviewing possible troop placements in the northern Negev Desert.[18]

By their nature, all such contacts were informal, and in Gronich's case kept secret from the US authorities. Officially, relationships between the US and Israeli militaries remained nonexistent. Hence, in its formative years the IDF displayed not a single characteristic that could be said to owe anything to American influence. It based its policies with respect to the conscription of reservists on models derived from Switzerland and the pre–World War II German expe-

rience; it owed its heavy emphasis on using draft terms as opportunities for patriotic indoctrination to lessons derived from the Soviet army;[19] and the principles underlying professional Israeli military conduct were in origin almost
entirely British. In the latter case especially, the spectrum was enormous. IDF
rank-and-file saluted their officers in the British style; they were governed by a
military code of justice that transcribed entire pages of the relevant British man-
uals; they used Hebraized versions of British military terms for everyday artifacts
("jerry cans," "bully beef," "mess tins"); and they prepared for air-raid attacks
based on their studies of British experiences during the Blitz.

How much—if at all—early IDF operational concepts also reflected British
teachings, and especially the strategy of "indirect approach" promulgated by
Basil Liddell Hart, is a matter of some contention. Most observers now accept
that far more influential was the impact exerted by memories of the ways in
which the Wehrmacht had performed blitzkrieg operations during World War
II.[20] What remains significant, however, is that it was to British staff colleges, at
Devizes, Camberley, and Farnborough, that the earliest cohorts of IDF senior
officers (Moshe Dayan, Yitzhak Rabin, and Ariel Sharon) were sent to advance
their military education. And from the mid-1950s, some of their successors,
such as Uzi Narkis, also attended equivalent institutions in France and (after
some understandable reluctance) in Germany. In this period, not one applied
for entry to a US military academy. This is hardly surprising, since personnel
as a rule followed matériel. During the early 1950s, the British gradually re-
laxed their earlier embargo on arms sales to Israel. Germany too became a significant source of battle platforms. Most forthcoming of all, however, were the
French, especially once Gamal Abdel Nasser began supporting the Algerian
rebels. By the eve of the Sinai campaign, France had become the IDF's principal
source of armor and aircraft, a situation that necessarily brought increasing
numbers of IDF officers into contact with French ideas of how to best use these
armaments.[21]

By contrast, Israel's relations with the United States—which had soured when
the two sides failed to reach a security pact in 1955 and were brought to a nadir
by the Suez crisis a year later—were in the military sphere simply nonexistent.[22]
Moreover, there seemed little prospect of change. As matters stood, the Americans
certainly were not prepared to sell the IDF weapons of any significance, and
neither did they seem to have much to offer in the way of ideas. Until as late as
the mid-1960s, US military theorists seemed to be obsessed with Armageddon-
like scenarios of an intercontinental ballistic nuclear exchange with the USSR.
This was of no relevance whatsoever to their Israeli contemporaries, whose
minds were focused on another round of conventional battles between the IDF
and its Arab neighbors. No wonder, therefore, that not a single American military thinker is mentioned in either of the two most influential works on Israeli

strategy written before 1967: Yigal Alon's *Masach shel Chol* ("Curtain of Sand," first edition 1960) and Yisrael Ber's *Bitachon Yisrael—Etmol, ha-Yom u-Machar* ("Israel's Security: Yesterday, Today, and Tomorrow," 1966).

From Hawk Missiles to F-16s

By the mid-1960s, the tone of the relationship had altered significantly, so much so that the United States—although still not Israel's senior military partner— was definitely becoming a major influence on Israel's military capabilities. In part, the change can be attributed to the overall shift in the US policy toward the Middle East that began during Eisenhower's second term but was given greater impetus under the aegis of Kennedy and Johnson.[23] But that overarching cause was supplemented by the more specific (albeit oblique) impact on US-Israeli military relations exerted by the completion in the early 1960s of the nuclear reactor that, with French help, Israel constructed in the greatest secrecy at Dimona.

The Dimona installation, although an obvious strategic asset from Israel's point of view, was in strictly military terms also a considerable headache. Principally, this was because it imposed on the IDF the need to ensure its total protection against hostile assault, especially from the air. A sudden hit-and-run raid by Egyptian or Jordanian planes, resulting in even one bomb explosion on or near the reactor ("a bolt from the blue," in Israeli military parlance), was the IDF General Staff's greatest nightmare, to the avoidance of which its members devoted much time and discussion throughout the late 1950s and early 1960s. After considerable hemming and hawing, just one solution seemed possible. Israel had to obtain a state-of-the-art air defense system, and more specifically a battery of surface-to-air radar-based missiles.[24] After scouring the not very large international market for such goods, the choice eventually fell on the American Hawk missile, which had entered US Army service in 1959. Ben-Gurion presented a formal application to purchase Hawks during his meeting with John F. Kennedy at the New York Waldorf Astoria Hotel on May 30, 1961.

Why the US government ultimately agreed to the Hawk sale in 1962 still remains obscure. (Did the Americans demand a quid pro quo in terms of American inspection of the nuclear facility? Was Kennedy looking to establish a new balance of strategic power in the Middle East? Or did he just want to curry favor with Jewish voters in the forthcoming midterm elections?)[25] Far less debatable are the consequences of that decision. Most obviously, it signified America's willingness to supply Israel, for the first time, with significant weapons systems. Although at this stage the inventory was limited entirely to "defensive" armaments, the Hawk sale set in motion a process that over the next two years expanded to include overtly offensive weapons, too. As Avraham Ben-Zvi's exhaustive study emphatically points out, "The process by which [post-1962] arms sales to Israel was shaped and delineated was cyclical (and occasionally dialectical) rather than linear."[26] Nevertheless, even before the Yom Kippur War, the momentum had become irreversible. In February 1966 the United States agreed to complete the sale to Israel of Patton tanks, whose supply via West Germany had been interrupted by Arab pressure; in May it announced a new agreement to provide Israel with Skyhawk jet bombers; and—after considerable delay—in October 1968 Johnson declared his agreement to supply the Israeli air force with fifty Phantom F-4 jets by the end of 1970.

Virtually unnoticed at the time, but of great long-term significance for Israel's military culture, were what might be termed the collateral personnel consequences of the Hawk sale and its successors. Since no Israeli antiaircraft unit had any experience whatsoever in operating weapons as sophisticated as the Hawk, specially selected teams of troops had to be sent out to Fort Bliss, Texas, in August 1963 to learn their trade. That soon became standard practice. As a result, successive generations of Israeli pilots, armored corps commanders, artillerymen, and engineers, many at an early stage of their careers and some while still in draft service, completed extended tours of duty in bases and training camps across the continental United States. They brought back with them not just a familiarity with US military idioms and commands ("ejection seats," "cease firing") but also a knowledge of American military culture and organization—and very often an infatuation with all things American that soon would be shared by the vast majority of their countrymen. By the 1990s, when the chief of the IDF General Staff was Ehud Barak, who had received a master's degree from Stanford University, this atmosphere would greatly facilitate the import into the IDF of the American organizational fad of total quality management. [27]

Channels of Person-to-Person Influence, 1970–2010

Other expressions of the American "soft-power" contribution to Israeli military likewise deserve to be considered extensions of the foundations thus laid in the mid-1960s. In some instances, the process was stimulated by a one-off demonstration of American munificence, itself stimulated by the need to fulfill a specific contractual undertaking. Such was the case, most obviously, with respect to the Ovda and Ramon air bases constructed in the Negev by the US Army Corps of Engineers in the early 1980s to replace those the IDF relinquished in the Sinai under the terms of the 1978 Camp David Accords. Certainly the construction itself generated several moments of tension (especially when the US

Army engineers refused to allow the Histadrut to monitor the employment conditions of the Portuguese laborers imported to the Negev under American contracts).[28] At the military level, however, the experience created numerous opportunities for extended person-to-person contacts that could not otherwise have been sustained, and hence facilitated a process of mutual understanding.

Not incidentally, the project also set a new bar for other IDF facilities. Henceforth, it became standard practice to ensure that all IDF bases in the Negev (such as the older artillery training grounds at Shivta, the new noncommissioned officers' base, Bislach, outside Yerucham, and the armored school at Tzukei Ovda near Eilat) would be built to the criteria of comparative luxury that the Americans had introduced at Ovda and Ramon. Gone, then, were the days of the old British Nissen huts, which still disfigured many Israeli installations as late as the 1970s. Henceforth, even raw recruits could expect to be housed in air-conditioned buildings, custom built to suit the local climate.

Other channels of person-to-person military contact proved to be more persistent. In the late 1960s the IDF abandoned its earlier traditions of dispatching its senior personnel exclusively to either Britain or France for advanced officer training. Instead, American institutions became the destination of first choice. No precise figures are available, but it would appear that over the past four decades several scores of Israeli military personnel have attended either the US Army War College at Carlisle, Pennsylvania, the US Air Force Academy at Colorado Springs, or the US Army Combined Arms Center at Fort Leavenworth, Kansas. Smaller numbers have also intermittently participated in programs at the National Defense University, at the Johns Hopkins School for Advanced International Studies, and at the John F. Kennedy School of Government at Harvard.[29]

Initially, the IDF seemed to regard these postings more as a reward for past service than as a foundation for future development. Indeed, until as recently as the late 1980s, most of the recipients of these "benefits" were in the twilight of their military careers.[30] Perhaps for that reason, the procedures of recommendation, selection, and placement seem on the Israeli side to have been haphazard, with the buddy system (*proteksia*) counting for more than academic criteria. Consequently, officers frequently arrived at their destinations without the requisite language skills or a clear idea of what their forthcoming curriculum might entail.[31] A report published by the Israel State Comptroller in 2001 revealed that not until the mid-1990s did the IDF establish an umbrella unit responsible for integrating all of Israel's international military contacts, including those that dealt with attendance at overseas military establishments, and not until five years later was the framework thus established made robust enough to withstand the pressure of bureaucratic turf wars.[32] Personnel attached to the staff of this body are convinced that the new unit has not only helped improve the quality of the senior IDF officers who are now dispatched to American destinations but, more substantially, it has also sensitized them to an international exchange of ideas. The graduates return with a sense of belonging to an international security community, a fraternity of professionals who share a common language and mode of thought.[33]

Successive memoranda of understanding have formalized the ties between the US and Israeli security establishments. The earliest such agreement was signed soon after the 1973 war, laying the basis for regular exchanges of information between the Research and Development Office in the Israel Ministry of Defense and the Directorate of Defense Research and Engineering in the US Department of Defense.[34] Subsequent frameworks included the Joint Political-Military Group, established in 1983 and officially designated "the forum in which the two states discuss and implement . . . joint cooperative efforts such as combined planning, joint exercises and logistics"; the Joint Security Assistance Planning Group (established in 1988), "the forum in which the two states review Israel's requests for security assistance in the light of current threat assessments and US budgetary capabilities"; and the Strategic Dialogue group, established in 2001, which brings together senior military teams from both sides on a biannual basis.[35] And all this is in addition to innumerable one-on-one meetings and conversations that in recent years have become almost commonplace, not least at the very highest levels. In June 2010 it was reported that Lieutenant General Gabi Ashkenazi, then chief of the IDF General Staff, and Admiral Michael Mullen, then chair of the US Joint Chiefs of Staff, "speak on a secure line connecting their respective offices every week, and meet somewhere in the world every several months."[36]

The Flow of Ideas, 1970–2010

Most contacts between Israeli and US military personnel doubtless focus on rather humdrum matters: exchanging technical know-how, sharing intelligence data, and—most time-consuming of all—scheduling routine visits to each other's relevant units and command centers. Over the long haul, nevertheless, a more profound process of mutual learning has also taken place, with the two sides engaging in dialogues about the challenges presented by changes in the military's technological, organizational, and social environments. Typically those dialogues, oral and written, take the form of practical inquiry, with each side seeking to benefit from the other's experience, principally by analyzing specific instances of its recent battlefield performance.

Given the shared nature of their intellectual objectives, it might have been expected that the US and Israeli militaries would adopt broadly similar analytical approaches. Observation suggests, however, that such has not been the case, though certainly some overlap can be discerned. More striking, however, is the evidence indicating that, on balance, the two sides have exhibited contradictory preferences with respect to both the *modes* and principal *topics* of inquiry.

First, with respect to modes of inquiry: at the risk of generalization, it can be said that, by and large, the Americans have preferred what might be termed "firsthand observation." Necessarily, many of their official and quasi-official reports on Israeli military performance lean heavily on secondary sources. However, as recent American studies of IDF performances in the Second Lebanon War (2006) and Operation Cast Lead (2008) show, the authors clearly attempted to visit the region and gain their own sense of what had transpired, principally by interviewing as many Israeli officers and defense officials as possible.[37] Other studies have been even more assiduous in this respect. Indeed US sources—and especially military agencies—have dispatched their own teams of after-action analysts not solely to speak to IDF commanders, but also to inspect Israeli battlefields and thus collect raw data of their own.

This methodology was first employed immediately after the 1967 war, resulting in one classified study by the Joint Technical Coordinating Group for Munitions Effectiveness, established by the Joint Chiefs of Staff in 1963, and another titled "Comparative Analysis of Armored Conflict Experience" by the Historical Evaluation and Research Organization, under contract to the US Army.[38] Each succeeding round of Arab-Israeli conflict generated similar interest. Thus, immediately after the 1973 war, an American team of armored warfare experts, led by General Donn Starry and chaperoned by senior IDF officers, toured the battlefields of Sinai and the Golan, bringing back data that were also carefully perused by General William DePuy, the first commander of the US Army's Training and Doctrine Command (TRADOC).[39] Visiting Lebanon soon after the Israeli-Syrian air battles of 1982, US Secretary of Defense Caspar Weinberger asked to inspect the utility of Israeli unmanned aerial vehicles (UAVs)— whereupon he was shown an IDF video recording of his stopover with US forces in Beirut the previous day.[40]

But most sustained of all has been US military interest in studying firsthand how the IDF has coped with the phenomenon of low-intensity warfare, particularly during the first and second Intifadas. Long before US forces began to confront similar situations in Iraq and Afghanistan, senior US officers visited Israel—sometimes clandestinely—to observe counterinsurgency operations. (An outstanding example was Lieutenant General William Boykin, the legendary and controversial commander of Delta Force. His autobiography, which does not once record him visiting Israel, contains a photograph whose caption reads, "On operations in Israel, 1987. We wore Israeli army uniforms to reduce the appearance of an American military presence.")[41] Understandably, such visits became more frequent and less covert after 9/11, when American officials at the highest levels of government acknowledged that the strategic challenges facing the United States were akin to those with which Israel has had to wrestle for decades.[42] Indeed, once the invasions of Afghanistan (2001) and Iraq (2003) got under way, the presence of US military units at Israeli training facilities became almost routine. Thus, in 2007 it was announced that US Marines and soldiers were about to train on a regular basis at "Baladia City," a mock-up of a typical Arab township built in 2005 by IDF engineers in the Negev.[43]

For the most part, the procedures the IDF adopted to learn from American military experiences have been very different. Few Israeli officers have ever visited (or been allowed to visit?) an ongoing or recent American battlefield site. One of the exceptions—typically—was Moshe Dayan, who for a week in August 1966 (almost eight years after he retired as chief of the IDF General Staff) accompanied units of the First Air Cavalry Division on jungle patrols in Vietnam.[44] Otherwise the IDF has acquired most of its information on US military performances secondhand, via the written word. This tradition stretches back into the 1950s, and its development can be traced with a fair degree of precision by an analysis of IDF publications. *Maʾarchot,* the premiere IDF journal, founded as a Haganah bulletin as early as 1939, had always printed translations of foreign material, and in 1953 began issuing an independent bimonthly supplement, titled *Tziklon,* for that purpose. Articles that had originally appeared in US military journals (*Combat Forces Journal, Armor, Infantry School Quarterly,* the *Military Review*) were regularly featured, providing historical analyses of US military actions in both World War II and Korea and reports on recent weapons developments.

Tziklon ceased publication in the early 1960s (after 113 issues), but the tradition that it had sustained did not die out. Translations of foreign materials, including those that originated in the United States, continued to appear in a new publication under the same title (thirteen issues between August 1976 and May 1985); in a substitute, titled *Tatzpit* (eight issues, 1984–1992); and thereafter in *Maʾarchot* itself. A statistical survey of the articles published in *Maʾarchot* between February 1993 (issue no. 328) and June 2010 (issue no. 431) reveals that just over 15 percent consist of translations from foreign journals, most of which are American—the spectrum now includes *Parameters, Armed Forces Quarterly,* and *Foreign Affairs.* An additional 12 percent, although written by Israeli authors, focus specifically on analyzing either US military operations (especially the two Iraq campaigns, Kosovo, and Afghanistan) or on strategic concepts of American origin ("revolution in military affairs" or RMA, "jointness," and "swarming"). In both areas, then, the United States had clearly replaced Europe as the source of most IDF military thought.

A comparative study of the most widely read American military journals suggests that the intellectual exchange was, in this respect, virtually a one-way street. Notwithstanding the intensity of publicity given to Israeli feats of arms in the American professional and lay literature, in its entire history *Military Review* has published only eleven articles of specific relevance to the IDF, two of which were criticized by readers for being riddled with inaccuracies.[45] But even that record is better than that of *Armed Forces Quarterly*, which has printed just three articles on the IDF, and of *Parameters*, which has printed only two. If the search is restricted to Israeli authors, the results are even more pronounced: just one in each case.[46]

No less significant than the discrepancies in the methodologies employed by the Israeli and US militaries to learn from each other's experiences is the asymmetry in the nature of the topics in which they seem to be interested. Here, too, some overlap can be discerned. Nevertheless, the differences of emphasis are unmistakable. For the most part, American students of Israeli battlefield performance have focused on specific applications of force, usually at the tactical level—which is where the IDF was widely considered to excel before 1973 and where it occasionally scored successes during the two Intifadas. They did not look to the Israeli experience to provide inspiration for doctrinal innovations or novel strategic concepts—understandably, since in this area the IDF record has always been considered to be far less distinguished.[47] In this respect, even US military reactions to the 1973 war were typical. Recent research conclusively buries the myth that Generals William DePuy and Donn Starry, TRADOC's first two commanders, conceived their notions of "active defense" and the "air-land battle" in a sudden flash of inspiration on the Golan Heights. On the contrary, "many of the concepts that make up DePuy's doctrine were developed, conceived, and articulated prior to the Yom Kippur War." The contribution of the Israeli experience was far more mundane. It provided DePuy with a means of "gaining leverage in negotiating Army budgets and convincing the infantry generals (in the field commands and TRADOC) of the need to change training methods and increase the role of armor."[48]

A similar perspective dominates US secondhand analyses, as articulated in written materials. Thus, analyses of the "war on terrorism," in *Joint Forces Quarterly* (JFQ) for instance, highlight the IDF's revolutionary use of UAVs and its resort to targeted killings, but other than in an article by the only Israeli author among the journal's contributors, *JFQ* says very little about the strategic philosophy that might underlie Israel's approach to counterinsurgency operations.[49] Even when examples drawn from the Israeli experience do figure prominently in professional American studies of such subjects as close air support, no attempt is made (or perhaps thought necessary) to ask whether Israeli commanders might have developed a doctrine of strategic weight in these areas.[50] Invariably, references to the IDF are noticeable by their almost total absence from broad overviews aimed at distilling for possible American use general principles regarding military organization and contemporary applications of force from the writings of overseas practitioners and observers.[51] The only exception—one so highly controversial that it surely proves the rule—is the notion of "operational shock," a Soviet military concept that was developed and adapted during the late 1990s by retired Brigadier General Shimon Naveh, a highly talented IDF infantry commander who in 1994 received a doctorate in military thought from King's College, London. Initially Naveh's views were praised as insights of genius by some American observers. But although he continued to be engaged as a part-time consultant at the US Army's School of Advanced Military Studies at Fort Leavenworth, later comments, especially after the IDF's poor performance in the 2006 Lebanon war, have been less complimentary.[52]

In recent years especially, the predominant IDF approach to the American experience has been very different. Necessarily, as has been the case ever since the 1950s, there continues to be great interest in tactical-level issues—of which the most prominent are the technological attributes of new means of transport and firepower, and in the ways in which American commanders have deployed, supplied, and utilized the individual weapons and units at their disposal.[53] However, whereas for many decades inquiry virtually stopped there, such is no longer the case. The available evidence suggests that in addition, Israeli analysts now also seek to probe the doctrinal and theoretical implications of recent US military performance, and in so doing to pose questions that focus on the operational and strategic levels.

This development seems to have been first prompted by Operation Desert Storm in 1991, which resulted in a victory whose impact on Israeli military thinking was still being recalled over a decade later.[54] Analyses of the roots of the stunning US attainments in that campaign became a staple item of Israeli military literature and were then followed by further reports on US performances in Kosovo, Operation Iraqi Freedom, and the war in Afghanistan. As in the past, much of the information was transmitted via translations of American materials. In some instances the translations encompassed entire books, such as Thomas Keaney and Eliot Cohen's *Revolution in Warfare? Air Power in the Persian Gulf* (Hebrew version by Ma'archot publishing house, 2000), or Sean Naylor's analysis of Operation Anaconda in Afghanistan (*Not a Good Day to Die*) and Douglas Macgregor's *Transformation Under Fire,* both of which were published in full in Hebrew under the imprint of the IDF Staff College in 2007. More often, the efforts were relatively modest, consisting of synopses and/or shorter articles on major themes of current interest. One example is Eliot Cohen's introductions to the transformations envisaged in warfare as a consequence of changes in computer-driven communications, popularly known as the revolution in military affairs (RMA). Another is David Fatuna's studies of "jointness," the expression coined by the US armed forces to describe cross-service cooperation in all stages of the military process, from research through procurement and into operations.[55]

Just as prominent, and far more interesting, were specifically Israeli interpretations of these concepts. These were often accompanied by discussions of the ways in which their applications could be—indeed, in some views, had to be—assimilated by the IDF. At issue, then, were not merely the possible merits and uses of particular items of current American ordnance. Rather, the scope was much broader and extended to surveys of the lessons that the American experience held for reorganizing the IDF and the revisions of its fighting doctrines. Did the RMA now make it possible for the IDF to adopt a less labor-intensive approach to the battlefield, and hence to forgo at least some of its traditional reliance on reservists? Did the new balance between air and ground forces supposedly demonstrated to such effect in the Balkans require the IDF to consider the Israeli air force (renamed the Israel Air and Space Force in 2003) as its principal strategic arm, and not as primarily an ancillary to infantry and armor? Did the vision of "jointness" and "network-centric warfare," as taught in US military academies, mandate a new Israeli philosophy with respect to the location of combat commanders, who could perhaps better "manage" the battle from the rear rather than, as had been traditional, from the front?[56] Did not "swarming," as first preached by John Arquilla and David Ronfeldt in a 1997 RAND Corporation book-length study titled "In Athena's Camp: Preparing for Conflict in the Information Age," prescribe a reorganization of IDF forces?[57]

Even without being privy to discussions in the General Staff, it is clear that opinions on such issues within Israel's military elite had by the first decade of the new millennium become deeply divided. Hints of these disputes can be discerned in occasional reports of IDF planning branches published by Israel's state comptroller.[58] Far less oblique is the evidence contained in military-related publications. Transparently seeking to ensure that their opinions received a proper hearing, senior representatives of rival camps clearly felt no compunction about airing their views in such forums. *Ma'archot* was one major platform. Others consisted of presentations to academic symposia, contributions to edited volumes on trends in military thought, and—albeit less frequently—book-length studies.[59]

Too Much of a Good Thing?

Ultimately the IDF's poor performance in the Second Lebanon War of 2006 brought these debates to an abrupt halt. Sometime during the previous decade, it was thereafter generally agreed, Israeli military thought had taken a wrong turn and now had to get back to basics. As is always the case with retrospective investigations into the parentage of failures, fingers were pointed in numerous directions. The Winograd Commission, for instance, spread blame widely, citing false economics (reductions in reserve training), mismanaged organizational reform (which resulted in a top-heavy command structure), a misplaced trust in air power, and perhaps above all, a tendency on the part of field commanders to frame their orders in accordance with the intricate jargon associated with the American notion of "effects-based operations" rather than in plain speech intelligible to their subordinates.[60] Other critics were even more specific, explicitly attributing the IDF's hesitation to undertake ground operations during the early stages of the 2006 war to the ways in which the chief of staff, Major General Dan Halutz (not incidentally a former commanding officer of the Israeli air force), had misinterpreted the attainments of US air power in the Kosovo campaign.[61]

Perhaps, however, the root causes went even deeper. Several decades of intimate contact with US military forces, commanders, weapons, and thinking might, in the most profound of ways, have subverted the IDF's independence of thought. Although still capable of displaying tactical ingenuity, at the strategic and doctrinal levels members of Israel's security elite seem to have become overwhelmed by the American mind-set. American military concepts, even those discredited in the United States (such as "effects-based operations"),[62] were imbibed with an innocence once reserved for biblical truths. Likewise, American operations were often analyzed with uncritical acclaim. Perhaps because they lacked any firm theoretical grounding in the fundamentals of strategic thought, Israeli commanders became intoxicated with faddish American terminology.[63] Consequently, they seem not to have considered the possibility that—as one analyst very belatedly pointed out—the "American way of war," if at all viable, might be appropriate only to the armed forces of the United States.[64] This failing still persists. When in 2008 the Israeli government decided to draw up a plan for reorganizing the IDF and Ministry of Defense, the tender was awarded to a firm of American consultants.[65]

Given such developments, there are reasons for wondering whether the almost umbilical bonds that tie the IDF to US military sources perhaps have become too tight. Quite apart from making Israel dangerously dependent on supplies of American military hardware, the alliance might also have stifled independent Israeli military thought. In the long term, the latter threat may be no less insidious than the former. For several years now Israeli strategic planners have recognized the need to attain as large a degree of self-reliance as possible in the realm of weapons systems—most notably, since 1991, by developing autonomous satellite capabilities. Perhaps the time has come for the same incentive to motivate an effort to wean the IDF away from dependence on the "soft power" and intellectual dimension of the relationship.

Notes

1. Karen L. Puschel, *US-Israel Strategic Cooperation in the Post-Cold War Era* (Boulder, CO: Westview, 1992), pp. 88–89.

2. For a personal account, see an interview with the commanding officer of one such battalion in "Operational Leadership Experiences," Combat Studies Institute, Fort Leavenworth, Kansas, 2008, http://cgsc.cdmhost.com/cdm4/browse.php?CISOROOT=/p4013coll13&CISOSTART=1,221.

3. Andrew J. Shapiro (assistant secretary, US State Department), "The Obama Administration's Approach to U.S.-Israel Security Cooperation: Preserving Israel's Qualitative Military Edge," remarks at Brookings Saban Center for Middle East Policy, Washington, D.C., July 16, 2010, www.state.gov/t/pm/rls/rm/144753.htm.

4. Section 201 of the law virtually guaranteed the IDF's regional hegemony by mandating that all presidents take measures to ensure that "the sale or export of [the] defense articles or defense services will not adversely affect Israel's qualitative military edge over military threats to Israel."

5. Shapiro, "The Obama Administration's Approach."

6. Jeremy M. Sharp, "US Foreign Aid to Israel," CRS Report for Congress, no. RL 33222, Washington, D.C., December 2009.

7. Shapiro, "The Obama Administration's Approach."

8. Puschel, *US-Israel Strategic Cooperation,* pp. 18–20.

9. For example, Steven L. Spiegel, "US Relations with Israel: The Military Benefits," *Orbis* 30 (Fall 1986): 475–497. Gil Ehrenkrantz, "How the United States Has Benefited from Its Alliance with Israel," *MERIA Journal,* June 2010, www.gloria-center.org/meria/2010/06/ehrenkranz.html#_ednref1.

10. In addition to the Yom Kippur War, the major "arms + cash" milestones are generally recognized to be the special aid packages of 1979; the memorandum of understanding of 1984; the designation of Israel as a "major non-NATO ally" in 1998; the supplementary aid bill of 2003; and the ten-year military aid

agreement signed by President George W. Bush in 2007. Eytan Gilboa and Efraim Inbar, eds., *US-Israeli Relations in a New Era* (London: Routledge, 2009).

11. Michael B. Oren, "Orde Wingate: Friend Under Fire," *Azure* 10 (2000): 39.

12. It has been calculated that some 30,000 males volunteered to enlist in the Jewish Brigade. Yoav Gelber, *Between the British, Germans and Arabs* (in Hebrew), Vol. 4 of "The History of Volunteering" (Jerusalem: Yad Yitzchak Ben-Zvi, 1984), pp. 299–303. So too did almost 4,000 women. Anat Granit-Hakohen, "Hebrew Woman to the Flag! The Service of Female Members of the Yishuv in the British Forces During World War II" (in Hebrew; Jerusalem: Yad Ben-Zvi, 2011).

13. Eliot Cohen, *Supreme Command* (New York: Anchor Books, 2002), pp. 147–152.

14. Shlomo Slonim, "The 1948 Embargo on Arms to Palestine," *Political Science Quarterly* 94, no. 3 (Fall 1979): 495–514.

15. Charles Behrend Sonneborn, "Catalyst for Israel: A Biography of Rudolf Sonneborn" (unpublished manuscript, 2002), Leo Baeck Archives, New York, http://digital.cjh.org/R/?func=dbin-jump-full&object_id=560046&local_base=GEN01.

16. Avi Cohen, *History of the Air Force in the War of Independence* (in Hebrew; Tel Aviv: Ministry of Defense Publications, 2004), vol. 3, pp. 729–747. For US contributions to other branches of service, Jeffrey and Craig Weiss, *I Am My Brother's Keeper: American Volunteers in Israel's War of Independence, 1947–1949* (Angleton, PA: Schiffer, 1998).

17. As "Mickey Stone," Marcus assumed responsibility for keeping open the road between Tel Aviv and Jerusalem (a task to which Ben-Gurion attached supreme importance). See Benny Morris, *1948: A History of the First Arab-Israeli War* (New Haven, CT: Yale University Press, 2008), pp. 227–229.

18. Interview with Gronich, 2001. Israel has never granted Gronich adequate recognition. Indeed, he was suspected by some of the Yishuv old guard of being an American spy and in 1949

virtually hounded out of the country. He returned to the United States, retired from military service, and went into the movie business. In the 1990s he permanently set up home in Israel, where he died at age eighty-seven in 2003.

19. Yitzchak Greenberg, *The Israeli Reserves Army: Laying Down the Foundations, 1949–1950* (in Hebrew; Sdeh Boker: Ben-Gurion Research Center, 2001).

20. Liddell Hart did much to promulgate the myth of his own influence, especially after the Six-Day War, when IDF victories seemed to vindicate his ideas. For a more skeptical view, which argues that few Israeli generals ever bothered to read a page written by Liddell Hart (or anyone else, for that matter), see Tuviah Ben-Mosheh, "Liddell Hart and the IDF—A Reappraisal," *Journal of Contemporary History* 16 (1981): 369–391.

21. Yitzchak Steigman, *From the War of Independence to Kadesh: The IAF, 1949–1956* (in Hebrew; Tel Aviv: Ministry of Defense Publications, 1990), pp. 132–144. In general, Edward Luttwak and Dan Horowitz, *The Israeli Army* (London: Allen Lane, 1976), p. 93.

22. Robert Schulzinger, "The Impact of Suez on US Middle Eastern Policy," in *The Suez-Sinai Crisis, 1956*, ed. Selwyn Troen and Moshe Shemesh (New York: Columbia University Press, 1990), pp. 251–265.

23. Avraham Ben-Zvi, *Decade of Transition: Eisenhower, Kennedy, and the Origins of the American-Israeli Alliance* (New York: Columbia University Press, 1998).

24. Ezer Weizmann, *On Eagles' Wings* (in Hebrew; Tel Aviv: Maariv, 1975), pp. 226–229.

25. Compare Ben-Zvi, *Decade of Transition,* with Avner Cohen, *Israel and the Bomb* (New York: Columbia University Press, 1998), p. 111.

26. Avraham Ben-Zvi, *Lyndon B. Johnson and the Politics of Arms Sales to Israel: In the Shadow of the Hawk* (London: Cass, 2004), p. 3.

27. Stuart A. Cohen, "Restructuring the Militia Framework of the IDF," *Journal of Strategic Studies* 18 (December 1995): 78–93; Isaac Gur-Ze'ev, "Total Quality Management and Power/Knowledge Dialectics in the Israeli Army," *Journal of Thought* 32 (1997): 9–36.

28. John Wall, "Managing Construction of Israeli Air Bases in Negev," *Journal of Management in Engineering* 1 (1985): 233–243; and Frank Schubert, *Building Air Bases in the Negev: The U.S. Army Corps of Engineers in Israel, 1979–1982* (Washington, DC: Office of History, US Army, 1992).

29. The IDF does not release data on the number of personnel dispatched overseas, and may not keep consolidated records. The *Historical Facts Book* issued by the US Department of Defense (latest edition 2009) is only slightly more informative. It lists (p. 134) eighty Israeli officers who have been registered as students in the United States under the International Military Education and Training Program since FY 1950. But there are obviously other sources of funding, about which I have not been able to obtain information.

30. Interview with Colonel Yossi Hochbaum, Doctrine and Instruction Division in the Operations Branch, IDF, April 2010.

31. Interview with Colonel Leonard Wong, US Army War College, Carlisle, Pennsylvania, January 2010.

32. Israel State Comptroller, *Annual Report no. 52a* (in Hebrew; Jerusalem: Government Printing Office, 2001), pp. 90–91.

33. On this concept, see Emanuel Adler and Michael Barnett, "A Framework for the Study of Security Communities," in *Security Communities,* ed. Emanuel Adler and Michael Barnett (Cambridge: Cambridge University Press, 1998), pp. 29–65.

34. The origins of this agreement, and the snags that hindered its initial implementation, are sketched in a frank autobiography by one of its principal Israeli architects, retired General Uzi Eilam, *Keshet Eilam* ("Eilam's Arc"; Tel Aviv: Miskal, 2009), pp. 213–236.

35. David Ivry, "United in Vision, Strategic Partnership & Friendship," in *Peace—Dream or Vision: A Decade Since the Assassination of Prime Minister Yitzhak Rabin,* ed. Aviva Palter (Netanya: S. Avraham Center for Strategic Dialogue, 2007), pp. 130–134.

36. Anshel Pfeffer, "Mullen to Make Unplanned Stop in Israel After Afghanistan Visit,"

Ha'aretz, June 26, 2010. The first chair of the Joint Chiefs to visit Israel was General John Vessey Jr., in January 1984.

37. For example, Stephen D. Biddle and Jeffrey A. Friedman, *The 2006 Lebanon Campaign and the Future of Warfare: Implications for Army and Defense Policy* (Carlisle, PA: SSI Publications, US Army War College, 2008); two publications compiled for the RAND National Defense Research Institute by David E. Johnson, *Preparing and Training for the Full Spectrum of Military Challenges* (2009) and *Military Capabilities for Hybrid War: Insights from the Israel Defense Forces in Lebanon and Gaza* (2010); and Lieutenant Colonel Scott C. Farquhar, ed., *Back to Basics: A Study of the 2nd Lebanon War and Operation CAST LEAD* (Fort Leavenworth, KS: US Army Combined Arms Center, 2009).

38. Personal communication, Professor Kenneth M. Pollack, who cites both works in his *Arabs at War: Military Effectiveness, 1948–1991* (Lincoln: University of Nebraska Press, 2002), pp. 628–629.

39. Eilam, *Keshet Eilam*; James Kitfield, *Prodigal Soldiers* (New York: Simon & Schuster, 1995), p. 153. The war also produced a further crop of Historical Evaluation and Research Organization studies, for example, "Artillery Survivability in Modern War" (1976), listed at www.dupuyinstitute.org/tdipub1hero.htm.

40. Dore Gold, *Israel as an American Non-NATO Ally* (Tel Aviv: Jaffee Center, 1992), p. 33.

41. William G. Boykin, *Never Surrender* (New York: Faith Words, 2008), photo inserts.

42. Four days after 9/11, in a principals' meeting at Camp David, George Tenet, then head of the CIA, concluded that "our situation is more like that of the Israelis." Bob Woodward, *Bush at War* (New York: Simon & Schuster, 2002), p. 89.

43. See www.marinecorpstimes.com/news /2007/06/marine_israel_combattraining_ 070624.

For an IDF report of the use made by the marines of the facility, see *Bayabasha* (journal of IDF Ground Forces Command), no. 6 (June 2008), http://mazi.idf.il/5221–6401-HE/IGF.aspx.

44. Dayan had gone to Vietnam as a temporary war correspondent for the Israeli daily *Ma'ariv*. He later collated his reports in the book *Vietnam Diary* (in Hebrew; Tel Aviv: Dvir, 1977).

45. See, respectively, Major Richard Gabriel, "The IDF in Lebanon," *Military Review* (April 1985): 77–79, and *Military Review* (April 2003): 95, for a multiauthor article on the integration of women into IDF combat units.

46. Lieutenant Colonel (ret.) David Eshel, "Counter Attack in the Sinai. 8 October 1973," *Military Review* (November 1993): 55–66; Major General (ret.) Jacob Amidror, "Israel's Strategy for Fighting Terror," *Armed Forces Quarterly* (Autumn 2002): 117–123; and Martin Van Creveld, "Why Israel Doesn't Send Women into Combat," *Parameters* (Spring 1993): 5–9. Also relevant is Brigadier General Ben-Zion Farhi (Military Advocate General, IDF), "Current Legal Trends in the Areas Administered by Israel," *Military Law Review* (Summer 1986): 47–60.

47. Interview with US military analyst, January 2010. For a critique of the anti-intellectualism characteristic of IDF officers, see Martin Van Creveld, *The Sword and the Olive: A Critical History of the IDF* (New York: PublicAffairs, 1998), pp. 314–317; and Stuart A. Cohen, *Israel and Its Army: From Cohesion to Confusion* (London: Routledge, 2009), pp. 101–104.

48. Saul Bronfeld, "Fighting Outnumbered: The Impact of the Yom Kippur War on the U.S. Army," *Journal of Military History* (April 2007): 465–498. On the post-Vietnam innovations instigated by DePuy and Starry, see John L. Romjue, *From Active Defense to AirLand Battle: The Development of Army Doctrine, 1973–1982* (Fort Monroe, VA: TRADOC, 1984).

49. Compare Ralph Sanders, "UAVs: An Israeli Military Innovation," *Joint Forces Quarterly* (Winter 2002–2003): 114–118, and Peter M. Cullen, "The Role of Targeted Killing in the Campaign Against Terror," *Joint Forces Quarterly* (January 2008): 22–29 with Amidror, "Israel's Strategy for Fighting Terror."

50. See, for example, Breton Greenhous, "The Israeli Experience," in Benjamin Cooling, *Case Studies in the Development of Close Air Support* (Washington, DC: US Air Force, 1990), pp. 491–534.

51. *JFQ* has devoted several entire issues to topics of broad strategic relevance, such as "force transformation," "asymmetric warfare," and "lawfare." Each analysis draws on the experience of numerous militaries—to the almost total exclusion of the IDF. Sean J. A. Edwards, *Mars Unmasked: The Changing Face of Urban Operations* (Santa Monica: RAND, 2000), deletes from its list of relevant case studies the IDF experience in Beirut (1982), which had figures in its predecessor: R. D. McLaurin, et al., *Modern Experience in City Combat* (Westport, CT: Praeger, 1987).

52. Compare Lieutenant Colonel (ret.) Timothy Challens, "Emerging Doctrine and the Ethics of Warfare," paper presented at the 2006 International Military Ethics Symposium, Springfield, Virginia, www.usafa.af.mil/jscope /JSCOPE06/Challans06.html, and Robert J. Molinari, "Winning the Minds in 'Hearts and Minds'; A Systems Approach to Information Operations as Part of Counterinsurgency Warfare," School of Advanced Military Studies Monographs, US Army Command and General Staff College, Fort Leavenworth, 2006, http:// cgsc.cdmhost.com/cdm4/item_viewer.php?CIS OROOT=/p4013coll3&CISOPTR=353, with Milan N. Vego, "A Case Against Systemic Operational Design," *Joint Forces Quarterly* (April 2009): 69–78, and Justin Kelly and Michael Brennan, *Alien: How Operational Art Devoured Strategy* (Carlisle, PA: SSI Publications, US Army War College, 2009), www.strategicstudies institute.army.mil/pubs/display.cfm?PubID= 939.

53. Thus, the most important military lesson that Dayan derived from his Vietnam experience was the potential inherent in the helicopter, as both gunship and transport. *Vietnam Diary*, pp. 64–85. Avi Kober, too, found that until 2000, "the leading strategic dimension in [Ma'archot] articles was technological." Avi Kober, "The Intellectual and Modern Focus in Israeli Military Thinking as Reflected in Ma'arachot Articles, 1948–2000," *Armed Forces & Society* 30 (2003): 155.

54. Comments to this effect by Colonel Aviad Sela (commanding officer of USA Department in the Division of Strategic Planning in IDF Planning Branch), "The USA Influence on the IDF's Qualitative Edge" (in Hebrew), *Ma'archot* 383 (May 2002): 42–49.

55. See, respectively, *Ma'archot* nos. 305 (1998) and 408 (2006).

56. Amnon Barzilai, a particularly well-informed correspondent, reported on the turbulence generated by such queries in IDF thinking, in *Ha'aretz*, May 6, 2003, p. B1.

57. The notions in this work were relayed to an Israeli audience in Hayim Assa and Yedidyah Ya'ari, *Lohamah Mevuzeret* ("Diffused Warfare: War in the 21st Century") (Tel Aviv: Maskil, 2005). Baldly summarized, "swarming" advocates exploiting modern command and communications abilities to attack the enemy by means of a series of coordinated military strikes launched in phases ("pulses") from numerous directions by small and dispersed units that are linked in a single communications network.

58. For example, Report no. 51a (2001) on the doctrine and training division in the General Staff, pp. 109–147.

59. For evidence in *Ma'archot*, see issue nos. 352 and 354 (both 1997) and 371 (2000) on the RMA; 340 (April 2005) and 371 (July 2000) on air power; 352–353 (August 1997) on the operational level of strategy; 374–375 (February 2001) and 404 (July 2005) on US performances in Iraq; 365 (August 1999) and 368 (December 1999) on Kosovo; 378–379 (September 2001) and 401 (June 2005) on jointness. See also, for example, General Yitzchak Ben-Yisrael, "The RMA in the Iraq War," in *After the Iraq War*, ed. S. Feldman (in Hebrew; Tel Aviv: Ministry of Defense, 2004), pp. 69–89; Brigadier General (ret.) Shimon Naveh, "Asymmetric Conflicts: An Operational Critique of Hegemonic Strategies," in *The Limited Conflict*, ed. H. Golan and S. Shay (in Hebrew; Tel Aviv: Ma'arachot, 2004), pp. 101–145; Assa and Ya'ari, *Lohamah Mevuzeret*; Shlomo Nir, *Man to Man* (in Hebrew; Tel Aviv: Misgav, 2004).

60. Winograd Commission, *Final Report*, January 2008, pp. 393–413 and 545–576, www .vaadatwino.co.il/reports.html#null. "Effects-based operations" had originally emerged in US military circles during the 1991 Gulf War. It was based on the hypothesis that the objectives of

war could be achieved by disrupting the enemy's command structure and forces, and not necessarily by destroying assets and infrastructure. Victory would result from the creation of "effects" that caused disorientation and paralysis. These notions were transmitted to senior Israeli military circles by means of the Operational Theory Research Institute, which was founded as an IDF think tank in 2001 under the command of Brigadier General Shimon Naveh. On the controversies generated by this body, and by Naveh himself, see Cohen, *Israel and Its Army,* pp. 104–105.

61. Captain "Victor" (IDF Intelligence), "How the IDF Became Enthralled with Fire and Neglected Maneuver" (in Hebrew), *Ma'archot* 415 (November 2007): 4–7; and Colonel Itai Brun (commanding officer, Dado Center for Interdisciplinary Military Thought), "What Happened to Maneuver?" (in Hebrew), *Ma'archot* 420–421 (September 2008): 13–16.

62. James N. Mattis, "USJFCOM Commander's Guidance for Effects-Based Operations," *Parameters* (Autumn 2008): 18–25.

63. Avi Kober, "The IDF in the 2nd Lebanon War: Why the Poor Performance?" *Journal of Strategic Studies* 31 (2008): 3–40.

64. Ron Tira (former senior officer in the IAF's special operations and intelligence wings), *The Limitations of Standoff Firepower-Based Operations,* INSS Memorandum no. 89, Tel Aviv, 2007, pp. 66–67; *The Struggle over the Nature of War,* INSS Memorandum no. 96, 2008, pp. 121–124.

65. McKinsey & Company, "Harvest Time" Program, presented November 25, 2009, http://dover.idf.il/IDF/English/News/today/09/11/25 02.htm.

In fairness, however, it should be noted that the same company had earlier undertaken a similar project for the UK armed forces.

8

Apocalypse Now?

THE IRANIAN NUCLEAR THREAT AGAINST ISRAEL

Steven R. David

ALONE AMONG THE COUNTRIES OF THE WORLD, Israel's very existence is openly challenged. Leaders of countries, groups, and international organizations periodically call for its destruction. Some of these calls represent "soft" threats in that they do not seek Israel's physical annihilation. Proposals to make Israel a binational state "for all its citizens" or to simply allow a non-Jewish majority to emerge in Israel also fall into this category. Other threats, however, call for the physical destruction of Israel in which most if not all of its inhabitants would be killed or expelled. Defeat in conventional war would likely bring about such an outcome. This is a fate Israel has dodged repeatedly since its first conflict, the 1948 War of Independence—a war that if Israel had lost would have ended the Zionist experiment then and there. Today, however, neither calls for a one-state solution or even the prospect of massive war pose the greatest threat to Israel's existence. Rather, if Israel is to undergo what has been termed "state death,"[1] the cause is most likely to be attack by nuclear weapons, and the country wielding those weapons is most likely to be Iran.

There are several reasons nuclear weapons pose an existential threat to Israel, including the nature of nuclear weapons themselves, Israel's vulnerability to a nuclear attack, the growing capability of many of Israel's enemies to develop nuclear weapons, the desire of many of these same countries and groups to eradicate Israel, and the possible failure of deterrence to ward off a nuclear attack. One is left with a dire situation in which those whose most cherished dream is to destroy Israel are rapidly gaining the means to do so, with Israel lacking the means or the will to stop them.

The Uniqueness of Nuclear Weapons

Nuclear weapons are unique because so much destructive power is contained in a small package. A single nuclear weapon the size of a suitcase can obliterate a city and all its inhabitants. The bomb that destroyed Hiroshima was "only" twelve kilotons, far smaller than many nuclear weapons that are likely to be used today. There has never been anything like this in history. Making matters worse, the massive power of nuclear arms is typically combined with delivery systems, such as missiles and jet aircraft that can reach their targets in a matter of minutes. As such, what is new about nuclear weapons is not so much their ability to destroy but, as Thomas Schelling observed, their ability to wreak "sudden destruction." Because destruction is nearly instantaneous, it is more likely to happen. In theory, one can destroy an entire society with knives, killing each member one after the other. In practice, however, resistance, fatigue, moral revulsion, or simply the passage of time would make such total destruction improbable. It is not hard to imagine, though, a leader pushing one button that results in the total annihilation of a society in a matter of minutes. Because it is easy to conceive of, it is easy to do, making nuclear destruction of another state an all too thinkable proposition.[2]

Israel would be especially vulnerable to nuclear destruction because it is so small and its population highly concentrated. Israel is only a little more than 8,000 square miles, slightly smaller than New Jersey. More than 75 percent of its Jewish population is wedged into a narrow coastal strip from Ashkelon to Nahariya. The three cities of Jerusalem, Tel Aviv, and Haifa alone make up nearly half the population and are the economic, political, and cultural heart of Israel. Only a handful of nuclear weapons, perhaps no more than three, would be enough to end Israel as a Jewish state. Although no country could withstand a nuclear strike with equanimity, few match Israel in terms of its sheer vulnerability to a state-ending attack. Japan survived the destruction of Hiroshima and Nagasaki, and went on to become a prosperous economic powerhouse. The destruction of Tel Aviv and Jerusalem, on the other hand, would fatally wound Israel in a way that would make recovery highly improbable. Even if Israel was not destroyed, the mere threat of a nuclear attack could gravely hurt its future. Living in the shadow of nuclear assault, especially by a state like Iran that has openly sought Israel's eradication, could erode Zionism by encouraging Jewish emigration and discouraging immigration. The best and the brightest Israeli citizens may choose to live somewhere less prone to nuclear annihilation. Some argue this is already happening.[3]

Many countries and groups in the Middle East seek nuclear capability. Nuclear programs of one sort or another exist in Egypt, Syria, Saudi Arabia, Jordan, and Libya. None, however, are far enough along in the development of nuclear weapons to pose any real danger. In two cases—Iraq in 1981 and Syria in 2007—when it looked like enemies of Israel were getting close to making nuclear arms, Israel destroyed their reactors with fighter-bombers, crippling their capability to become nuclear-armed states. The threat that it would do so again should another adversary come close to developing nuclear weapons hangs forever in the air. Several militant groups have also expressed an interest in acquiring nuclear weapons, with al-Qaeda the most ominous possibility.[4] However, making nuclear weapons, and particularly manufacturing the fissile material necessary for a nuclear explosion, is beyond the capability of any substate group. So, although theft or purchase of nuclear weapons by terrorists remains an ongoing concern, Israel need not worry about nonstate actors making nuclear weapons on their own.

What Israel does worry about, and with good reason, is the prospect of Iran's acquiring nuclear weapons. This concern stems first from Iranian leaders' calls for Israel's destruction. At a speech delivered at the World Without Zionism Conference, held in 2005, Iranian President Mahmoud Ahmadinejad said, "The occupying regime [Israel] must be wiped off the map." Although others have attempted to declare that the translation was not accurate, editors of the *New York Times* ascertained that was indeed what he said, a contention supported by official Iranian translations including the one on Ahmadinejad's own website.[5] That Ahmadinejad famously denies that the Holocaust has ever happened—a view shared by many in the Iranian government—only supports the notion that this leader is prepared to depart from reality when the fate of the Jewish people is involved. Other Iranian leaders have also weighed in with incendiary comments. In December 2001, former Iranian president Akbar Hashemi Rafsanjani (who is often characterized as a moderate) declared, "If one day the Islamic world is also equipped with weapons like those that Israel possesses now, then the imperialist's strategy will reach a standstill because the use of even one nuclear bomb inside Israel will destroy everything. However, it will only harm the Islamic world. It is not irrational to contemplate such an eventuality."[6] These statements, along with crowds routinely chanting, "Death to Israel" (along with "Death to America"), suggest that many in Iran do indeed wish to eradicate Israel from the face of the earth.

The Iranian Nuclear Program

If Iran wants to destroy Israel, few would dispute that it is rapidly acquiring the nuclear weapons to do so. Iran's nuclear program is long-standing, but it is only in the past decade or so that it has really taken off. The nuclear program began with help from the United States, which was eager to support Iran, then under the pro-American shah. In 1957, the United States concluded a nuclear cooperation agreement with Iran as part of its Atoms for Peace Program and, a decade later, sold Iran a small, five-megawatt reactor designed for research. Spurred on by American encouragement, the shah announced in 1974 plans to build twenty-three nuclear reactors, a huge number for any country but particularly high for a state whose ample oil and gas resources seemingly precluded a need for nuclear power. At the time of his downfall in 1979, the shah had concluded contracts for several nuclear reactors, with one reactor, at Bushehr, nearly completed.[7] All this momentum came to naught when the Ayatollah Khomeini came to power and promptly ended all developments in the nuclear field, calling them "un-Islamic."[8] The catastrophic Iran-Iraq War of 1980 to 1988 changed Khomeini's mind about the advisability of nuclear weapons. In a previously classified letter, Khomeini wrote to former Iranian president Rafsanjani at the end of the war declaring that Iraq's use of chemical weapons and the indifference of the international community demonstrated Iran's need to restart its nuclear program.[9] The resulting program remained largely secret until 2002, when an Iranian exile group revealed that Iran had been working for decades on enriching uranium in Natanz as well as producing a heavy water reactor.[10]

The revelation of these secret programs strongly suggests that Iran was pursuing two paths, the successful completion of either of which would result in the development of a nuclear weapon. Producing a nuclear bomb is no simple task. Most critical is amassing sufficient quantities of fissile material, either plutonium or highly enriched uranium, both of which require major efforts to be made bomb-ready. Plutonium is an artificial element produced as a by-product in nuclear reactors. To get enough plutonium for a bomb, one needs a nuclear reactor to create the plutonium and a reprocessing plant to separate the plutonium from the uranium rods. Iran planned to produce several nuclear reactors, each of which would produce enough plutonium for a nuclear bomb. Iran's first power reactor, built by the Russians at Bushehr, was completed in the summer of 2011. Although the Bushehr reactor will produce substantial quantities of plutonium, it is not a cause for major concern since it will be under International Atomic Energy Agency safeguards and the Russians have promised that all the spent fuel will be returned to them. Other nuclear reactors, however, may not enjoy such close supervision, raising the question of whether Iran could divert plutonium for weapons use. Although there is no evidence that Iran has a reprocessing plant to remove the plutonium, such a task is not difficult (it can be done through a simple chemical process), and the plant can be concealed from prying eyes. An additional worry is Iran's decision to build a heavy water reactor. These kinds of reactors use natural (not enriched) uranium as a fuel, making it easier for a country to operate the reactor without outside oversight. Several countries including Israel and India have used heavy water reactors as their route to nuclear development.

Although Iran's construction of a heavy water reactor is cause for worry, the path Iran has chosen to concentrate its efforts in developing nuclear weapons capability is by enriching uranium. Enriching uranium to the point where a nuclear explosion can be achieved is no easy task. The isotope of uranium needed for a nuclear bomb—U-235—exists naturally but makes up only 0.7 percent of uranium. For a bomb, that 0.7 percent needs to be enriched, or purified, to much higher levels. There are several ways this can be done, the most common being to convert uranium to a gas and funnel the uranium through thousands of centrifuges where the lighter U-235 isotope gradually becomes separated from the heavier (and nonfissionable) U-238 isotope. Uranium enriched or purified to around 3 percent can be used as a fuel for many reactors, while uranium enriched to around 90 percent can be used for a nuclear bomb. The same centrifuges required to enrich uranium for the peaceful use of nuclear energy can be employed to further enrich the uranium to make a bomb; hence, there is no clear way to distinguish a peaceful enrichment program from one dedicated to making nuclear explosives. This enables countries like Iran to maintain a large enrichment capability to make bomb-quality uranium, all the while maintaining they are just making fuel for peaceful nuclear reactors.

Making matters worse, Iran has already amassed a large quantity of uranium enriched to 3 percent. The physics of enrichment are such that it is much easier to purify uranium from 3 percent to 90 percent than it is to go from natural uranium to 3 percent. Iran can therefore continue to lightly enrich uranium consistent with the provisions of the Nuclear Non-Proliferation Treaty (of which it is a signatory), gradually increasing its supply. If the Iranian leadership decides to develop a nuclear weapon, it can use the existing stocks of 3 percent enriched uranium as a base (and some enriched to 20 percent) and then further enrich the uranium to 90 percent, thus acquiring the capability to build a nuclear bomb.

There is no doubt that Iran has a major program in uranium enrichment capable of making enough fissile material for a bomb. By the end of 2009, Iran had already amassed over 8,000 centrifuges in Natanz, giving it the capability to produce two or more nuclear weapons per year.[11] Moreover, Natanz is not the only enrichment plant run by the Iranians. In September 2009 President Barack Obama, along with French President Nicolas Sarkozy and then British Prime Minister Gordon Brown, announced that Iran was building a hidden enrichment facility in a mountain near the holy city of Qom. Neither the Qom nor the Natanz plants were revealed to International Atomic Energy Agency inspectors as required by the Non-Proliferation Treaty. It is true that a 2007 US National Intelligence Estimate concluded that Iran had halted work on a nuclear weapon in 2003, but this assessment has been largely discredited, with even the American government distancing itself from it. Intelligence agencies from Israel, Britain, and France have all asserted that Iran is actively working on nuclear weapons, a conclusion given support by the International Atomic Energy Agency itself. Although an exact date of Iran's acquiring nuclear arms is difficult to pinpoint, the revised American estimate of between 2012 and 2015 is most likely on the mark.[12]

Having developed nuclear weapons, Iran would have few difficulties launching them against Israel. Iran has about one hundred Shahab-3 ballistic missiles, some of which have ranges up to 1,300 miles, enabling them to hit virtually any target in Israel.[13] Iran is working on other ballistic missiles with even greater ranges and payload, enhancing its ability to strike at Israel with more weapons. Iran is also developing cruise missiles—essentially flying torpedoes—that could be launched from ships or from ground sites close to Israel armed with nuclear warheads. Although cruise missiles travel with less speed than ballistic missiles, they still fly at several hundred miles an hour while hugging the ground, making interception very difficult. Russia is supplying Iran long-range bombers, including the Tu-22 Backfire and the SU-24 Fencer, each of which have the range to reach Israeli targets.[14] Iran's ties with militant groups at war with Israel, most notably Hamas and Hizbollah, offer opportunities to launch short-range missiles into Israel and possibly even smuggle a nuclear device into the Jewish state.

How an Iranian Nuclear Weapon Threatens Israel's Existence

The view that Iran is well on its way toward acquiring nuclear weapons capable of reaching Israel by a variety of means is not in serious dispute. The question remains, however, as to how much of a threat to Israel's existence a nuclear-armed Iran would be. After all, the United States has confronted nuclear adversaries throughout its history, with no major ill effects. These rivals included the Soviet Union, which at one point aimed over 10,000 nuclear weapons at the American heartland, and China, which had far fewer weapons but was led by a radical regime that openly discounted the dangers of nuclear war. Many scholars, most notably the political theorist Kenneth Waltz, have argued that far from causing war, nuclear weapons bring about peace.[15] In this view, leaders recognize that nuclear conflict with other nuclear-armed states would be suicidal and therefore would never be undertaken. A nuclear-armed Iran may bluster and posture, but at the end of the day, its leadership would recognize that attacking Israel with nuclear weapons would mean the end of Iran as a country, to say nothing of their personal demise as well. Just as nuclear weapons helped keep the peace during the tensest days of the Cold War, so will it do so in the Middle East of today.

There are many problems with this rosy scenario, most of which stem from the view that the success of nuclear deterrence during the Cold War might not apply to contemporary Iran. Deterrence will not halt an Iranian strike if the country's leadership decides to launch a first strike that disarms Israel's retaliatory forces. That Israel is a tiny country whose land-based missiles and aircraft are concentrated in a relatively small area supports an Iranian belief that a "disarming" first strike could be achieved. Such a strike could come out of the blue but probably would arise from some crisis. One can envision a situation where Israel and one of Iran's proxies, such as Hizbollah, were engaged in a shooting war that threatened to escalate. Iran might then launch its nuclear weapons first, especially if it believed Israel was preparing to launch a strike on its own. Having two hate-filled countries facing each other, each armed with nuclear weapons and each believing it could disarm the other, is truly the mother of all nightmares. If Iran did launch first and successfully disarmed Israel, little would stand in its way of finishing the job and totally annihilating the Jewish state. After becoming a nuclear power, therefore, Iran could conceivably develop nuclear forces that threaten Israel's retaliatory nuclear arms and, should the Iranians become convinced that they have achieved a disarming first-strike capability, there would be little to stop them from launching an attack.

Although it would be foolish to eliminate this possibility, the prospect of a rational Iranian leadership believing it could disarm Israel's nuclear retaliatory capability is difficult to accept. Israel maintains a robust nuclear force of some one hundred to two hundred nuclear warheads deployed on a triad of weapons, each leg of which would likely survive an Iranian assault to deliver a devastating counterstrike of its own. On land, Israel maintains a fleet of Jericho ballistic missiles, with ranges that reach over 2,000 miles, enabling the country to attack virtually any target in Iran. The missiles are stored in limestone caves, complicating any effort to destroy them before they can be launched. In the air, Israel has squadrons of F-15 and F-16 fighters, nuclear capable and (with in-flight refueling) able to reach any point in Iran and return to Israel. The aircraft reside in blast-proof hangars and can be ready to take off at a moment's notice, before any Iranian missiles could reach Israel. Most important, Israel has three Dolphin submarines from Germany and is planning to purchase three more. Each submarine has twenty-four cruise missiles, each of which can be launched with a nuclear warhead while the submarine remains submerged.[16] These submarines are undetectable, making them invulnerable to any Iranian attack. Even if Iran launched a devastating nuclear strike that disarmed Israel and eradicated the country, the Israeli submarines would be able to wreak total destruction on Iran in return. No rational Iranian leadership could convince itself that it could hit Israel with nuclear weapons without committing national suicide. Insofar as nuclear deterrence works, the first-strike option for Iran is off the table.

The second reason nuclear deterrence might not keep Israel safe is the fear that the Iranian leadership, because of fanatical religious beliefs, may simply be impossible to deter. Deterrence is the ability to persuade someone not to do something, by threatening them with unacceptable punishment if they do. The key word in this definition is "unacceptable." American leaders during the Cold War justifiably assumed that Soviet leaders would deem the destruction of their society (and of themselves) unacceptable regardless of the harm they could inflict on the United States. Soviet leaders assumed the same for their American counterparts. These assumptions could be made because the American and Soviet leaders, despite their many differences, were rational in the sense that they were sensitive to costs. Nothing was worth the destruction of their country, their way of life. Since both sides recognized that a nuclear strike would be suicidal, and since no national interest could possibly justify bringing about one's own destruction, deterrence held.

The view that the Iranian leadership cannot be deterred rests on the assumption that those controlling the nuclear weapons are driven by fanatical religious beliefs so that it makes sense to destroy Israel even if it means bringing about their own annihilation. The notion of Iran as a "suicide nation" has its roots in the view that many of the Iranian leaders believe in the Hidden Imam, the last of the Twelve Imams who, as a child, supposedly did not die but is awaiting a return to earth. Those who share this belief see the return of the Hidden Imam in a similar vein as some Christians view the Second Coming, that is, he will return (from his "occultation") to restore order and peace to a world gone wrong. Indeed, Shia belief has Jesus also appearing (after the Hidden Imam) to set the world on the right course. Many Iranian leaders embrace the belief of the Hidden Imam, especially those who follow the Ayatollah Mohammad-Taqi Mesbah-Yazdi, an ultraconservative figure who supports suicide bombings and believes Zionists are the source of all evil.[17] Iranian President Ahmadinejad, a disciple of Yazdi, is known to be a fervent believer in the Hidden Imam, saying in November 2005 that "the most important task of our Revolution is to prepare the way for the return of the Twelfth Imam." During the war with Iraq, Ahmadinejad served as a volunteer with the Basiji, the fanatical Iranian group that sent children and older men wearing "keys" to heaven on marches across Iraqi minefields with predictably horrific results. The Basiji, who also believe in the Hidden Imam, remain a potent political force in Iran and are among Ahmadinejad's strongest backers.[18]

What does all this have to do with nuclear deterrence? The fear is that Ahmadinejad and many other Iranian leaders' belief in a Hidden Imam will cause them to pave the way for his return. Before the Hidden Imam will reappear, the world has to undergo a massive, cataclysmic struggle. Only then will the Imam come to earth and create a paradise for believers while condemning the infidels to a horrific fate. That belief, combined with the celebration of martyrdom of the Basiji, and a tradition of anti-Semitism in Shia thought, suggests that Ahmadinejad might provoke a nuclear war with Israel, creating the upheaval necessary to hasten the Imam's return. As the prominent scholar of Islam, Bernard Lewis, said, "If they [the Iranians] kill large numbers of their own people, they think they are doing them a favor. They are giving them a quick free pass to heaven and its delights, the divine brothel in the skies."[19] If such beliefs are indeed held by those who control Iranian nuclear weapons, deterrence is worthless.

The notion that Iranian leaders are impossible to deter is hotly contested by a wide range of military and political analysts. They first reject the notion that the Iranian leadership is led by religious extremists who welcome martyrdom. It is true that many Iranian leaders are deeply religious, but then again, so are many American leaders. Few argued that George W. Bush, a devout Christian, should not be entrusted with nuclear weapons because of fears that he may seek to provoke Armageddon, so why then make similar arguments about Iran's leaders? Moreover, even if some in the Iranian government may be reckless in their use of nuclear arms, launching a nuclear weapon is a complex undertaking that involves several steps and many people. In Iran, the Supreme National Security Council, the Revolutionary Guard Corps, and the Supreme Leader, Ali Khamenei, would likely play a critical role in giving the order to initiate a nuclear attack. The prospect that all of them would be gripped by messianic fever to commit an action they know to be suicidal is hard to accept.

The specter of an irrational Iran embracing martyrdom becomes all the more far-fetched when examining Iranian behavior since the 1979 revolution. Although the Iranian leadership has used volatile rhetoric (especially with regard to Israel) and has spoken often of the need to pursue Islamist goals, its behavior has been relatively pragmatic and conservative. Far from seeking to promote Islamic revolution throughout the world, Iran has often behaved with restraint. It is a major supporter of both Hizbollah and Hamas, but stood idly by when each was pummeled by Israel in the wars of 2006 and 2009. Iran claims to be concerned about the plight of Muslims the world over but kept a low profile while Russia slaughtered thousands of Muslim Chechens over the past twenty years. The United States is regularly denounced as the "Great Satan" and Israel as the "Little Satan" but Iran has been careful to avoid direct conflict with either country. Iran seeks to spread its influence throughout the Arab world but has been moderate in its efforts for fear of provoking a backlash from the overwhelmingly Sunni states. Iran's distaste of dealing with infidels has not constrained its efforts to pursue economic and diplomatic ties with Russia and China. Even the quest for nuclear weapons can be seen as a means of defending

Iran against very real threats from nuclear-armed adversaries, such as the United States and Israel. Seen in this light, the best guide to Iranian policy is not religiously driven extremism but rather the desire of a leadership to survive in a very dangerous neighborhood. That survival requires that Iran not let either religious dogma or intense hatred of Israel to get out of hand. Instead, Iran, like all other nuclear-armed states, will do whatever it can to not allow nuclear war to erupt, either by design or by miscalculation. Nuclear deterrence, it would seem, will be alive and well in Tehran, as it is with all other countries facing nuclear-armed adversaries.[20]

A third path by which Israel may become the target of Iranian nuclear weapons is if Iran transferred nuclear weapons to militant groups who in turn used them against Israel. Iran has already sent thousands of missiles to the Lebanese militant group Hizbollah, which went to war with Israel in the summer of 2006. Iran has also been a key supporter of Hamas in Gaza, which fought Israel in the winter of 2008–2009. Both Hamas and Hizbollah openly call for Israel's destruction. If Iran provided either group with nuclear weapons, it is conceivable they would use them against Israel. Attacking Israel with nuclear weapons would not pose an insurmountable problem for either group. A suicide aircraft, a boat headed for shore, a device smuggled in a shipping container, or maybe a primitive cruise missile could all be employed. Since the nuclear weapon would not come directly from Iran, the Iranian leadership might be convinced they could avoid retaliation. A loose nuke, after all, could come from several sources, including transfer by a sympathetic military officer in Pakistan, theft from Russia, or purchase from North Korea. A Hamas or Hizbollah nuclear strike then serves two ends: it delivers a mortal blow to Israel while preserving deniability for Iran.

Though tantalizing, the idea that Iranian leaders would transfer nuclear weapons to Hamas, Hizbollah, or anyone is far-fetched. Much progress has been achieved in the world of nuclear accountability—determining the source of a nuclear weapon by examining the aftereffects of an explosion. Iran could never be certain that Israel would be unable to determine that it supplied the nuclear weapon, all the more so because Israel would not demand proof that would stand up in a court of law. Rather, the Israelis would simply have to *suspect* Iran was behind a nuclear attack to order a devastating retaliation. The very fact that such an attack occurred might be enough for the Israeli leadership to respond against Iran, a possibility any Iranian leadership could not discount. It is notable that although Iran has transferred missiles and other conventional weaponry to Hamas and Hizbollah, it has refrained from providing chemical or biological weapons, correctly seeing them as a red line not to be crossed. If Iran transferred nuclear weapons to Hizbollah or Hamas, it would be placing its survival in the hands of groups it cannot control, an action that any rational Iranian government would almost certainly reject.

Israel also faces a threat from an Iranian nuclear strike stemming from miscalculation. During the Cold War the United States and the Soviet Union, despite the relative moderation of their leaders, arguably came close to nuclear war on several occasions, most notably during the Cuban Missile Crisis. One can easily envision a similar cycle of miscalculation, excessive risk-taking, and inadvertent escalation, only this time the outcome might lead to war. The relationship between Iran and Israel is far worse than ever was the case between the two superpowers. Even at the height of the Cold War, the United States and the Soviet Union recognized each other and had embassies in each other's capital, and neither called for the destruction of the other. Iran, on the other hand, refuses to recognize Israel, there are no diplomatic relations between the two countries, and leaders of Iran regularly call for the obliteration of the Zionist enemy. In addition to supporting Hamas and Hizbollah, Iran almost certainly was behind the bombing of the Israeli embassy in Argentina in 1992 and the Jewish community center there two years later. None of this makes the leaders of Iran irrational. But given the enormous hatred the Iranian leadership has for Israel and the lack of direct communications between the two countries, the prospects for miscalculation leading to nuclear war are far greater than ever was the case between Washington and Moscow. One has only to envision a crisis erupting between Iran and Israel, both armed with nuclear weapons, each fearing the other will seek an advantage by striking first, to recognize that deterrence is a very fragile hedge against the eruption of nuclear war.[21]

A fifth path by which Israel would become the target of an Iranian nuclear weapon is through an unauthorized or accidental strike. As with all nuclear-armed states, the Iranian leadership will seek to keep tight control over its nuclear arsenal. Just who would exercise that control is unclear. Iran's command structure is marked by overlapping structures, many of which pursue competing agendas.[22] Nevertheless, it is believed that ultimate control rests with the Supreme Leader Ali Khamenei, who is the head of state and commander in chief of the armed forces.[23]

Khamenei's relatively moderate rhetoric regarding Israel, such as his 2005 statement that Iran does not wish to militarily destroy Israel, are reassuring (assuming he is speaking the truth), but there are concerns that others in the nuclear chain of command may think differently. Khamenei's control of nuclear forces is exercised through the Islamic Revolutionary Guard Corps (IRGC), a group known for its extreme views regarding Israel. The IRGC is led by General Mohammad-Ali Jafari, who has openly called for the destruction of Israel.[24] Ahmadinejad, by virtue of his position as president and former member of the IRGC, is also likely to play some role in nuclear planning. Having these two men so close to the nuclear trigger cannot be comforting for Israel.

Given Khamenei's central role in nuclear planning, how likely is it that an Ahmadinejad, Jafari, or some unknown military commander could launch a nuclear weapon at Israel without governmental approval? It is impossible to know for certain, but the overall picture is not reassuring. If Iran develops nuclear weapons, it will confront the "always/never" dilemma described by political scientist Peter Feaver.[25] Feaver argues that all leaders, but particularly leaders of countries with new nuclear forces, need to be certain that their nuclear weapons will always be used if the order is given to do so, but never be used against their wishes. The problem is that efforts to ensure one goal undermine those of the other. If Khamenei wanted to be certain that Iranian nuclear weapons would never be used without his express authorization, he might limit to himself the authority to order a launch. That way some hate-filled colleague or wayward colonel would not be able to precipitate a nuclear war on his own. However, if Khamenei wanted to be sure that Iranian weapons would always be ready to strike if the order was given, then he might extend authority to launch to many subordinates so that an attacker could not "decapitate" Iran's ability to use its nuclear weapons by killing the leaders authorized to do so. Given Iran's fears of an Israeli (or American) preemptive strike, Khamenei may well decide that a nuclear-armed Iran should lean toward the "always" side of command and control, making the prospect of an unauthorized strike that much more likely. Since an unauthorized strike may involve only a small number of individuals or even a single person, there is a much greater likelihood of irrationality, fanaticism, or miscalculation undermining deterrence.

Nuclear deterrence will also play no role in the event of an accidental launch. During the Cold War, both the United States and the Soviet Union experienced many accidents involving nuclear weapons. They included the crashing of nuclear-armed aircraft, nuclear weapons being engulfed in flames, and false alerts of nuclear attacks.[26] Even after the Cold War, frightening incidents continue to occur, such as the transport of cruise missiles across the United States without anyone realizing they were nuclear armed. For new nuclear-weapons states, the likelihood of an accident is far greater than that experienced by the United States and the USSR. Modern American nuclear weapons have what is called the "one-point safety rule," in which there is less than one chance in a million that a weapon will go off due to explosion or fire.[27] There is little possibility that an Iranian nuclear bomb will be made to this standard. If an Iranian nuclear weapon goes off accidentally, it may be misinterpreted as an Israeli attack, prompting an Iranian strike, thus throwing both countries into nuclear war. Aside from the weapons themselves, a false radar warning signaling an impending attack might push the Iranians to launch their missiles so they are not caught on the ground. Once launched, these missiles cannot be recalled, resulting in an accidental nuclear war. Whatever the situation, a new Iranian nuclear force will not have the technology, safeguards, and restraints that (barely) got the superpowers through the Cold War. Perhaps humankind's luck will continue and no nuclear weapon will be detonated or launched by accident. But given the primitive nature of what would be Iran's new nuclear force, no one can be confident that our good fortune will continue.

Finally, and perhaps most likely, Israel could be destroyed by Iranian nuclear weapons launched by a collapsing regime. There is no certainty that the present Iranian government will last much longer. Major demonstrations rocked the regime in the summer of 2009, leading many to conclude that it had seen its last days. The Iranian government was able to suppress that budding revolt, but it still faces a young, restive population, of whom many are opposed to Islamic rule, and a struggling economy that shows few signs of recovery. Just as the shah's Iran was declared by President Jimmy Carter to be an "island of stability" just before it fell, so too might the rule of the mullahs be brought to an abrupt and violent end. The key question is how the Iranian leaders will react when they know their hold on power (and maybe their lives) have come to an end. Will they go quietly? Or perhaps, with nothing to lose, will they take Israel down with them, even if it means the end of Iran? After all, if the Islamic Republic is to be no more, what better way to justify its and their existence than by destroying the hated Zionists once and for all?

It may be that an Iran with nuclear weapons will behave as other nuclear-armed states have. It will recognize that attempting to launch a disarming first strike against its enemies is too risky, no interest is worth the death of their own nation, and transferring nuclear arms to militant groups outside their control is madness. It will ensure that nuclear weapons will never be used in an unauthorized manner; miscalculations and accidents cannot be permitted to occur; and it is better to let a regime fall than to bring about the destruction of the Iranian people. This would be an Iran that is deterrable and containable, an Iran where nuclear-weapons possession might not exactly be welcome but probably would not lead to any cataclysmic changes. To most observers, this is the most likely outcome of a nuclear-armed Iran.

The problem, however, is that no one can be sure that this reassuring picture is accurate. Each of the threats posed by a nuclear Iran to Israel's existence is plausible. An Iranian leadership may well decide in time of a crisis that it must launch first, lest its weapons be disarmed. The prospect of certain death may not deter leaders who hate Jews more than they love life. Elements of the Islamic Revolutionary Guard Corps, used to transferring missiles and other weapons to Hamas and Hizbollah, might continue in that tradition with the nuclear arms they have come to control. A rational, deterrable Iranian leadership may nevertheless fail to prevent some lower-level fanatic from starting a nuclear war, or mistakenly assume an accidental detonation of a faulty nuclear bomb was actually an Israeli attack. An Iranian leadership faced with the loss of all may not wish to go quietly, but rather eliminate the Zionist enemy as their gift to posterity.

Even if one concludes that an Iran armed with nuclear weapons will behave in a responsible, prudent, and rational manner, and even if one assumes that all the scenarios that have Iran launching a nuclear attack against Israel are unlikely to happen, how certain must one be of this to accept Iran's ascension to the nuclear club? Can policy makers in Jerusalem conclude that if there is "only" a 20 percent or even 10 percent chance of Iran behaving recklessly, then it is acceptable to allow it to become a nuclear power? There is no more important function of government than to protect its citizens. As such, the mere possibility of an Iranian nuclear attack against Israel warrants the most serious consideration as to what can be done to prevent such a threat from becoming reality.

Staying Alive: Responding to the Iranian Threat

Stopping Iran from developing nuclear weapons will not be easy, as the Iranian leadership sees nuclear arms as the key to their survival. By acquiring nuclear weapons, Iran is able to deter a nuclear strike from its enemies, especially Israel and the United States. A nuclear-armed Iran would be less likely to be a target of an American invasion, a lesson Saddam Hussein failed to appreciate, much to his regret. Although the mullahs are not popular in Iran, their efforts to acquire nuclear arms are embraced across the Iranian political spectrum. Most Iranians see efforts to halt their nuclear technology as another form of Western imperialism, of keeping Iran down, preventing it from assuming its rightful place as a regional hegemon. By agreeing to halt nuclear developments, especially in the light of Israel's acknowledged nuclear arsenal, the Iranian leaders would be surrendering to their worst enemies. Such an open sign of capitulation would be politically disastrous, giving fuel to the perception that the mullahs are weak and ripe for overthrow.

Although halting the Iranian nuclear program will be difficult, it is not impossible. Policy makers have suggested a range of approaches that some say hold out the hope of preventing Iran from developing nuclear weapons or, if they do, from attacking Israel. These approaches include diplomacy, economic sanctions, creation of a nuclear-free zone in the Middle East, various coercive actions short of war, establishment of an effective defense, and a military strike. Israeli policy would play only a marginal role in the first two paths but would be central to the others. Although there is disagreement as to which approach to follow, there is a consensus that none of the choices is promising, with the challenge being to choose the least bad option.

Diplomacy is attractive as a relatively cost-free, nonviolent approach to persuading Iran not to develop nuclear weapons. Those advocating a diplomatic approach suggest that the United States attempt to meet the legitimate fears of the Iranian leadership by guaranteeing that America will not seek to topple them. The United States could also help matters by toning down its anti-Iranian rhetoric and seeking a dialogue based on mutual respect and noninterference in Iranian internal affairs. America's European allies can help by actively seeking warmer relations with Iran, a position for which they are especially well qualified since they do not carry the negative baggage of the United States, with its history of anti-Iranian policies and strong support for Israel. With its hold on power reassured, the hope is that Iran will be willing to forgo its nuclear aspirations and reap the benefits of closer ties with the West.

Diplomacy may be worthwhile to pursue, but few believe it will convince the Iranians to halt their nuclear program. The diplomatic route has already been followed, with nothing to show for it. In 2004, Britain, France, and Germany succeeded in getting Iran to halt its enrichment of uranium and agree to more intrusive inspections of its nuclear programs by the International Atomic Energy Agency. That agreement, however, came about less due to the persuasive powers of European diplomats than Iran's fears that the United States, feeling flush after a successful invasion of Iraq, would next turn its military force to Iran. Once the United States got bogged down in Iraq and the threat of American intervention in Iran evaporated, the mullahs quickly reneged on the agreement with the Europeans, restarted their enrichment of uranium, and again restricted the scope of IAEA inspections. American diplomacy has fared no better. Many complained that the Bush administration's harsh words (including Iran in the "axis of evil") poisoned relations between the two countries and that a more conciliatory approach would transform the hostile relationship. Nevertheless, Barack Obama came into office and attempted to warm relations with Iran, only to be summarily rebuffed. Given that the mullahs feed off their hostility to the United States, for them to compromise with the "Great Satan" would be to undermine much of their legitimacy. An American guarantee not to seek the toppling of the Iranian regime most likely would not be believed and would be rejected even if the Iranian leaders thought it genuine. Keeping lines of communication open makes sense, as does attempting to limit hostile discourse. It makes less sense to believe that diplomacy will cause the Iranian leaders to change any of their policies regarding the development of nuclear weapons.

At first glance, economic sanctions appear to be a powerful tool to influence Iran's decision on whether to move ahead with nuclear weapons development. Iran is very much a part of the globalized world, depending on trade and investment to keep its economy afloat. Oil exports alone make up fully 80 percent of Iran's state budget and without them Iran's economy would collapse. Although a major oil producer, Iran needs to import 40 percent of its refined gasoline products. Cutting off those imports would lead to widespread shortages of gasoline for transport and industry, bringing the Iranian economy to a screeching halt. So, why hasn't the United Nations called for an embargo on Iranian oil? Why haven't the countries of the world agreed not to sell Iran any refined gasoline? The answer is obvious: too many countries want to buy Iranian oil, sell it refined gasoline, or simply do business with Iran because it serves their interests. China buys oil and natural gas from Iran, Russia is selling Iran nuclear reactors while helping the country develop its oil and natural gas reserves, and many European states fear a rise in the price of oil should Iranian petroleum be removed from the market. Stopping Iran's production of nuclear weapons is less important to much of the world than making money. As such, when the United Nations imposes sanctions on Iran, as it has done on four occasions thus far, they are modest, focusing on the Iranian Revolutionary Guard and mullahs, but not to the extent that anyone is seriously harmed or inconvenienced. Sanctions imposed by the European Union and the United States in 2010 have been more biting. Gasoline imports to Iran have been cut, access to most foreign banks has been denied, and shipping has been curtailed due to difficulties of acquiring insurance.[28] Still, few believe these measures will be enough to convince the Iranians to give up their nuclear plans. Economic sanctions might indeed work to persuade the Iranian leadership to change course, but only if key countries of the world agree to act in ways that would cripple the Iranian economy. That has not happened yet and there are few signs that it will.

Diplomacy and sanctions are largely out of Israel's hands to pursue, but an area where Israeli policy can make a difference is the demand—from Egypt and other states—that Israel give up its own nuclear force and agree to a nuclear-free zone in the Middle East. On its face, the argument for Israeli nuclear disarmament is compelling. Israel is one of only three countries (India and Pakistan are the others) that have refused to sign the Nuclear Non-Proliferation Treaty, which commits its signatories not to develop nuclear arms. Israel has refused to sign the treaty because it maintains a robust nuclear force that it believes is necessary for its security. Nevertheless, demanding that Iran, which has signed the treaty, to forgo nuclear development while turning a blind eye to Israel strikes many as hypocritical. Why should Israel be allowed nuclear weapons and not Iran? If progress in convincing Iran to end its nuclear program is to be made, many argue, Israel also must agree to give up its nuclear arms.

As convincing as this argument may sound, it fails to persuade on several counts. Unlike Iran, Israel has not threatened its neighbors with extinction. It has maintained its nuclear force responsibly, not using or attempting to intimidate its neighbors with its still undeclared nuclear arsenal. More important, it is highly unlikely that Israel would ever agree to give up its nuclear weapons. Its conventional military forces are vastly outnumbered and outspent by the countries of the Middle East, many of which refuse to recognize Israel's right to exist. There is no evidence that an Israeli decision to divest itself of nuclear arms would convince Iran to halt its nuclear development, nor would Israel believe Iran if such a declaration were made. Iran has already violated its commitments to the treaty by maintaining a secret enrichment facility, and there is little reason to believe that Iran would behave more responsibly if Israel acceded to the treaty. Though demanding a nuclear-free zone may score debating points, it is not going to happen and would almost certainly not change Iran's nuclear plans in the unlikely event that it did.

If Israel has little confidence in deterrence, there is always the option of defending itself from an Iranian nuclear strike, of physically guarding against an attack. Israel is one of a very few countries that deploy an anti–ballistic missile system, the Arrow, designed to destroy incoming warheads. Unlike the American anti–ballistic missile system, which destroys warheads by direct impact, the Arrow relies on an optical sensor and a proximity-fused warhead that need come within only forty or fifty yards to destroy the target. Israel also uses American-supplied advanced Patriot missiles that can intercept warheads at lower altitudes than the Arrow, as well as a system code named Magic Wand, for which little information is available in the open literature.[29] Though they are impressive on paper, there is no assurance that these systems will work. The effectiveness of *any* anti–ballistic missile system is in serious doubt. The destructive power of nuclear weapons is so awesome and Israel is so vulnerable to a nuclear attack that any warheads that got through would cause catastrophic damage. That some warheads would penetrate Israel's defensive shield is a near certainty. The challenge of an anti–ballistic missile system is similar to "hitting a bullet with a bullet." If that is not difficult enough, a country like Iran could take counter-measures, such as employing decoy warheads or launching staggered attacks. If convinced that Israel could shoot down its ballistic missiles, Iran retains the option of using other delivery systems, such as cruise missiles, aircraft, or smuggling, for which an anti–ballistic missile system is useless. Although it makes sense for Israel to continue to deploy and continue to improve its ballistic missile defense system, it cannot assume that the system will keep it safe from an Iranian attack.

Israel can pursue a range of coercive actions short of war, perhaps in coordination with the United States, to mitigate or eliminate the Iranian nuclear threat. Israel could, for example, seek to intimidate or eliminate Iranian nuclear scientists in order to halt or delay Iran's nuclear program. In the 1960s, Israel sent letter bombs to German scientists developing ballistic missiles for Gamal Abdel Nasser's Egypt, effectively ending the program. The number of Iranian scientists, however, is far too large and the difficulties of attacking them far too great for such an operation to be successful. Regime change appears to be an attractive option given the resistance to the mullahs, as seen in the widespread protests in the summer of 2009. The emergence of a democratic government in Iran may not end its quest for nuclear arms, but the threat it would pose to Israel would be substantially lessened. Regime change, however, is very difficult to bring about (think of the US experience in Iraq), and by destabilizing the Iranian regime, Israel may dramatically increase the threat of an Iranian attack. Blockading Iran holds out the hope of pressuring the Iranian government by threatening to eviscerate its economy. Such an action, however, would require active American participation, likely would provoke a violent Iranian response, and would not be welcomed by Iran's trading partners and oil importers. None of these policies holds out much hope of improving Israel's plight and would probably make a dire situation far worse.

The final and most discussed option is a military strike against Iran's nuclear facilities. Israel would prefer such an attack to come from the United States, but that appears increasingly improbable. If a military strike is to be launched against Iranian facilities, it almost certainly would be Israel acting alone. Israel has taken this kind of action before. In 1981, Israeli bombers destroyed Iraq's nuclear reactor, Osirak, in a daring raid that set back Saddam Hussein's nuclear program for many years, and in 2007 Israel destroyed a clandestine nuclear reactor in Syria, apparently built with the cooperation of North Korea. An Israeli strike against Iran would be far more complex, but not necessarily impossible. A number of studies suggest that such a strike could be successful, albeit with many risks.[30] Though details vary, the general consensus is that Israel would use around one hundred F-15E, F-16I, and F-16C fighters perhaps in combination with its Jericho ballistic missiles to hit a wide range of Iranian nuclear targets, including the centrifuges at Natanz and near Qom, and the heavy water reactor project at Arak. The aircraft might fly over several countries, including Turkey, Syria, and Iraq or Saudi Arabia (perhaps with Saudi permission). The mission would likely require midair refueling for the jets to reach their targets and return home. A successful strike would delay Iran's nuclear development for several years, during which time international pressure might convince Iran not to continue with its nuclear development or perhaps allow for regime change in which a more palatable Iranian leadership would emerge. At the very least, the imminent production of nuclear weapons would be halted.

Although a military strike holds out the hope of stopping Iran's nuclear program, success is far from assured, while its consequences are likely to be staggeringly harmful to Israel, the United States, and the world community. Halting Iran's drive to acquiring nuclear weapons will be far more difficult than Israel's preventive strikes against Iraq and Syria. Instead of destroying a single nuclear reactor, Israel would need to attack a wide range of targets scattered throughout a large country. Since Iran is enriching uranium to produce bomb-quality fissile material, Israel must destroy thousands of centrifuges, many of which are dispersed, concealed, hardened against attack, and located in or near areas inhabited by large numbers of civilians. To highlight just one problem, even if Israel located a tunnel in which centrifuges are kept, it still would not be able to determine whether the tunnel veered left, right, or downward to target its bombs and missiles.[31] America's refusal to supply Israel with all the weapons it wanted adds to Israel's problems of launching a successful strike.

Once the military operation was over, Israel (and much of the rest of the world) would continue to face daunting uncertainties and challenges. Following the strike, Israel would not be certain just how much damage it had inflicted. There may be hidden sites left untouched by Israeli bombs, or targets that were hit may not have been destroyed. Even a strike that succeeded in hitting all the critical targets would not end Iran's nuclear development program forever. At best, there may be a delay of a couple of years, after which Israel would find itself in the same position, debating whether to strike yet again. Nor would Iran suffer such an attack without responding. Iran could unleash tens of thousands of missiles against Israel, via its Hamas and Hizbollah allies. It may choose to launch its Shabab missiles at Israel, perhaps targeting the nuclear reactor in Dimona (though it's unclear whether Iranian missiles have the requisite accuracy). Iran may lash out against the United States for real or perceived cooperation with Israel, galvanizing its proxies in Iraq to make life even more difficult for American forces. The proximity of Iran to the Saudi oil fields and the Straits of Hormuz provides ample opportunities for mischief, including attacking oil tankers, disrupting traffic in the straits, or even attacking the Saudi oil fields themselves. Before Iran fired a shot, the price of oil would skyrocket, angering Israel's friends and foes. The world may rally around Iran, a country that committed no aggression and yet suffered a grievous attack that killed many Iranian civilians. The news media would be filled with pictures of dead and wounded Iranian women and children, raising anti-Israeli feelings to a fever pitch and making the Jewish state an even bigger pariah than it is today. Israel's relations with the United States could well deteriorate. Jews throughout the world could be subject to Iranian (and Islamic) vengeance. All this, for a "successful" Israeli strike against Iranian nuclear facilities.

What to Do

Israel is in an incredibly difficult position. Iranian leaders have been open about their desire to destroy Israel and are well on their way toward achieving the capability to do so. The United States and the international community are not likely to take the steps necessary to halt Iranian nuclear development, and in any case, Israel cannot count upon them to do so. At the end of the day, only Israel has the will and capability to delay the Iranian nuclear program, but only at a terrible cost. Striking at Iran will unleash a Pandora's box of troubles for an already besieged Israel, perhaps even leading to a rupture of relations with the United States, Israel's strongest strategic asset. Doing nothing invites an Iranian attack that could kill millions and end Israel's existence. The world advocates restraint but if Israel were to be destroyed, most would get over it and not a few would welcome its demise.

What then will Israel do? Israeli leaders, mindful of the many disasters that would occur in the wake of an attack, will not strike until they conclude an Iranian development of nuclear weapons is certain. Making this determination is not as problematic as it may seem. Iran has already amassed a large quantity of low-enriched uranium that it would need to convert to bomb-quality material. Doing so, in what is called a "breakout," will take time—several months, according to the Israelis, a year in the view of American officials. The United States believes that efforts at a breakout would be detected by international inspectors within weeks, allowing time for a disarming attack before any weapons could be built.[32] There are of course costs to Israel of waiting for evidence of a breakout to occur before acting. Israel and the United States may disagree as to what constitutes unequivocal signs of Iranian nuclear development. The Iranians may achieve a breakout sooner than expected or they may be enriching uranium in some secret location beyond the eyes of the inspectors. Nevertheless, the advantages to Israel of waiting for a sign of a breakout are compelling. The United States would be more willing to assist an Israeli strike or even launch an attack on its own if Washington were convinced of an inexorable Iranian effort to develop nuclear weapons. At the very least, an Israeli strike in the context of an Iranian dash to make nuclear arms in violation of the Non-Proliferation Treaty would soften American and international condemnation of an Israeli attack. If Israel is to undertake the cataclysmic step of launching a strike on Iran, better to do it when Iranian intentions are not in doubt, thus removing a major objection to Israeli actions.

The alternative to an Israeli strike is for Israeli leaders to do nothing and allow Iran to develop nuclear capability. An Israeli decision not to launch a military attack is what the American foreign policy establishment and especially those of the realist school of international relations believe Jerusalem should and will ultimately choose. Realists argue that leaders (including those in Iran) are rational and deterrable. In this view, Israel will recognize that Iranian leaders do not mean what they say about destroying Israel and would not pursue policies that they know are suicidal. Not striking holds out the possibility that Israel may get lucky and escape serious harm, versus the certainty of catastrophic ills that would befall the Jewish state should a military strike be launched. Just as America tolerated a fanatic Maoist China with nuclear weapons and accepted the previously "unacceptable" acquisition of nuclear arms by the rogue North Koreans, so too will Israel acquiesce in a nuclear capability for Iran.

Although certainly possible, this realist prediction of Israeli restraint may be wrong. Most observers who see Israel striking Iran argue that Israeli fears of Iranian irrationality, of Iran not behaving like a "normal" state, will push Israel to attack. Less attention is paid to the prospect of Israel departing from the norms of expected behavior, acting in ways different from other countries that have not shared its historical traumas. In this view, Israel is not like other nations. It was created in the aftermath of the Holocaust with the mission of "never again" allowing the destruction of the Jewish people to take place. Only seventy years after the Holocaust, the leader of a hostile state is once more openly calling for the extermination of 6 million Jews. Only this time, the Jewish people have the means, however problematic, to prevent that threat from happening. Seen in this light, the decision to launch an attack on Iranian nuclear facilities appears virtually inevitable. The comforting realist vision of successful nuclear deterrence and containment may indeed work for the United States, Russia, China, and others. Nevertheless, if Israel and Iran are truly different, if they are driven by demons that do not afflict much of the rest of the world, then realist predictions of a peaceful stalemate will not apply to the Israeli-Iranian relationship.

In the end, the likelihood remains that Israel will allow Iran to become a nuclear-armed state. The obstacles to militarily disarming Iran and the consequences of even a successful strike are just too overwhelming. That said, an Israeli strike (or even an American one) cannot be ruled out, something the leadership in Tehran must take very seriously. What is clear is that whatever Israel does, the decision it makes on Iran may well be the most consequential it has ever made. The best Israel can hope for, to paraphrase Winston Churchill, is to choose the worst possible option except, that is, for all the others.

Notes

1. For a scholarly examination of the demise of countries, see Tanisha M. Fazal, *State Death: The Politics and Geography of Conquest, Occupation, and Annexation* (Princeton, NJ: Princeton University Press, 2007).

2. Thomas C. Schelling, *Arms and Influence* (New Haven, CT: Yale University Press, 1969), esp. pp. 19–20.

3. Leonard Weiss, "Israel's Future and Iran's Nuclear Program," *Middle East Policy* 16, no. 3 (Fall 2009): 82.

4. Graham Allison, *Nuclear Terrorism: The Ultimate Preventable Catastrophe* (New York: Times Books, 2004). Allison reports on al-Qaeda's meeting with two officials from Pakistan's nuclear program just one month before the 9/11 attacks in which the development of nuclear weapons was discussed. See pp. 20–24.

5. Ralph Sanders, "Israel and the Realities of Mutual Deterrence," *Israel Affairs* 15, no. 1 (January 2009): 82. For the *New York Times* piece, see Ethan Bronner, "Just How Far Did They Go, Those Words Against Israel?" *New York Times,* June 11, 2006.

6. Bret Stephens, "Iran Cannot Be Contained," Commentarymagazine.com, July–August 2010, p. 4.

7. Ehsaneh I. Sadr, "The Impact of Iran's Nuclearization on Israel," *Middle East Policy* 12, no. 2 (Summer 2005): 59. The Bushehr reactor would not be completed until the summer of

2011 and it would be under Russian—not American—auspices.

8. Leonard Weiss, "Israel's Future and Iran's Nuclear Program," *Middle East Policy* 16, no. 2 (Fall 2009): 81.

9. Scott Sagan, Kenneth Waltz, and Richard K. Betts, "A Nuclear Iran: Promoting Stability or Courting Disaster?" *Journal of International Affairs* 60, no. 2 (Spring/Summer 2007): 148, remarks by Scott Sagan.

10. Weiss, "Israel's Future and Iran's Nuclear Program," p. 80.

11. David Albright and Jacqueline Shire, "Iran's Growing Weapons Capability and Its Impact on Negotiations," www.armscontrol.org/act/2009_12/AlbrightShire, p. 8.

12. Ibid., pp. 8, 9.

13. Maseh Zarif, "Potential Delivery Systems for Iran's Nuclear Program," www.irantracker.org/nuclear-program/potential-delivery-systems-irans-nuclear-program, p. 2.

14. Sanders, "Israel and the Realities of Mutual Deterrence," p. 82.

15. Kenneth N. Waltz, "More May Be Better," in Scott D. Sagan and Kenneth N. Waltz, *The Spread of Nuclear Weapons: A Debate Renewed* (New York: Norton, 2003).

16. Sanders, "Israel and the Realities of Mutual Deterrence," p. 87.

17. Stephens, "Iran Cannot Be Contained"; Erich Follath, "Is War Between Iran and Israel Inevitable?" *Salon*, June 23, 2009, www.salon.com/news/opinion/feature/2009/06/23/iran_israel.

18. For a brief but insightful account of Ahmadinejad, the Basiji, and the Hidden Imam, see Mattias Kuntzel, "Ahmadinejad's Demons," *New Republic*, April 24, 2006, pp. 15–23.

19. Sanders, "Israel and the Realities of Mutual Deterrence," p. 89.

20. For a similar view, see James Lindsay and Ray Takeyh, "After Iran Gets the Bomb," *Foreign Affairs* 89, no. 2 (March/April 2010): 33–49.

21. For a similar argument, see Barry Rubin's remarks in Barry Posen, Barry Rubin, James M. Lindsay, and Ray Takeyh, "The Containment Conundrum," *Foreign Affairs* 89, no. 4 (July/August 2010): 164.

22. Mehran Kamrava, "Iranian National Security Debates: Factionalism and Lost Opportunities," *Middle East Policy* 14, no. 2 (Summer 2007): 84.

23. Anthony H. Cordesman and Adam C. Seitz, "Iranian Weapons of Mass Destruction: Doctrine, Policy, and Command" (working paper, Center for Strategic and International Studies, January 12, 2009), p. 8, 090112_iran_wmd_policy.pdg

24. Ibid., p. 4.

25. Peter D. Feaver, "Command and Control in Emerging Nuclear Nations," *International Security* 17, no. 3 (Winter 1992/93): 160–187.

26. The role of accidents is explored by Scott Sagan in Sagan and Waltz, *The Spread of Nuclear Weapons.*

27. Steven E. Miller, "Assistance to Newly Proliferating Nations," in *New Nuclear Nations: Consequences for U.S. Policy,* ed. Robert D. Blackwill and Albert Carnesale (New York: Council on Foreign Relations, 1993), p. 116.

28. David E. Sanger, "Bucking History, Obama Tries to Make Progress on Several Fronts in the Mideast," *New York Times,* September 1, 2010, p. 1.

29. Ian Siperco, "Shield of David: The Promise of Israeli National Missile Defense," *Middle East Policy* 17, no. 2 (Summer 2010): 131, 132.

30. See, for example, Abdullah Toukan and Anthony H. Cordesman, "Study on a Possible Israeli Strike on Iran's Nuclear Development Facilities," Center for Strategic and International Studies, March 14, 2009, http://csis.org/files/media/csis/pubs/090316_israelistrikeiran.pdf; Efraim Inbar, "The Need to Block a Nuclear Iran," *Middle East Review of International Affairs* 10, no. 2 (2006), pp. 85–104.

31. Gabriel Schonfeld, "Darkness at the End of the Tunnel: Penetrating the Iranian Underground," *Weekly Standard*, June 30, 2008.

32. Mark Mazzetti and David E. Sanger, "Israel Assuaged on Iran Threat, U.S. Officials Say," *New York Times,* August 20, 2010, p. A1.

9

American Influence on Israeli Law

FREEDOM OF EXPRESSION

Pnina Lahav

Introduction

From the inception of the Zionist movement, as the nineteenth century came to a close, Jewish families in Eastern Europe split. Some thought that only return to the Jewish homeland could resolve the plight of Jews in exile; others held that mass migration to Western countries, particularly the United States, would be the more realistic means to a good and meaningful life.[1] This difference of opinion soon translated into a tension of cultures and values. For the first half of the twentieth century, even as the Zionist movement cultivated American Jews in an effort to encourage US support for a Jewish state, many of its leaders rejected any lessons they could draw from the American experience, let alone American law. In their minds, America stood for unfettered capitalism and rugged individualism, values diametrically opposed to their dedication to building a utopia in the holy land, based upon social justice and collective solidarity. As the discussion below reveals, Israelis have come to appreciate what America has to

I wish to thank Alon Harel, Moshe Negbi, and Zvi Triger for making valuable comments on this piece, and Carolyn Mattus, Yulia Shilovitsky, and Avi Robinson for research assistance. All errors are mine alone.

offer in more than one way. American legal values and choices increasingly gained influence and prestige.

The legal system of Palestine inherited by the British Mandate in 1922, and left mostly in place when Israel declared independence in 1948, was shaped by Ottoman law and British colonialism. Therefore, it was quite untouched by American influences.[2] Even today the basic Israeli legal structure and the content of its norms is largely rooted in either British colonial legislation (e.g., the penal code, the law of corporations, the law of evidence, tort law) or European influences, which is the heritage of the Europe-oriented Israeli legal elite (e.g., the law of contracts, the law of sales). In matters of constitutional design, the most glaring difference between the United States and Israel is the continuing Israeli resistance to a comprehensive written constitution. Ever since they achieved independence, Israelis have been discussing the need for a constitution. Each decade has seen its own set of proposals for a preferred version, but so far none has been adopted. Instead, Israel went to West Germany to borrow the term "basic law" while giving it a unique Israeli content. Rather than passing one comprehensive basic law, as the Germans have done, Israelis opted for a series of statutes they called basic laws, which were adopted over time. Thus, Basic Law: the Knesset, Basic Law: the Government, Basic Law: the Courts, and in the 1990s, Basic Law: Human Dignity and Freedom came into being.[3] From the perspective of constitutional design, these basic laws reflect a system radically different from that of the United States.

To begin with, these laws are not firmly entrenched.[4] The Knesset may amend most of their provisions with a simple majority. This makes them radically different from the US Constitution, where the amendment process is cumbersome and demanding. Additionally, there are several differences rooted in the form of governance. For example, in the US the president is elected for four years and, barring impeachment, is not dependent on the approval of Congress. In Israel, the principle of separation of powers is flexible, with the cabinet staying in power at the pleasure of the Knesset. Furthermore, the cabinet reflects a coalition: the variety of parties representing a majority of the 120 Knesset members. Fundamental disagreements between the coalition partners affect the range of policy choices open to the prime minister.

Similarly, there are several differences between the Israeli court system and the American judicial branch. The jury is not and has never been a part of the Israeli judicial system. Judges are appointed by a committee that includes members of the judiciary, the bar, the Knesset, and the cabinet. The Supreme Court of Israel operates as both an appellate high court and a "high court of justice." The latter is an institution introduced by the British Mandate but has since acquired a distinctly Israeli flavor. It allows ordinary citizens to challenge governmental action directly to the highest court without first going through the lower courts. Israelis are fond of this mechanism and make extensive use of it.[5] The courts, as we shall see below, have come increasingly to consult American precedents as they contemplate the legal problems before them.

This brings us to Israeli legal education. As I have argued previously, legal education in Israel has seen a substantial transformation. In the 1950s it was largely based on European models with strong English overtones. Today an American student visiting one of the elite Israeli schools will find himself or herself quite at home. Israeli law professors are very familiar with American law and make extensive use of it. Their students, then, are not treading terra incognita as they visit an American legal institution or read American legal scholarship.

Similarly, Israeli law firms, particularly the big ones engaged in international business, have adopted the model of the American law firm and emulate its structure and patterns.[6] Again, an American lawyer visiting one of these firms may find the environment quite familiar, and vice versa.

It appears, therefore, that one may confidently trace a historical pattern. Following its establishment, Israel's legal system bore very little resemblance to the American legal system. Over the decades, as Israel has forged a bond with the United States, partially due to political realignments and partially because of the universal process of globalization, American influence became more welcome and accepted. Today, just as one sees everywhere in Israel the fingerprints of American politics and culture, so may one detect the fingerprints of American law. A caveat, however, is in order: both American law and Israeli law are complex systems, coats of many colors. One should beware of overly broad generalizations. One should be mindful of the complexity and not assume too much coherence in the flow of influence from one side of the ocean to the other.

This essay addresses one area where the American influence on Israeli law has been quite evident: freedom of expression. The First Amendment to the US Constitution provides that "Congress shall make no law abridging the freedom of speech or of the press." This language invites speculation: what does "no law" mean? How should "abridge" be interpreted? How much should be included in the word "speech"? Throughout the nineteenth century, the First Amendment was not interpreted to protect much expression.[7] After the First World War, however, the US Supreme Court developed a robust jurisprudence elaborating both a theoretical base and a set of doctrines designed to protect an expansive array of speech rights. This jurisprudence was also held to apply to the several states.[8] In the twenty-first century no one doubts the significance of free speech as a core American constitutional value deserving and begetting zealous judicial protection.[9]

Five years after it was established, Israel's Supreme Court adopted this American legacy as its own. The transplantation was neither mechanical nor utterly successful. Still, it did take root and has been developed in ways that echoed developments in the United States. Today there is little doubt about the Israeli legal commitment to freedom of expression. I shall trace the American influence through representative cases in each of the six decades of Israel's life as a sovereign state.[10]

The 1950s: *Kol Ha'am v. Minister of the Interior*

Imagine a legal system where the press is regulated by a special statute that requires each newspaper to obtain a license prior to publication. Further, imagine that a public official (the minister of the interior, in Israel's case) is vested with the power to suspend the license and close down the newspaper if he determines that the newspaper was publishing materials that may cause a breach of the peace. In other words, the law gives the minister unbridled discretion. Imagine, too, that the polity has just emerged from a bloody war, is surrounded by enemies, and is facing a world skeptical of its right or strength to exist. Imagine that the state is anxious to find allies and supporters, but attracts none, that it yearns for unity and solidarity and feels that controversy and contentiousness are harmful. If such a legal system has no written constitution and a five-year-old hesitant and restrained Supreme Court, how would importing American jurisprudence of free speech be possible?

Simon Agranat, the Israeli Justice who authored the opinion in *Kol Ha'am v. Minister of Interior,* offered the answer.[11] Agranat was born in Louisville, Kentucky, and grew up in Chicago, Illinois. He attended the University of Chicago both as an undergraduate (majoring in history) and as a law student. An avid Zionist, he immigrated to Palestine in 1929, shortly after obtaining his law degree. Agranat's fervent Zionism did not prevent him from deeply loving and appreciating what the United States had to offer. These qualities helped him when he came to write the opinion in this seminal case, which all agree has laid the solid foundations of Israeli administrative and constitutional law, moving Israel's legal system away from colonial authoritarianism and toward democratic liberalism.

The newspaper *Kol Ha'am* (The People's Voice) belonged to the Israeli Communist Party and promoted the party's platform. On January 14, 1953, it published an editorial alleging that Israel had offered to send 200,000 troops to support the American effort in the war against North Korea. The specific allegation was false, but it was true that Israel's government at that time was in the process of abandoning its "neutral" or "independent" position in matters of foreign affairs and beginning to support the United States. From the vantage point of the twenty-first century, these facts seem trivial. But one should be careful not to fall into the trap of ahistoricism. In the early 1950s, Israel had a robust left-wing political camp composed of several influential parties. The Cold War was raging and these parties tended to side with the Soviet Union. Israel's government and its left-leaning ruling party, Mapai, wished to maintain a neutral stance, both to secure the support of its left wing and out of concern for the large Jewish population behind the Iron Curtain. Thus, although Israel was beginning to seek American friendship and support, it was not yet willing to openly declare allegiance to American leadership. Into this complex web came the *Kol Ha'am* editorial, both criticizing vehemently and blowing out of proportion David Ben-Gurion's overtures toward the United States. Ben-Gurion was so vexed that he found it necessary and appropriate to deny the allegations from the podium of the Knesset. That step would be equivalent to the US president holding a press conference to deny certain news reports—a step indicating how seriously the need for denial was taken. In addition, the minister of the interior also decided to invoke the law and suspend the newspaper. When *Kol Ha'am* petitioned the Supreme Court, it was asking the Court to step into a rather hot political crisis. To aggravate matters for the Supreme Court, a three-month-old precedent, from the pen of the chief justice, held that the press ordinance gave the minister of the interior absolute discretion and that therefore there was no room for judicial intervention.[12]

In a unanimous opinion by a panel of three justices, Agranat ignored the precedent and invalidated the suspension order. The legal stepping stones he used were declaring that Israel was committed to the value of free expression, and elaborating on the theories that justify the need for this freedom in a democracy. The principle of free expression, he said, is particularly robust in the area of censorship or prior restraint. Therefore, the broad discretion vested in the minister of the interior, inherited from the British Mandate, must be judicially structured to balance between this pillar of democratic theory and the perceived need to protect valid interests such as the prevention of breach of the peace or national security. The formula for the appropriate balance, he held, was the probable danger test. Three elements testify to the heavy influence of American law on this opinion. First, the Supreme Court relied on the opinions of Justices Oliver Wendell Holmes and Louis Brandeis for the development of the foundations of the justifications for freedom of expression. Second, the Supreme Court relied on what was at the time the most recent American rendition of the clear and present danger test, found in *Dennis v. United States.*[13] The *Dennis* formula taught that if the government wished to suppress political expression, it had to show that "the gravity of the evil" sought to be averted (e.g., the overthrow of the government with force and violence) "discounted by the improbability that it might occur" was such as to allow official suppression.[14] Agranat similarly called for an assessment of the "probability" that the danger might indeed occur. This in fact has been the test Israeli courts have applied in matters of free expression to this day.[15] Third, and most important for the development of Israeli constitutionalism, Agranat located the principle of free speech in Israel's Declaration of Independence.[16] The Declaration, he said, may not be a part of the positive law, but it is the fountain from which all legitimacy flows. It possesses enormous persuasive power. This last move was also peculiarly American, but somewhat more subtle than the previous two. In endowing the Declaration of Independence with interpretive inspiration, Agranat was actually (but not explicitly) relying on the man he held in profound admiration: American Civil War president Abraham Lincoln. In his Gettysburg Address, Lincoln invoked the great legacy of the United States as a nation "conceived in liberty," spoke of the "new birth of freedom," and tied this freedom to democratic values by stating that it was a government of, by, and for the people. Agranat planted these ideas on Israeli soil. The Zionist dream to establish a Jewish state was precisely a dream for "new birth of freedom." Israel was a nation "conceived in liberty," and as such it was dedicated to democratic values. It was an audacious move, quite stunning in the Israeli climate of the 1950s, a move that could not have been imagined by one not immersed in American history and culture. The bold assertion that the purpose of the polity was liberty, and that liberty meant a democratic regime demanding a large measure of free expression, was very American and, in the early 1950s, not widely accepted outside of America's borders. Agranat was confident that Israelis, too, were eager to lift the stone off the well of freedom and to drink the fresh water of liberty.

It is important to emphasize that the importation of American law did not amount to mindless imitation. The best proof lies in the result itself. In the United States of the early 1950s, McCarthyism was roaring, and anybody suspected of harboring sympathy toward communist ideology was labeled disloyal. In *Dennis v. United States,* the case invoked by Agranat in *Kol Ha'am,* the US Supreme Court sustained the conviction of the Communist Party leadership. Agranat refused to let the ugly demons of McCarthyism fly over Israeli soil. He indeed adopted the Dennis legal formula but applied it to protect communist speech. *Kol Ha'am* was allowed to continue its raucous criticism of the government with impunity. A few years later the Israeli Communist Party died a natural death, and its mouthpiece, *Kol Ha'am,* faded into oblivion.

1960s: *Yeredor v. Central Elections Committee, 1965*

The case of *Kol Ha'am* depicted the cleavages of political opinion among the political majority of Jews in Israel, communists included, but *Yeredor* went to the heart of the Arab-Israeli conflict.[17] As a result of the bloody war that followed Israel's Declaration of Independence, Israeli Arabs found themselves demoted from their status as a majority in the land to that of a minority. In the 1950s, a small group of political activists formed El Ard ("the land" in Arabic), but the group was outlawed by the government. In 1964, members of this group, together with Jewish political activists, formed a political party called the Socialist List and applied to run in the upcoming elections to the Knesset. The government objected on the grounds that five members on the list were also members of the outlawed organization El Ard, suspected of aiming to destroy the Jewish state and restore the status quo ante. The Central Election Committee sided with the government and banned the party.[18] The question before the Supreme Court was whether Israeli law permitted banning a political party, thereby violating the right to be elected, and by way of extension, whether the right to elect a party of one's choice was also negatively implicated.[19]

The dilemma the Supreme Court faced was that the statute regulating elections did not vest the Central Elections Committee with authority to ban a party. There was no explicit statutory language authorizing the ban. The government was asking the Supreme Court to recognize that it had the inherent authority to ban a political party, or in other words, to make a determination that amounted to judicial legislation.

The Supreme Court, again through Justice Agranat, who by then was chief justice, held that the Central Elections Committee did indeed possess the power to ban a party.[20] Among other arguments, Agranat relied again on Israel's Declaration of Independence. This time, however, he did not tilt the balance in favor of liberty. He invoked the part of the Declaration that asserted that Israel was a Jewish state and had it trump the freedom of expression. The identity of the Israeli polity, Agranat declared for the first time in a judicial opinion, consisted of a fusion of both Jewish and democratic elements. One could not purge any parts of this formula. No party in the Knesset, he held, could doubt Israel's legitimacy as a Jewish state or advocate its extinction. Because the Supreme Court agreed with the Central Elections Committee that the applicant party intended to deny the legitimacy of Israel as a Jewish state, it concluded that the party could be banned.

This form of legal argument exposes a fundamental difference between Israel and the United States. Indeed, the method of mining the fundamental principles underlying the system was the same—like Abraham Lincoln before him, Agranat invoked the Declaration of Independence to justify his holding. But whereas in the case of *Kol Ha'am* Agranat pointed to a principle that Israel shared with the United States, the principle of democracy, in *Yeredor* he allowed a very different principle to take center stage: that Israel is a Jewish state. In American law, one does not find such a substantive ethnic attribute of the American polity that is strong enough to override the democratic process. By contrast, Israel is a country always struggling to balance between the universal and the particular, between its commitment to democracy and its determination to remain a Jewish state. In *Yeredor* the Supreme Court allowed the particular to trump the universal and excluded the Socialist List from the electoral process.

Still, President Lincoln entered the deliberations of the *Yeredor* case as well. During the American Civil War Lincoln justified the emergency suspension of the writ of habeas corpus without congressional approval, in direct violation of the Suspension Clause found in Article I of the Constitution, as follows: "It forces us to ask: 'Is there, in all republics, this inherent and fatal weakness? Must a government, of necessity, be too strong for the liberties of its own people, or too weak to maintain its own existence?'"[21] In other words, Lincoln argued that the safety of the republic justified the temporary suspension of the writ. Here, too, Agranat was implying, violating the equal-protection principle inherent in the election law was justified to protect the Jewish state. In 1985 the Knesset amended the election law to allow the Central Election Commission to ban parties.[22]

It is important to note the differences between the reliance on American law in *Kol Ha'am* and in *Yeredor*. In *Kol Ha'am* Agranat used Lincoln's appeal to the Declaration of Independence to incorporate the principle of free expression into Israeli law. In *Yeredor*, Agranat used Lincoln's unilateral arrogation of emergency powers to the executive branch to justify the power of the Central Elections Committee to ban political parties. Thus, whereas *Kol Ha'am* aligned itself with the more sunny disposition of American constitutionalism, *Yeredor* opted for the authoritarian, suppressive potential inherent in American constitutional interpretation. Both tracks, indeed, are available for importation. Both American and Israeli laws are complex enough systems to permit such choices.[23]

The 1970s: The Yom Kippur War and the Law of Defamation

Two years after *Yeredor* was decided, Israel experienced one of the most traumatic events in its nineteen-year history, an event that came to define its identity to this day. The Six-Day War in June 1967, preceding a most terrifying "waiting period," ended with a glorious victory. Israel emerged as a dominant military power in the Middle East and created the now-intractable dilemma concerning the future of the occupied territories. Under the leadership of Prime Minister Golda Meir, born in Russia but raised in Milwaukee, Wisconsin, US-Israeli relations became cozy. American influence on Israeli politics, culture, and economy was increasingly evident. And yet, while Israelis were basking in the splendor of their military prowess and economic prosperity, they failed to foresee the gathering storm. The 1973 Yom Kippur War, a surprise attack launched simultaneously by Egypt and Syria, inflicted severe harm on Israel, tore the people's confidence to pieces, and exposed the country's imminent vulnerability. It also exposed an arrogant and conceited leadership, blind to the writing on the wall. Following intense public pressure, a commission of inquiry was appointed, headed by Chief Justice Simon Agranat, to investigate the causes for "the mishap." At the same time, the United States itself experienced an unparalleled political crisis. Shattered by the failed war in Vietnam and the revelations of massive governmental deceit to keep the war going, Americans were facing the Watergate scandal and President Richard Nixon's disgraceful fall from power. The crown of glory went to the press, which heroically exposed government misconduct and insisted on official accountability. By contrast, the Israeli press at that time was rather smug and complacent. Indeed, *Kol Ha'am* protected freedom of the press, but Israeli press culture did not take bold advantage of that freedom. Publishers and journalists saw themselves as the long arm of the government and felt comfortable adhering to its strategy and guidelines. Any doubtful voice was silenced by the military censor, acting under the Defense (Emergency) Regulations, which were also inherited from the British Mandate.[24] Expectations of unity and solidarity shaped the popular understanding of democracy, and aggressive watchdogs were not welcome. After the Yom Kippur War, this self-image began to change. The press observed the American Fourth Estate's vigorous challenges and felt remorseful and inadequate. Israelis were angry with their government, and journalists translated their anger into an increasing willingness to raise serious questions about government policy. When the Agranat Commission began probing the political and military performance that led to the Yom Kippur War, the media coverage became hypercritical and aggressive.[25] The members of the commission, among them Justices Agranat and Moshe Landau, were not accustomed to this level of aggressive, even acrimonious criticism. As a result, they felt it was only natural to appeal to the minister of justice and to the attorney general to protect them from this watchdog that had suddenly been turned loose. They expected the attorney general to muzzle the press. Herein we see the tensions inside Israeli law related to various paths open to the decision makers. The attorney general could choose the conventional path that Israel had inherited from the British Mandate. This path empowered the government to invoke the law of contempt of court and either punish reporters who "crossed the line" or at least issue a warning that might chill their enthusiasm for criticizing aggressively. The other path was to follow the American model and limit the power of contempt of court because of "the profound national commitment to the principle that debate on public issues should be uninhibited, robust, and wide-open, and that it may well include vehement, caustic, and sometimes unpleasantly sharp attacks on government and public officials."[26]

Much to the disappointment of the Agranat Commission, Attorney General Meir Shamgar preferred the American to the English solution. Shamgar's decision to tolerate hostile press coverage inaugurated a new era in the relationship between the government and the press in Israel that was closer to the American model. Israel's press is still rather protective of its government and tends to be deferential in matters of national security, but it is now more self-conscious of its professional duty to keep a critical eye on governmental affairs.[27]

From the perspective of the history of Israel's Supreme Court, the 1970s signaled the end of one era and the beginning of another. Agranat and several of his brethren retired. New justices were appointed, who were either born in or had grown up in Israel, but who eyed the American system of government and its legal culture with appreciation and affection. Shamgar, the attorney general who valued the freedom of the press, joined the Supreme Court and in 1983 would be appointed chief justice. Meanwhile, Yitzhak Rabin, architect of the victory in the Six-Day War and an admirer of the American constitutional system, particularly the strong powers vested in the president, was now prime minister. Rabin's new attorney general, Aharon Barak, the outstanding former dean of the faculty of law at Hebrew University who had spent time at Harvard Law School, would also soon join the Israeli Supreme Court. Barak would succeed Shamgar as chief justice in 1995. These two men are pivotal to the continuation of our story because of their determination to pursue the path Justice Agranat took in 1953 and further consult American jurisprudence, particularly that related to freedom of expression.[28]

Back to freedom of expression in Israel of the 1970s. As a junior justice in the mid-1970s, Shamgar attempted to modify the Israeli law of defamation by incorporating into it the important 1964 holding in *New York Times v. Sullivan*.[29] In that case, a unanimous US Supreme Court held that when public officials sue the press for defamation, the First Amendment operates as a shield to protect the journalist. To succeed in a defamation claim, the public official must prove that the journalist had actual knowledge that the report was false or exercised reckless disregard of the falsehood (the doctrine known as the "actual malice" rule). This holding has been recognized as one of the cornerstones of First Amendment law in the United States and has survived both the conservative Burger and Rehnquist courts.[30]

The Israeli case *Ha'aretz v. Electric Company* involved the CEO of a governmental company.[31] The director was criticized for authorizing the electric company to purchase for him an expensive American car with fancy amenities. The purchase occurred during a time of economic recession in Israel. Following public outcry, the director announced that he would sell the car, but he appeared to take his time. The newspaper *Ha'aretz* criticized this state of affairs, and the electric company sued, claiming that the director's reputation was injured. In court, Shamgar interpreted the Israeli defamation law in light of *New York Times v. Sullivan*; he even provided the same justifications that Justice William Brennan provided in his American opinion. Justice Shamgar's opinion prevailed in the first round, but Israel's court then decided to invoke a procedure called "further hearing," which allowed reconsideration of a ruling with an expanded panel of justices. Five justices now reconsidered the case, and Shamgar found himself dissenting. Writing for the majority, Justice Landau, then deputy chief justice and soon to be chief justice, held that the Israeli law of defamation was closer to the British model than to the American model. Therefore, a firm distinction between facts and opinion required that facts journalists reported must be correct. Only a "fair comment" or opinion was immune to a lawsuit by the public official. The enlarged panel found *Ha'aretz*, the leading daily at the time, liable for defamation. By historical accident, the matter came before the Israeli Supreme Court as the Nazi Party in Illinois was litigating its right to march in the town of Skokie. The town was populated by Holocaust survivors who strongly opposed the idea that Nazis could be allowed to march in their streets. Both the state and the federal courts refused to carve an exception to the principle that the First Amendment insisted on content neutrality, and did not allow a municipality to silence a view, no matter how reprehensible.[32] Justice Landau was shocked. As he rejected Shamgar's view and held that *Ha'aretz* had defamed the director of the electric company and owed him compensation for injuring his reputation, Landau added, "[Skokie] was decided because the Justices saw themselves bound by the First Amendment. We should better reflect on that phenomenon."[33]

The Landau-Shamgar debate brought to the surface the ever-present tension within the Israeli legal community. One camp, represented by Landau, preferred a cautious path loyal to the English common law, which values order and civility over social dynamism, and therefore would opt for a more restrained public debate. The other camp, represented by Shamgar, wished to encourage Israeli development into a vibrant, energetic democracy, willing to risk some cacophony to allow a wider spectrum of views and ideas and encourage accountability and transparency. We shall return to this point below.

The 1980s: Kahane Comes to Israel

The 1980s intensified the tension between the two camps. An American-born rabbi named Meir Kahane forced the Israeli polity to make a choice in at least one area: racist speech.[34] Kahane was a relatively well known figure in New York Jewish circles. He founded the Jewish Defense League, an organization prone to violence, feeding on the tension between Jews and African Americans at the end of the 1960s. He also attracted public attention through his fight on behalf of Soviet Jewry. In 1971, Kahane immigrated to Israel, settled in the occupied territories, and became politically active. His agenda included a racist component: he advocated an Israel populated by Jews alone, considered Israeli Palestinians as "others," and encouraged ethnic discord. Although Jewish-Israeli prejudice against Palestinian Arabs was a part of Israeli society prior to Kahane's arrival in Israel, his charismatic presence and daring tactics considerably aggravated Jewish-Arab relations. The 1980s saw several legal battles concerning the legitimacy of racist speech in Israel, mostly related to Kahane and his followers. By and large, the courts favored wider latitude for free speech, whereas the Knesset and other government institutions favored curbing racist speech. In 1985, the Knesset amended Section 7 of Basic Law: the Knesset, to ban political parties that incite racism.[35] Another amendment to the Knesset's procedure prohibited submission of a bill that contained racist language.[36] In 1986, racist speech became a criminal offense punishable by a five-year prison term.[37] Israel's Knesset preferred to follow the example of Europe and the United Kingdom, jurisdictions that banned racist speech, rather than that of the United States.[38]

Comparing the Israeli activity in this area to that obtaining in the United States allows us to assess the extent and the limits of American influence on Israeli law. Today racist speech, as distinguished from hate crimes, is largely protected under the First Amendment.[39] That has not always been so. In 1952, the US Supreme Court held that a state acts within its police powers when it bans racist speech.[40] Thereafter, the Court expanded the protection of speech, even to racist speech, but at the same time expanded civil rights.[41] Consequently, for a while Americans thought the civil rights movement had won and racism was a thing of the past.[42] During the 1980s some legal scholars began to argue that "words wound" and that therefore regulating racist speech should be permissible.[43] This debate was taking place at precisely the same time the Israelis were deliberating this question. The Israeli Supreme Court, in several opinions involving Kahane, ruled that freedom of expression should prevail. As we saw, however, the Knesset was of a different opinion.[44] We see a fundamental difference between the US and the Israeli constitutional systems. In Israel, as in the United States, the Supreme Court has great power to interpret statutes and influence the legal culture. However, the Israeli Knesset does have the final say. If the members of the Knesset form a majority, their votes prevail and their legislative judgment overrides that of the Supreme Court. Not so in the United States. In both Israel and the United States, racism is a fact of life and has been found to be toxic. Both polities attempted to curb it through the law. The movement to outlaw racist speech succeeded in Israel but failed in the United States, where neither Congress nor state legislatures may trump the Supreme Court's interpretation of the Constitution.[45] Only a constitutional amendment, which is achieved through a difficult and rarely successful process, may do so.

But if in the matter of regulating racist speech Israel deliberately chose a different path and criminalized racist expression, in the matter of censorship it exhibited a more marked willingness to adopt US ideas. Two important cases of the 1980s display this point.

Yitzhak Laor is a noted Israeli poet and writer. In the early 1980s he wrote a play titled *Ephraim Goes to the Army.* The play scratched an open wound: the performance of Israeli soldiers in the occupied territories. In sharp and poignant dialogue, the play denounced Israeli brutality against the Palestinians.[46] The Film and Theater Censorship Board, a relic of the mandatory period, was outraged by the play and banned its production. The 1984 opinion in *Laor v. Film and Theater Censorship Board* overturned the ban and has become a landmark case.[47] Interestingly, the Censorship Board internalized the *Kol Ha'am* test and argued that the "probable danger" doctrine, rather than the bad tendency test or some "reasonable" yardstick, was the appropriate legal tool by which to evaluate the ban. The board found depicting Israelis as brutal occupiers, even resembling Nazis, both inflicted immeasurable pain on the Jewish population and created a probable danger that Palestinian Israelis would resort to violence. Again, the reader may ask herself if the social, political, and historical differences between the United States and Israel warranted a different judicial approach. Was it relevant that the US population did not suffer the emotional proximity to the trauma of the Holocaust that Israelis experienced? Or that Americans are not familiar with a domestic occupation and, furthermore, since 1971 American males have not been obliged to perform military service? Still, Americans have experienced the trauma of slavery, of Jim Crow laws, and of extensive lynching and yet remained loyal to the principle of free expression. The Israeli Supreme Court must have felt that the American principles, rooted in the theory of democratic self-government, should serve Israel as well. The Supreme Court made several references to American law, quoted both American scholars and judicial opinions, and emphasized three important American constitutional doctrines. First, the Supreme Court emphasized the need to apply a balancing of interests test that would be structured so that the value of free speech would be appropriately assessed. Second, the Supreme Court emphasized that it would review the facts de novo rather than defer to the judgment of the Censorship Board when free expression was at stake. Third, the Supreme Court made use of the means/ends relationship prong of the strict scrutiny test, often applied by US courts when a constitutional right is allegedly violated. The Supreme Court held that if a less drastic means was available to the decision makers, they should not resort to censorship. None of these devices was new to Israeli law. The innovation lay in the subordination of the Film and Theater Censorship Board to the jurisprudence of free expression and in the factual context. The future of the occupied territories has been an increasingly contentious question in Israel. Israelis wished to think of the government in the West Bank as "enlightened occupation," and the play meant to specifically puncture this belief. The Supreme Court's opinion, therefore, touched a raw nerve, but evidently the justices felt that Israelis were mature enough to overcome the indignation and permit a climate of free expression. The Knesset eventually abolished the Censorship Board related to theatrical plays. Today only film censorship survives. We shall return to this issue when we address cases of the twenty-first century. [48]

A 1988 case seals the trilogy for this decade. Laor presented the army in a very unfavorable light. But even though the play walked a fine line between fact and fiction, it was still theater, and portrayed low-level officers. The case resulted in limitations on the board, an archaic body about which Israelis did not care much. *Shnitzer v. the Military Censor* was an altogether different matter.[49] It involved an institution at the heart of the security establishment: the mythical Mossad. It challenged the authority of the military censor, until then an authority quite immune to popular scrutiny. An article by Aluf Ben, then a young, irreverent reporter and today *Ha'aretz*'s editor-in-chief, discussed recent dissatisfaction among the Mossad upper echelons, and situated the upcoming appointment of a new Mossad chief in the context of this discontent. The article also wished to name, and describe, the head of the Mossad, until then inaccessible to public scrutiny, and only known by his first initial.[50] In accordance with the law, the article was submitted to the military censor, who repeatedly banned publication. *Ha'ir*, a local magazine and a part of the Ha'aretz group slated to publish the piece, petitioned the Supreme Court. The question was, To what extent was the press entitled to tell the Israeli people the truth about one of their central institutions? In a unanimous opinion of three justices, Chief Justice Barak held that the military censor, like the rest of the executive branch, was subject to judicial review. The censor was obliged to apply the "probable danger test" before he could censor journalists. In a review de novo, the Court examined the article and decided that the probable danger test was not met and that therefore the magazine was entitled to publish the piece. The Court relied heavily on the 1953 case of *Kol Ha'am* and other Israeli precedents. The landmark American case involving the Pentagon Papers also made an appearance, and one has a feeling that the Israeli Supreme Court was eager to adopt its spirit and approach.[51] The Pentagon Papers case rejected the Nixon administration's request for an injunction against the *Washington Post* and the *New York Times* when the two newspapers began to publish top-secret documents related to the Vietnam War. The case pushed the envelope in its insistence on accountability and transparency in government and in allowing the people access to the belly of governmental operations. The Israeli Supreme Court must have been proud of its bold move, placing Israel squarely in the camp of vibrant Western democracies, eager to nurture the principle that the ruled must keep watch over their rulers.

The 1990s: Basic Law—Human Dignity and Freedom and the Assassination of Yitzhak Rabin

We must now divert from our narrative to flag two important constitutional events in the 1990s that are indirectly connected to freedom of expression: the passage in 1992 of Basic Law: Human Dignity and Freedom and the assassination of Prime Minister Yitzhak Rabin in 1995.

This law raises important questions: First, are the rights it recognizes more privileged than those rights it fails to mention? Second, does the law confer upon the courts the power to invalidate subsequent legislation that violated the rights recognized therein? In other words, does the new Basic Law confer upon the courts the power of judicial review?[52]

The Basic Law does not mention the right to freedom of expression or the right to equal protection of the laws, which is an important subject that is not addressed in this chapter. The original plan was to submit to the Knesset additional but separate Basic Laws that would guarantee freedom of speech and freedom of association. In all probability this plan aimed to prevent the legislation from becoming contentious and to enhance the chance that the Knesset would adopt a bill guaranteeing at least some rights.[53] The lesson for the reader is that to the extent that the Knesset looks to the United States for inspiration, it picks and chooses from that legacy what it wishes to adopt. The US Bill of Rights begins with the First Amendment. Israel's Knesset kept its silence about free speech, neither endorsing nor rejecting the right. This does mean that the pull of American culture notwithstanding, Israelis are marching to their own drummer. Some have suggested that the right to freedom of expression may be "found" in the concept of human dignity, which is the cornerstone of Basic Law: Human Dignity and Freedom. We shall return to this issue momentarily.

Another central question relates to judicial review. Did the Basic Law endow the courts with the power to invalidate legislation?[54] It was certainly silent on this issue just as the US Constitution was silent when William Marbury sued James Madison over the withholding of his commission to a judgeship. In *Marbury v. Madison,* now a cornerstone of American constitutional law, Chief Justice John Marshall determined that the federal courts did possess the power to invalidate legislation if they concluded that it violated the constitution. No one has doubted this proposition ever since.[55] In 1992, Chief Justice Aharon Barak gave a speech later published under the title "The Constitutional Revolution." He suggested that the Basic Law created a Bill of Rights and conferred upon the courts the power of judicial review. Soon thereafter, in *Bank Hamizrahi v. Migdal,* a panel of nine justices accepted Barak's idea and held that Israeli courts could invalidate legislation that violated the Basic Law.[56] The fingerprints of *Marbury v. Madison,* as well as the two centuries of American debate, make a strong presence in this case. The terms "judicial activism" and "judicial restraint" entered the Israeli legal menu, and any Israeli law student feels at ease discussing their pros and cons.[57]

The other central event in the 1990s was the assassination of Prime Minister Yitzhak Rabin on November 4, 1995, at a peace rally in Tel Aviv. The assassination of the prime minister, hero of the Six-Day War, and architect of the Oslo peace process by a young man who hoped he would thereby undermine Rabin's policies was an earth-shattering event. It ignited a fierce debate about the contours of free speech in Israel and the distinction between protected expression and incitement. In the aftermath of the assassination, the Israeli law of incitement has been amended several times to reflect the Knesset's fear that the principle of free expression might be used by undemocratic or nationalist forces who do not value the principles of democracy. The same debate was repeated during the prime ministership of Ariel Sharon when plans for evacuating settlements from the Gaza Strip were carried out. It is quite likely that we have not seen the end of this debate and that the political turmoil accompanying any decision about the future of the occupied territories will bring about renewed calls for a vigorous application of the criminal law against incitement, countered by defenders of free speech.[58]

Basic Law: Human Dignity and Freedom made an appearance in a highly controversial case, symbolically concluding the twentieth century. It had to do with the Holocaust, memory, history, and Zionist ideology. It also raised questions about postmodernism, the relativity of truth, and whether a sharp line between fact and fiction must be preserved even at the expense of artistic freedom. Hannah Senesh has been a mythical figure in Israel and in the Jewish world.[59] A young woman, a budding poet, and a courageous soldier, she was recruited by the British to parachute behind enemy lines in Hungary and make contact with the remnants of the Jewish community then being transported by Adolf Eichmann to the death camps. She was caught by the Gestapo, tortured, and executed. In Israeli mythology she stands for noble heroism. Furthermore, she is contrasted with Rudolf Kasztner, leader of the Jewish community in Hungary, who many suspected of collaborating with the Nazis.[60] Motty Lerner, a playwright, wrote a play about the Kasztner affair and included a statement by Kasztner that Senesh broke under aggressive interrogation and gave away the names of her fellow paratroopers. The question before the Supreme Court was whether Senesh's brother, Giora, had the right to enjoin Israel's Broadcasting Agency, which is a governmental institution, from including the statement in the play. It should be emphasized that Lerner and the Broadcasting Agency attached an announcement that the play was a work of fiction, a docudrama. Giora Senesh argued that even a fictional assault on his sister's memory was intolerably painful and should not be permitted. In a 2–1 opinion, the Supreme Court declined to order the Broadcasting Agency to delete the damaging statement.[61]

The entire Supreme Court agreed that Senesh was not broken during the interrogation and did not divulge the names of her comrades. This proved to be an important pillar of the opinion. The basic Zionist narrative was confirmed by the Supreme Court. Because the Supreme Court expressed confidence in Senesh's heroism, it was free to pose her fight for freedom in Nazi-occupied Europe as compatible with, rather than antithetical to, the freedom of expression that her brother's petition attacked. The Senesh Court, therefore, did not confirm the stain on Senesh's reputation, but rather augmented Senesh's struggle to free the world from tyranny, any tyranny. Barak's first step was to anchor the right to freedom of expression in Israeli law. Without analyzing the question, Barak assumed that the term "human dignity" in Basic Law: Human Dignity and Freedom included freedom of expression. He also enlisted canonical precedent (*Kol Ha'am*), the deepest roots of Jewish culture (prophecy as a phenomenon of speaking truth to power), and the dual nature of Israel as a Jewish and democratic state.[62] These three fundamental arguments are all authentically Israeli and rather independent of American influence. Together they prove the level of maturity and confidence that the Israeli judiciary had reached at that point, skillfully using the tools in the arsenal of the polity itself to resolve significant questions.

However, America was peeping behind the veil in subtle and less subtle ways. The *Kol Ha'am* case itself, as discussed above, was based on considerable US intellectual sources. It is indeed interesting to see how it has now been detached from its mooring in US law and culture and has attained an Israeli life of its own. American legal influence was apparent as well. The Israeli Supreme Court quoted Justice Brennan's famous statement in *New York Times v. Sullivan* that speech must be "uninhibited, robust and wide open."[63] Later it also quoted Justice Brandeis's equally famous statement in *Whitney v. California* that "only an emergency justifies repression."[64] More important, the Supreme Court held that the legal analysis at hand required balancing. The right to free expression had to be balanced against the person's right to dignity and reputation, as well as against the interest of the public in avoiding a breach of the peace. The tool of "balancing" basic values and interests was deployed by Justice Brennan in *New York Times v. Sullivan* and has influenced American constitutional law since the New Deal. One of its most famous proponents on the US Supreme Court was Justice Felix Frankfurter. Then, and now, the tool of balancing has been controversial, and lately it has been emphatically rejected by Justice Antonin Scalia but embraced by Justice Anthony Kennedy.[65] In the Senesh case, Chief Justice Barak, true to his jurisprudential philosophy, had taken a stand in favor of balancing and against a formalistic approach to constitutional law. Today, balancing has permeated Israeli constitutional analysis so extensively that its roots in American jurisprudence are nearly forgotten.[66]

It is interesting, at this point, to reflect on the Senesh case in the company of *Ha'aretz v. Electric Company*, decided in the 1970s.[67] In *Ha'aretz*, the Supreme Court upheld truth as a cherished value, opined that the right to reputation is as important as the right of the press to criticize public officials, and boldly distanced itself from the American idea that uninhibited speech is good for democracy. The *Senesh* majority rejected this view, thereby embracing the American position. But *Senesh* also included a strong dissent by Justice Mishael Cheshin. This dissent, along with the fact that public pressure propelled the Broadcasting Agency to delete the controversial paragraph, may indicate that underneath the surface there are forces in Israel who feel uncomfortable with this level of freedom and prefer a higher level of regulation of speech. This discomfort is related not only to matters concerning national security, but also to matters of history and culture.

As mentioned above, the decision in the Senesh case was delivered in 1999, thereby symbolically bidding farewell to the twentieth century. That same year, at the dawn of the new century, Chief Justice Barak delivered another critical opinion for the Supreme Court, denying the power of Israel's security services to engage in torture without explicit Knesset authorization.[68] Could he be thinking of the techniques applied against Hannah Senesh, a young woman noble and pure? At the time, Israel's battle against terrorism did not touch the American nerve, but soon enough, with the trauma of September 11, 2001, the question of torture came to haunt Americans. They became interested in the Israeli experience. Herein appears a reverse phenomenon: Israeli influence on American law. Barak's opinion has been studied by American legal scholars and judges as they contemplated an answer to the question of whether the US Constitution might be interpreted to permit torture.[69]

The First Decade of the Twenty-First Century

Terrorism continued to be a very serious problem for Israel in the first decade of the twenty-first century. This review concludes with two cases dealing with varieties of censorship in the context of the war against terrorism: one decided in 2003 following Operation Defensive Shield, and the other decided in 2009 as Operation Cast Lead came to an end.

By then, Chief Justice Barak had retired from the bench. His impact on the legal system of Israel, and in particular on the value of free expression as interpreted in the Israeli context, had been immense. Barak had also kept close ties with the United States and had been very familiar with its legal system. He was replaced by Chief Justice Dorit Beinisch. It is interesting to note that while the Supreme Court of Israel was dominated exclusively by males until 1974, it has been much more open to the nomination of women than the US Supreme Court. Today, in addition to Chief Justice Beinisch, four women serve on the Supreme Court, compared with the three women now serving on the US Supreme Court.[70] The two opinions reviewed below were written by women.

A suicide bomber exploded amid innocent civilians celebrating the Passover Seder at a hotel in the town of Netanya. Many were killed and more were wounded. It was one more deadly attack in a string of suicide bombings. In retaliation, Israel launched Operation Defensive Shield.[71] A particularly fierce battle ensued in the refugee camp located in the West Bank town of Jenin. Scores were killed and wounded on both sides, and the destruction was immense. On the heels of the battle, an Palestinian-Israeli filmmaker, Muhammad Bakri, visited the site with the intent of giving voice to the Palestinian side of the story. His film, *Jenin Jenin,* was a blood-chilling "*J'accuse*" against the Israeli military.[72] In accordance with Israeli law (recall that following *Laor,* discussed above, the board of censorship of theatrical plays was abolished but the board of film censorship was retained),[73] the Board of Film Censorship convened, deliberated, and banned the film. The film director petitioned the Supreme Court, and the ban was invalidated. The board argued that the film posed "a danger to the public peace and its feelings."[74] The main point around which the arguments revolved was that the film placed Israel and the individual soldiers fighting on its behalf in an extremely offensive and odious false light, and that it was based not on facts but on lies and misrepresentations.

The three justices of the panel, Dalia Dorner, Ayala Procaccia, and Asher Grunis, indeed agreed that the film was offensive and that it did not reflect the truth. However, they insisted that the board did not have a monopoly on the truth, and its function is not to shield the Israeli public from falsehoods. Although the Supreme Court rejected the filmmaker's argument that the statute authorizing the censorship board was unconstitutional,[75] it applied the limitation provision of the Basic Law and found that the ban was not applied for a legitimate purpose, and furthermore was not proportional.[76] The reasoning of the Supreme Court made it clear that it was well aware of the changes in the media environment in the twenty-first century. It pointed out that the board had no power to prevent the showing of the film outside of Israel, and that in the age of globalization and the Internet, anyone willing to pay $30 (note that the court used the currency of the American dollar, not the Israeli shekel) could purchase the film. The Supreme Court opined that validating the ban might even invite the suspicion that Israel was trying to hide something from international public opinion, and thus might tarnish Israeli reputation further rather than defending its name. From the perspective of American influence on Israeli law, this is an interesting point. Furthermore, the fact that American public opinion is so crucial for Israel's well-being appears between the lines. It was the American sweeping revolution in technology that turned the world into a global village and made the film available for all to purchase and watch. American technology thus made the act of banning futile and even self-defeating.[77] From this practical perspective, it was not even necessary to use American law to reach the result. American pragmatism was enough.

As we have seen, the Court in *Jenin Jenin* did not need American law to justify an antipathy to censorship. It already had its own long line of precedents, starting with *Kol Ha'am,* and it had Basic Law: Human Dignity and Freedom to guide it in evaluating the legality of governmental action. But the *Jenin Jenin* Court did invoke American cases. Justices Holmes and Brandeis's dissents reappeared, and their famous quotes were on full display. Justice John Harlan's seminal opinion in *Cohen v. California* was also invoked to express "the hope [recall that Israel's national anthem is "The Hope"] that use of such freedom will ultimately produce a more capable citizenry and a more perfect polity."[78] But it should be emphasized that along with the discussion of US law there were also discussions of English and Australian law.[79] This fact displays another difference between Israeli and American law. In the United States there is currently a raging debate about the usage of foreign law. Some even argue in favor of amending the Constitution to prohibit the tool of consulting foreign law.[80] In this respect, Israelis are closer to their continental relatives; they are curious and open, willing to consult any legal solution to the problem at hand.[81]

Two final anecdotes embedded in the *Jenin Jenin* opinion help us reflect on the American/Israeli connection. One of the US Supreme Court justices quoted by Justice Dorner was Justice William O. Douglas, speaking in 1949 in *Terminiello v. Chicago.*[82] Terminiello, an anti-Semitic priest, vexed the Jewish community in Chicago with his offensive remarks against Jews. On the heels of the Holocaust, these remarks sparked rage and indignity. The US Supreme Court invalidated the priest's conviction for breach of the peace, with Justice Douglas speaking for the majority. Shortly thereafter, Justice Douglas visited Israel and met with the justices of the newly established Supreme Court. "Didn't you go too far in *Terminiello?*" asked the Chicagoan Justice Agranat. Justice Douglas retorted, "We can afford it. Can you?"[83] Agranat commented that this answer reverberated in his mind for many years to come. Almost fifty years later, in *Jenin Jenin* the circle was closed. When Justice Dorner was quoting Douglas in *Terminiello,* she was also advising that "we can afford it." Indeed, Israel has come a long way since its establishment in 1948. Justice Procaccia, the other woman on the panel, ended her splendid concurring opinion with another quote, from the most famous legal celebrity in America: Alan Dershowitz. The Harvard law professor is not only prolific but also extremely influential in both the United States and Israel. His quote, strategically placed at the end of Procaccia's opinion, advised, "The solution is to answer bad speech with good speech, and to have the good speech prevail in the marketplace of ideas."[84] Dershowitz is one of Israel's most eloquent and persuasive defenders. Was Justice Procaccia saying that with friends like these, we do not need censorship? That his extraordinary advocacy would combat the impact of *Jenin Jenin*? That here we have an illustration of what Justice Brandeis meant by saying "more speech" is the best cure for "noxious doctrine"?

The final case in this review ends the first decade of the twenty-first century: *Society of Foreign Journalists v. Minister of Defense*. The journalists, presumably Americans among them, sought access to the Gaza Strip before, during, and after Operation Cast Lead. The Supreme Court rejected their petition but expressed satisfaction with the government's statement that access would be guaranteed. The opinion was very short and did not rely on any precedents. No one would have expected a different outcome. One cannot expect the judiciary to interfere in security considerations as war is raging.[85] Clearly the American military would not grant more access to journalists in either Iraq or Afghanistan. The interesting American fingerprint on the opinion is related to language. Israelis are proud of their Hebrew. They flag it as one of the most durable and valuable achievements of Zionism. And yet Hebrew is permeated with foreign terms. Here Chief Justice Beinisch describes the Supreme Court's contribution to the negotiations between the journalists and the military: "We offered [the government] to consider the 'pool' system as a solution to granting access. . . . The government stated that . . . it will allow the entrance of eight foreign journalists . . . applying the 'pool' system." Indeed, the word "pool" appears between quotation marks, as if to indicate that it does not belong. The chief justice was writing a short opinion spontaneously and in a great hurry, without taking the time to check whether there was a Hebrew translation for the term. But she did seem comfortable using American English in her opinion, while not feeling the need to rely on any American source. This, too, reveals American influence on Israeli law.[86]

Conclusion

The second decade of the twenty-first century is barely upon us, and therefore it is premature to analyze any emerging trends in the field of free expression. It is, however, important to mention briefly two recent developments. First, the ubiquitous presence of technology as well as the Internet resulted in what has come to be known as the Anat Kam affair. Kam, a soldier, surreptitiously obtained classified documents from her military office and shared them with *Ha'aretz* reporter Ury Blau. In 2011 Kam was convicted of espionage. It is not yet clear whether Blau will be indicted for revealing the content of classified documents. It remains to be seen whether this episode results in a reaffirmation of the rationale of the Pentagon Papers case or in a more restrictive jurisprudential approach that insists on the limits of free expression when balanced against national security concerns.[87] American influence may affect the Israeli courts as they confront this issue, but it is important to realize that in the United States itself the issue of how to deal with the leakage of classified documents is extremely controversial.

The second phenomenon that may come to characterize the second decade of the twenty-first century has a more distinct Israeli flavor. It has to do with a wave of legislation and legislative activity (bills not passed or bills pending) that does not directly address freedom of expression yet indirectly chills the freedom of speech. One example is the Nakba Law, passed in March 2011, which empowers the minister of finance to curb governmental funding of institutions commemorating the Palestinian trauma rooted in the 1948 war. If this legislative agenda gains momentum, Israeli democracy may embark on a path more in keeping with the McCarthy era in the United States and less with the progressive spirit of the United States, associated with James Madison, Thomas Jefferson, and Louis Brandeis.[88]

There is a basic tension within Zionism that nurtures all aspects of Israeli society and culture, including law. It is a tension between Utopian Zionism and Catastrophe Zionism. In a nutshell, Utopian Zionism reflects the idea of Israel as a light unto the nations, a state based on universal values and guided by moral principles, in accordance with the vision of the great biblical prophets of Israel. This idea is specifically stated in the Israeli Declaration of Independence and permeates early Zionist thought.[89] Judicial opinions invoking the soaring confidence that freedom of speech will lead to better citizenry and a better polity capture the ideals of Utopian Zionism. Catastrophe Zionism, rooted in the historical experience of persecution, defenselessness, and isolation culminating in the Holocaust, yield an Israel guided by the particular rather than the universal: it is a nation dominated by the overwhelming urge to survive, and therefore subordinates all other considerations to the supremacy of survival. In biblical terminology, this worldview is captured as "a people that dwells alone and shall not be reckoned among the nations."[90] Judicial opinions influenced by this vision emphasize security above other values, aggressively defend the classical Zionist narrative, and view dissent as disloyal and subversive. Good examples are the decisions by the censorship boards in *Laor* and *Jenin Jenin* versus the Supreme Court's opinions in these cases, which agreed that the play and film, respectively, were offensive, and yet held that they should be protected under Israel's constitutional umbrella. A similar tension is played out as this chapter is being written, between those who would like to chill the speech of Israeli professors critical of Israel, and those who insist that Israel must tolerate and respect their right to speak.[91]

It is hard to predict how this clash will unfold. As described in this chapter, Israel has gone a long way toward protecting and tolerating even the most painful criticism. This trend may well be reversed, however. In making the decision of whether to maintain the current climate of freedom or to embark on a suppressive path, Israel will not necessarily consult other legal systems. Long are the days since the leadership of the Yishuv, in the days before statehood, eyed Americans with critical reserve. So, too, gone are the days when American free speech jurisprudence served as a model for Israelis to look up to and to emulate. By now Israel is quite mature, and has enough assets in its own library to guide it through difficult times. American law is still very interesting to Israelis, but it no longer plays the crucial role it played in the first decades of statehood.

Notes

1. I use the term "split family" both metaphorically and empirically. Many members of the Zionist elite in Palestine had relatives in the United States. Examples include David Ben-Gurion, Golda Meir, Berl Katznelson, and Moshe Dayan. See, for example, Deborah Dash Moore and I. S. Troen, *Divergent Jewish Cultures: Israel and America* (New Haven, CT: Yale University Press, 2001).

2. For law during the Mandate period, see Ron Harris, et al., *The History of Law in a Multi-Cultural Society: Israel, 1917–1967* (Hants, England: Ashgate Publishing, 2002); Assaf Likhovski, *Law and Identity in Mandate Palestine* (Chapel Hill: University of North Carolina Press, 2006).

3. For a full list of the Basic Laws, see http://knesset.gov.il/description/eng/eng_mimshal_yesod1.htm. For an interesting overview see A. Gross, "Global Values and Local Realities: The Case of Israeli Constitutional Law," in *Toward a Universal Law for Humanity*, ed. D. Davis, A. Richter and C. Saunders (Oxford: Hart Publishing, forthcoming).

4. An entrenched provision in a Basic Law would typically require a supermajority (80 out of the 120 members) or an absolute majority (61 members). Compare with Article V of the US Constitution, which requires that a proposal to amend be adopted by a two-thirds majority of both houses of Congress and ratified by a three-fourths majority of the states. Article V also stipulates that no state shall lose its equal

representation in the Senate without its own consent.

5. For the emergence of judicial review of legislative action, see below, p. 201, and A. Rubinstein and B. Medina, *The Constitutional Law of the State of Israel* (Tel Aviv: Shocken, 2008), and references there. See also Pnina Lahav, "Israel's Supreme Court" in *Contemporary Israel: Domestic Politics, Foreign Policy, and Security Challenges*, ed. R. Freedman (Boulder: Westview Press, 2009).

6. Gad Barzilai, "The Ambivalent Language of Lawyers in Israel: Liberal Politics, Economic Liberalism, Silence, and Dissent," in *Fighting for Political Freedom*, ed. T. C. Halliday et al. (Oxford: Hart Publishing, 2007), pp. 247, 247–249. See also Pnina Lahav, "American Moment(s): When, How, and Why Did Israeli Law Faculties Come to Resemble Elite US Law Schools?" *Theoretical Inquiries in Law* 10 (2009): 653.

7. David Rabban, *Free Speech in Its Forgotten Years, 1870–1920* (Cambridge: Cambridge University Press, 1999).

8. Through the process of incorporation, which began with Gitlow v. New York, 268 US 652, 666, 45 S.Ct. 625, 630 (1925).

9. See 2010 term, Roberts Court, for example, Citizens United v. Federal Election Commission, 558 US 50 (2010), and United States v. Stevens, 130 S.Ct. 1577 (2010).

10. Space does not allow a thorough review of the Israeli case law. Though I tried to focus on the most significant cases, it is quite possible

that others may disagree with my choices and place the emphasis on additional cases not herein reviewed. For further study, see David Kretzmer, "The Influence of the First Amendment Jurisdiction on Judicial Decision Making in Israel," in *Constitutional Bases of Political and Social Change in the United States*, ed. Shlomo Slonim (New York: Praeger, 1990), p. 295; and A. Reichman, "The Voice of America in Hebrew? The Reliance of Israeli Courts on American Jurisprudence in Matters of Freedom of Expression," in *Be Quiet, Someone Is Speaking*, ed. Michael D. Birnhack (in Hebrew; Tel Aviv: Tel Aviv University Faculty of Law, 2006). Ha'ayin Ha-Shvi'it, a website covering the Israeli media, has extensive coverage and a bibliography of matters related to the press in Israel, www.the7eye.org.il/Pages/home.aspx; the human rights portal at www.humanrights.org.il /main.asp?MainCategoryID=5 reviews cases related to freedom of expression (all in Hebrew). See also discussion in Rubinstein and Medina, *Constitutional Law of the State of Israel*, and references there; and discussions in David Kretzmer and Francine Kershman Hazan, *Freedom of Speech and Incitement Against Democracy* (Netherlands: Kluwer Law International, 2000); Gary Jeffrey Jacobsohn, *Apple of Gold: Constitutionalism in Israel and the United States* (Princeton, NJ: Princeton University Press, 1992); Aharon Barak, *The Judge in a Democracy* (Princeton, NJ: Princeton University Press, 2008); and Moshe Negbi, *Freedom of the Press in Israel: Values in the Legal Mirror* (in Hebrew; Jerusalem: Jerusalem Institute for Israel Studies, 1995).

11. HCJ 73/53, 87/53, Kol Ha'am Ltd. v. The Minister of Interior [1953], 7 PD 871 (in Hebrew), I Selected Judgments of the Supreme Court of Israel 90 (1948–1953) (in English). See Pnina Lahav, *Judgment in Jerusalem: Chief Justice Simon Agranat and the Zionist Century* (Berkeley: University of California Press, 1997), pp. 107–112. See also Orit Rozin, "*Kol Ha'am*: A Portrait of a Struggle," in Birnhack, *Be Quiet, Someone Is Speaking*, p. 71.

12. *Kol Ha'am* Ltd. v. Minister of Interior (known as the first Kol Ha'am case).

13. Dennis v. United States, 341 US 494, 507 (1951).

14. Ibid., p. 510.

15. The term "probability" was translated into Hebrew as "near certainty," and this is how it appears in English translations of Israeli opinions. However, the reader should keep in mind that "near certainty" is not an independent Israeli construct, but rather the Hebrew translation of "discounted by its improbability."

16. The official title is "The Declaration of Establishment of the State of Israel," but it is popularly referred to as the Declaration of Independence. For the American origins of the Declaration, see Y. Shachar, "Jefferson Goes East: The American Origins of the Israeli Declaration of Independence," *Theoretical Inquiries in Law* 10 (2009): 589.

17. Elections App. 65/1 Yaakov Yeredor v. Chairman of the Central Election Commission for the Sixth Knesset [1965], 19(3) PD 365. Copy of English translation on file with the author.

18. For a review, see Lahav, *Judgment in Jerusalem*, pp. 181–195 and references there. See also R. Harris, "State Identity, Territorial Integrity, and Party Banning: A Pan-Arab Political Party in Israel," *Socio-Legal Review* 4 (2008): 19.

19. Like Whitney v. California, 274 US 357, 377 (1927), *Yeredor* may be viewed as a freedom of association case, rather than as a strictly freedom of expression case. However, the centrality of the case cannot be appreciated without understanding its ramifications for freedom of expression.

20. Justice Sussman joined Chief Justice Agranat in this result, drawing inspiration from the German Basic Law. Justice Chaim Cohn issued a powerful dissent, arguing that only a statute could permit the ban.

21. *Yeredor*, p. 388, quoting *State Papers by Abraham Lincoln* (1907), 9. Agranat ended this quote by stating, "The reply given to this question by the glorious President [Lincoln], in theory and in practice, is known to all." Agranat, Lincoln Speech of July 4, 1861, ibid.

22. Basic Law: The Knesset (Amendment 9), http://knesset.gov.il/laws/special/eng/ basic2 _eng.htm.

Amendment of section 7A

    1. In the Basic Law: The Knesset, the following section shall be inserted after section 7 "Prevention of participation of candidates' list 7A. A candidates' list

shall not participate in elections to the Knesset if its objects or actions, expressly or by implication, include one of the following:

    (1) negation of the existence of the State of Israel as the state of the Jewish people;

    (2) negation of the democratic character of the State;

    (3) incitement to racism."

For a discussion, see Barak, *Judge in a Democracy*, pp. 28–32.

23. Examples of the "dark" disposition of US law to suppress rights are the wave of convictions under the Espionage Act during World War I: O'Brien v. United States, 391 US 367, 382, 88 S.Ct. 1673, 1681 (1968), and more recently Holder v. Humanitarian Law Project, 130 S.Ct. 2705, 2730 (2010). See Geoffrey R. Stone, *War and Liberty, An American Dilemma: 1790 to the Present* (New York: W. W. Norton, 2007).

24. Defense Emergency Regulation, Article 98 (1945), reprinted in *Palestine Gazette* no. 1442, p. 1080 (Supp. II, 1945). For discussion of the modifications implemented to ease the censorship, see Pnina Lahav, *Press Law in Modern Democracies: A Comparative Study* (New York: Longman Publishing Group, 1985), pp. 274–277. See also Z. Segal, *Freedom of the Press: Between Myth and Reality* (Tel Aviv: Papyrus,1996), Moshe Negbi, *Freedom of the Press in Israel*, and Zaki Shalom, "Golda Meir's Meeting with the Editors in Chief at the Dusk of the Yom Kippur War," *Iyunim BiTkumat Yisrael* 20, no. 299 (2010) (in Hebrew).

25. For more about the Agranat Commission, see Lahav, *Judgment in Jerusalem*, p. 223.

26. New York Times Co. v. Sullivan, 376 US 254, 270, 84 S.Ct. 710, 721 (1964). See also Landmark Communications Inc. v. Virginia, 435 US 829, 844 (1978).

27. It is important to observe that since September 11, 2001, the US press has also displayed the characteristics of timidity and deference to the government. In addition, like the American press, Israel's press today is self-consciously motivated by profit, a factor that mitigates its self-understanding as a watchdog of the government.

28. See discussion in Lahav, "Israel's Supreme Court," p. 135.

29. *New York Times Co. v. Sullivan.*

30. See, for example, Hustler Magazine v. Falwell, 485 US 46, 57, 108 S.Ct. 876, 882 (1988).

31. CA 723/74 Ha'aretz Newspaper Publishing Ltd. v. Israel Electric Company Ltd. [1977] 31(2) PD 281; FH 9/77 Israel Electricity Co. Ltd. v. Ha'aretz Newspaper Publishing Ltd. [1978] 32(3) PD 337. For a discussion of Ha'aretz v. Electric Company, see Pnina Lahav, "American Influence on Israel's Jurisprudence of Free Speech," *Hastings Constitutional Law Quarterly* 9 (1981): 21, 69–99.

32. National Socialist Party of America v. Village of Skokie, 432 US 43, 44, 97 S.Ct. 2205, 2206 (1977); see also Philippa Strum, *When the Nazis Came to Skokie: Freedom for Speech We Hate* (Lawrence: University Press of Kansas, 1999).

33. *Israel Electricity Co. Ltd. v. Ha'aretz Newspaper Publishing Ltd.*, p. 347. For an elaboration, see Lahav, "American Influence," pp. 99–108.

34. For the Kahane phenomenon, see Ehud Sprinzak, *The Ascendance of the Israeli Radical Right* (New York: Oxford University Press, 1991), pp. 211–251.

35. Recall that in *Yeredor*, the Court found that the Knesset Elections Committee had inherent powers to ban a party. Twenty years later, the Knesset amended the law to permit the exclusion of political parties, supra n.22.

36. Rubinstein and Medina, *Constitutional Law of the State of Israel*, vol. 2, p. 733.

37. Section 144 B Penal Code, amended in 1986 to include this offense: Penal Law, 5737–1977 (Amendment 20), 8 LSI 144B (1986) (Israel).

38. See David Kretzmer, "Freedom of Speech and Racism," *Cardozo L. Rev.* 8 (1987): 445; Amnon Reichman, "The Passionate Expression of Hate: Constitutional Protections, Emotional Harm and Comparative Law," *Fordham International Law Journal* 31 (2007): 76; Raphael Cohen-Almagor, "The Scope of Tolerance: Regulating Hate and Racial Speech in Israel," *Cardozo Journal of International and Comparative Law* 405 (2009): 17.

39. R.A.V. v. City of St. Paul, 505 US 377, 391, 112 S.Ct. 2538, 2547 (1992).

40. Beauharnais v. Illinois, 343 US 250, 266, 72 S.Ct. 725, 736 (1952).

41. See Brandenburg v. Ohio, 395 US 444 (1969) (striking down as unconstitutional an

Ohio criminal syndicalism statute that punished the plaintiff for a speech he made in which he stated, "Send the Jews back to Israel").

42. *Beauharnais* was never overruled but has not been followed. See, for example, *Village of Skokie*, p. 43; *Brandenburg v. Ohio*, p. 446,

43. Matsuda, et al., *Words That Wound* (Boulder, CO: Westview Press, 1993).

44. HCJ 742/84 Kahane v. Shlomo Hillel, and 5 others [1985], 39 (4) PD 85; HCJ 24/86, HCJ 669/85 Kahane v. Shlomo Hillel, and 5 others [1986], 40 (4) PD 393; HCJ 400/87 Kahane, MK v. Shlomo Hillel [1987], 41 (2) PD 729; HCJ 399/85 Kahane, MK v. Broadcasting Authority [1987], 41 (3) PD 255. See R. Cohen-Almagor, *The Boundaries of Liberty and Tolerance: The Struggle Against Kahanism in Israel* (Gainesville: University Press of Florida, 1994).

45. City of Boerne v. Flores, 521 US 507, 516, 117 S.Ct. 2157, 2163 (1997).

46. For a poignant analysis of the effects of the occupation on Israel, see David Kretzmer, *The Occupation of Justice, the Supreme Court of Israel and the Occupied Territories* (Albany: State University of New York Press, 2002).

47. HCJ 14/86 Laor v. Films and Plays Censorship Board [1987] PD 41(1) 421.

48. In 1991 the Knesset repealed the authority of the board over theatrical productions. Penal Law, 5737–1977 (Amendment No. 35), 8 LSI 144B (1991) (Israel). See also D. Barak-Erez, "The Law of Historical Films: In the Aftermath of *Jenin Jenin*," *University of Southern California Interdisciplinary Law Journal* 16 (2007): 495.

49. HCJ 680/88 Shnitzer v. Chief Military Censor [1989] 42(4) PD 617.

50. Prior to oral argument, the parties agreed that the question of naming or describing the head of the Mossad would not be subject to litigation. The Court therefore avoided this matter. *Shnitzer*, p. 623.

51. Ibid., sections 13–17. New York Times Co. v. United States, 403 US 713 (1971) (the Pentagon Papers case).

52. For Basic Law: Human Dignity and Freedom, see www.knesset.gov.il/laws/special/eng/ basic3_eng.htm. Basic Law: Human Dignity and Freedom, S.H. 1391. But see Section 10 *Validity of Laws*: "This Basic Law shall not affect the validity of any law (*din*) in force prior to the

commencement of the Basic Law," http://knesset.gov.il/laws/special/eng/basic3_eng.htm.

53. Guy Bechor, *Constitution for Israel* (in Hebrew; Or Yehuda: Maariv, 1996), p. 198.

54. The question only relates to the judicial power to invalidate statutes passed by the Knesset (a matter of constitutional law). Government regulations were always subject to review by the courts (a matter of administrative law).

55. Marbury v. Madison, 5 US 137, 177 (1803).

56. CA 6821/93 United Mizrahi Bank Ltd. v. Migdal Cooperative Village [1995] PD 49 (4) 221.

57. For retired Chief Justice Barak's defense of judicial review, see Barak, *Judge in a Democracy.*

58. See M. Kremnitzer and M. Ghanayim, "Incitement, Not Sedition: Sedition in the Criminal Law" (working paper no. 7, Israel Democracy Institute, November 1997), www.idi.org.il /PublicationsCatalog/Documents/PP_7 /התתסה20%,הדרמה.pdf (in Hebrew). See also Michal Buchhandler-Raphael, "Incitement to Violence Under Israeli Law and the Scope of Protection of Political Speech Under Israeli Freedom of Speech Jurisprudence: A Comparative Analysis and an Alternative Perspective, http://works.bepress.com/cgi/viewcontent.cgi ?article=1000&context=michal_buchhandler _raphael.

59. A Google search on September 20, 2010, in English yielded 47,100 entries.

60. See Lahav, *Judgment in Jerusalem*, pp. 121–144; L. Bilsky, *Transformative Justice, Israeli Identity on Trial* (Ann Arbor: University of Michigan Press, 2004), p. 19; Y. Weitz, *The Man Who Was Murdered Twice: The Trial and Death of Dr. Israel Kasztner* (in Hebrew; Jerusalem: Keter, 1995).

61. HCJ 6126/94 Giora Senesh v. the Chairman of the Broadcasting Agency [1999] Takdin Elyon 99 (2) 806. In keeping with aggressive methods of advertising and the fierce competition for viewers, the broadcasting agency repeatedly showed the short segment where Kasztner made the accusation, in full knowledge that this was the most provocative and counterfactual part of the play.

62. One interesting development in the reasoning of the Court had to do with a subtle change of emphasis. Rather than relying on the Declaration of Independence as a source of democratic values and therefore of free expression, as was

done in *Kol Ha'am*, the Court relied on Jewish sources. Thus, the Court emphasized the tradition of the prophets, who spoke truth to power, and contrasted this legacy with Maimonides's emphasis on the right to reputation. Ibid.

63. Ibid., p. 811. It should be noted that in relying on *New York Times v. Sullivan*, the Court also cited Chief Justice Shamgar's opinion in *Ha'aretz v. Electric Company*, which was overruled in the further hearing. Despite the overruling, it appears that Shamgar's approach did persist in Israel's jurisprudence.

64. Ibid., p. 817: "To courageous, self-reliant men, with confidence in the power of free and fearless reasoning applied through the process of popular government, no danger flowing from speech can be deemed clear and present, unless the incidence of the evil apprehended is so imminent that it may befall before there is opportunity for full discussion. If there be time to expose through discussion the falsehood and fallacies, to avert the evil by the processes of education, the remedy to be applied is more speech, not enforced silence. Only an emergency can justify repression. Such must be the rule if authority is to be reconciled with freedom"; Whitney v. California, 274 US 357 (1927), 377.

65. See Kathleen M. Sullivan, "Foreword: The Justices of Rules and Standards," *Harvard Law Review* 106 (1992): 22; see also *United States v. Stevens*, p. 1585.

66. But it should be noted that there is an important gate through which an Israeli balancer must walk: the limitation provision of Basic Law: Human Dignity and Freedom. Section 8 provides that "there shall be no violation of rights under this Basic Law except by a law befitting the values of the State of Israel, enacted for a proper purpose, and to an extent no greater than is required." Available at http://knesset.gov.il/laws/special/eng/basic3_eng.htm. In *Senesh*, Barak meticulously applied this provision to the question of whether the Broadcasting Agency may be ordered to delete the controversial statement to prevent a breach of the peace. For Barak's philosophy of balancing, see Barak, *Judge in a Democracy*, pp. 164–176.

67. See discussion of authoritarian legislation inherited from the British mandatory regime and the lack of respect for free expression in the 1950s, supra.

68. The Public Committee Against Torture in Israel v. Government of Israel [1999], 43(4) PD 817.

69. Ibid., see Lahav, "Israel's Supreme Court," p. 136. Itamar Mann and Omer Shatz, "The Necessity Procedure: Laws of Torture in Israel and Beyond, 1987–2009," *Unbound, Harvard Journal of the Legal Left*, 2010, www.legalleft.org/wp-content/uploads/2011/02/2-necessity_procedure.pdf. On the cusp of the twenty-first century, Israel's Supreme Court also addressed the legal contours of crimes of sedition (incitement to terrorist activity). In two cases decided on the same day in 2000, CA 8613/96 Jabareen v. State of Israel, 54(5) PD 193 [2000] and CA 1789/98 State of Israel v. Benjamin Kahane 54(5) PD 145 [2000], the Court narrowed the definition of incitement in the Prevention of Terrorism Ordinance (1948) but let stand a broad definition of sedition in the Penal Code. These companion cases reflect the tension within Israeli law between the American, more permissive First Amendment jurisprudence and the more restrictive British and continental approach. See Daphne Barak-Erez and David Scharia, "Freedom of Speech, Support for Terrorism, and the Challenge of Global Constitutional Law," http://ssrn.com/abstract =1735007, pp. 12–14. It is interesting that the authors place Israel in the European rather than in the American camp. In my opinion the authors' decision is based on their conception of Israeli free-speech jurisprudence as reflected by legislation. An examination of the analysis in both *Jabareen* and *Kahane* reveals the deep influence of US jurisprudence on these opinions.

70. Israel's Supreme Court has fifteen justices, and thus one-third women, as does the current US Supreme Court. However, in the past decade, the Israeli Court had a larger number of women than the US Court. Note that Justice Elena Kagan, the third woman on the US Supreme Court, joined her two sisters only in 2010.

71. For a collection of cases related to this war, see *Judgments of the Israel Supreme Court: Fighting Terrorism Within the Law*, published by Israel's court system and the Ministry of Foreign Affairs, undated (English translation).

72. HCJ 316/03 Muhammad Bakri v. Censorship Board [2003] Takdin Elyon 2003 (3) 353. See also Barak-Erez, "Law of Historical Films."

73. See discussion of the 1980s in this chapter.

74. *Bakri v. Censorship Board,* p. 355.

75. Because it violates Section 8 of Basic Law: Human Dignity and Freedom.

The Court held that given the result in the case, it was not necessary to address this issue. Implied in this dictum was the opinion that the right to free expression is embedded in the term "human dignity." Basic Law: Human Dignity and Freedom, pp. 353–363, Dorner opinion.

76. Limitation clause, Basic Law: Human Dignity and Freedom.

77. *Bakri v. Censorship Board,* pp. 353, 361.

78. Harlan also connected freedom of expression to "individual dignity," thereby making it more relevant under Basic Law: Human Dignity and Freedom: "[the protection of expression is rooted] in the belief that no other approach would comport with the premise of individual dignity and choice upon which our political system rests," quoting Cohen v. California, 403 US 15, 26 (1971), Justice Dorner's opinion, p. 360.

79. Justice Dorner and Justice Proccacia.

80. See Adam Liptak, "Ginsburg Shares Views on Influence of Foreign Law on Her Court, and Vice Versa," *New York Times,* April 12, 2009, p. A14.

81. A subsequent lawsuit in defamation against the Jerusalem and Tel Aviv cinemateques ended with a settlement whereby the cinemateques paid the plaintiffs, army reservists who fought in Jenin, the sum of 40,000 Israeli shekels; "Reservists to Receive Compensation for 'Jenin, Jenin' Screening," Ynet, November 11, 2007. A lawsuit in defamation by five reservists was rejected by the district court on the ground that the plaintiffs were not mentioned in the film. This decision is presently pending on appeal before the Supreme Court. E-mail from Moshe Negbi, on file with the author.

82. *Bakri v. Censorship Board,* p. 362.

83. Lahav, *Judgment in Jerusalem,* p. 106.

84. Alan Dershowitz, *Shouting Fire* (Boston: Little, Brown, 2002), p. 187. Justice Grunis joined both the opinions and the result, and thereby Dershowitz's quote was the penultimate segment of the Jenin Jenin opinion.

85. But Justice Dorner's observation in *Jenin Jenin* should ring in the minds of the decision makers, especially in the aftermath of the Goldstone Report: "During the war and in the following days the entrance of reporters to the camp was prohibited. One could only learn about the events in hindsight, from testimonies of persons involved, from the investigations of various groups and from eye-sight. *The media blackout contributed to the controversy, which is still raging, about what really happened there*" [emphasis added], *Bakri v. Censorship Board,* para. 2.

86. In 1982, the same Association of Foreign Journalists petitioned for unregulated access when the settlement town of Yamit was evacuated following the peace agreement with Egypt. The Court similarly rejected the petition. But Association of Foreign Journalists v. Government of Israel, H.C.J. 236/82 P.D. 36 (2) 637, did not use the American word "pool," and instead used the Hebrew description of "presence of a certain number of media representatives." Dorit Beinisch (now chief justice) was the solicitor general defending the government in this case.

87. See http://en.wikipedia.org/wiki/Anat_Kamm-Uri_Blau_affair. See discussions in Moshe Negbi, *Freedom of the Journalist and Press Freedom* (Tel Aviv: Open University, 2011), and Ilana Dayan, "Released on Probation," *Ha'aretz,* September 14, 2011, for startling discussions of the constraints experienced by the Israeli press. Both Negbi and Dayan are highly regarded Israeli journalists. In Hebrew.

88. See Mordechai Kremnitzer and Shiri Krebs, "From Illiberal Legislation to Intolerant Democracy," *Israel Studies Review* 26 (2011): 4. See also other entries in the same volume for further discussion of this phenomenon.

89. The Declaration of the Establishment of the State of Israel: "The State of Israel will . . . be based on freedom, justice and peace as envisaged by the prophets of Israel." *Official Gazette:* Number 1; Tel Aviv, 5 Iyar 5708, 14.5.1948, p. 1, http://knesset.gov.il/docs/eng/megilat_eng.htm.

90. Numbers 23:9, King James version.

91. See, for example, "Israeli Civil Rights Groups See Themselves as Under Siege," *New York Times,* September 9, 2010, www.nytimes.com/2010/04/06/world/middleeast/06israel.html. It is interesting to note, however, the similarity between this development and McCarthyism, and that Israelis do understand this resemblance.

10

American Orthodox Jews and the State of Israel

Steven Bayme

WHILE SERVING ON A PANEL on the religious-secular divide in Israel some years ago at the conference of the Association for Israel Studies, an Israeli panelist turned to me and noted, "I want to distinguish between the normal and the non-normal Orthodox." Somewhat bewildered as to whether I should feel flattered by her sensitivity to my position as an Orthodox Jew or chagrined by her well-intentioned distinction, I proceeded to note how for American Orthodox Jews, Israel had become a major resource for development of personal Jewish identification and commitment to Jewish peoplehood—goals that surely ought to be cherished by secular and religious Israelis alike. Conversely, at Yeshiva University commencement exercises in May 2010, Israeli Ambassador Michael Oren opened his keynote address by recounting questions most frequently asked of Israeli ambassadors. Oren noted that what he found most annoying was the question frequently asked of him by American Jews as to why he had decided to leave America for Israel in the first place. He concluded by saying, "Here [at Yeshiva University] no one would pose such a question."

Although these trends in American Orthodox attachment to Israel have developed fairly recently, Zionism itself has long enjoyed consensual support within the ranks of American Orthodoxy. As far back as 1902, Rabbi Moses Margolies, the nationally prominent rabbi at New York's prestigious Kehilath Jeshurun Orthodox synagogue, served as a delegate to the conference in Boston of the Federation of American Zionists.[1] More significantly, the Union of Orthodox Rabbis, otherwise notorious for its separatism and refusal to cooperate with the non-Orthodox movements, mourned the passing of Theodor Herzl and hailed the promulgation of the Balfour Declaration.[2]

To be sure, there were divisions, both politically and theologically. In 1947 Agudath Israel of America opposed the declaration of Israeli statehood.[3] Jewish day schools were, and in some respects remain, divided over the teaching of Israel and the celebration of Israel Independence Day. Even today representatives of Satmar Hassidism routinely picket Zionist demonstrations, such as the Israel Day parade, claiming that the very idea of a Jewish state prior to the coming of the Messiah constitutes theological heresy and a serious violation of Talmudic oaths abjuring the Jews from returning to Palestine en masse, rebelling against the nations, and attempting to hasten the messianic era.[4] Nonetheless, the *Jewish Observer,* the longtime albeit now-defunct organ of Agudath Israel of America, consistently expressed concern for the security, safety, and well-being of Israel even while evincing great hostility toward Israeli secularism.[5] Similarly, American ultra-Orthodox yeshivot remained generally ambivalent about Israel yet supported Israel on security grounds and sent students to study in Israeli yeshivot. One survey of students in such American yeshivot indicated that 18 percent planned to settle in Israel. Inside the yeshiva world, Israel as a state lacked distinctive theological or religious importance but constituted a positive force for protecting and ensuring the security of a critical mass of Jews.[6]

More specifically, new trends within American Orthodoxy over time became evident: Haredi anti-Zionism soon fell into eclipse to the point of virtual disappearance. To be sure, the Satmar expressed their anti-Zionism quite loudly but quickly became a marginal force within Jewish communal discourse. Second, and perhaps of even greater long-term import, Orthodoxy, once considered moribund and on the verge of demographic decline, experienced a remarkable resurgence in late twentieth-century America and appears poised to assume even greater significance in Jewish communal affairs and politics. Last, as both Haredi and Modern Orthodoxy grew demographically, historical lines of demarcation between them on Zionism increasingly became blurred. Excepting the marginal and increasingly irrelevant Satmar, Modern Orthodox and Haredi Orthodox alike perceive their futures as closely intertwined with the future of Israel as a Jewish state.

More generally, Orthodox attachments to Israel over time became much stronger than those of Reform and Conservative Jews. Theologically, Modern Orthodox Jews perceived Israel as the "beginning of redemption" and introduced the perhaps questionable halachic innovation of reciting the Hallel prayer on Israel Independence Day.[7] This trope of Israel's redemptiveness signaled retention of the image of Israel as messianic and utopian even as the facts on the ground indicated otherwise.[8] Increasingly, Orthodox Jews looked at Israel and liked what they saw. The presence of close family members and friends in Israel only deepened these attachments.

To be sure, Orthodox Jews did have issues with Israeli society. Specifically these concerns focused upon Orthodox alienation from the Israeli cultural Left, which in turn saw in Orthodoxy echoes of the older shtetl Jew, which Zionism was designed to repudiate. Israeli politicians who spoke Hebrew flawlessly but could not recite prayers such as the kaddish, or who made personal concessions to religious practice solely for the sake of preserving a governmental coalition, elicited primarily Orthodox scorn and ridicule.

Yet what was remarkable about Orthodoxy's attachment to Israel spoke to its own self-perception of verve and self-confidence. Secure in their Jewish identity, Orthodox Jews felt no sense of inferiority to Israelis yet fully identified with Israel as a sovereign state of the Jewish people. Ironically, the "true partnership" between Israel and American Jewry long advocated by leading non-Orthodox Jewish intellectuals and communal leaders in fact attained its fullest realization among the Orthodox, who, cognizant of how a Jewish state transformed the very terms of Jewish life, were most eager to join hands with that Jewish state in constructing a viable Jewish future.[9]

The Orthodox rabbinate in particular functioned as a leading sector in formulating Orthodox attachments to Israel as a Jewish state. The Modern Orthodox Rabbinical Council of America looked to its dean and halachic decider, Rabbi Joseph B. Soloveitchik, for guidance on how to understand theologically Israel's position in world Jewry. In a 1956 Yiddish address titled "My Beloved Knocketh," Soloveitchik distinguished between a covenant of fate and a covenant of destiny. All Jews share in a covenant of fate, but not all share in the covenant of destiny, namely our place as God's holy people. Soloveitchik confessed that he had little interest in state politics; nor was he inspired by a state "like all other nations." Rather, he defined Israel's mission as elevating the covenant of shared fate, symbolized by the exodus from Egypt (freedom from bondage), into a covenant of shared destiny, symbolized by Sinaitic revelation of becoming a holy people.[10]

More specifically, and in pronounced contrast to Haredi colleagues, Soloveitchik assigned theological significance to Israel as a Jewish state. Although the birth of Israel did not constitute revelation, it did connote an expression of divine will and spirit, manifested through a series of six "knocks at the door." These included the political rebirth of Israel as a sovereign state, a military victory of the few against the many, and a refutation of traditional Christian theology that Jews had been deprived of their sovereignty subsequent to their rejection of Jesus. In turn, the birth of Israel had slowed the assimilation of American Jewry, demonstrated to the world that Jewish blood was by no means cheap, and that

Jews now enjoyed a permanent refuge from oppression, best expressed in the Law of Return.[11] The extremists among the secular Zionists had erred in seeking to eradicate the shared fate with Diaspora Jewry, while moderate Zionists erred in thinking that Israel's birth would put an end to contemporary anti-Semitism.[12] In effect, Soloveitchik adopted the mantle of Israel-Diaspora partnership on the project of enlarging the covenant of shared fate to include the covenant of shared destiny.

Soloveitchik's close colleague and occasional critic, Rabbi Emanuel Rackman, then vice president for university affairs at Modern Orthodoxy's flagship institution, Yeshiva University, and subsequently president and chancellor of Bar-Ilan University in Israel, was the first to pick up the cudgels of Soloveitchik's challenge. Rackman hoped for the development and broad application of Jewish law to the modern conditions of a nation-state. For example, he underscored the need for a universal Jewish family law, much as Israel lived by a common Jewish calendar.[13]

Rackman's vision of Israel as venue of a truly *Modern* Orthodoxy inspired many. It connoted both linking state and society with Jewish law and tradition and seeking adaptability within the halacha itself to modern conditions. Israel connoted an incredible opportunity to demonstrate the salience of Judaic heritage within a democratic Jewish state. Sadly, such proposals ran aground against an increasingly vocal and rigid Israeli Chief Rabbinate. After 1967 in particular the rabbinate began issuing pronouncements concerning the future of the territories, to the consternation to Soloveitchik and others, who felt such positions were best left to security and military experts rather than to the halachists.

Similarly, the monopoly of the Chief Rabbinate over issues of personal status— "Who is a Jew?"—alienated many in Israel from Judaism itself as it did many in the Diaspora, who felt they would not qualify as Jews given the halachic criteria the Chief Rabbinate employed. By 1991, Rackman wrote that the Orthodox stranglehold on Jewish family law had proven disastrous for Jewish unity and that he envisioned a resulting backlash against Jewish law itself.[14] These positions, as well as several other controversies, distanced Rackman from the Rabbinical Council of America, which continued to recognize the Chief Rabbinate of Israel as chief halachic decider for the Jewish state.

Yet even as theological and halachic disputes shaped the relationship of the Orthodox rabbinate to Israel, American Orthodox Jews themselves were arriving in Israel—both for short-term and long-term stays—in ever-increasing numbers.

In terms of permanent aliyah to Israel, the disproportionately Orthodox percentage of American Jewish immigrants to Israel, popularly known as olim, is especially striking. In the two decades prior to the Six-Day War, approximately one-third of American olim were Orthodox, compared to some 25 percent who were Conservative and 7 percent Reform. Surprisingly, during those decades an additional one-third of olim were religiously unaffiliated, suggesting the continuing strength of secular Zionism during the early decades of Israel's existence. After 1967 the Orthodox percentage of American olim increased to 42 percent in the 1970s and approximated 66 percent in the 1980s.[15] More recent indications suggest that among current olim, almost 80 percent are Orthodox. As of 1987, for example, 10 percent of Ramaz alumni reside in Israel.[16] Taking 1967 as a baseline, of the Flatbush Yeshiva class of that year of 125 graduates, 15 currently reside in Israel, as do 30 percent of 1967 graduates of the Maimonides School (Brookline, Massachusetts).

These data suggest the increased influence of day-school graduates in future Jewish communal life. The day-school population itself has increased exponentially over the past two generations. In 1960, at the height of the baby boom, Jewish day schools enrolled 30,000 students, or 5 percent of the population of Jewish students receiving any form of Jewish education. Today over 200,000 students attend Jewish day schools, constituting over 40 percent of the school population.[17]

More specifically, the particular schools cited above constitute the "Ivy League" of Jewish day schools. From their earliest days in the 1930s and 1940s, Maimonides, Flatbush, and Ramaz defined themselves as Religious Zionist institutions inculcating a love for Israel and the Jewish people as central curricula components. All three schools underscore the importance of Hebrew language instruction. Jewish study classes were conducted entirely in Hebrew, a "sink or swim" approach that caused difficulties for both instructors and students yet produced students fully fluent in Hebrew as the language of Jewish culture and civilization. Moreover, these three institutions are all justly proud of their "dual curriculum," insisting upon excellence in both Judaic and secular realms. The afore-mentioned dean of Modern Orthodoxy, Rabbi Joseph B. Soloveitchik, founder of the Maimonides school, embodied this vision of combining excellence in two realms. Similarly the emphasis upon coeducation at all grade levels at Maimonides signaled an innovative—even radical—commitment to equal education across gender lines on the grounds that separate could never be equal. In this respect, as in its Zionism, Hebraism, and commitment to secular education, Maimonides, like Flatbush and Ramaz, was a distinctively Modern Orthodox educational institution and defined the relationship with Zionism and Israel as inherent components of a truly *Modern* Orthodoxy.[18]

The rates of aliyah among day-school graduates suggest the relative ease of Orthodox aliyah and absorption within Israel. The presence of close friends and family provide Orthodox olim with a nurturing environment, enabling newcomers to manage the difficult processes of immigration and acculturation. Moreover, the motivation for Orthodox aliyah lies more in self-fulfillment as a Jew rather than in fear of anti-Semitism, which is hardly a motivating factor for aliyah among most American Jews.[19] Most important, American Orthodox Jews perceive an Israel with which they may identify wholeheartedly and therefore find it easier to contemplate undertaking the major financial and personal sacrifices involved in successful aliyah.

Last, facilitating this process is the extremely high visitation rate to Israel for American Orthodox Jews. Fourteen percent of Orthodox Jews have visited Israel a minimum of five times and an additional 15 percent have visited ten or more times. Among Ramaz alumni, 95 percent have visited Israel at least once, and two-thirds at least four times. These percentages are staggering when one considers that two-thirds of American Jews have never visited Israel at all and only 13 percent of Conservative and 9 percent of Reform Jews have been to Israel a minimum of five times.[20] Multiple visits provide opportunities for greater acculturation, developing fluency in Hebrew, and nurturing of social bonds, all of which become critical to successful aliyah. Put another way, Orthodox attachment to Israel, social structure, education (including the oft-cited one-year post–high school programs in Israel), language training, and familiarity with Israelis are all factors conducive to Orthodox aliyah.

Within Israel, Orthodox Jews have made notable contributions to the development of Israeli society. Leading Modern Orthodox rabbis have settled in Israel and have led significant institutions there, including Gesher, an organization dedicated to bridging the religious-secular divide among Israeli teenagers; Pardes Institute of Jewish Studies; and Bar-Ilan University. Politically, Orthodox Jews have been prominent both in dovish groupings, for example, Meimad, and more hawkish movements, for example, Women in Green. The concept of synagogue as community center, best expressed in Israel as the Young Israel movement, is largely an American export. Perhaps most surprisingly, synagogue initiatives promoting greater gender equality, such as the Yedidya synagogue in Jerusalem and the Shira Hadasha minyan, were established largely with the leadership of Orthodox olim.[21]

To be sure, media coverage frequently focuses upon extremism within the ranks of Orthodox olim. One common stereotype is that of Meir Kahane as paradigmatic of "crazy Americans." More scientific research, however, indicates that Orthodox olim, products of American university educations, frequently are numbered not among the most extreme but rather among the most moderate voices in Israel in behalf of liberal and democratic values.[22]

Although aliyah may be the most dramatic illustration of the depth of Orthodox attachment to Israel, the one-year post–high school pre-college study programs in Israeli yeshivot have in fact been more transformative—both as a stepping stone to subsequent aliyah and as a force shaping the world of contemporary American Orthodoxy. Commonly referred to as the "gap year" programs, these have grown exponentially in recent decades. Barely existing prior to 1967, they have since spawned an entire cottage industry of institutions catering to American students spending their first year after high school in an Israeli yeshiva and often continuing their stay to a *shanah bet,* or second year, before returning to study at an American university. In 1979 Ramaz High School reported that of its fifty-nine graduating seniors, ten were attending such a program in Israel—almost 17 percent. By 1982 the percentage had increased to 25 percent and by 2006 to an astounding 67 percent of the Ramaz graduating class.[23]

In fact, at other schools the percentage was even greater. In 1994 Yeshiva University's Wang High School for Boys reported that 88 percent of its graduating seniors were attending an Israeli yeshiva.[24] By 2002, 65 percent of all day-school graduates in the New York City area were attending one or another of these programs.[25]

One should not understate the transformative impact of this experience. First, within an incredibly short period of time a new norm had been created. Orthodox students and their parents perceived the Israel experience as a necessary step in one's Jewish education. High schools at present routinely schedule "Israel evenings," at which representatives of Israeli yeshivot actively recruit the next year's students. At Yeshiva University, 73 percent of undergraduates—both male and female—have studied on these programs.[26]

Clearly aliyah has increased in some measure due to the programs. Among Americans at Yeshivat Shaalvim in the 1980s, 18 percent ultimately chose permanent aliyah.[27] For others, multiple trips to Israel have become routine. Thus, of day-school graduates 40 percent have been to Israel a minimum of three times in contrast to only 3–5 percent of supplementary school graduates. Still others change their choices of where to attend university during their stay in Israel.[28] At Yeshiva University one-third of the students that attended one-year programs during the course of the year had shifted their college plans and enrolled instead at Yeshiva University, with its intensive programs of Torah study.[29] To be sure, these changes in plans have drawn considerable ethical criticism given existing commitments to a particular school, which in turn prevented other students from attending in their place.

Moreover, upon returning, the behaviors of many students have altered the face of contemporary Orthodoxy. Males often opt for the black hat and the large kipa and demonstrate externally their fringes, or tzitzit, usually defined as an undergarment. Females opt for long sleeves and dresses, creating a mode of distinctive Orthodox appearance. Perhaps most striking have been head coverings for married women, a practice virtually nonexistent in a previous generation. Where only 17 percent of their mothers wore the head covering, three-quarters of female graduates of one-year programs either do so or intend to do so after marriage.[30]

Beyond changes in behavior lie fundamental changes in worldview, especially toward secular studies. University education is often perceived as a trial to be passed or a necessary step to earn a living, rather than a broadening experience of encountering new ideas and different cultures.[31] The case some years back of the "Yale five"—all graduates of one-year programs who refused to reside in Yale dormitories—provides one illustration of the trend to perceive university education in utilitarian terms rather than as a source of values and ideas.[32] Similarly, Yeshiva University itself became a different place once the one-year programs became popular. As an undergraduate there in the 1960s, I generally encountered only a handful of students studying Talmud at night in the Bet Midrash. Returning to teach a decade later, I discovered that that very same Bet Midrash now contained a minimum of two hundred students attending nightly. In turn I wondered whether university-level secular education could occur if the library appeared so empty during evening hours.

As a phenomenon, these changes, often referenced as "flipping out," are quite surprising. For one thing, students are often the products of coed high schools that are considerably dissonant with single-sex institutions. Surprisingly, however, students generally do not rebel. To the contrary, the percentage scoring highly on levels of religiosity and religious practice nearly doubles for those who attend one-year programs in contrast to those who do not. These changes remained in place a full twelve months following their return from their sojourn in Israel.[33]

Conversely, however, little change appears to exist in the level of Zionism and pro-Zionist activity. Students report modifications in religious outlook and behavior, but surprisingly Zionist commitment does not appear to be a critical dimension of the educational impact. The curricula of the one-year programs place great emphasis upon intense religiosity and text study. Religious Zionism, by contrast, appears to receive relatively short shrift.[34]

What does appear to have occurred is spiritual transformation. The faculty are very much at odds with the lifestyle of their students' homes and with the culture of the day schools that they attended in the United States. Far removed from American homes, Modern Orthodox Jewish communities, and American society, these institutions are able to shape an environment very dissonant with the one in which students were raised. As my own daughter wrote to me shortly after her arrival on such a program, "This place is much more religious than you or I ever imagined." Another parent, asking one of the deans at the one-year program her son attended to support her position that following a *shanah bet* experience her son would remain committed to attending an Ivy League institution rather than Yeshiva University, received only the dismissive comment to the effect that her son had discovered the spiritual bankruptcy of his parents' Modern Orthodox lifestyle. Reportedly Rabbi Soloveitchik himself, when questioned about these developments in the late 1970s, expressed his dismay at the wedge these schools were driving between students at the one-year programs and the homes in which they were raised.[35]

This is not to suggest that the students become Haredi. Most profess identification with "centrist Orthodoxy"—hence the popularity of Yeshiva University among graduates of the programs. Nonetheless, the changes are quite profound. Whether it be attitudes toward college, gender relations, dress codes, or, perhaps most important, reverence of rabbinical authority over parents, graduates of these programs are changed Jews and changed human beings. Separatism from non-Orthodox Jews has only increased, exacerbating a divide within a broader Jewish community. Without becoming Haredi, these students are expressing their agreement with Haredi values while disparaging those of their Modern Orthodox, to say nothing of their non-Orthodox, peers. For example, where 60 percent of students prior to attending a program in Israel report comfort levels with mixed swimming and attending movies with sexual content, after a year of such study, only 12 percent report such comfort levels.[36]

Interestingly, dissent over the one-year programs remains quite muted within Modern Orthodox communal settings in the United States. To be sure, parents do often vent their irritation over how their children have become so much more intensely observant than they themselves and long for greater "normalcy" in gender relations. On the whole, however, the day schools and their leadership are quite proud of their students' commitment to spending a year in Israel studying at a yeshiva. They glory in a larger picture of deepening attachment to Israel and the Jewish people and value the experience of a transitional year between high school and college at a yeshiva. In turn, they perceive Modern Orthodox institutions in the States as strengthened immensely by graduates in the years following their return from Israel. If anything, they note with pride how the Conservative and Reform movements wish they, too, could elicit the same intensity and commitment among their graduates as do the Orthodox.

If the one-year programs have received nearly a free pass among Orthodox leaders, Americans living in the West Bank settlements have given rise to considerably greater controversy. Approximately 15 percent of West Bank settlers are Americans.[37] Although strongly Orthodox, many do settle in secular towns, such as Ariel, whose long-term mayor, Ron Nachman, a secular Israeli, frequently courts American Jewish leaders and has created a support group, American Friends of Ariel. Dr. Chaim Waxman, a sociologist who studied Americans on the West Bank some years back, underscored their liberal educations and values, noting that only 15 percent rejected democratic values. To be sure, Waxman conceded that only 30 percent would extend equal rights to Arabs.[38] In some cases their higher education and flawless English have enabled them to serve as eloquent public spokespeople for the settlements and their ideology before American media and audiences.

Reaction to the West Bank settlers within the American Orthodox rabbinate has also been diverse. In general, American Orthodoxy was the group most ambivalent about the Oslo process and the prospect of a Palestinian state. Orthodox rabbis in turn mounted financial, moral, and political support for the settlers' movement with some congregations going so far as to "twin" or "adopt" particular settlements. The Lubavitcher Rebbe was particularly outspoken in urging retention of all territories acquired during the 1967 war.

Yet there were also dissonant voices among the leadership of American Orthodoxy. As noted earlier, Rabbi Joseph B. Soloveitchik, ideological leader of Modern Orthodoxy, urged that rabbis leave questions of the territories to political and military experts and cautioned that the excessive sanctity placed upon land constituted a new idolatry.[39] Rabbi Norman Lamm, longtime president of Yeshiva University, expressed great concern about messianism. He urged instead greater theological humility regarding Israel and its victories, avoided extremist positions, and preferred agnosticism on whether Israel's triumphs constituted messianic redemption.[40]

To be sure, some also found considerable support for extremism within American Orthodox circles. In a 1986 American Jewish Committee survey of American Jews, Professor Steven M. Cohen discovered that only 14 percent of American Jews supported Meir Kahane but that 30 percent of Orthodox Jews did so.[41] American Orthodoxy provided Kahane with his financial base, including during his tenure in Israel. At Yeshiva University, Kahane remained a featured speaker as late as 1984, long after he had been ostracized and marginalized by American Jewish communal institutions generally.

Other Orthodox Jews of American origin did tend toward radical activity within Israel. Miriam Levinger, a transplanted New Yorker, settled in Hebron and, together with her husband, Avraham Levinger, became leaders in the radical protests of Gush Emunim, the West Bank settlers' movement.[42] Era Rapaport, former mayor of Shiloh, joined the settlers' underground in a plot to attack and maim Arab mayors they perceived as inciting terrorism. To be sure, Rapaport confesses his struggles with the values of his Western and liberal education of equal rights and the dignity of human life. Nevertheless, he spent considerable time in the States invoking the support of prominent rabbis in America for his activities as a member of the 1980s underground.[43]

In contrast, other Americans subsequently regretted their involvement in radical activity. Yehudah Ben-Meir, an ordained rabbi and a professor of psychology, joined the leadership of Gush Emunim and attempted to impose its agenda upon the National Religious Party. Years later he regretfully concluded that "the monster has turned on its maker."[44] Rav Aharon Lichtenstein, Soloveitchik's son-in-law, who emigrated to Israel in 1971 to become dean and rosh yeshiva at Yeshivat Har Etzion, became well known for his dovishness and support for the Oslo process. West Bank settlement leader Elyakim Haetzni derided Lichtenstein by saying he may not qualify to be counted among "those faithful to the land of Israel."[45]

Still others were frightened by Gush Emunim, its self-righteousness, and its linkage with extreme nationalism, and bitterly resented how it had hijacked Religious Zionism. Following the assassination of Prime Minister Yitzhak Rabin, President Norman Lamm of Yeshiva University noted, "We must always bear in mind the warning of the sages that one must not respect even a Rav when chillul Hashem [desecration of the Lord's name] is involved. . . . There is no such thing as acceptable terrorism for the sake of Torah or the sake of Israel."[46]

Lamm's comments directly contradicted those of some of his more rightist colleagues. In the months preceding Rabin's assassination, at least one Orthodox rabbi in Brooklyn had raised the question of potential violence against the prime minister on the grounds that he was a *rodef,* one who endangered the Jewish people. In Teaneck, New Jersey, several prominent people in an Orthodox congregation resigned from membership in response to the rabbi's engaging in regular tirades against the Israeli government and its pursuit of the Oslo process.

Generally, however, American Orthodox leadership exerted greater pressure on domestic issues than on questions of the future of the territories. Orthodox Jews elevated questions of personal status—marriage, divorce, burial, and most important, the definition of who exactly qualified as a Jew—to existential issues on which their voice would be heard clearly and loudly. As early as 1948 the Rabbinical Council of America (RCA) intervened in support of the Chief Rabbinate of Israel as halachic decider for the Jewish state, a position it has sustained to this day.[47] Even when the Chief Rabbinate, increasingly under Haredi control, has taken extreme positions on personal status issues within Israel, the RCA's perspective has remained consistent: support the Chief Rabbinate as halachic decider of Israel. Such unqualified support, to be sure, has often distanced the RCA from more liberal Orthodox colleagues, to say nothing of Conservative or Reform ones.

Moreover, on the specific issue of who is a Jew, raised legislatively in 1988, many within the Orthodox rabbinate in America maintained that the Haredi parties had overplayed their hand. By demanding specific definition of who qualifies as a Jew in accordance with the halachic criteria of Haredi rabbinic leaders and seeking Knesset legislation specifying as much within the Law of Return, many felt that the politicization of this issue within Israeli society was unnecessarily driving a wedge between Israel and world Jewry.

The problems inherent in the proposed legislation were multifold. First, by invoking the Knesset as legislative body, the Haredim were flexing political muscles given a multiparty system that rewarded small parties within governing coalitions. Second, symbolically, the proposal of a change in the definition of who is a Jew under the Law of Return would delegitimize non-Orthodox rabbis in the United States. Last, the Law of Return itself did not have any halachic ramifications in any case. As far back as 1950 it had allocated the right of immediate citizenship to a number of non-Jewish groupings, including gentile family members of would-be olim. Little wonder that many concluded that as the architect of the proposed legislation, the Lubavitcher Rebbe was waging the wrong battle in the wrong place at the wrong time. Rabbi Haskell Lookstein, for one, while opposing "Orthodox bashing" and excessive criticism of the Lubavitcher Rebbe during the "who is a Jew?" agitation, urged that the matter be kept out of the hands of the Knesset and claimed that the Chief Rabbinate itself should handle all cases that arose on an individual basis. Lookstein in effect opposed legislation defining a Jew while at the same time upholding the principle of the supremacy of the Chief Rabbinate in halachic matters within Israel society.[48]

On foreign affairs, as noted, American Orthodoxy was somewhat less likely to intervene in Israeli political questions. For example, the agitation within Israel concerning return of the Sinai peninsula to Egypt and dismantling of the settlements there in 1982 elicited only minimal Orthodox protest in the States. An Israeli Orthodox politician, Rabbi Chaim Druckman, did urge American Orthodox audiences to protest the Sinai withdrawal but met with little success.

During the Oslo years, Orthodox protest was more outspoken—especially given the putative return of the West Bank to Palestinian sovereignty as opposed to the Sinai peninsula, which held no halachic status or sanctity under Jewish law. Thus, in the 1990s, some Orthodox congregations opted to "adopt" the settlements. By 1995 a real fissure had developed between Orthodox and non-Orthodox Jewish politics. Whereas over two-thirds of American Jews generally at that point supported the Oslo process, only 31 percent of Orthodox Jews did so.[49] The politics of American Orthodox Jews during the Oslo years were aligned fairly closely with those of Israeli Orthodox Jews. The National Council of Young Israel and the Orthodox Union were in fact prepared to criticize publicly the pursuit of Oslo by the Israeli government, going so far as to lobby in Washington against American aid for the Palestinian Authority in direct opposition to the wishes of the pro-Oslo Israeli government.[50] Chabad-Lubavitch, the prominent worldwide Hassidic grouping famed for its impressive outreach activity in accordance with the instructions of the late Lubavitcher Rebbe, broke ranks with the Netanyahu government after its 1998 acceptance of the Wye Accords. Most other Orthodox organizations and groupings, however, followed the lead of legally elected and democratic governments of Israel irrespective of their private misgivings concerning their policies.

By contrast, many significant Orthodox rabbis either openly supported the Oslo process or were neutral toward it. Yeshiva University President Lamm urged that we not apply halachic discourse to Oslo—an echo of the admonition of Rabbi Soloveitchik regarding the future status of the territories.[51] Rabbi Lookstein joined Shvil Ha-Zahav (Golden Mean), a small grouping of influential Orthodox rabbis who supported Oslo in the name of moderation rather than extremism.[52] In Israel itself, the noted American rosh yeshiva, Rav Aharon Lichtenstein, openly opposed his colleagues who called upon religious soldiers to disobey orders during the Oslo process.[53]

American Orthodoxy, however, was most sorely tested in its response to the Hebron massacre in 1994 perpetrated by Baruch Goldstein and the 1995 assassination of Prime Minister Rabin. Kahanist groupings in Brooklyn expressed tolerance if not approval for Goldstein himself, who was a graduate of Brooklyn's famed Yeshiva of Flatbush. The animus against Rabin within the Orthodox world intensified greatly in the months preceding his assassination. One Orthodox rabbi in Teaneck, New Jersey, referenced the Israeli government as a "Rabin Judenrat."[54] Following the assassination, the National Council of Young Israel boycotted a memorial event for Rabin, claiming it had been politicized into a pro-Oslo rally.[55]

Yet these events also spurred considerable soul-searching within Orthodox ranks. Rabbi Louis Bernstein, longtime leader of the RCA and one-time college instructor of Goldstein, stated unequivocally, "We have sinned," referring to the failure of Jewish education to instill humanistic values. The then-president of the Orthodox Union, Dr. Mendy Ganchrow, claimed he was "deeply grieved" by the Rabin assassination.[56]

Most eloquent was Lamm, who engaged in self-criticism, noting that Orthodox rabbis had created the atmospherics that led to the assassination. He offered an unequivocal condemnation, claiming there could be zero tolerance for extremist rhetoric. Sadly, a decade later, following Lamm's retirement, one of his most senior roshei yeshiva invoked the language of political violence in response to a question concerning the potential partition of Jerusalem. Lamm, to be sure, had warned unequivocally against Orthodox self-righteousness and those who cloak their extremist positions in the mantle of Torah. Acknowledging that both Goldstein and Yigal Amir, Rabin's assassin, were products of the leading institutions of Modern Orthodoxy and themselves seemingly were outstanding representatives of the Modern Orthodox lifestyle, Lamm insisted that Orthodox institutions reevaluate their teachings and expressly repudiate the polarizing language that had so poisoned the atmosphere against Rabin. In turn, Lamm emphasized the values of tolerance and mutual understanding.[57] Whether his initiatives in fact changed the culture of Yeshiva University, let alone the Orthodox community, to this day remains very much an open question.

The most recent flare-up of tensions along these lines concerned the Gaza disengagement. Both the RCA and the Orthodox Union, after considerable debate, supported governmental decisions on Gaza. Immediately following the disengagement, enormous protest ensued concerning Amona, a small bloc of West Bank settlements whose inhabitants engaged in civil disobedience and violent confrontations with police. The Orthodox Union issued a strongly worded protest to Prime Minister Ehud Olmert about the police activity while downplaying the provocative tactics of the protesters.[58]

What in fact was the difference between these actions so close in time? First, Amona was on the West Bank rather than in Gaza. Second, the trauma of the Gaza disengagement was so severe in its impact upon Religious Zionism both in Israel and the United States that the pent-up hostilities during the disengagement found their outlet in Amona. Last, Amona served notice upon Olmert and future Israeli governments that additional disengagements would evoke only severe Orthodox hostility.

Where, then, are we in the relationship of American Orthodoxy to Israel? First, American Orthodoxy is well positioned to assume increasingly greater roles within Jewish communal leadership. Only 8 percent of American Jews self-identify as Orthodox, but 17 percent of those under age thirty-five do so. Within affiliated Jewish homes, 38 percent of children under age eighteen are living within Orthodox-identified homes. Only the Orthodox enjoy a positive birthrate of three children or more per family, with ultra-Orthodox and Hassidic homes enjoying significantly higher birthrates.[59]

Thus, for demographic reasons alone, Orthodox Jewry is likely to become a plurality—if not a majority—of those eager to play active roles within Jewish communal life. In this context the depth of Orthodox attachment to Israel becomes even more critical. At present, one cannot begin to contemplate a successful pro-Israel demonstration or Israel Day parade without the strong participation of Orthodox Jews. They are highly committed to Israel, perceive Israel as the historical Jewish homeland, visit frequently, and are passionate in their pro-Israel advocacy. Last but not least, they are probably the only major sector within American Jewry to be fluent in Hebrew, the national and historical language of the Jewish people and the Jewish state.

However, the specter of an Orthodox ascendancy within the American Jewish pro-Israel community carries with it significant risks. One danger is political. If only Orthodox Jews form the base of American Jewish support for Israel, politicians cool to Israel may easily disregard the Jewish vote. Liberal candidates for office may note that Orthodox Jews will not vote for them anyway while non-Orthodox Jews are unlikely to vote based primarily upon a politician's record on Israel. Conversely, conservative candidates may claim that the Jewish vote, tiny as it is, is unlikely to go their way, save among the Orthodox, because Jews, especially younger Jews, generally do not care enough about Israel to make it their political priority. Put another way, when the base of pro-Israel support in America becomes narrowly concentrated within the Orthodox community, by definition that base has been sorely attenuated.

Second, the Orthodox agenda itself concerning Israel risks becoming identified with a narrowly based religious nationalism. Will Orthodoxy become the primary base of Israeli politicians who oppose future territorial concessions and thereby endanger Israel's demographic future as a majority Jewish state? Will Orthodox Jews support efforts to broaden religious legislation within Israel, thereby enhancing the divide with American Jews, who value the virtually unlimited religious liberty existent in America and are disturbed when they encounter an Israel in which the Orthodox enjoy a monopoly over laws of personal status?

Last, Orthodox Jewish attachment to Israel exposes the broader cleavage in America between Orthodox and non-Orthodox Jews. Increasingly these two sectors operate on different dimensions, each failing to fathom the values and priorities of the other. These cleavages weaken the Jews as a people, undermine commonality among Jews, and result in attenuated Jewish influence in American politics.

Orthodox leadership possesses a powerful tool in its attachment to Israel. Whether it will harness that attachment to strengthen America's ties to Israel, nurture a stronger concept of Jewish peoplehood, and enrich itself through an ongoing relationship with Israel, or whether that attachment may in fact weaken American political support for Israel, divide Jew from Jew, and undermine the collective basis of the narrative of the Jewish people remain questions for the future. Even more important, questions remain open as to whether Religious Zionism may rise to the challenge of building a Jewish state upon the twin principles of Judaism and democracy, or will it retreat to a more utilitarian vision of Israel as useful but by no means critical to modern Jewish identity? Will Religious Zionism articulate a humanistic vision that all mankind is created in the image of God, or a dualistic worldview that divides the world between Jews and others? Most important, can Religious Zionism reclaim a vision of Jewish messianism as constructing a Jewish vision of social order and justice in a Jewish state rather than attempting to "force the end" through illegal and even violent actions? At this crossroads in Zionist history, those questions and the struggle for Orthodoxy's future remain very much open.

Notes

1. Jeffrey S. Gurock, *American Jewish Orthodoxy* (Hoboken, NJ: Ktav, 1996), p. 120.

2. Ibid., pp. 121–125.

3. Louis Bernstein, *Challenge and Mission* (New York: Shengold, n.d.), p. 211.

4. Norman Lamm, *Seventy Faces* (Hoboken, NJ: Ktav, 2002), vol. 2, pp. 185–186.

5. Daniel Gutenmacher, "Agudath Israel of America and the State of Israel," in *Israel and Diaspora Jewry*, ed. Eliezer Don-Yehiya (Ra-

mat Gan: Bar-Ilan University Press, 1991), p. 111.

6. William Helmreich, *The World of the Yeshiva* (New York: Free Press, 1982), pp. 232–233.

7. Rafael Medoff, "Rav Chesed: The Life and Times of Rabbi Haskell Lookstein," in *Rav Chesed*, ed. Rafael Medoff (Jersey City, NJ: Ktav, 2009), vol. 2, pp. 485.

8. For the somewhat different views of Rav Aharon Lichtenstein concerning the

redemptiveness of Israel, see Shalom Berger et al., *Flipping Out?* (New York: Yashar Books, 2007), pp. 55–56.

9. Steven Bayme, *Jewish Arguments and Counterarguments* (Hoboken, NJ: Ktav and American Jewish Committee, 2002), pp. 369–384.

10. Joseph B. Soloveitchik, *Kol Dodi Dofek (My Beloved Knocketh)*, trans. David Z. Gordon (New York: Yeshiva University Press, 2006), p. 84.

11. Ibid., pp. 31–42.

12. Ibid., pp. 81–82.

13. Emanuel Rackman, *A Modern Orthodox Life* (Jersey City, NJ: Ktav, 2008), pp. 183–184, and, more generally, 142–143.

14. Ibid., p. 241.

15. Statistics cited in Chaim Waxman, *American Aliyah* (Detroit: Wayne State University Press, 1989), pp. 84, 94–100.

16. Medoff, *Rav Chesed*, p. 487.

17. Alvin Schiff, *Beyond the Melting Pot* (New York: Devora Publishing, 2009), p. 255.

18. On the Maimonides School, see Seth Farber, *An American Orthodox Dreamer* (Hanover, NH: University Press of New England, 2004), pp. 68–69. On Ramaz, see Medoff, *Rav Chesed*, pp. 370–371. See also Nathalie Friedman, "The Graduates of Ramaz: 50 Years of Day School Education," in *Ramaz School: Community, Scholarship, and Orthodoxy*, ed. Jeffrey Gurock (Hoboken, NJ: Ktav, 1989), pp. 82–123; and Gurock, "The Ramaz Version of American Orthodoxy," ibid., pp. 40–82. The Flatbush Yeshiva High School was established in 1950. For background and a survey of alumni through 1971, including commitment to Israel and the Hebrew language, see Joseph Heimowitz, "Jewish Education Makes a Difference—A Study of the Graduates of a Yeshivah High School," *Jewish Education* 47, no. 2 (Summer 1979): 28–34.

19. Waxman, *American Aliyah*, p. 134. See also Yair Sheleg, *The North American Impact on Israeli Orthodoxy* (New York: American Jewish Committee and Argov Center of Bar-Ilan University, 1999), p.1.

20. Waxman, "American Orthodoxy, Zionism, and Israel," in Berger et al., *Flipping Out?* p. 158.

21. Sheleg, *North American Impact on Israeli Orthodoxy*, pp. 3–5, 7–8, 10–11, 12–14, 18–20.

22. Ibid., pp. 27–29.

23. Medoff, *Rav Chesed*, pp. 486–487.

24. Waxman, "American Orthodoxy, Zionism, and Israel," p. 188.

25. Sam Heilman, *Sliding to the Right* (Berkeley: University of California Press, 2006), p. 113.

26. Berger et al., *Flipping Out?* p. 12.

27. Data cited in Heilman, *Sliding to the Right*, p. 337.

28. Ibid., p. 114.

29. Berger et al., *Flipping Out?* p. 12.

30. Heilman, *Sliding to the Right*, p. 118.

31. Ibid., p. 119.

32. Sam Freedman, *Jew vs. Jew* (New York: Simon & Schuster, 2000), Chap. 5, esp. pp. 254–261.

33. Berger et al., *Flipping Out?* pp. 33, 61–62.

34. Ibid., pp. 27–28, 33–34.

35. Schiff, *Beyond the Melting Pot*, pp. 575–576.

36. Berger et al., *Flipping Out?* pp. 44–46.

37. Steven T. Rosenthal, *Irreconcilable Differences?* (Hanover, NH, and London: Brandeis University Press, 2001), p. 127.

38. Chaim Waxman, "Those Crazy Americans?" *Midstream* 32, no. 3 (March 1986): 31. See also my exchange with Waxman on the subject, *Midstream* 32, no. 8 (October 1986): 59–60.

39. Rackman, *A Modern Orthodox Life*, p. 202.

40. Lamm, *Seventy Faces*, vol. 2, pp. 213–216.

41. Cited in Robert I. Friedman, *The False Prophet* (Brooklyn, NY: Lawrence Hill Books, 1990), p. 6.

42. Robert I. Friedman, *Zealots for Zion* (New York: Random House, 1982), pp. 12–13. See also Jerold S. Auerbach, *Hebron Jews* (Lanham, MD: Rowman & Littlefield, 2008), p. 105.

43. Era Rapaport, *Letters from Tel Mond Prison* (New York: Free Press, 1996), pp. 21–24, 27–28, 196–197.

44. Gershom Gorenberg, *The Accidental Empire* (New York: Henry Holt, 2006), p. 268.

45. Cited in Ian Lustick, *For the Land and the Lord* (New York: Council on Foreign Relations, 1988), p. 128.

46. Lamm, *Seventy Faces*, vol. 2, pp. 180–181.

47. Bernstein, *Challenge and Mission*, pp. 215–235.

48. Medoff, *Rav Chesed*, pp. 501–502.

49. Rosenthal, *Irreconcilable Differences?* p. 130.

50. Mendy Ganchrow, *Journey Through the Minefield* (Silver Spring, MD: Eshel Books, 2004), pp. 227–230.

51. Lamm, *Seventy Faces,* vol. 2, p. 235.

52. Medoff, *Rav Chesed,* p. 493.

53. Akiva Eldar, *Lords of the Land* (New York: Nation Books, 2007), pp. 328–329.

54. Rosenthal, *Irreconcilable Differences?* pp. 127–131. On Goldstein, see Auerbach, *Hebron Jews,* pp. 123–141.

55. Ganchrow, *Journey Through the Minefield,* p. 236.

56. Ibid., p. 233.

57. Lamm, *Seventy Faces,* vol. 2, pp. 220–229.

58. Waxman, "American Orthodoxy, Zionism, and Israel," pp. 199–200.

59. Jonathan Ament, *American Jewish Religious Movements* (New York: United Jewish Communities, 2005), see tables on pp. 5, 21, 24. See also Ukeles Associates, *Young Jewish Adults in the U.S. Today* (New York: American Jewish Committee, 2006), pp. 79–83; and Jonathan Ament, *Israel Connections and American Jews* (New York: United Jewish Communities, 2005), p. 26, table 5.

11

The Relationship Between American Evangelical Christians and the State of Israel

Neil Rubin

> As a Zionist and as one who, in the Christian community, is probably the most out-spoken supporter of Israel and the Jewish people the world over, I would say that I have become a radical on this issue. I think that radicalism is needed at this point in history to compensate for the injury that has been inflicted upon the Jewish family, often in the name of God, by religious zealots.[1]
>
> —REV. JERRY FALWELL

IN 1971, THE ISRAELI GOVERNMENT delivered a modern prophet to an excited crowd of mostly first-time visitors to the state of Israel. Some 1,500 evangelical Christian pastors were gathered in Jerusalem's newly renovated convention center—a space provided free of charge by Golda Meir's government—for the first Christian Zionist conference in the Jewish state. So there was more than a little buzz in the air when Israel's eighty-five-year-old legendary first prime minister, David Ben-Gurion, greeted the crowd. It was, as organizer Gaylord Briley said, a "ringside seat at the second coming."[2]

In June 1981, shortly after Israeli air force jets had pulled off a daring surprise attack that destroyed Iraq's soon-to-be-operational nuclear reactor, Israeli Prime Minister Menachem Begin knew where to turn to rally support in the United States for a strike certain to create pressure on Washington to condemn the unilateral Israeli action. His first call was not to President Ronald Reagan, widely regarded as much more pro-Israel than Jimmy Carter, his immediate predecessor, but to his friend the Reverend Jerry Falwell.[3]

Then, in early April 2002, when President George W. Bush called on Israel to act with restraint in the wake of a horrible wave of suicide bombings (including a particularly gruesome one at a hotel Passover seder attended by many immigrant families from the former Soviet Union), Christian Zionists were quick to respond. Hundreds of thousands of them dispatched letters and e-mails to the White House that reflected the words of an April 11, 2002, letter sent to Bush from some of their leaders—all of whom were supporters of the president. It read in part:

> We would ask you to end pressure on Israeli Prime Minister Ariel Sharon so that he has the time necessary to complete the mission he has undertaken—the elimination of terrorist cells and infrastructure from the West Bank territories.

The White House refrained from more public criticism of Israel as it began its Operation Defensive Shield, designed to root out terrorist infrastructures in West Bank cities.[4]

Who are these American evangelical Christians? Why and how did they become an indisputable force in national politics in general and in Washington's relationship to Israel in particular? Why has their pro-Israel passion created such angst among American Jews as well as anger among other Christians? And what does their action of recent decades portend for the future when it comes to US policy toward Israel?

Evangelical Theology and Political Activity

In size alone, one cannot question the importance of the American evangelical community. In 2008, 26.3 percent of the country's adults—roughly one in four—self-identified themselves as belonging to an evangelical church, while 48 percent of the country belongs to other churches.[5] Today the National Association of Evangelicals, founded in 1942, claims to represent more than 45,000 churches from forty denominations. Its definition of an evangelical is a broad one. "Evangelicals," it declares, "take the Bible seriously and believe in Jesus Christ as Savior and Lord."[6] More to the point, Christian Zionists, nearly all of whom are evangelicals, are generally known as millennarians for their belief that Jesus will usher in a 1,000-year kingdom of peace upon his return. This is based on a reading of the New Testament's Revelations: 20–22, which depicts great battles between Jesus and Satan, including a 1,000-year reign of peace until the final victorious fight against Satan and his followers. The periods leading up to this time frame are known as "dispensations," and those who believe in it are often known as "dispensationalists."[7]

Evangelicals, as the numbers show, are far from the only Protestants. Yet, in general terms they differentiate themselves from members of Protestant mainline churches—such as Episcopalians, Lutherans, Methodists, and Presbyterians—in their approach to theology and political behavior. Evangelicals tend to be more conservative politically and religiously, while the opposite seems true for the majority of mainline Protestants. In fact, exactly 50 percent of the members of evangelical churches say they are Republican or lean in that direction, while only 34 percent fit in that category for Democrats.[8] This means that the GOP starts political campaigns with a presumption that it already has the lion's share of evangelical votes.

Logic suggests that all Christians are interested in the birthplace of Jesus and the venue where their sacred scripture says he will return to usher in a messianic era. How that interest should manifest itself remains a heated debate within the broader Christian community as it engages the very human political world. For evangelicals, however, there is an unquestionably disproportionate pro-Israel sentiment. In fact, in 2003 and 2004, the Pew Forum on Religion and Public Life found that although only 35 percent of all Americans believed the United States should support Israel over the Palestinians, 52 percent of white evangelicals (a strong majority of the community) agreed with the statement. The more socially conservative and religiously observant the evangelical (for example, Pentecostals and charismatics), the stronger the support for Israel. In fact, 64 percent of these traditionalists agreed to favor Israel, while only 18 percent disagreed.[9]

Such a response to world political events must fit into the religious *weltanschauung* of evangelical Zionists. As such, every conversation regarding the whys of their pro-Israel stands includes a citation of Genesis 12:3, which reads:

> And I will bless them that bless thee, and him that curseth thee will I curse; and in thee shall all the families of the earth be blessed.[10]

Thus, to dispensationalist evangelicals—a group that believes God has not forsaken his covenant with the Jewish people—the way to gain their own blessings from God is to favor the children of Abraham, which is understood as the Jewish people then and now. As Rev. John Hagee, one of today's most influential Christian Zionist leaders, has written, "No pronouncement of Scripture is clearer or more decisive. God smiles on the friends of the descendants of Abraham, and they enjoy heavenly favor."[11]

This biblical verse is clearly the prism through which evangelical dispensationalists see world events as well. Back in 1981, as the Soviet Union seemed to be an immovable, permanent force in global affairs, Falwell cited Genesis 12:3 when he called Moscow's "harassment and persecution of Jews . . . a fatal mistake." For the Christian Zionist, it took but a decade to prove such a declaration as the Soviet Union came to an inglorious end.[12]

Theology does not stand alone when it comes to the Christian Zionists' reasons for supporting Israel. In the Jewish state, many not only find a place where religious diversity and holy sites are legally protected by the government (unlike in most Arab/Muslim countries), but they also see a bulwark against Islamic fundamentalism, which threatens the Judeo-Christian values of which they often speak. Similarly, they see in Jerusalem's government a democracy amid a world of theocratic totalitarianism. As Rev. Pat Robertson said, "We [evangelicals], like all right-thinking people, support Israel because Israel is an island of democracy, an island of individual freedom, an island of the rule of law, and an island of modernity in the midst of a sea of dictatorial regimes, the suppression of individual liberty, and a fanatical religion intent on returning to the feudalism of eighth-century Arabia."[13]

One relatively recent study has made this quite clear. A 2002 survey commissioned on behalf of Stand for Israel found that although 35 percent of evangelicals say the most important reason to support Israel is New Testament prophecy, 24 percent do so because Israel is a democracy and an additional 19 percent do so because the Jewish state is a "long-standing" US ally in fighting terrorism. When one combines the last two factors—arguably related—a majority of American evangelicals favor Israel for geopolitical reasons over theological ones.[14]

How Evangelicals Entered the Political Mainstream

The evangelical passion for Israel fits into the overall pattern of the community formally reentering the political realm, particularly via the rise of pastors clearly comfortable in the glare of national media, such as Falwell and Robertson. A staunch proponent of Prohibition in the 1920s, the movement experienced a setback when public sale of alcohol was again legalized in 1933 with the passing of the Twenty-First Amendment to the US Constitution, overturning the Eighteenth Amendment, which outlawed the sale of alcohol other than for medicinal or scientific purposes. However, the blow that pushed the movement from high levels of political activism was clearly the 1925 Scopes Monkey Trial in Dayton, Tennessee. After dramatically losing a highly publicized battle to prevent the teaching of the theory of evolution in public schools, evangelical activism in the political sphere retreated.[15]

Even Rev. Billy Graham, who by the 1950s had become the most well-known evangelical leader in the country—eventually becoming a confidant of presidents—

primarily focused on social issues instead of political ones, maintaining "the pietist position that churches and religious leaders should stay out of politics and confine themselves to more 'spiritual matters,'" which they thought would be more effective in solving social problems.[16]

By the 1970s, with church membership growing (in part as a counterreaction to the liberal activism of the previous decade), evangelicals were finally reemerging on the political scene. This came in the form of Falwell's Moral Majority, formed in 1979, and Robertson's Christian Coalition, formed in 1989. The Moral Majority, as Falwell said, was a home for anyone of any religion who was "pro-life, pro–traditional family, pro-moral, and pro-American." In that last category, he said, came the call for "a stand in support of strong national defense and unswerving support for the State of Israel."[17] Only one year after forming the group, Falwell was already seen as a factor in delivering a conservative Christian base to GOP presidential candidates (despite saying his group would back candidates of any party that favored its views).[18] For his part, Robertson's Christian Coalition declared its commitment to "represent the pro-family point of view before local councils, school boards, state legislatures and Congress."[19]

Both Falwell and Robertson—the most visible American evangelical leaders in political circles from the 1980s through the first decade of the twenty-first century—also were busy laying the groundwork for a future generation of leaders who would reflect their views. In the 1970s, each founded an accredited university based on evangelical precepts but that also presented degreed study programs in the same disciplines as did secular universities. Nearly four decades after its 1971 start, Falwell's Liberty University, based in Lynchburg, Virginia, offered its almost 12,000 students (not counting 34,000 taking online courses) sixty accredited programs in addition to competing in NCAA Division I sports. In 1998, a $4 million donation to Liberty University paid for all 3,000 freshmen to participate in an Israel study tour.[20] Likewise, Robertson's Regent University in Virginia Beach, Virginia, founded in 1978, today has about 5,000 students.[21] In 2007, Zev Chafets reported that former Israeli prime minister Ehud Barak was listed as a faculty member at Robertson's university.[22]

By 2006, while Falwell and Robertson remained active on the pro-Israel front, they were slowly being eclipsed by John Hagee, a San Antonio, Texas-based pastor who made defending Israel his raison d'être. That year, the longtime pro-Israel advocate formed Christians United for Israel (CUFI), whose sole purpose was to advocate in Washington, D.C., and around the country on behalf of Israel. Less than one year after his group's founding, Hagee had made enough of an impression on the American Israel Public Affairs Committee (AIPAC) to gain an invitation to address the group's high-profile annual policy conference. He told them, with his booming voice and impeccable cadenced timing in full force, "Ladies and gentleman of AIPAC, it's a new day in America. The sleeping giant of Christian Zionism has awakened; there are 50 million Christians standing up and applauding the State of Israel. . . . We are bound together by Torah—the roots of Christianity are Jewish. We are spiritual brothers and what we have in common is far greater than the things we've allowed to separate us over the years."[23]

Aside from the political realm, another indication of the rise of evangelicals in American society in general can be measured by the phenomenal success of evangelical-related themes in television shows, books, and movies—the fate of the state of Israel and the modern Jewish people always part of the equation. In 1970, Hal Lindsey published the book *The Late Great Planet Earth,* which revolved around dispensationalist theology to explain everything from the Cold War to the rise of New Age religions. At one point he wrote that in the earth's final days, everything would focus on "the most important sign of all—that is the Jew returning to the land of Israel after thousands of years of being dispersed. The Jew is the most important sign to this generation." According to the *New York Times,* the book was the best-selling nonfiction title of the 1970s. By 2006, it had sold more than 15 million copies and had been translated into more than fifty languages. Meanwhile, the *Left Behind* book series by authors Tim LaHaye and Jerry B. Jenkins (who wrote similar children's books) also focused on end-of-time scenarios. The first one was printed in 1995. By 2006 the series had sold more than 55 million copies. The last six in the series all debuted at number one on the major best-seller lists, such as those of the *New York Times, Publisher's Weekly,* and the *Wall Street Journal.*[24]

History of Evangelical Views on a Jewish State

The modern establishment of an independent Jewish state in the land of the Hebrew Bible and the New Testament has been important to evangelicals since long before the country's founding on May 15, 1948. Six decades prior to that date, the groundwork for such support was in motion.

The ideology behind this began taking root in North America through the work of John Nelson Darby, the Anglo-Irish evangelist widely created with popularizing dispensationalism. According to him, God created a number of dispensations, or time periods, each of which creates a test for humans, which they inevitably fail. The first started with the creation of human beings but ended when Adam ate of the fruit of the tree of knowledge of good and evil and was then cast out of the Garden of Eden by God. The second began at that moment but ended when God punished humanity's inherent wickedness via the great flood. Noah's saving a remnant of humanity and the animal world, however, began the third dispensation, which is the current one.

For Darby and his subsequent followers, there was a direct message in all this when it came to the Jewish people, which had been scorned for many centuries by the Catholic Church and many Protestant groups for their rejection of the divinity of Jesus of Nazareth. Darby said that the Jewish failure to acknowledge Jesus as the Messiah "was not an unprecedented crime against God" but the continuance of "a well-worn pattern of human failure. The punishment for this failure is not rejection by God, but the end of one dispensation and the beginning of another."[25]

This is an unequivocal rejection of the "supercession" or "replacement theology" that had been dogma for much of the Christian world until this point. That notion declares that because of the Jewish spurning of Jesus, God's blessing in the Hebrew Bible to the descendants of Abraham had now been given to the followers of Jesus. In other words, for many Christians other than Darby, God broke his covenant with the Jewish people because they rejected his Messiah. For centuries, that engendered a hatred for Jews among many Christian denominations.

Darby's work set in motion the rise of an evangelical Christianity that for more than a century has had a marked impact on American religious life, one that rose, ebbed, and again plays a prominent role in national conversations. It all began taking root in 1875 through the first Niagara Bible Conference, a two-week retreat for conservative church leaders in Niagara Falls, New York. Within a few years, the annual event was controlled by dispensationalists. In 1878, the group drafted a statement of core tenets that included the following summary:

> The Lord Jesus will come in person to introduce the millennial age, when Israel shall be restored to their own land, and the earth shall be full of the knowledge of the Lord.[26]

One participant in the Niagara group, C. I. Scofield, set out to spread the word by publishing a Bible with detailed annotations and references to theologically bolster the conservative perspective. In 1909, the first *Scofield Study Bible* was published and became "perhaps the most important single document in all fundamentalist literature."[27]

Meanwhile, political action was afoot as well. Dispensationalists set about to raise their profile in public life by persuading leading American opinion and policy makers to endorse their efforts in helping create a modern state of Israel. One of the more prominent efforts was the Blackstone Memorials, named for their originator, William Eugene Blackstone. Blackstone had toured Palestine in 1889–1890 and written *Jesus Is Coming,* one of the first evangelical best sellers. The first Blackstone Memorial, penned in 1891, was signed by 431 prominent citizens, including financiers John D. Rockefeller and J. P. Morgan, future president William McKinley, US Supreme Court Justice Melville Fuller, congressmen, and editors of major newspapers in Baltimore, Boston, Chicago, Philadelphia, and New York.[28] A second Blackstone Memorial was drafted and circulated in 1916 to push President Woodrow Wilson to support the concept of a Jewish state in Palestine. The document was given to Wilson, the son of a Presbyterian minister, in May 1917. He "received it gladly" and supported the Balfour Declaration of the United Kingdom, which called for a "national home for the Jewish people in Palestine" when it was issued in November 1917.[29]

In 1927—six years before the Nazi Nationalist Socialist Party took power and twenty-one years before David Ben-Gurion's dramatic public reading of Israel's Declaration of Independence—the Assemblies of God, which today claims 63 million members and almost 3 million US members, making it the world's largest Pentecostal denomination—adopted a series of "Fundamental Truths." Number 14 stated, "The revelation of the Lord Jesus Christ from heaven, the salvation of national Israel, and the millennial reign of Christ on the earth is [sic] the scriptural promise and the world's hope (2 Thess. 1:7; Rev. 19:11; Rom. 11:26, 27; Rev. 20:1–7)."[30]

Near the end of World War II, with both the Zionist movement attaining prominence and the horrible depths of the Holocaust becoming clear, the Assemblies of God adopted a detailed resolution condemning anti-Semitism and clearly favoring a state of Israel. It included this language: "Every child of God who finds joy in the revealed will of our Father delights in the glorious promise of Israel's restoration [as an independent Jewish state]."[31]

Not surprisingly, the stunning 1967 Six-Day War victory of Israel over its Arab neighbors electrified the evangelical community, much as it had the world Jewish community. As John F. Walvoord, president of Dallas Seminary and an influential dispensationalist Bible teacher, said at the time, the conquest of Jerusalem by Israeli forces was "one of the most remarkable fulfillments of biblical prophecy since the destruction of Jerusalem in 70 A.D." In an issue of *Moody Monthly* devoted to the war, a variety of authors said the conflict convinced them that God had fought on Israel's side and that Israel had now moved one step closer to its rendezvous with the Antichrist, whose appearance was pivotal in the coming of Armageddon. This period also saw the rise of evangelical support for the West Bank/Gaza/Golan Heights settlement policies of subsequent Israeli governments (until the Rabin-Peres administration of 1992–1996 began curtailing such activities). Dispensationalists seemed to overwhelmingly justify such building on biblical grounds, citing Psalms 83:1–8, in which Israel's enemies seek to destroy it but fail.[32]

For the most part, the National Association of Evangelicals began subtly tilting toward Israel while trying to keep a neutral public stand in the first decade after the Six-Day War. In 1970, in its resolution on the Middle East, it recognized "the rights of all nations in the Middle East, both Israeli and Arab, to exist as sovereign nations from the perspective of biblical and historical positions." Eight years later, it called for "border modifications that will insure the safety and security of all countries involved" while affirming "that the gifts and the calling of God are irrevocable, that God has not rejected His people Israel nor forsaken the Arabs, but will yet fulfill His promise."[33]

The next major phase of Christian Zionism's advocacy for Israel came on November 10, 1975, when the UN General Assembly passed Resolution 3379, which declared, "Zionism is a form of racism and racial discrimination."[34] Evangelicals joined their Catholic and mainstream Protestant coreligionists' anger with particular ferocity. Dr. Arnold T. Olson, president of the Minneapolis-based Evangelical Free Church of America, said the resolution was "another nail in the coffin of an institution seemingly bent on destroying itself. . . . In other countries we call it nationalism and praise it as patriotic, but when it comes to Israel it is branded as racism." Dr. A. Jase Jones, director of the Southern Baptist Convention's Department of Interfaith Witness of the Home Mission Board, sent a letter to UN Secretary General Kurt Waldheim that accused those who voted for the document of having "degraded the high principles of . . . that noble institution."[35] The evangelical press was no exception. *Christianity Today* bluntly said the move "threatened to make the U.N. appear irresponsible, prejudiced and anti-Semitic."[36]

Six years later, there was another major opportunity for American evangelicals to show their support for Israel. In 1981, Israel's air force destroyed a nuclear reactor in Iraq believed to be close to being operational, which quickly brought international condemnation, including from the Reagan White House. Within twenty-four hours, Begin had called Falwell and asked for his support with US public opinion. Falwell pledged his support, congratulating his friend for "putting one right down the smokestack."[37] The next year, when Israel went to war with Lebanon, Falwell had some choice words for those who would oppose the Jewish state, saying that "God would smite any nation that raises its hand against Israel, even the United States."[38]

One of the greatest challenges to date for pro-Israel evangelicals—and indeed for some American Jews as well—came in the form of the September 13, 1993, White House handshake between Israeli Prime Minister Yitzhak Rabin and Palestine Liberation Organization Chairman Yasser Arafat. Suddenly Israel was engaged in a process that, if successful, would certainly see the state of Israel return lands captured in 1967 to the Palestinians. That challenged both Jewish and Christian theological dogma in that it meant relinquishing land that was promised by God to the Jewish people, and doing so for a very uncertain peace.

The struggle to support Israel's democratically elected government in peace negotiations, which inevitably includes the possibility of Israel giving up land to the Palestinians, has been difficult. Christian Zionists are said to respect the decisions of Israeli leaders in general terms so long as the Israeli public supported such efforts, but the rancor of Israeli public life has always made such a determination difficult. As David Brog observes, "This does not mean that the Christian Zionists morphed into peace enthusiasts. They remained largely skeptical and sometimes expressed their doubts and concerns."[39] In fact, Falwell openly pondered mobilizing US churches to oppose the Clinton administration's pressure on Israel to withdraw from the West Bank.[40]

This issue also exposed a fault line in Jewish advocacy for Israel, one that entered into the evangelical-Jewish relationship. During the August 2005 Israeli unilateral withdrawal from the Gaza Strip, New York Assembly member Dov Hikin, who is both a Democrat and an Orthodox Jew, joined with Rev. James Vineyard of Oklahoma City, Oklahoma, to raise more than $600,000 to publicly express their opposition. The campaign included placing newspaper ads and leading other evangelical pastors on study missions to Israel. Vineyard was quoted at the time as saying, "The judgment of God will fall on America if this [Gaza withdrawal] goes through."[41] That seemed to be on Robertson's mind in January 2006 when Israeli Prime Minister Ariel Sharon was struck down with a stroke that led to a coma. The evangelical leader suggested on his *700 Club* television show that it was divine intervention for masterminding Israel's controversial unilateral civilian and military withdraw from the Gaza Strip the previous August. Within a week, Robertson apologized in a letter to one of Sharon's sons.[42]

When the issue of land for peace was again being discussed in 2007, this time by Israeli Prime Minister Ehud Olmert, Robertson was asked in an interview with the *Jerusalem Post* if he had told Olmert to not give up biblical land in the West Bank. Robertson reportedly responded, "The Israelis have to be responsible for what their leaders do. It's up to them as a free society to determine the course of action of their nation. . . . I don't think the holy God is going to be happy about someone giving up his land. But that would be between Mr. Olmert and his God. It isn't for me to say."[43]

Regardless, Christian Zionists clearly have a strong affinity for Israel's right-wing (and mostly Orthodox) settlers. In fact, from 2000 to 2010, at least forty American groups gave more than $200 million in tax-deductible donations to Israeli settlements. Although not all of the funds came from Christian groups, much of the support certainly did, in the form of dollars as well as volunteers. As but one example, twice a year American evangelicals show up at a Jewish-owned West Bank winery in Har Bracha to help harvest grapes. For his part, Hagee says a "large majority" of the donations from CUFI target Israeli efforts within the pre-1967 borders. Yet, a few years ago he reportedly donated $250,000 to expand a dormitory at the Har Bracha yeshiva.[44] Likewise, in 1995 another Christian Zionist leader, Ted Beckett of Colorado Springs, Colorado, started Christian Friends of Israeli Communities, which was designed to provide "solidarity, comfort, and aid" to what were then 220,000 Jews living in the West Bank and Gaza Strip. By the late 1990s, he had paired about forty churches with settlements on the way to his goal of 150 such matches.[45]

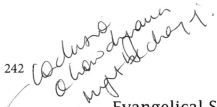

Evangelical Splits on Israel

Evangelicals, however, are not fully united when it comes to being pro-Israel and essentially giving little weight to Palestinian nationalist aspirations. This stems from two central reasons: concerns over the fate of evangelical Christians working in Arab and Muslim countries, and a feeling that God would want them to advocate on behalf of the oppressed—in the mind of some evangelicals, the Palestinians fall into that category.

So, for example, Ted Haggard, president of the National Association of Evangelicals, admitted during the 2006 Second Lebanon War that Israeli leaders had been "pressuring him" to make a statement of support, which he did not do publicly. As he explained to Associated Press reporter Rachel Zell, "Our silence is not a rejection of Israel or even a hesitation about Israel. Our silence is to try to protect people. There's a rapidly growing evangelical population in virtually every Islamic country. Much of it is underground in the countries that are more radicalized, and many of the Christians survive based on their neighbors' just ignoring the fact that they don't go to mosque."[46]

Further, though a healthy percentage of evangelicals favor a biblical Israel in terms of boundaries, meaning from the Mediterranean Sea to the Jordan River, a number of influential leaders and their followers publicly advocate for a two-state solution—one that would see a Jewish state (primarily within the pre-1967 borders) coexist with a Palestinian state composed of the Gaza Strip, the West Bank, and East Jerusalem.[47] So on July 29, 2007, thirty-four evangelical leaders sent President Bush a letter—released to the *New York Times*—that stated:

> Historical honesty compels us to recognize that both Israelis and Palestinians have legitimate rights stretching back for millennia to the lands of Israel/Palestine. Both Israelis and Palestinians have committed violence and injustice against each other. The only way to bring the tragic cycle of violence to an end is for Israelis and Palestinians to negotiate a just, lasting agreement that guarantees both sides viable, independent, secure states.[48]

In addition, in November 2007, the Bush administration held the one-day Annapolis Conference, which was designed to jump-start the languishing peace process. In conjunction with that effort, more than eighty evangelical leaders signed a statement that called for a democratic Israel as well as a democratic Palestinian state "with a flourishing economy that offers economic opportunity to all its people." They added:

> We call on all evangelicals, all Christians, and everyone of good will to join us to work and pray faithfully in the coming months for a just, lasting two-state solution in the

Holy Land. . . . And we covenant to pray for the leaders of all nations engaged in this effort, hoping for them the blessing of the Lord, who said, "Blessed are the peacemakers."[49]

Such tensions within the evangelical community have been seen in particular in the left-leaning evangelical magazine *Sojourners,* which primarily focuses on social justice issues. In 2000, the publication ran a piece by Rev. Peter Walker, noting that "Zion-theology could lead to problems." He wrote that in his reading of sacred texts, "thinking that Jerusalem is somehow different from other cities can too easily become an excuse to avoid universally valid aspects of biblical morality."[50] And in a 2003 article, Leslie C. Allen and Glen Stassen wrote, "Most Zionists claim that God's eternal covenant with Abraham and his descendants (Genesis 12, 15) means that Israel must have undivided political sovereignty over all the land mentioned there. . . . Their claim is biblically erroneous. God's covenant and promise of the land in Genesis is given to Abraham and his descendants, not only to Israel." The title of their article, "How Christian Is Zionism?" speaks volumes as to their perspective.[51] Finally, in 2003 the scholar Donald Wagner, in a lengthy *Sojourners* piece, wrote, "Perhaps the most glaring weakness in the Christian Zionist program is its failure to relate to or defend Palestinian Christians, who are fleeing their homeland in record numbers not due to Islamic extremism, but because of Israel's brutal occupation policies."[52]

Evangelical Splits with Other Christians

The battles within the evangelical community, however, are minor when compared to those with mainline Protestants. Indeed, a major dividing line in the stands of the groups can be seen in how they relate to the Middle East. Today, if Christian Zionists are known for their somewhat unquestioning pro-Israel stands, mainline Protestants are known for entering into anti-Israel boycott, divestment, and sanctions efforts (known as the BDS movement). In fact, for the past decade such initiatives have garnered headlines at numerous national gatherings of mainline churches.

So it was that in July 2004, the Presbyterian Church (USA) voted to "study" divesting from its investments portfolio companies doing business with Israel. A few months later, the Episcopal Church voted for a "year-long study" boycotting companies linked to "Israeli occupation." One month after that, the General Synod of the United Church of Christ voted to examine ways of using "economic leverage" against Israel to influence the Palestinian-Israeli dispute.[53] And in the same time period, the Anglican Church (with which the Episcopalians are affiliated) called on other denominations to undertake similar "studies." The next year, the Virginia and New England Conferences of the United

Methodist Church approved resolutions calling for an investigation into whether they had holdings in companies that profited from Israel's occupation.[54] Clearly a major fault line between mainline and much of evangelical Protestant thinking had been exposed.

In such efforts, the mainline Protestants were primarily echoing the words of their Middle East counterparts, from whom they gain firsthand perspective about the Arab-Israeli conflict. A flare-up of the issue came in 2006 when the leaders of four Christian communities in Jerusalem issued "The Jerusalem Declaration on Christian Zionism." In it, they condemned Christian Zionism as

> a modern theological and political movement that embraces the most extreme ideological positions of Zionism, thereby becoming detrimental to a just peace within Palestine and Israel. . . . In its extreme form, it places an emphasis on apocalyptic events leading to the end of history rather than living Christ's love and justice today. . . . With urgency we warn that Christian Zionism and its alliances are justifying colonization, apartheid and empire building.[55]

The response was quick in coming. One week later a joint response was put out by three leading Christian Zionist groups: Bridges for Peace, Christian Friends of Israel, and the International Christian Embassy Jerusalem. Their six-point rebuttal was equally forceful. They wrote:

> A Christian Zionist believes in a literal interpretation of the Bible and rejects replacement theology that definitely played a pivotal role in the persecution of the Jews through the centuries and undergirded the Holocaust. . . . Christian Zionists do not base their theological position on end-time prophecy, but on the faithful covenant promises of God given to Abraham some four thousand years ago. They do not have a "thirst for Armageddon," and do not claim to know the sequence of events that will lead to it.[56]

Israel and the Evangelicals

The Christian world may be wracked with controversy regarding its proper role in the Palestinian-Israeli conflict, but Israeli governments have long welcomed the support of the evangelical community.

An important component of this activity is not just to acquire political support, but also to continue to bring large numbers of Christian tourists to Israel. In fact, shortly after the 1967 war the Israeli government sent Yona Malachy from its Department of Religious Affairs to the United States to study the feasibility of evangelicals as an Israeli ally. He quickly noted that the community was "fiercely friendly and not afraid to say so."[57] As discussed in the introduction, the appearance of a figure with no less than the mythical stature of David Ben-Gurion at the first large evangelical gathering in Israel was a powerful symbol.

By 1980, the Israelis were open enough to a pro-Israel evangelical embrace to allow for the construction in Jerusalem itself of the International Christian Embassy Jerusalem (ICEJ). The operation was founded by Dutch Christian Zionist Jan Willem van der Hoeven when thirteen countries moved their embassies to Tel Aviv from Jerusalem to protest Israel's formal annexation of East Jerusalem. Today the ICEJ serves both as a base for Christian Zionists visiting the Holy Land and supports their political advocacy for Israel abroad. It has helped raise tens of millions of dollars to bring many thousands of Jews from the former Soviet Union to the Jewish state, has twin community relationships with West Bank Jewish settlements, and has stood solidly against any territorial concessions to the Palestinians.[58] The ICEJ has always enjoyed high-profile Israeli government support, as nearly every prime minister since its inception has either personally addressed the embassy's annual Sukkot gathering (as have leading American evangelicals) or sent a letter to be read.[59]

Further cementing the relationship, in early 2004 Israeli Knesset members Yuri Shtern (National Union Party) and Yair Peretz (Shas) formed the Knesset Christian Allies Caucus "to build a direct line of communication, cooperation and coordination between the Knesset and Christian leaders around the world." By 2010, the group had seventeen Knesset members from across the Israeli political spectrum, representing parties including Kadima, Labor, Likud, National Union, and Yisrael Beitenu.[60]

The importance of evangelical tourism to Israel's economy is obviously important. In 2004, while serving as Israel's minister of tourism, Benny Elon estimated that despite the second Intifada about 400,000 evangelicals had traveled to Israel the previous year alone.[61] In fact, acknowledging the hundreds of millions of dollars this brought into the state's economy, Israeli tourism officials have targeted the evangelical community for decades. In 1990 the Ministry of Tourism, claiming that Christian pilgrims already made up 25 percent of the Jewish state's tourists, began paid commercials on American Christian television and radio stations that urged listeners to come "walk in the footsteps of Jesus." A large billboard picturing Jerusalem with the words "Come see his old neighborhood" was even put up in Atlanta, Georgia.[62]

Politically, the relationship between evangelical and Israeli leaders grew exponentially when Menachem Begin became prime minister in 1977. Although not personally religious, Begin headed his country's secular nationalist camp, which saw Israel's post-1967 borders as vital to the Jewish state for both historic and security reasons. However, he always had respect for and good relations with religious leaders, Jewish and non-Jewish.

Indeed, Begin found a kindred soul in political aspirations for Israel in Falwell. Their relationship began in 1978 when the Israeli invited the American to visit the Jewish state on an all-expenses-paid trip. The next year, back on another trip to the Holy Land paid for by the Israelis, Falwell endorsed the settlement-building policies of Begin's Likud Party and even planted trees in what became known as the Jerry Falwell Forest. One year later, Begin presented his new friend with the Vladimir Jabotinsky Medal, named for Begin's ideological mentor and the founder of Zionist Revisionism, which based itself on an unapologetic Jewish presence throughout the lands of biblical Israel.[63] Likewise, fellow Likud Prime Minister Benjamin Netanyahu knew that Falwell was a trusted ally and that American evangelicals could help blunt pressure from the Clinton White House. The strategy to use the evangelicals as a foil against the White House was designed and pushed by Netanyahu's chief political adviser, the media-savvy, American-born David Bar-Ilan.[64]

Sometimes such relationships between the Israelis and evangelicals came to the dismay of mainstream American Jewish groups. As but one example, in early 1998, Netanyahu came to the United States to discuss with President Bill Clinton Israel's next phased withdrawal from the West Bank. But his first stop in America was to confer with neither congressional supporters nor American Jewish leaders. Rather, he met with 1,000 evangelical Christians gathered at Falwell's behest. In a gesture that could not have been to the liking of the Democratic White House, the crowd saluted Netanyahu as "the Ronald Reagan of Israel," the former Republican US president being an iconic figure for the politically conservative community. For his part, Falwell promised Netanyahu the support of 20,000 evangelical pastors who would "tell President Clinton to refrain from putting pressure on Israel" to adhere to the Oslo Accords.[65] Then Netanyahu met privately with Falwell and leaders of the Southern Baptist Convention. As the American-Israeli journalist Gershom Gorenberg has written, "As a foreign leader visiting Washington, Netanyahu could hardly have been ruder to his host, the American president."[66]

The American Jewish Response

American Jews took notice in the early 1970s as the evangelicals reemerged on the political scene. The first step was to formally acquaint the leadership of the two communities. To that end, in late 1973 representatives of the American Jewish Committee began contacting evangelical figures to cosponsor with the American Institute of Holy Land Studies a three-day National Conference of Evangelical Christians and Jews. The New York City–hosted event convened twenty-three evangelical and twenty Jewish leaders from various denominational and political perspectives. Rabbi James Rudin, an American Jewish Committee interfaith staffer, noted in his summary that "both faith groups must continue to express positive support for and solidarity with the people and the State of Israel to insure her survival and security."[67]

Nonetheless, many Jews as well as their national organizations were far from willing to fully drop their concerns regarding evangelical domestic beliefs. American Jewish opposition to trusting the professed unconditional evangelical love for Jews and Israel was based on three historical patterns: the already mentioned end-time theology that sees a strong Jewish state as both figurative and literal cannon fodder for Armageddon; the Christian (and particularly evangelical) emphasis on proselytizing (including the funding of Hebrew Christian groups, which includes and targets people who were born Jewish); and a strong difference on domestic agendas such as abortion, gun control, and separation of religion and state (Jews and evangelicals are almost polar opposites on those issues, with a strong majority of the former supporting a much more liberal approach).

As a result, the initial mainstream Jewish organizational reaction to the increased evangelical role in politics was primarily hostile. In 1981, with the Moral Majority but two years old, the American Jewish Congress's leaders said that though they were "mindful" that the evangelical leaders and spokesmen "defend and support the State of Israel," that was "irrelevant to our assessment of their domestic programs. The damage done by their efforts to curtail domestic freedom is not made less by their views on Israel."[68]

When it came to proselytizing, there seemed to be confusion among major evangelical bodies. For example, on March 4, 1995, the Alliance of Baptists passed a statement on Jewish-Christian relations that rejected supercessionism and lamented how "regrettably, in recent years this effort at Jewish-Baptist dialogue has been reduced to a theology of conversion."[69] However, on June 14, 1996, in its "Resolution on Evangelism," the US Southern Baptist Convention—the largest American evangelical denomination—voted in favor of the need to "direct our energies and resources toward the proclamation of the Gospel to the Jews."[70] The next year, the Southern Baptist Convention told its members to direct "their energies and resources toward the proclamation of the gospel to the Jewish people." In 1999, the group's International Mission Board recommended increasing the efforts during Rosh Hashanah and Yom Kippur because Jews were said to be "in a great state of spiritual receptivity" during that period.[71]

Likewise, a perception of evangelical anti-Semitism continued to hamper the relationship. When asked in 1997 if they thought that the Christian Right was anti-Semitic, 47 percent of American Jews responded either "most" (22 percent) or "many" (25 percent), meaning that nearly half felt that many evangelicals were anti-Semitic.[72] By 2001—well into the second Intifada—the distrust rose even higher, despite evangelicals' being in the forefront of defending the Jewish state nationwide. That year the American Jewish Committee survey reported that 54 percent of American Jews felt that "most" or "many" on the Christian Right were anti-Semitic individuals.[73] Though the new Intifada had given rise to a heightened debate among Jews regarding pro-Israel evangelical support, the evangelical support for President George W. Bush was greeted with great suspicion by most American Jews, who feared an advance of conservative social policies favored by Christians.

Evangelicals are fully aware of the Jewish mistrust. One way they seek to assuage it is by directly addressing the issue of anti-Semitism. As Hagee said at a 2002 speech given at the Embassy of Israel in Washington, D.C., "Anti-Semitism is a sin, and sin damns the soul. It is time for Christians to stop praising the dead Jews of the past—Abraham, Isaac, and Jacob, while slandering the Jews that live across the street. They are the same family."[74]

By the first decade of the twenty-first century, the issue of evangelical support for Israel was clearly a much-discussed one in national Jewish circles. The trigger to the reassessment of the Jewish-evangelical relationship was twofold: the wide acknowledgment that the Christian Right was a strong supporter of the Bush administration, and the evangelical support for Israel during the outbreak of the second Intifada in late September 2000, which coincided with increasing criticism of the Jewish state from mainline Protestants. To help the Jewish community navigate the issues in 2002, the Jewish Council for Public Affairs—the national umbrella group representing some 150 Jewish community relations councils and organizations—began formally studying American Christians' relationship to Israel through its Israel Advocacy Initiative. That same year, the Anti-Defamation League published the booklet *Meeting the Challenge: Church Attitudes Toward the Israeli-Palestinian Conflict*.[75] Six years later the Jewish Council for Public Affairs published the comprehensive booklet *Looking at Them Looking at Us: A Jewish Understanding of Christian Responses to Israel*.[76]

It was not uncommon for the mistrust to be evident in how Jewish groups closely monitored and responded to statements by leading evangelicals. In May 2008, Union of Reform Judaism head Rabbi Eric Yoffie wrote to Hagee after numerous reports of Hagee's saying that the Holocaust was part of God's plan to force the Jews to go to Israel because many Jews defied the call of the Zionists to settle in their ancient homeland.[77] Hagee eventually publicly apologized in an exchange of letters with Anti-Defamation League head Abraham H. Foxman in which the Christian leader pledged "to work to express my faith in a way that is sensitive to and respectful of others."[78]

A month earlier, Yoffie chose as a topic for his address to the annual convention of Reform rabbis "Christian Zionism: Is It Good for North American Jews and Good for Zionism?" He offered a limited acceptance of such support but warned that embracing it could compromise both the pro-Israel cause and the

Reform movement. "The central principle of pro-Israel advocacy in America for half a century has been that it must be moderate, centrist, and insistently bi-partisan, able to draw advocates from both sides of the political aisle," he wrote. As such, he called on his colleagues to not participate in CUFI "Night to Honor Israel" programs.[79]

This was not Yoffie's first foray into dialogue with evangelical leaders. In April 2006, Yoffie had taken his concerns over the rhetorical battle between Jewish liberals and Christian conservatives on domestic matters directly to Falwell. In doing so, he addressed Liberty University's student body and was then hosted by Falwell at a luncheon.[80]

Foxman, the national director of the Anti-Defamation League and arguably the most visible and influential Jewish professional in the country, seemed to vacillate when it came to how American Jews should respond to evangelical support for Israel given the two communities' generally opposing views on domestic issues. In a 2002 op-ed for North American Jewish newspapers titled "Why Evangelical Support for Israel Is a Good Thing," he wrote, "There is no quid pro quo. At no point have we had to choose between our fundamental principles concerning the role of religion in America and our appreciation for their standing with Israel."[81] But in late 2005—well into nearly a year of controversy over the Mel Gibson film *The Passion of the Christ,* which Foxman said stoked anti-Semitic canards—he called a summit of Jewish leaders to discuss evangelical Christianity's aggressiveness on church-state issues.[82] By 2007, he seemed prepared to give much more weight to domestic concerns than in the past. In another column sent to Jewish newspapers, this one titled "Jews and Evangelicals: Support for Israel Isn't Everything," he wrote, "The theological reasons for why they stand with Israel, as a precursor to the Second Coming and Armageddon, take a backseat to current realities. . . . We will not be silent or cower to threats on the issue of separation of church and state."[83]

Nonetheless, as American Jewish Committee head David Harris has said, "Many Jews and many Israelis are very open-eyed about the driving religious philosophy of the evangelicals and why they want Israel to exist. The end of time may come tomorrow, but Israel hangs in the balance today." Likewise, his Anti-Defamation League counterpart, Foxman, has added, "Israel is fighting for security, isolated in a hypocritical world. It's no time to say [to evangelicals] 'You're not a perfect friend.'"[84]

One group of Jews that in general has much fewer concerns with the evangelical-Jewish pro-Israel alliance is the most traditional segment of the community. Indeed, Orthodox Jews are often seen at pro-Israel evangelical events, such as Hagee's CUFI gatherings. Although they remain a minority—between 10 percent and 15 percent in most Jewish population surveys—Orthodox Jews in recent decades have become more visible and active in political affairs.[85]

Sensing the political power and humanitarian assistance such support could bring from so many people (an estimated 60 million to 70 million Americans alone), some American Modern Orthodox rabbis—often to the uneasiness of their colleagues—created groups that allied with the Christian Zionists on both international and domestic issues. In the former category was the Yeshiva University–ordained Rabbi Yechiel Eckstein's International Fellowship of Christians and Jews (IFCJ). The success of the effort is evident. Founded in 1983 to improve evangelical-Jewish ties and to provide humanitarian relief to Jews in Israel and the former Soviet Union, from 1994 to 2004 the group was estimated to have raised about $100 million in aid for such causes. By 2004, the IFCJ was getting 2,000 to 2,500 pieces of mail a day, "most of them with checks." At that point, the group estimated that it had raised about $100 million in financial support for Israel from its donor base of 365,000 individuals and groups.[86] And three years later, the IFCJ was ranked by the *Chronicle of Philanthropy* among America's top four hundred charities and by the Israeli newspaper *Ha'aretz* as the Jewish state's second-largest charitable foundation.[87]

Open Questions for the Future

American evangelicals—particularly many of their more prominent leaders—have made Christian Zionism a hallmark of their public activism for the past four decades. Early on, pro-Israel stands were integral to the political rise of Falwell and Robertson, and remain so today to people such as Hagee, arguably the primary successor in this area. There is no reason to believe such emphasis will come to a halt anytime soon. In fact, it is likely to increase as graduates of evangelical institutions such as Liberty University and Regents University take their place in local and national organizations and Hagee's CUFI remains strong. In addition, with adherents of Christian Zionism being a base for the Republican Party, and American Jews taking a smaller but still significant role in the Democratic Party, it is hard to imagine that the pro-Israel agenda will not find a welcome home in the campaigns of nearly every candidate for the US House of Representatives, the US Senate, and the presidency itself.

There is, however, a matter of priorities when it comes to the nation's halls of power. As the Obama presidency has shown (particularly when compared to those of Bill Clinton and George W. Bush), serious questions can be raised as to the strength of emotional attachment the resident of the Oval Office has toward the Jewish state. This could be a wedge issue for the so far largely unsuccessful GOP efforts to gain support from a majority of American Jews, who are disproportionately important in the electorate due to their geographical concentration and financial contributions. Clearly there are already borderline anti-

Israel voices on the hard Left, which offers near-blanket support for Democratic candidates akin to how traditional evangelicals support Republican ones. If the pro-Israel cause becomes increasingly a Republican issue instead of a bipartisan one, would future Democratic administrations be as willing to defend Israel in international forums as their predecessors have done?

Also, with the rise of Christian conservatives on domestic issues—particularly as they play out in smaller, less urbanized regions of the country—tensions between national Jewish and evangelical groups may occasionally flare up, as they have over separation of religion and state issues as seen in debates over teaching creationism alongside evolution in public schools—in some ways echoing the 1925 Scopes Monkey Trial in Tennessee.[88]

In addition, with the continued growth in American Christianity of traditional evangelical communities over mainline Protestants, will the Jewish rejection of such domestic stands lead to frustration and potentially the seeding of anti-Semitism—a fear reflected in the Jewish response to the strongly positive evangelical reaction to the 2004 film *The Passion of the Christ*? Likewise, will continued Jewish nervousness about the evangelical embrace irritate the evangelical rank-and-file, making them markedly less enthusiastic than their leaders?

Meanwhile, if Israeli-Palestinian negotiations succeed in advancing a comprehensive deal, one whose implementation will invariably call for large amounts of aid from Washington and perhaps even a US military monitoring presence, will evangelicals support the choice of the democratically elected government of Israel that gives up Jewish control of the biblical heartland? If not, will their opposition be passive or much more active? The latter form could involve using a proven ability to raise many millions of dollars to fund the activities of West Bank Jewish anti–peace treaty activists, a camp whose most radical members have already shown a penchant for violence against their own government's wishes.

Finally, will Christian voices calling for more attention to the plight of the Palestinians gain a greater foothold in the evangelical community, bringing new pressures on the state of Israel from what Jerusalem now sees as a critical ally in maintaining US support?

Dispensationalists may have a proscribed understanding of how world history will play out, but the answers to these questions are anything but clear.

Notes

1. Merrill Simon, *Jerry Falwell and the Jews* (Middle Village, NY: Jonathan David Publishers, 1984), pp. 5–6.

2. Zev Chafets, *A Match Made in Heaven.* (New York: Harper Perennial, 2007), pp. 37–38.

In 1971, Carl Henry, former editor of *Christianity Today,* hosted a "prophecy conference" in Jerusalem for 1,500 delegates from thirty-two countries. Ben-Gurion, ever one to encourage support of the state of Israel, was reportedly happy to attend. In fact, when he died in 1973, the evangelical author Hal Lindsey's book *The Late Great Planet Earth* was on a reading table in his cottage at Kibbutz Sde Boker.

3. Chafets, *A Match Made in Heaven*, p. 66.

4. David Brog, *Standing with Israel: Why Christians Support the Jewish State* (Lake Mary, FL: Frontline, 2006), pp. 144–145. The signers included American Values head Gary Bauer, the Reverend Jerry Falwell, the Reverend John Hagee, and Religious Roundtable founder Ed McAteer.

5. "U.S. Religious Landscape Survey: Religious Beliefs and Practices: Diverse and Politically Relevant June 2008," Pew Forum of Religion & Public Life, p. 8. By comparison, 23.9 percent said they belong to a Roman Catholic Church, 18.1 percent to a mainline Protestant church, and 6.9 percent to a historically black church. The category "other religions" was under 5 percent with the remainder claiming no religious membership.

6. "What Is an Evangelical?" www.nae .net/church-and-faith-partners/what-is-an -evangelical. For the complete self-definition, see "Statement of Faith," www.nae.net/about -us/statement-of-faith.

7. *New Testament in Modern English,* trans. J. B. Phillips (New York: Macmillan Company, 1958). For a primer on dispensationalists, sometimes called "millennialists," see Timothy P. Weber, *On the Road to Armageddon: How Evangelicals Became Israel's Best Friend* (Grand Rapids, MI: Baker Academic, 2004), pp. 9–11, 19–26. For a brief review of Jews and Israel in "Armageddon theology," see Phil Zuckerman, "Jews and the Christian Right," *Journal of Jewish Communal Service* 73, no. 1 (Fall 1966): 24–26. There is a complex differentiation among groups of pre-millennialists, post-millennialists, and dispensational millennialists (or dispensationists).

8. "U.S. Religious Landscape Survey," p. 85. Meanwhile, 41 percent of mainline Protestants say they favor the GOP while 43 percent favor the Democrats. Catholics, however, favor the Democrats by a rate of 48 percent to 33 percent. It is important to remember that no denomination is without diversity, though majority trends are clear.

9. James Rudin, *The Baptizing of America: The Religious Right's Plans for the Rest of Us.* (New York: Thunder's Mouth Press, 2006), p. 111.

10. *The Holy Scriptures* (Philadelphia: Jewish Publication Society of America, 1955), p. 23.

11. John Hagee, *Beginning of the End, Final Dawn over Jerusalem, Day of Deception* (Nashville, TN: Thomas Nelson Publishers, 2000), p. 20.

12. Brog, *Standing with Israel,* p. 70, citing Falwell in Martin Schram, "Jerry Falwell Vows Amity with Israel," *Washington Post,* September 12, 1981.

13. Brog, *Standing with Israel,* p. 80, citing Robertson's speech to the Herzliya Conference in Herzliya, Israel, December 17, 2003.

14. Memo from George Mamo to Ethan Felson, "American Christians and Support for Israel," April 13, 2005. The memo was provided by Felson, Jewish Council for Public Affairs interfaith point person, for this chapter. Mamo is the senior vice president of the International Fellowship of Christians and Jews, which runs Stand for Israel. The poll was conducted by the Tarrance Group, which bills itself as a GOP polling firm.

15. George M. Marsden, *Fundamentalism and American Culture* (Oxford: Oxford University Press, 2006), pp. 184–195.

16. Ibid., p. 233.

17. Simon, *Jerry Falwell and the Jews,* pp. 108–109.

18. John Herbers, "Ultraconservative Evangelicals a Surging New Force in Politics," *New York Times,* August 17, 1980.

19. For more on the Christian Coalition's stands, see www.cc.org/about_us.

20. Weber, *On the Road to Armageddon,* p. 219.

21. For more information on the schools, see their websites at www.liberty.edu and www .regent.edu.

22. Chafets, *A Match Made in Heaven*, p. 17. A search on August 10, 2010, revealed that Barak was no longer listed.

23. John Hagee, "AIPAC Policy Conference Address," March 11, 2007, Washington, D.C. Also see Neil Rubin, "'A Biblical Mandate': A Leading Evangelical Makes His Case to Amer-

ican Jews as to Why He Is Strongly Pro-Israel," *Baltimore Jewish Times*, July 28, 2006, pp. 44–45. Although Hagee said he had expected about 500 people to show up for his first CUFI conference and address, there were about 3,000 participants.

24. Brog, *Standing with Israel*, pp. 58–59, citing Hal Lindsey, *The Late Great Planet Earth* (Grand Rapids, MI: Zondervan, 1970). The website for the books, www.leftbehind.com, claims 66 million books sold by mid-2010. The original twelve-volume series has been followed by a similar series for children, nonfiction books, political books, and military books.

25. Brog, *Standing with Israel*, p. 45.

26. Ibid., p. 53.

27. Ibid., p. 55, citing James Barr, *Fundamentalism* (Philadelphia: Westminster Press, 1978), p. 5.

28. Weber, *On the Road to Armageddon*, pp. 103–104. Weber writes, "Though the memorial got plenty of press coverage, President [Benjamin] Harrison and Secretary [of State James] Blaine virtually ignored the document, and the little diplomatic notice it received faded quickly," p. 105.

29. Ibid., p. 105.

30. Moshe Aumann, *Conflict & Connection: The Jewish-Christian-Israel Triangle* (Jerusalem: Geffen Books, 2003), pp. 70–71.

31. Ibid., p. 71.

32. Weber, *On the Road to Armageddon*, pp. 184–185. On day four of the war—the day after Israel Defense Forces captured Jerusalem's Old City—the Moody Bible Institute's radio station broadcast a two-hour program on the war's prophetic significance.

33. "Middle East 1970," National Association of Evangelicals, www.nae.net/resolutions/246-middle-east-1970, and "Middle East 1978," National Association of Evangelicals, www.nae.net/resolutions/247-middle-east-proposed-resolution-1978.

34. "The Anti-Zionist Resolution at the United Nations," in *Israel in the Middle East: Documents and Readings on Society, Politics, and Foreign Relations, 1948–Present*, ed. Itamar Rabinovich and Yehuda Reinharz (Oxford: Oxford University Press, 1984), pp. 309–312. The document was eventually overturned in 1991 at the

urging of President George H. W. Bush, who saw the move as helpful in starting the Madrid Process, which brought Israeli and Arab leaders into face-to-face negotiations for the first time since the 1949 Rhodes Armistice talks.

35. Judith H. Banki, *The UN's Anti-Zionism Resolution: Christian Responses* (Washington, DC: American Jewish Committee, 1976), p. 41. Waldheim, when he later was elected to the ceremonial role of president of Austria, was accused of purposely hiding his World War II service in the German army.

36. Ibid., p. 49. Also see Kenneth A. Briggs, "Resolution in U.N. on Zionism Scored: Christian Leaders Call for Defeat of Measure Pending in the General Assembly," *New York Times*, November 9, 1975; and memo of Marc Tanenbaum to Bert Gold, "Christian Responses to UN Resolution on Zionism-as-Racism," American Jewish Committee, November 20,1975, www.ajcarchives.org/ajcarchive/DigitalArchive.aspx.

37. Chafets, *A Match Made in Heaven*, p. 123.

38. Rudin, *Baptizing of America*, p. 113.

39. Brog, *Standing with Israel*, p. 197.

40. Laurie Goodstein, "Falwell Offers to Mobilize Churches to Oppose Israeli Pullback," *Washington Post*, January 21, 1998. Regarding compromises, evangelicals greeted Netanyahu during a trip to the United States at that time with chants of "Not one inch!"

41. Rudin, *Baptizing of America*, p. 124.

42. "Robertson Apologizes to Sharon Family," *New York Times*, January 13, 2006.

43. Chafets, *A Match Made in Heaven*, p. 204.

44. Jim Rutenberg, Mike McIntire, and Ethan Bronner, "Tax-Exempt Funds Aid Settlements in West Bank," *New York Times*, July 5, 2010.

45. Weber, *On the Road to Armageddon*, pp. 225–226. The effort includes pen pals, fund raising, and lobbying.

46. Chafets, *A Match Made in Heaven*, p. 210. As Haggert told Chafets a few weeks later, "I didn't speak out immediately because we needed to move some people around, that's all. . . . In the era of universal media, some sixteen-year-old fanatic in a village might hear or read some statement I make, pick up a machine gun, and kill a nun or a missionary."

47. In doing so, these leaders also echo the position of the Israeli peace camp led by the group

Peace Now and represented in the Knesset by Zionist parties, such as Meretz. The official platforms of the Labor and Kadima Parties also call for a two-state solution but leave the fate of East Jerusalem to the negotiations. Interestingly, to date these evangelical groups have not seemed to try to form an alliance with these pro-"land for peace" parties, perhaps in part due to the pro-Palestinian element within their communities.

48. "Letter to President Bush from Evangelical Leaders," *New York Times,* July 29, 2007.

49. David Neff, "Evangelical Leaders Reiterate Call for Two-State Solution for Israel and Palestine," *Christianity Today,* November 2007, www .christianitytoday.com/ct/2007/novemberweb -only/148–33.0.html. Signatures included those of leading representatives of the National Association of Evangelicals (Bruce Jones), activists (Jim Wallis of *Sojourners*), and academics (Duane Litfin, president of Wheaton College).

50. Peter Walker, "O Jerusalem, Jerusalem," *Sojourners,* September–October 2000. It's worth noting that although not published until the early fall, Walker likely had the July 2000 Camp David peace negotiations, which focused on dividing Jerusalem, in mind.

51. Leslie C. Allen and Glen Stassen, "How Christian Is Zionism?" *Sojourners,* July–August 2003.

52. Donald E. Wagner, "Short Fuse to Apocalypse?" *Sojourners,* July–August 2003.

53. Chafets, *A Match Made in Heaven,* p. 81.

54. In addition, in June 2005 the Virginia and New England Conferences of the United Methodist Church approved resolutions calling for an investigation into whether they had holdings in companies that profited from Israel's occupation.

55. "The Jerusalem Declaration on Christian Zionism," statement by the patriarch and local heads of churches in Jerusalem, August 22, 2006. The document was signed by Jerusalem's Latin patriarch, Jerusalem's Syrian Orthodox patriarch, the Episcopal bishop of Jerusalem and the Middle East, and the bishop of the Evangelical Lutheran Church in Jordan and the Holy Land, available at http://int.icej.org /media/jerusalem-declaration-christian-zionism.

56. "A Defense of Christian Zionism in Response to the Bishops' Declaration," August 29, 2006. The document was signed by the heads of Bridges for Peace, Christian Friends of Israel, and the International Christian Embassy Jerusalem, available at http://int.icej.org/media /jerusalem-declaration-christian-zionism.

57. Weber, *On the Road to Armageddon,* p. 221. Also see Yona Malachy, *American Fundamentalism and Israel: The Relation of Fundamentalist Churches to Zionism and the State of Israel* (Jerusalem: Hebrew University, 1978). To support Israel's settlement policies, evangelicals often cite Psalm 83:1–8, which describes Israel's enemies united and massing to do battle against it, and Obadiah 17–20, which speaks of Israel's triumph over its enemies.

58. Bill Broadway, "The Evangelical-Israeli Connection," *Washington Post,* March 27, 2004.

59. An exception to the rule was Prime Minister Ehud Barak, whose brief tenure in office is likely responsible for this. Also, the only Sukkot that fell during his term in office was in mid-October 2000, which was only two weeks into the second Palestinian Intifada. That obviously was his major concern.

60. For more, see the KCAC website at www .cac.org.il.

61. Broadway, "The Evangelical-Israeli Connection." Elon is a Modern Orthodox Jew who lives in the West Bank settlement of Beit El.

62. Peter Steinfels, "Religion Notes," *New York Times,* February 24, 1990.

63. Weber, *On the Road to Armageddon,* pp. 218–220. Some observers, including Weber, write that Begin even gave Falwell a Learjet to use while promoting the pro-Israel cause across the United States. However, Zev Chafets, who was Begin's American-born press spokesman during the 1970s, has called that notion a "myth." As he wrote, "The prime minister of Israel doesn't have planes to give away. Begin himself flew El Al and he would have gone coach if his security detail had let him." Chafets, *A Match Made in Heaven,* p. 66.

64. Gershom Gorenberg, *The End of Days: Fundamentalism and the Struggle for the Temple Mount* (Oxford: Oxford University Press, 2000), p. 166.

65. Donald Wagner, "Evangelicals and Israel: Theological Roots of a Political Alliance," *Christian Century,* November 4, 1998, p. 1020.

66. Gorenberg, *The End of Days*, p. 162.

67. See exchange of letters between Julius Briller of the American Jewish Committee and Dr. G. Douglas Young of the Institute of Holy Land Studies, October 23 and November 7, 1974. Also see "Draft: Program Prospectus: Evangelical Christians, 1975," in American Jewish Committee archives, www.ajcarchives.org /ajcarchive/DigitalArchive.aspx.

68. "Jewish Congress Assails the 'Evangelical Right,'" *New York Times*, October 25, 1981.

69. See "Ecumenical & Interfaith" on the Alliance of Baptists website, www.sitemason.com /files/f6GcW4/statementchristiansjews2003.pdf. The Alliance of Baptists was founded in 1987 as a breakaway group from the Southern Baptist Conference, protesting the perceived growing lack of traditionalism in the latter group.

70. See "Resolution on Jewish Evangelism" on the Southern Baptist Convention website, www.sbc.net/resolutions/amResolution.asp?ID =655.

71. Chafets, *A Match Made in Heaven*, p. 49. Chafets mocks the effort by writing, "The American Jewish community faces problems, but mass conversion to evangelical Christianity is not one of them. . . . Nowadays, at least half marry non-Jews. What Jews don't do is get born again. There are probably more ex-Jewish Buddhists than Baptists in the United States."

72. *1997 Annual Survey of American Jewish Opinion* (New York: American Jewish Committee, 1997), p. 20.

73. *2001 Annual Survey of American Jewish Opinion* (New York: American Jewish Committee, 2001), p. 9. In part, this came from the support of then-governor George W. Bush in his 2000 presidential campaign, in which he made strong outreach to evangelicals while American Jews overwhelmingly supported Democratic challenger Vice President Al Gore.

74. Brog, *Standing with Israel*, p. 74, citing a Hagee speech at the Embassy of Israel in Washington, D.C., December 14, 2002.

75. Eugene Korn, *Meeting the Challenge: Church Attitudes Toward the Israeli-Palestinian Conflict* (New York: Anti-Defamation League, 2002).

76. Yehiel Poupko, *Looking at Them Looking at Us: A Jewish Understanding of Christian Responses to Israel* (New York: Jewish Council for Public Affairs, 2008).

77. Eric Yoffie letter to John Hagee, May 21, 2008, http://urj.org//about/union/leadership /yoffie//?syspage=article&item_id=6072.

78. "ADL Welcomes Pastor Hagee's Clarification of Remarks on Jews and the Holocaust," June 13, 2008, http://www.adl.org/PresRele /HolNa_52/5299_52.htm.

79. Eric Yoffie, "Christian Zionism: Is It Good for North American Jews and Is It Good for Zionism?" http://urj.org//about/union/leader ship/yoffie//?syspage=article&item_id=6073.

80. Chafets, *A Match Made in Heaven*, pp. 189–194. The meeting came at the behest of Chafets, who asked Falwell if he would host Yoffie, who happened to be one of his childhood friends. For Yoffie's remarks, see "Remarks by Rabbi Eric Yoffie at Liberty University," April 26, 2006, http://urj.org//about/union/leadership /yoffie//?syspage=article&item_id=6100.

81. Abraham H. Foxman, "Why Evangelical Support for Israel Is a Good Thing," www .adl.org/Israel/evangelical.asp, July 16, 2002.

82. Chafets, *A Match Made in Heaven*, p. 142. Reflecting the tensions and competition within the Jewish world over this and other issues, Chafets wrote, "Some who attended thought Foxman had gone too far [in his criticism of evangelicals on domestic matters]. Others simply didn't feel like serving in Abe's army."

83. Abraham H. Foxman, "Jews and Evangelicals: Support for Israel Isn't Everything," Jewish Telegraphic Agency, January 16, 2007.

84. Broadway, "The Evangelical-Israeli Connection."

85. The ultra-Orthodox, or Haredi, group Agudath Israel, which has a political party in Israel's Knesset, opened its Washington office in 1988. Likewise, the Modern, or "centrist," Orthodox group, the Orthodox Union, opened a public affairs office in Washington in 1990. The OU's public affairs offices had already been in operation in the organization's New York City headquarters for several years, but the organization recognized the need to be part of the lobbying scene in the nation's capital for its voice to be heard. See Chapter 10 in this volume.

86. Broadway, "The Evangelical-Israeli Connection." For more on Eckstein, see Zev Chafets,

"The Rabbi Who Loved Evangelicals (and Vice Versa)," *New York Times,* July 24, 2005, and John W. Kennedy, "The Ultimate Kibbutzer," *Christianity Today,* February 2009.

87. Chafets, *A Match Made in Heaven,* p. 120.

88. There is a key difference in the eras. Today some evangelicals want creationism—which most scientists see as a religious doctrine—taught not to the exclusion of evolution, which is seen as a scientific theory, but side-by-side with it.

12

The Quest for Impact

LESSONS LEARNED FROM THE AMERICAN JEWISH PEACE CAMP

Mark Rosenblum and Dan Fleshler

THE EXPLOSIVE GROWTH OF J STREET, the self-described political arm of the "pro-Israel, pro-peace" movement in the United States, has been met with both acclaim and controversy. It has prompted breathless claims, from critics and supporters alike, that there is something novel and utterly daring about the mobilization of American Jews who define themselves as pro-Israel and are willing to publicly criticize Israeli policies.[1]

In fact, the phenomenon of American Jews organizing pro-Israel peace groups is hardly new. Since the early 1970s, a number of groups and organizations that have supported Israel's peace camp and opposed various Israeli policies have emerged in the United States.

This chapter will analyze the birth, growth, and challenges faced by four peace groups: Breira, Americans for Peace Now, Israel Policy Forum, and J Street. It will examine whether the experience of these organizations offers insights into the prospects for the continued growth and success of the current pro-Israel peace camp in the United States.

This chapter is by no means a systematic history of the American Zionist Left.[2] Rather, it is a selective analysis of some organizations that have received the attention—and often raised the hackles—of more traditional American Jewish groups and affected the organized Jewish community's discourse about the Arab-Israeli conflict. Some have had an influence—albeit, arguably, a modest one—on the domestic political context of America's Middle East policies, while others have affected Israeli-Palestinian relations by legitimizing moderate Palestinian nationalists.

We will briefly review the distinct historical "moments" in which each group was born and some of the events in both the Middle East and United States that affected the groups. We will also discuss some of their activities and identify broad trends that help to account for their successes and failures. However, this chapter will not examine managerial strengths or weaknesses, fund-raising and communications operations, or other factors that help to determine the sustainability of nonprofit organizations. Rather, we will focus on broader patterns and lessons that may offer insights into the future of the American Jewish peace camp, and the variables that may determine the extent of its influence.

Based on what America's "pro-Israel, pro-peace" camp has experienced thus far, we have identified several distinct characteristics and factors that are necessary for such groups to sustain themselves and affect not only the broader Jewish community, but the American government as well. What they require are:

1. The participation of individuals from American Jewish organizations that are generally considered to be part of the mainstream community, including synagogue groups, federations, and established Zionist organizations.
2. Israeli policies and behaviors that are objectionable to a broad swath of American Jews, such as the continuing occupation of the West Bank, settlement expansion, and the absence of a serious Israel peace initiative. The perceived imperative to *oppose* something has been and remains the sine qua non of any Jewish peace group's success in the United States.
3. Israeli allies, either in the form of social movements—for example, Shalom Achshav (Peace Now)—politicians, or government officials pursuing diplomatic rapprochement with Israel's neighbors. The ability to point to Israelis, especially those with security credentials, who share the values and goals of pro-Israel peace groups provides a degree of reassurance to American Jews who are concerned about Israel's future, yet reluctant to speak out against Israeli policies.
4. A viable, credible Arab negotiating partner for Israel, and the perception that such a partner exists.
5. An American administration that is intent upon facilitating a peace process. Among diplomats with experience in the Middle East, proactive, bold American diplomacy is viewed as essential to ending the Israeli-Palestinian conflict.[3] American administrations need the political leeway to lean on both sides of the conflict, rather than just one side,

and to suggest ideas that neither party is happy about but both can live with. Yet hands-on American engagement not only is essential to a viable peace process; it is also needed to foster support in the American Jewish community for the pro-Israel peace camp, which—experience has shown—finds it hard to grow when there is little hope. The prospect of effective American diplomacy has been a key source of hope.

The Breira Moment

Israel's near-defeat in the 1973 Yom Kippur War prompted a furious reaction from the Israeli public, which demanded that leaders at the highest echelons of government be held accountable for prewar complacency and a lack of preparedness. Mass demonstrations, an official commission that called for the dismissal of several high-ranking Israeli military officials, and the eventual resignation of Prime Minister Golda Meir and Defense Minister Moshe Dayan all helped to legitimize dissent against Israeli government policy.

The acrimonious public discourse after the Yom Kippur War intensified deepening ideological gaps within Israel. The ideological Left was represented by a small, isolated, yet vocal Israeli peace camp, while the Right coalesced around the Israeli settlement movement and its principal organization, Gush Emunim. As Michael Staub puts it, "For Israeli leftists and arguably more moderate elements of the population as well, the 'earthquake' (as many Israelis derisively called the Yom Kippur War) underscored that no lasting peace could be achieved without an exchange of land."[4]

During the aftershocks of this earthquake in late 1973, a diverse group of liberal and left-wing American Jews founded Breira ("alternative"). Its stated purpose was "to legitimize public dissent within the American Jewish community concerning the profound issues that confront us as Jews in the Diaspora" and to challenge increasingly vocal, right-wing American Zionists.[5]

From the start, Breira insisted that it was not part of some alienated Jewish fringe, but that it emanated from the heart of the Jewish community. Although its initial statement called for Israel to "make territorial concessions," it also stated that Breira drew inspiration from the "idealism and thought of many early Zionists with whom we identify."[6] Over the course of its four-year history, Breira's members and sympathizers included a who's who of decidedly respectable, liberal American Jews. These included leading rabbis, such as David Saperstein of the Reform movement's Religious Action Center, Balfour Brickner of the Stephen Wise Free Synagogue, and a good many Hillel directors; leading Zionist activists, such as Joachim Prinz, chair of the World Conference of Jewish Organizations; and intellectuals, such as Irving Howe, Nathan Glazer, Charles

S. Liebman, and Jacob Neusner. Interestingly, its ranks also included Jews who would eventually move into leadership positions of the communal establishment, including John Ruskay, now the CEO of the UJA-Federation of New York. Breira also included people affiliated with the New Left and small countercultural Jewish organizations, such as the Jewish Peace Fellowship and the Committee on New Alternatives in the Middle East, which was founded in 1970 by leaders of the anti–Vietnam War movement, including Noam Chomsky.[7]

Although American Jewish organizations' angry reactions to Breira have received attention from both scholars and activists,[8] the fact that much of the Jewish community accepted Breira's participation in debates about Israel during its first three years is rarely noted. Its publications and speakers—including invited guests from Israel—publicly lambasted Gush Emunim and the Israeli occupation, held that Palestinian nationalism was not something Jews could quash or wish away, and—most significantly—criticized the Israeli government's intransigence. Yet, for much of its existence, according to Staub, "there was a widespread sense that although Breira was raising unpleasant issues, those issues were important and indeed a segment of the Jewish community agreed with Breira's positions." Although Breira prompted fierce resistance and anger from the outset, American Jewish media outlets like the *National Jewish Post and Opinion* and *Washington Jewish Week* initially treated it respectfully.[9]

The organization's downfall was precipitated when in November 1976, a group of American Jews met with two Palestinians with close ties to the PLO: Issam Sartawi, a member of the Fatah Revolutionary Council, and Sabri Jaryis, a leading Arab-Israeli author. The meeting was organized by the American Friends Service Committee. Although its participants included people from B'nai B'rith and the American Jewish Congress, there were also two Breira executive committee members, Rabbis Max Ticktin and Arthur Waskow. The story of the confidential meetings was leaked, eventually reaching the *New York Times*.

The condemnations from a broad range of Jewish groups, media outlets, and scholars were fast and furious,[10] and Breira was singled out as the target. At the time, the idea of legitimizing the PLO was beyond the pale in the American Jewish establishment and much of Israel. It was perceived as an unredeemable enemy of Israel, an anti-Semitic organization sworn to the Jewish state's destruction. According to Yehoshafat Harkabi, the chief of Israel's military intelligence from 1955 to 1959 whose views were widely quoted in American Jewish circles at the time—and who later became Peace Now's ally—the PLO Covenant was "politicidal" and "genocidal."[11] In this atmosphere, Breira's leaders and principal organizers were portrayed as radical, New Left activists who were fiercely hostile to Israel. Those with mainstream credentials were depicted as naive dupes. As the firestorm spread, B'nai B'rith tried to fire employees who were members of Breira, and the conservative movement's Rabbinical Assembly refused to allow two Breira members to sit on its executive council. Breira's first national conference, in March 1977, was violently disrupted by the Jewish Defense League.

The organization quickly collapsed. There was more than one reason, including occasional insensitivity to American Jewish fears and sensibilities.[12] But the main reasons were that Breira lacked the ability to point to a credible Arab peace partner, and the group's fellow travelers in Israel who called for talks with the PLO were lonely voices in the wilderness. As Steven Rosenthal explains, "As long as all Arab states vowed to destroy the Zionist entity there was no room for the kind of flexibility Breira advocated. Moreover, the potentially disastrous implications of the retention of the West Bank for Israel's political and cultural future were not generally evident."[13]

The Peace Now/Americans for Peace Now Moment

If the Yom Kippur War was an earthquake, the diplomatic outreach of Egyptian President Anwar Sadat to Israel had an even larger seismic impact on the Israeli consciousness. When Sadat proclaimed his willingness to speak to the Israel Knesset and then visited Israel in 1977, he was greeted with open arms by the vast majority of Israelis and their Jewish supporters in the Diaspora. At long last, the leader of the most important state in the Arab world was willing to end Israel's utter isolation and pariah status in the Middle East, and the pent-up frustration from decades of international ostracism was released in a collective, communal surge of hope, gratitude, and tears.

Sadat's principal reason for striving for peace with Israel was to restore the Egyptian territory and national pride that had been lost in the 1967 war. Sadat concluded that regaining the Sinai and Egyptian honor required Egypt to wean itself off its dependence on the Soviet Union and to develop a new economic and strategic alliance with the United States. Though the Soviets could deliver weapons, the United States could deliver Israeli territorial concessions. He also sought to protect his political position in the inter-Arab arena by taking up the issue of the broader Arab-Israeli conflict, particularly the Palestinian issue. The kind of comprehensive settlement he envisioned was, to put it mildly, not acceptable to Israeli Prime Minister Menachem Begin.

A large segment of the Israeli public wondered why, after the initial exultation over Sadat's outreach, after the drawbridge between Israel and the Arab world had been lowered, Begin seemed determined to raise it. In response, 348 Israeli reserve officers and soldiers sent him a widely publicized letter, noting that:

> We are writing this with deep anxiety, as a government that prefers the existence of the State of Israel within the borders of "Greater Israel" to its existence in peace with good neighborliness, will be difficult for us to accept. A government that prefers existence

of settlements beyond the Green Line to elimination of this historic conflict with creation of normalization of relationships in our region will evoke questions regarding the path we are taking. A government policy that will cause a continuation of control over millions Arabs will hurt the Jewish-democratic character of the state, and will make it difficult for us to identify with the path of the State of Israel.[14]

A small group of signatories and their friends borrowed the name "Peace Now" from an advertising copywriter and called a meeting in Tel Aviv. Hundreds turned out and a grassroots protest movement was born. Initially this news barely made a dent on most American Jews. But Begin's election and rhetoric had already begun to plant the seeds of a counterpart to Peace Now in the United States. According to Dan Fleshler:

After supporting for decades an Israeli government dominated by the Labor Party, which they assumed—rightly or wrongly—had gone out of its way to extend its hand for peace, much of American Jewry was utterly flabbergasted by Begin and his Likud-dominated Cabinet. The new Israeli government was suddenly in the hands of people who had inherited the tradition of the uncompromising, "Iron Wall Israel" advocated by Begin's mentor, the Revisionist leader Ze'ev Jabotinsky. . . .

In the prevailing American Jewish narrative, Israel had always offered its hand in peace to the Arabs and had consistently been rebuffed. . . . But Begin appeared to be matching . . . Arab . . . recalcitrance by announcing his intention to expand settlements in occupied territories.

Likud's ascendancy created a "crisis of allegiance for American Jewry," as Samuel Freedman described it. In the organized American Jewish community, within a year after Begin's election, "local leaders found themselves forced to defend Israeli positions they could not understand. Contacts with non-Jewish dialogue partners—church leaders, civil rights leaders, labor leaders—were becoming testy. Synagogue rabbis reported distress among their congregants at what looked like Israeli reluctance to make peace," JJ Goldberg recounts.[15]

By the time Israel invaded Lebanon in 1982, discomfort with Likud policies had been growing apace within the American Jewish community, and it found occasional, tangible expression by prominent American Jewish leaders.[16] But it was Israel's behavior in the first Lebanese war that sparked the organized Zionist peace movement in the United States, which was, not surprisingly, inspired by growing protests in Israel.

Initial Israeli troop movements to stop PLO attacks from the north were widely supported in the Jewish state. But the Israeli Left and center were galvanized when it became clear that Defense Minister Ariel Sharon, IDF chief of staff Raful Eitan, and their colleagues harbored broader ambitions, and were pushing on to Beirut to remake Lebanon. Opposition to this adventurism by the security-conscious, dovish officers who led Peace Now helped to change the calculus of dissent in Israel, prompting many Israelis to overcome a habitual hesitancy to publicly protest against their government's military policies.

A series of street demonstrations organized by Peace Now, including one with more than 100,000 participants on July 3, 1982, called upon the Begin government to stop the war, talk to Palestinian national leaders, and dismiss Sharon. In September, after Lebanese Christian Phalangists allied with Israel massacred hundreds of Palestinians in the Sabra and Shatilla refugee camps, Peace Now— with the Labor Party and others—organized the largest demonstration in Israeli history, with approximately 400,000 people demanding that the Israeli government be held accountable.[17] Although anguish and fury over Israel's behavior in Lebanon prompted the largest rallies, the Peace Now movement was also sustained by opposition to the Israeli settlement movement and a demand that Israel not take steps to preclude eventual territorial compromise.

Although a chapter of Peace Now supporters had started in Chicago in 1981, after Sabra and Shatilla, the movement found willing and committed partners among American Jews across the country. During 1982 and 1983, Friends of Peace Now chapters began to organize in New York City, Boston, Baltimore, Raleigh-Durham, North Carolina, Los Angeles, Washington, D.C., and more than a dozen other cities. A national organization, originally called American Friends of Peace Now, was established in 1983. The group changed its name to Americans for Peace Now in 1988, and, for the sake of simplicity, we will refer to it as APN.

With op-eds, ad campaigns, and speakers from Israel, APN promoted a distinctly Zionist argument that, though somewhat provocative during its first decade, has now become part of the consensus narrative adopted by many Israeli centrists. Indeed, the present-day speeches of Kadima leader Tsippy Livni on Israel's future echo the language of Peace Now activists in the mid-1980s: if Israel clings to the territories and does not give voting rights to Palestinian Arab residents, it will cease to be a democracy; if it does give Palestinians voting rights, it will cease to be a Jewish state.

APN began with approximately $6,000 in the bank and approximately one hundred donors. It grew slowly but steadily, at first trying to organize more chapters around the country. APN eventually relinquished the chapter-based model in favor of engaging American Jewish leaders around the country, creating a national membership structure as well as three regional offices and a Center for Israeli Peace and Security in Washington, D.C. Although APN's membership was varied, its board and major volunteers in the mid-1980s included leaders from Jewish federations and other mainstream communal organizations, including Gerald Bubis, founder of the Hebrew Union College School of Jewish

Communal Service; Sanford Solender, former executive vice president of the UJA-Federation of New York; Richard Gunther, national cochair of Federation's Project Renewal, and Los Angeles cochair of Project Exodus; and Robert O. Freedman, graduate dean (and later president) of Baltimore Hebrew University. By the late 1980s, the board also included other prominent liberal Jews who had not previously been engaged with Israel's peace camp, such as feminist author Letty Cottin Pogrebin; Peter Edelman, a law professor and associate dean of Georgetown University Law Center; and Sara Ehrman, a Democratic Party activist and former AIPAC organizer. By 1993, the organization's annual budget was close to $1.3 million.[18]

There was some fierce opposition to specific APN positions and statements, including the group's call for Israel to talk with the PLO, a stance it arrived at in 1987. Nevertheless, it gradually gained enough respectability and a large enough membership base that in 1993, it was admitted into the Conference of Presidents of Major American Jewish Organizations, the most important umbrella organization in the American Jewish community.

This begs the question of why APN was able to gain legitimacy in the American Jewish community while calling for negotiations with the PLO, while Breira was ostracized, and ultimately collapsed, because it advocated dialogue with Palestinian nationalists. Like Americans for Peace Now, Breira's leadership had been composed of Zionists who were upset and agonized by the expanding occupation and the absence of peace diplomacy. But APN benefited from something that Breira had, for the most part, lacked: an organized movement of Israelis led and inspired by IDF reserve officers with security credentials.

Indeed, Israeli Peace Now activists included high-ranking soldiers who were deployed in Lebanon. An IDF officer and member of the elite Sayerat Matkal commando unit, Abu Vilan, was one of Peace Now's founders. In June 1982, while on the front lines with his troops as Israel steadily pushed to the north, Vilan sent word to his Peace Now colleagues that they should not launch mass demonstrations until the Israelis crossed the Litani River, which would demonstrate that Israel's defense establishment was pushing on to Beirut and lying to the public about its ambitions. The presence of such military leaders in Peace Now's ranks provided its supporters in the United States with a *hechscher*—a kosher seal of approval—and bolstered the case that they should be included in the American Jewish communal tent.

Along with this mainstream, grassroots Israeli movement, APN was also aided by intellectual Israeli allies with impeccable security credentials. By bringing these Israelis to the United States as speakers and calling attention to their work, APN activists countered the notion that they were a bunch of seditious graduate students rebelling against their parents, an image that had unfairly tarnished Breira. The Israeli allies who toured the United States on behalf of

APN included, for example, General Giora Furman, former deputy commander of the Israeli air force; Major General Shlomo Gazit, former head of Israeli intelligence; Major General Avraham Tamir, founding chief of the Policy and Planning Directorate of the IDF; and Colonel Mordechai Bar-On, former chief education officer of the Israel Defense Forces. The most important was probably the aforementioned Yehoshafat Harkabi, the legendary soldier/scholar and widely respected expert on the Palestinian national movement as well as anti-terrorism adviser to Prime Ministers Yitzhak Rabin and Menachem Begin.

Harkabi made a name for himself in the 1970s as Israel's premier strategic analyst, who documented that the PLO was a hard-line terrorist group intent on destroying Israel. Indeed, he was often quoted by American Jewish groups seeking to prove that Yasser Arafat and his cronies were modern-day Amalekites, the inherently evil biblical enemies that the Jewish people were obligated to destroy. But Harkabi evolved into a self-described "Machiavellian dove" who believed that territorial compromise with the Palestinians was essential to preserving Israel as a Jewish and democratic state.[19] He provided memorable, strategic sound bites that articulated the stark choices facing the Jewish state, for example, "Either Israel shall help birth a Palestinian state or it shall become the Palestinian state."[20]

This premise gained some adherents among American Jews, but what hampered APN's ability to gain even more traction on the Palestinian issue in the American Jewish community was the same obstacle that had stymied Breira: the perceived lack of moderate, Palestinian nationalist interlocutors. Both Peace Now and APN benefited from Sadat's conciliatory example. But needless to say, the Palestinian issue remained unresolved after the Camp David Accords between Israel and Egypt were signed. APN sought to address this core issue of the Arab-Israeli conflict by developing and nurturing contacts with moderate Palestinians and striving to give them legitimacy not only among American Jews but also in Israel.

Edward Said observes in *The Question of Palestine* that there were disagreements about long-term goals and short-term strategies among Palestinians living in the Diaspora, those living in the territories, and the remaining Palestinians who were citizens of the state of Israel. The "outsiders" in the Diaspora, generally represented by the PLO, were more hard-line on the question of a Palestinian right of return, had a more difficult time agreeing to a two-state solution, and didn't focus intently on the day-to-day problems of the "insiders." Palestinian nationalists who lived in the West Bank and in Israel proper included those who wanted to use negotiations over the territories as a springboard to a two-state solution.[21] This division was not well-known or understood even by many Israelis who favored the principle of territorial compromise in the 1980s, let alone by American Jews. APN played a role in introducing moderate West

Bank Palestinians to both publics, at a time when there was a law on the books prohibiting direct contact between Israelis and members of the PLO.

A number of prominent Palestinian leaders toured the United States under APN's auspices between 1982 and 1989, meeting with American Jews, Israeli security officials, and peace activists as well as US government officials. None of them were formal members of the PLO but they were all clearly Palestinian nationalists, and some had close contact with Arafat and other PLO officials. They included Faisal Husseini,[22] Ahmed Khalidi,[23] Ghassan Khatib,[24] Hanna Siniora,[25] Sari Nusseibah,[26] and Ziad Abu Zayyad.[27]

Of course, the main reason to introduce them to American Jewish audiences was to show that Israel had genuine partners for peace—Palestinian leaders who wanted to live side-by-side with Israel and renounced terrorism, yet who also insisted they were represented by Arafat and the PLO in the international arena. But the relationship between APN and these Palestinians was also part of a diplomatic strategy. During this period, with the encouragement of Peace Now, APN staff and board members were also engaging in Track Two diplomacy. They were trying to determine whether Arafat and the PLO would allow West Bank moderates to take a more prominent role and—via back-channel contacts with Arafat and his aides—were testing the PLO's willingness and capacity to support a two-state solution. In the diplomatic arena, this work with Palestinian moderates eventually paid dividends. Three people Arafat chose to head the Palestinian delegation at the Madrid Peace Conference in 1991 were West Bank/Gaza leaders with whom APN had established contacts and nurtured relationships: Husseini, Khatib, and Haider Abdel-Shafi.

The relationships developed with Palestinians by Peace Now and APN also resulted in joint advocacy activities. One of the most prominent occurred in December 1989. As violence during the first Palestinian Intifada escalated, more than 25,000 Israelis, Palestinians and supporters from abroad—including an APN delegation—linked hands around the Old City of Jerusalem. Israeli police confronted the demonstrators and the event ended with tear gas and recriminations.[28] Nevertheless, the rally sent a signal to the Arab world that there were Zionists and Palestinian nationalists who were willing to compromise.

However, that signal was not greeted warmly by an influential segment of the mainstream American Jewish community. APN took considerable risks by reaching out to Palestinian nationalists. Especially prior to the Oslo breakthrough in the summer of 1993, the notion of American Jews doing solidarity work with Palestinians who did not renounce the PLO was deeply troubling to many centrist, and even left-leaning, American Jews. To be sure, the reaction from the organized community to APN's outreach work was not nearly as angry as the apoplectic response to Breira. Nevertheless, despite the decidedly moderate messages from Husseini and his colleagues, APN's ability to tap into mainstream support was limited in part by its association with the PLO's allies in the West

Bank. These tensions were further exacerbated when the vigorous Middle East diplomacy of the George H. W. Bush administration prompted a confrontation with much of the American Jewish community: the loan guarantee controversy.

This controversy had its roots in the diplomacy leading up to the Madrid Peace Conference, which followed the Gulf War. Throughout 1991, President George H. W. Bush and Secretary of State James Baker sought Arab support for a Middle East peace conference in Madrid, Spain. To facilitate this effort, Bush and Baker tried to ensure that American loan guarantees for Israel would not be used to fund Jewish settlements in the West Bank. The government of Israeli Prime Minister Yitzhak Shamir refused to cooperate, claiming that new Israeli immigrants from Russia needed housing and that the West Bank was a logical place for it. In September, Bush asked for a 120-day delay on the loan guarantees before Congress considered the issue, but Shamir tried to go around him and secure the guarantees via legislation. That led to the now-storied press conference on September 12, 1991. A visibly angry President Bush criticized Shamir and invoked the "powerful forces" arrayed against him, asserting that "there were something like a thousand lobbyists on the Hill working the other side of this question. We've got one lonely little guy over here."[29]

American Jewish groups across the ideological spectrum were outraged. Helping Soviet Jewry was a sacred mission that was viewed as under attack. They felt that Bush was attacking the American Jewish community for exercising their constitutionally guaranteed right to petition their government. Moreover, they were upset by the open confrontation between the American and Israeli governments.

As American Jews from the major community groups descended upon Capitol Hill to lobby for the loan guarantees, APN was a lone dissenting voice. Peter Edelman, its cochair, testified in Congress on the matter. APN warned the Shamir government that its refusal to agree to a settlement freeze was endangering the US government's $10 billion loan guarantee. In addition, it warned that Shamir's position could lead to a clash with the White House that might compromise the strategic relationship between Israel and the United States.[30]

APN openly supported the American government's post–Gulf War peace initiative, which included a settlement freeze and was rejected by Shamir. In backing the US government in a public confrontation with Israel, and in breaking ranks with most of the Jewish community as it lobbied on behalf of Israel, APN had violated major taboos. Even dovish friends of APN, including Rabbi David Saperstein of the Reform movement's Religious Action Center and Theodore Mann of Project Nishma,[31] joined the struggle to secure the loan guarantees.

A significant number of individuals in the broader American Jewish community who would have been natural supporters of an attempt to stop settlement expansion could not overcome their discomfort with the Bush administration's squabbles with Israel, as well as with the American Jewish community. The principle that there should be "no daylight" between official American and Israeli positions would eventually become less popular among pro-Israel, American Jewish liberals, but at the time, it was inviolate. The only exception to this principle was articulated by the mavericks of APN, who alienated some potential supporters and allies with their criticism of the Shamir government's choice of settlement expansion over the $10 billion loan guarantee.

The Israel Policy Forum Moment

The Oslo peace process appeared to offer a perfect storm for APN and the Zionist Left in the United States. The Oslo years seemed to include all of the factors and variables necessary for dramatically expanding the peace tent in the organized American Jewish community:

1. An Arab partner for peace—or at least, for a time, the appearance of a partner in Yasser Arafat and a PLO that seemed to have reconciled itself to Israel's existence, at long last.
2. In Yitzhak Rabin, an Israeli leader with a mandate to explore territorial compromise, as well as the impeccable security bona fides needed to reassure much of the skittish Israeli public and Israel's supporters in America.
3. In Bill Clinton, an American leader who was popular in the American Jewish community and was prepared, at least to some extent, to facilitate a peace process that Israel desperately needed.
4. Fierce opposition to the Oslo process from militant Israeli settlers and their supporters in the United States, who galvanized and motivated peace process supporters to mobilize against them.

By all rights, this should have been APN's shining moment. However, the perception among the leadership of the Israeli Labor Party was that the organized, mainstream Jewish community was not sufficiently active in supporting Oslo and that liberals were deserting the field of pro-Israel advocacy, leaving the field to Likud sympathizers.

As a result, in 1993, with the encouragement of Labor Party officials, the Israel Policy Forum (IPF) was established. Its positions were similar to APN's, and the differences between the groups were based mostly on organizational cultures and the identities of their key leaders. Most of Israel Policy Forum's founders and its subsequent board members were wealthy American Jewish liberals, some of them leaders or former leaders of mainstream organizations, such as Robert K. Lifton, former president of the American Jewish Congress; Marvin Lender,

former chair of the United Jewish Appeal; and Jack Bendheim, a liberal Orthodox Jewish leader in New York City. Many of them were also major donors to
the Democratic Party and FOBs—Friends of Bill (Clinton). APN had FOBs as
well, but the IPF had shied away from involvement with APN. Some believed
that APN's positions and operational style were too radical to garner support
from the mainstream of the American Jewish community, where Labor's security
doves needed to make their case.

APN and IPF competed for donors and media attention but, along with Project Nishma and a few other groups, formed a de facto coalition to support the
Oslo peace process from the left wing of the organized American Jewish community.

However, that process foundered within a few years. All of the opinion pieces,
polls, newspaper ads, and exciting speakers from Israel that the peace camp
employed could not change the harsh, bleak realities of the conflict. What had
been a perfect storm turned into a killer storm after Rabin's assassination. Re-
lentless terrorism from Hamas in the mid-1990s brought about the election of
Likud leader Benjamin Netanyahu in 1996, leading to renewed turbulence in
US-Israeli relations and further complications for American diplomacy in the
Middle East.

Nevertheless, one of the characteristics of the pro-Israel peace camp in the
United States has been its persistent refusal to give up hope and its capacity to
function at unpromising diplomatic junctures. That was certainly true after Netanyahu assumed office, provoked Palestinian ire with a series of unilateral actions, and appeared to be backpedaling from Israeli commitments to further
redeployments in the West Bank that were part of the Oslo accords. In response,
both APN and IPF shifted focus and placed a high priority on a goal that had
rarely been articulated before: the mobilization of political support for proactive,
creative, and balanced American diplomacy. They had some success in this regard, especially during the Clinton administration's quarrels with the Netanyahu
government. It is worth reviewing what they accomplished during this period,
as it provides a useful precedent for J Street and the contemporary pro-Israel
peace camp.

Madeleine Albright's State Department reprimanded Netanyahu early in his
tenure in September 1996, when he reversed previous government policy and
sanctioned the opening of an ancient, Hasmonean tunnel under Jerusalem's Old
City. This enraged Palestinians, who viewed Israeli actions as disruptive to
Muslim holy sites on the nearby Temple Mount/Haram. Violence and rioting
ensued, in which fifteen IDF soldiers were killed and dozens more were injured;
approximately seventy Palestinians were killed and several hundred were
injured.[32] Two months later, President Clinton publicly criticized Israeli settlement expansion in the midst of negotiations over the status of Hebron. There

were other arguments, other challenges to Israel from US officials, and the IPF/APN coalition played a role in providing reassurance to Clinton that he would not be committing political suicide if he chided the Israeli government.

Beginning in the late summer of 1997, Secretary of State Albright issued public challenges to both Netanyahu and Palestinian Authority Chairman Yasser Arafat. In September, while in Israel, she called for a moratorium on settlements. Though the Conference of Presidents and other groups expressed concern, Albright received backing for this approach from American Jewish leaders who "concluded that a much more muscular U.S. role, even if it involves pressure on Israel, [was] necessary to revive negotiations over implementing the 1995 Oslo accords," according to the *Washington Post*.[33]

The *American Jewish Yearbook* of 1998 conveys the political dynamics at the time:

> The apparent growth of dissatisfaction with the Netanyahu government in American Jewish circles did not go unnoticed in the White House. On October 6, President Clinton, Vice-President Gore, and Secretary of State Albright held a "working dinner" with a small group of American Jews that lasted for three hours. Unlike such meetings in previous administrations, the guest list was not arranged by the Conference of Presidents of Major American Jewish Organizations; rather, the names were individually selected by the White House. Leaders of the mainstream Jewish organizations were there, but no noted "hawks." Conspicuous by their presence were three dovish activists: Jack Bendheim of the Israel Policy Forum, S. Daniel Abraham of the Center for Middle East Peace and Economic Cooperation (neither organization belonged to the Conference of Presidents), and Sara Ehrman, a close personal friend of the Clintons who was on the board of Americans for Peace Now.
>
> Clinton and Albright came away from the session convinced that Jews were not unanimously enamored of Israel's current government, held diverse views about the specific matters in dispute between Israel and the Palestinians, and would not necessarily react with outrage if Washington gently pressured Israel to make concessions for the sake of peace.[34]

It is impossible to quantify the extent to which this political protection mattered to the Clinton administration. The United States did press Netanyahu to yield 80 percent of Hebron to the Palestinian Authority as well as recognize that the PLO's National Covenant had been effectively amended and was no longer a negotiating obstacle. He was also cajoled to attend the Wye Peace Conference, where he agreed to further redeployments from the West Bank, although ultimately neither the "Hebron-plus" agreement nor the Wye Peace Conference actually fostered tangible, on-the-ground progress. What is significant for our purposes here is that the American Jewish peace camp demonstrated the capacity to provide political maneuvering room for an American president who was willing to publicly disagree with Israel. This was achieved by a smaller and less well-funded group of American Jews than the support base that now exists for J Street and the current pro-Israel peace camp. It may well be possible for the peace camp to do it again.

That is not to say that the Clinton administration was unconcerned about the domestic political backlash that would ensue from leaning too hard on the Israeli government, or that the United States was a sufficiently even-handed, honest broker when either Netanyahu or Ehud Barak was in power. But, as noted by longtime State Department hand Aaron David Miller, "Bill Clinton faced less pressure from domestic politics than any other president engaged in serious Arab-Israeli diplomacy. In fact, if there was any pressure from the Jewish community it came from groups like [Americans for] Peace Now and the Israel Policy Forum that were pushing him to go fast."[35] Indeed, Clinton was reportedly more concerned about domestic politics in Israel and the constraints it placed on Netanyahu and Barak than he was about American Jewish reactions to his diplomatic efforts.

But Bill Clinton alone could not salvage the Oslo peace process. It collapsed for a host of reasons beyond the scope of this chapter. They include structural flaws (the lack of third-party monitors to keep track of treaty violations and help the parties stay on course); Ehud Barak's brusque, take-it-or-leave-it negotiating style and the collapse of his governing coalition; Arafat's passivity and unwillingness to make necessary compromises; the Clinton administration's insistence on negotiations at Camp David before the Palestinians were ready; the lack of an American alternative in the event that permanent status negotiations failed; Israeli settlement expansion; and—last but certainly not least—the outbreak of the second Intifada. But according to both Barak and Clinton, it was Arafat, and Arafat alone, who was to blame.

As a result, the contention that "Barak offered Arafat a great deal, while Arafat responded with the Intifada" became the crux of the dominant narrative among American Jews and Israelis. Try as it might, the pro-Israel peace camp could not overcome this narrative, which expunged one of the key factors necessary to maintain support for the peace camp in the United States and Israel: a moderate Palestinian negotiating partner who was willing to compromise for the sake of a comprehensive peace settlement. The Jewish peace camp in both countries was dealt a serious blow, and the prospects for peace seemed even bleaker than they were after Rabin's assassination and the terrorism of the mid-1990s.

Prospects worsened during the George W. Bush administration, when another key factor—activist American peace diplomacy in the Middle East—was, with rare exceptions, absent. Especially after the attacks of September 11, 2001, Bush's approach to the Middle East rested on three M's:

1. Manichaeanism, a tendency to divide the universe into black and white, a "coalition of the willing" versus an "axis of evil."
2. Messianism, an abiding faith in the ability of democracy to solve the region's woes.
3. Militarism, the belief that America's terrorist enemies and their sponsors needed to know that they had no safe haven, and the United States would not hesitate to use its military might against any state that harbored them. To an American administration that took the reins during the Palestinian Intifada, equated Hamas with al-Qaeda, and included in its ranks neoconservatives with long-standing sympathies for Likud, diplomatic efforts toward a two-state solution were a low priority.

To be sure, there were occasional bright spots and glimmers of hope, such as the release of the Middle East Quartet's Road Map for Middle East Peace in 2002, the Annapolis Peace Conference in 2007, and the start of American efforts to train Palestinian security forces under Palestinian Authority Prime Minister Salam Fayyad.[36] But for much of Bush's tenure, America was missing in action when it came to Israeli-Palestinian diplomacy. Though the pro-Israel peace camp in the United States did not disappear, it suffered from the pessimism that prevailed in Israel and the territories, with only brief interruptions, during the Bush years.[37]

The J Street Moment

In the 1990s, both APN and IPF had occasional political victories and showed more political strength than is commonly attributed to them. However, they could not come close to rivaling the conventional pro-Israel lobby, that is, the American Israel Public Affairs Committee (AIPAC) and other organizations that wanted no "daylight" between Israeli and American positions. Individuals from both APN and IPF targeted money to support sympathetic members of Congress, but their efforts could not rival the formidable influence of AIPAC and its affiliated political action committees. Moreover, neither peace group had local chapters, and although APN did have a grassroots network, it was modest in comparison to AIPAC's.

In 2002, a new kid arrived on the liberal American Jewish block. Brit Tzedek v'Shalom attempted to build a larger grassroots base for the pro-Israel peace camp. It grew slowly but steadily and had forty chapters by 2008. However, its political clout still paled in comparison to that of the conventional pro-Israel lobby.

During George W. Bush's second term, a small group of wealthy, left-leaning American Jewish donors and Jewish activists decided that a significantly larger, more politically powerful pro-Israel peace camp was both necessary and possible.

After unsuccessful attempts to unite existing organizations—APN, IPF, and Brit Tzedek v'Shalom—in April 2008, a new organization was born: J Street.

J Street's principal mission was to foster balanced American diplomacy in the Middle East, at a time when the high price of lapsed diplomatic efforts was painfully clear. Although it was founded toward the end of the Bush administration, its growth—and the buzz it created—dramatically increased after the election of Barack Obama in November 2008.

Unlike the other pro-Israel peace groups, whose tax status limits their political activities, J Street is legally entitled to lobby without constraints. It has also set up a political action committee (PAC) to funnel money directly to political candidates and incumbents. In less than a year, it attracted close to 100,000 online supporters and raised more than $500,000 for congressional candidates, more than any other pro-Israel PAC in the country. In 2010, it absorbed Brit Tzedek v'Shalom as well as a small group devoted to organizing the pro-Israel peace camp on college campuses, the Union of Progressive Zionists, which became J Street University. As of April 2011, the organization had more than 150,000 online supporters, a nearly fifty-person staff, and grassroots political organizing capacities in much of the country. Though it has garnered some support from the mainstream, organized Jewish community,[38] it has also brought left-leaning Jews to the table who had little, if anything, to do with the Jewish communal world.[39]

Initially, J Street benefited from several of the requisite factors that had enabled other pro-Israel peace groups to gain traction within the American Jewish community. Netanyahu's perceived recalcitrance,[40] the extremist pronouncements of his foreign minister, Avigdor Lieberman, and the continued strength of the Israeli settlement movement were deeply offensive to large numbers of American Jews, and that helped to galvanize J Street's online supporters. By the time Obama took office, Palestinian Authority President Mahmoud Abbas and Prime Minister Salam Fayyad had demonstrated the existence of empowered Palestinian moderates with whom Israel could do business. The fact that violent civil strife in the territories had created two Palestinian polities—one in the Gaza Strip controlled by Hamas, and the other in the West Bank controlled by Fatah—was a terrible problem for the pro-Israel peace camp. However, in the euphoria over Obama's election and his administration's early, energetic diplomatic efforts, the problem was essentially shunted aside as a puzzle to be solved later.

The Jewish peace camp in Israel and the United States had yet another surge of hope when President Obama appointed George Mitchell as a high-level envoy devoted to the Israeli peace process, and when the administration confronted Netanyahu with the demand that Israel freeze all settlement construction. It appeared distinctly possible that Obama would be willing to take the political risks necessary to be the active, honest broker that the pro-Israel peace camp believed the region desperately needed.

As it grew, J Street ran into opposition within the organized Jewish community. Moreover, right-wing critics of J Street possessed online tools that were not at the disposal of those who had opposed Breira and APN in the 1970s, 1980s, and 1990s. J Street's unwillingness to defend Israel's 2008 military incursion in Gaza—Operation Cast Lead—was criticized even by some of the group's allies, including Rabbi Eric Yoffie, leader of the Union of Reform Judaism. Along with APN, J Street also opposed the American veto of a UN Security Council resolution that, among other things, condemned Israeli settlements. This provoked an even louder outcry from the conventional pro-Israel community and cost J Street the support of politicians who had previously accepted its endorsement, including Representative Gary Ackerman (D-NY).

In large part because of its visibility and its insistence on calling itself "pro-Israel" as well as "pro-peace," J Street quickly became a new lightning rod for right-wingers in Israel and the United States who could brook no criticism of Israeli policies from Diaspora Jews. It was even the focus of a highly publicized Knesset hearing, where Knesset members Dani Danon of Likud and Otniel Schneller of Kadima took turns rebuking the organization and denying it the right to consider itself Zionist or pro-Israel.

These and other controversies have become fodder for the Republican Party, which may try to use the association of congressional Democrats and President Obama with J Street as a weapon to peel away traditionally Democratic voters who are worried about Israel. "Up and down the ballot, from the presidential contest to local races, J Street will be the latest wedge the Republicans hope to drive between Jewish voters and the Democratic Party," predicted James Besser in February 2011.[41] Though this is suggestive of J Street's efficacy in changing the political dynamic in Washington and the American Jewish community, it is also a worrisome sign for the organization, which will lose its raison d'être if politicians and elected officials become too nervous about endorsing its positions or accepting money from its PAC.

The public relations storms that have swirled around J Street and the intercommunal controversies may well continue. If they do, they probably won't have a significant, adverse effect on much of the organization's core grassroots base. However, whether J Street can keep at least one foot in the Jewish communal tent, appealing to liberal, mainstream Jews who have grown increasingly wary of it, remains to be seen,

The Present Moment

Ultimately, the most important determinants for the pro-Israel peace camp's future are what will happen in Israel and the rest of the Middle East. As of this writing, it is not clear whether the key diplomatic and political factors that contributed to J Street's meteoric rise will remain intact. Indeed, they may well have been illusory. J Street has bet heavily on interventionist American diplomacy not only as a mechanism to foster diplomatic progress, but also as a rallying cry to garner members and donations. Given the gaps between the Israelis and Palestinians, and the ideological and territorial divisions among the Palestinians, it is difficult to believe that the bet will pay off in the remainder of Obama's first term.

George Mitchell gave up, resigning in May 2011 after two years of failed attempts to facilitate negotiations between Israel and the Palestinian Authority. Obama attempted to infuse new life into the peace process by announcing that a settlement should be based on the 1967 lines with mutually agreed-upon land swaps, and that the parties should focus on borders and security before tackling the issue of Jerusalem and the Palestinian refugees. But Obama appears to be politically hamstrung, and it is unlikely that he will push very hard for Israeli concessions as the presidential election season heats up.

Of course, there is always a chance that Obama will surprise his skeptics. Even during his first term, he might translate his sweeping rhetoric into implementable diplomatic mechanisms and personnel capable of dramatically advancing the American peace agenda in the Middle East. But that probably will not happen unless and until he is reelected. During a second term, it is possible that he will be less sensitive to the domestic political risks of bold Mideast diplomacy.

It would be presumptuous to predict what will occur in the Middle East in the weeks and months ahead. To put it mildly, it is difficult to be sanguine. As of this writing, Mahmoud Abbas has reportedly given up on the possibility that the United States will be an effective, forceful mediator. He has turned to the United Nations, and on September 23, 2011, submitted to the Security Council an application for Palestine to become a member state. Abbas's maneuvers at the UN have been rebuffed by Obama as well as Netanyahu, and if the Palestinians' UN membership bid fails in the Security Council, they likely will turn to the General Assembly for upgraded status as a nonmember state. The response of America's pro-Israel peace camp has been a renewed push for the Obama administration to facilitate serious bilateral negotiations, even though America's electoral calendar makes proactive diplomacy unlikely in the near future.

Moreover, the unity pact between the Palestinian Authority and Hamas has made it much more difficult for the pro-Israel peace camp to convince American Jews that Israel has a partner for peace. Both J Street and Americans for Peace Now have eschewed the convenient, popular argument that since "there is no partner," peace talks are impossible. While acknowledging the murderous behavior and genocidal, anti-Semitic ideology of Hamas, these groups have argued that a future Palestinian unity government should be judged primarily on the basis of its behaviors and policies on the ground.[42] They have echoed the arguments of prominent security experts in Israel.[43] But those arguments have fallen on deaf ears in the Israeli government and most of the organized American Jewish community.

Finally, although the potential effect of the so-called Arab Spring on the Palestinians is unclear at the moment, the prospects of massive demonstrations and civil disobedience in the territories and on Israel's borders—and a harsh counterreaction by the Israeli government—must be taken seriously.

None of this bodes well for either the region or for pro-Israel peace groups in the United States. They will not be able to sustain themselves indefinitely, or influence the American Jewish community and alter the political landscape, unless their constituents have some hope that peace in the Middle East is not an idle dream. Without an electoral manifestation of moderate national leadership in a reunified Palestinian national movement, along with an Israeli government that is serious about meaningful compromise, the prospects for a comprehensive settlement are slim. And the diminished likelihood that the United States can and will be an effective bridge builder between the parties, at least in the near term, could undercut the relevance of J Street, APN, and their allies.

Furthermore, like the parties to the conflict and the international community, the pro-Israel peace camp must confront another painful challenge: growing evidence that it may be too late for the two-state solution. Pessimists have been predicting that for years, and the Zionist Left has done its best to ignore those predictions. But with more than 500,000 Jewish settlers now in the occupied territories (including East Jerusalem), large gaps between the parties on core issues, and an American electoral calendar that probably does not permit the United States to address the conflict with sufficient urgency, more and more moderates on both sides have come to believe that the hourglass is running out on the negotiated two-state settlement. The option of one unified, secular, democratic state, once the goal of the international hard Left, is picking up support, particularly among Palestinians, including prominent Palestinians who had been advocates of a two-state solution.[44]

That said, rumors of the deaths of a viable peace process, a two-state solution, and an energized American Zionist Left may very well be premature. As Hussein Ibish, a senior research fellow for the American Task Force on Palestine, has put it:

> At some point a two state agreement could become practically impossible, although this has not yet occurred. The moment at which such a state of "impossibility" . . . will emerge is, contrary to many arguments by one-state advocates, not the function of a critical mass of administrative, topographical and infrastructural changes constructed by Israel in the occupied territories. Rather, it is that moment when a critical mass of

Israelis and Palestinians become convinced that such a peace agreement is no longer feasible or desirable. The two questions are linked, since entrenchment of the occupation greatly complicates any belief in the plausibility of a peace agreement to end it. However, political realities are fundamentally shaped by the confluence of political will and power. Longstanding and deeply rooted realities can be transformed by political actions based on necessity and consensus. The emergence of the State of Israel is a prime example of this process at work.[45]

In the past, the peace camp in Israel and the United States has encountered moments when it was difficult to envision a diplomatic path to a long-term solution. Pro-Israel peace groups found it hard to expand or to have much impact during those moments. Nevertheless, they managed to sustain a core constituency of Zionists committed to the goal of an enduring two-state solution and opposed to Israeli policies that precluded that possibility. That, in essence, is the task of the peace camp today.

There have been some positive developments that provide glimmers of hope and the basis for political activity by America's pro-Israel peace camp. One of them is the remarkable evolution of parts of the West Bank into an economically burgeoning state-in-the-making, with trained Palestinian security forces ready and willing to stamp out terrorist cells and protect Israeli lives. Palestinian Authority Prime Minister Salam Fayyad's experiment has, by and large, worked. It should be expanded, as Robert Danin, a former senior official with the State Department and White House, and former chief of mission for the Office of the Quartet Representative, Tony Blair, in Jerusalem, has suggested:

> Israel needs the PA to play a role within "Area C"—the 60 percent of contiguous West Bank territory still under exclusive Israeli control. . . . To date, Palestinian construction and development is forbidden by Israel in 70 percent of Area C and in the remaining 30 percent, it is nearly impossible for the Palestinians to obtain the required permission to build or repair infrastructure. . . . Israel should allow the PA to implement development projects and access its land and resources.[46]

The success of an even more ambitious Palestinian economic development program in the territories, coupled with expanded Palestinian security responsibility in Area C,[47] would send a signal to Israelis that, regardless of the diplomatic impasse, Palestinian partners are available for a two-state settlement. And, if coupled with a halt in Israeli settlement expansion, it would demonstrate to Palestinians that a political horizon still exists, even if gaps on permanent borders, the fate of Palestinian refugees, Jerusalem, and other issues still exist.

The Zionist peace camp can play a role in fostering these developments by urging the Obama and Netanyahu administrations to place a higher priority on what Danin calls "Fayyadism." As Danin asserts:

The United States, as the overseer of Israeli-Palestinian peacemaking, has tended to focus its high-level attention on negotiations, while leaving subordinates to do the important work on the ground to support Palestinian state-building. Focusing more political attention on the ground-up approach would help strengthen Fayyad's position among Palestinians, encourage Israel to invest more political capital in the state-building effort, and ultimately increase the chances that final-status negotiations will succeed.[48]

Another positive sign is the possible revival of the Arab Peace Initiative by the Arab League, whose member states are under increasing pressure from the newly empowered "Arab street" to help rescue the Palestinian people. The United States can and should facilitate some form of multilateral negotiations and press Israel to take advantage of this opportunity. Mobilizing support for such a regional initiative with potential international backing could be another focus of the pro-Israel peace camp.[49]

For more than three decades, the American Zionist Left in the United States has demonstrated a remarkable ability to adapt to the ebbs and flows of events in the Middle East. It remains to be seen whether it is adaptable enough to overcome the daunting obstacles of the present moment.

Notes

1. A *New York Times* story on May 5, 2010, depicted "a newly outspoken wing of Israel supporters" that "has begun to challenge the old-school reflexive support of the country's policies, suggesting that one does not have to be slavish to Israeli policies to love Israel. 'Most Jews have mixed feelings about Israel,' said Rabbi Tamara Kolton of the Birmingham Temple.' . . . 'They support Israel, but it's complicated. Until now, you never heard from those people. You heard only from the organized ones, the ones who are 100 percent certain: "we're right, they're wrong."'" Paul Vitello, "On Israel, US Jews Show Divergent Views, Often Parting from Leaders," *New York Times*, May 5, 2010.

2. For example, we omit other left-wing American Jewish groups that have also attracted followers and media attention, such as New Jewish Agenda, the Tikkun community, the Jewish Peace Lobby, and the Shalom Center. Nor do we touch upon non-Zionist groups in the American Jewish community, such as Jewish Voice for Peace.

3. See, for example, Daniel Kurtzer and Scott Lasensky, *Negotiating Arab-Israeli Peace: American Leadership in the Middle East* (Washington, DC: US Institute of Peace Press, 2007), based on a study group that included scores of veteran Middle East diplomats.

4. Michael Staub, *Torn at the Roots: The Crisis of Jewish Liberalism in Postwar America* (New York: Columbia University Press, 2004), p. 284.

5. Cited in Stephen Rosenthal, *Irreconcilable Differences? The Waning of the American Jewish Love Affair with Israel* (Hanover, NH: Brandeis University Press/University of New England, 2001), p. 36.

6. Cited in Rael Jean Isaac, *Breira: Counsel for Judaism* (New York: Americans for a Safe Israel), p. 2.

7. Staub, *Torn at the Roots*, pp. 291–292. See also Rosenthal, *Irreconcilable Differences?* pp. 36–37.

8. For example, in the opening plenary session of the 2011 J Street conference, Peter Beinart said, "In 1974, a group of young American Jews, mostly rabbis, created Breira, the first

American Jewish group to advocate a Palestinian state in the West Bank and Gaza Strip. They were vilified by the American Jewish establishment; their inaugural conference was physically attacked by the Jewish Defense League, and three years later they gave up." Peter Beinart, "Remarks to the Opening Plenary Session of the 2011 J Street Conference," J Street, February 26, 2011, http://conference.jstreet.org/Beinart.

9. Staub, *Torn at the Roots*, p. 293.

10. Rosenthal, *Irreconcilable Differences?* p. 38.

11. Yehoshafat Harkabi, interview by Mark Rosenblum, Jerusalem, Israel, March 28, 1978. A decade earlier in a 1968 article focusing on Fatah's doctrine, Harkabi offered similar language. He argued that while Fatah tried to avoid "notorious expressions" that were fashionable in Arab circles, like "throwing the Jews into the sea," they came back to "the Arab objective in its extremist version." According to Harkabi this "extremist version" that Fatah embraced was "destroying the state of Israel (what may be called a 'politicide') drives them to genocide." Yehoshafat Harkabi, "Fatah's Doctrine" (December 1968) in *The Israel-Arab Reader*, ed. Walter Laqueur and Barry Rubin (New York: Penguin, 2001), p. 122.

12. For example, when Jewish hostages were rescued by Israeli soldiers at Entebbe and the American Jewish community and much of the world rejoiced, Breira alienated potential supporters by announcing that Israel needed a "diplomatic Entebbe." Cited in Rosenthal, *Irreconcilable Differences?* p. 202.

13. Ibid., p. 41.

14. "Officer's Letter," Americans for Peace Now, March 1978, http://peacenow.org/entries /archive9.

15. Dan Fleshler, *Transforming America's Israel Lobby—The Limits of Its Power and the Potential for Change* (Washington, DC: Potomac Books, 2009), p. 116.

16. For example, an ad protesting right-wing Israel extremists appeared in the *New York Times* on July 2, 1980. Titled "Our Way Is Not Their Way," it was signed by fifty-six well-known American Jews, including three former chairmen of the Conference of Presidents of Major American Jewish Organizations. Cited

in Fleshler, *Transforming America's Israel Lobby,* p. 121.

17. David Shipler, *Arab and Jew, Wounded Spirits in a Promised Land* (New York: Random House, 1986), p. 500.

18. Mark Bilsky, interview by Mark Rosenblum, Washington D.C., June 2, 2011.

19. Yehoshafat Harkabi, interview by Mark Rosenblum, Jerusalem, March 28, 1978.

20. Ibid.

21. Edward Said, *The Question of Palestine* (New York: Times Books, 1979), pp. 118–141.

22. Faisal Husseini, son of the Palestinian guerrilla Abdel Qader Al-Husseini, was a Fatah activist who served time in Israeli prison. A prominent East Jerusalemite, Husseini would go on to lead the Palestinian delegation at the Middle East Peace Conference at Madrid. Husseini was also a member of the PLO Executive Committee, the member in charge of Jerusalem Affairs, and the head of the Jerusalem Committee of the Palestinian Committee for Final Status Negotiations. Husseini would also found the Orient House, the unofficial PLO presence in East Jerusalem. "Faisal Adbel Qader Al-Husseini (1940–2001)," *Orient House,* May 2001, www .orienthouse.org/about/husseini.html.

23. Ahmed Khalidi, a Palestinian scholar whose work focused on issues of security, would go on to serve as a Palestinian negotiator with Israel on security issues, and become a senior associate member of St. Antony's College, Oxford.

24. Ghassan Khatib would become a member of the Palestinian delegation at the Madrid conference and at the bilateral negotiations in Washington from 1991 to 1993. He would go on to hold numerous positions in the Palestinian Authority, including minister of labor and minister of planning. "Ghassan Khatib," Huffington Post, www.huffingtonpost.com/ghassan-khatib.

25. Hanna Siniora was the first Palestinian to meet Secretary of State George Shultz in an official capacity as a representative of the Palestinians in the West Bank and Gaza. He would become a member of the Palestinian National Council and an adviser to the Palestinian Delegation at Madrid. Siniora would also serve as the editor and publisher of influential Palestinian newspapers, including *Al Fajr* and the

Jerusalem Times. Hanna Siniora, "Curriculum Vitae," Israel Palestine Center for Research and Information, www.ipcri.org/files/hannacv.html.

26. Sari Nusseibeh was the chairman of the Union of Faculty and Staff at Birzeit University. He went on to become part of the Unified National Command of the Intifada (1988–1991), a member of the Steering Committee of the Palestinian Negotiating Team (1991–1993), and a member of the Palestinian National Council. He would also become a cofounder of the People's Peace Campaign and the PLO commissioner for Jerusalem affairs. Sari Nusseibeh, "Curriculum Vitae," Al Quds University, http://sari.alquds.edu/cv.htm.

27. Ziad Abu Zayyad was a leading advocate of Israeli-Palestinian coexistence. In 1986 he cofounded the Hebrew journal *Gesher* and engaged in extensive collaborative work with Israeli scholars. Abu Zayyad would become an adviser to the Palestinian negotiating team during the bilateral negotiations in Washington. He would also serve as a negotiator during the Gaza-Jericho negotiations, and as a member of the Palestinian Legislative Council from 1996 to 2006. "Short Biography of Ziad Abu Zayyad," in *Talking for Peace—A Karl Kahane Lecture Series,* Bruno Kreisky Forum for International Dialogue, www.frauenrat.co.at/tipps/tipp8.htm.

28. "Jews Join in Rally with Palestinians," *New York Times,* December 31, 1989, www.nytimes.com/1989/12/31/world/jews-join-in-rally-with-palestinians.html?src=pm.

29. George H. W. Bush, "The President's News Conference (September 12, 1991)," in *The American Presidency Project* [online], ed. John T. Woolley and Gerhard Peters, Santa Barbara, CA, www.presidency.ucsb.edu/ws/?pid=19969.

30. For additional context on the loan guarantee imbroglio, see Mark Rosenblum, "After Rabin: The Malaise of the Israeli Zionist Left," in *Contemporary Israel: Domestic Politics, Foreign Policy, and Security Challenges,* ed. Robert O. Freedman (Boulder, CO: Westview Press, 2009), pp. 58–65.

31. Project Nishma, founded in 1988, sought to familiarize American Jews with Israeli security experts who backed the Oslo peace process.

32. Benny Morris, *Righteous Victims: A History of the Zionist-Arab Conflict, 1881–2001*

(New York: Vintage Books, 2001), pp. 641–642.

33. Carlyle Murphy, "Some American Jewish Leaders Indicate Frustration with Netanyahu's Policies," *Washington Post,* September 19, 1997.

34. David Singer, *American Jewish Yearbook* (New York: American Jewish Committee, 1998), p. 115.

35. Aaron David Miller, *The Much Too Promised Land: America's Elusive Search for Arab-Israeli Peace* (New York: Bantam, 2008), p. 248.

36. The release of the "The Palestine Papers" by Al Jazeera in April 2011 indicated that the widespread perception of a diplomatic impasse during Ehud Olmert's administration was not accurate. The Jewish peace camp in Israel and the United States was unaware that, behind closed doors, Israeli and Palestinian negotiators had substantially narrowed the gaps between them. Though the gaps were significantly narrowed, they were not completely bridged. Olmert was forced to resign because of corruption allegations, and there remains considerable dispute about President Abbas's willingness and capacity to complete an agreement on all the final status issues. Netanyahu refused to begin negotiations at the point where they had ended.

37. The gloom was especially intense due to the discouraging victory of Hamas in legislative elections after Israel's disengagement from Gaza. Increased rocket attacks from the Gaza Strip, the kidnapping of Israeli soldier Gilad Shalit, the 2006 Lebanon War, and the eventual Hamas takeover of the Gaza Strip further dimmed the prospects for peace.

38. For example, J Street has a rabbinic cabinet with several hundred members.

39. A more thorough analysis of this period in American Jewish history would include other groups within the pro-Israel peace camp. APN remains vibrant, and the Israel Policy Forum has been absorbed into the Center for American Progress think tank but, as of this writing, is exploring the possibility of relaunching itself. Other groups, including the New Israel Fund, Meretz USA, and Ameinu, are also active partners in a liberal Zionist coalition.

40. After his election in 2009, Netanyahu was not universally panned by the peace camp in Israel. Some key figures among the Zionist doves, including Amnon Lipkin-Shahak, Gadi

Baltiansky, Gilad Sher, and Ami Ayalon, engaged in dialogue with "Bibi" and his aides, believing that only a right-wing prime minister had a chance to deliver on the peace process. But, although the pro-Israel peace camp in the United States greeted some of Netanyahu's statements positively, including a highly publicized speech at Bar-Ilan University in which he publicly endorsed the two-state solution, J Street, APN, and their allies found little to support in the Netanyahu government's policies and positions.

41. James Besser, "New DNC Pick Puts J Street in Spotlight," *Jewish Week*, April 12, 2011.

42. Interestingly enough, though the Israeli government has seemingly continued to defer offering any substantive peace initiative (particularly after the Fatah-Hamas reconciliation efforts), a slim plurality of the Jewish-Israeli public accepts the possibility of negotiating with a Palestinian government that includes Hamas. "The Peace Index," Israel Democracy Institute, May 2011, www.peaceindex.org/indexMonth Eng.aspx?num=205.

43. Efraim Halevy, former chief of the Mossad, recently called for Israel to engage Hamas in the wake of the Hamas-Fatah unity agreement. Halevy stated that "there will be no serious progress in the Israeli-Palestinian conflict without some way of including Hamas in the process so as to transform them from being part of problem to being part of the solution." Ethan Bronner, "Palestinian Factions Give Differing Views of Unity Pact," *New York Times*, April 28, 2011, www.nytimes.com/2011/04/29 /world/middleeast/29mideast.html?scp=1&sq =palestinian%20factions%20give%20differing %20views%20of%20unity%20pact&st=cse. In addition, an increasing number of Israeli security experts have called for engagement with Hamas. They include Kadima MK Shaul Mofaz, a former chief of staff who called for negotiating with Hamas as part of his 2009 peace plan; Major General (ret.) Shlomo Gazit, a former chief of military intelligence; Brigadier General (ret.) Shlomo Brom of the Institute for National Security Studies; Ami Ayalon, former Shin Bet chief and commander-in-chief of the Israeli navy; Yaakov Peri, a former Shin Bet chief; Major General (ret.) Giora Eiland, former head of

the IDF Operations Directorate, the IDF Planning and Policy Directorate, and the Israeli National Security Council; Colonel (res.) Shaul Arieli, former military commander in the Gaza Strip; Colonel (res.) Yuval Dvir, former military commander in the Gaza Strip; and Yossi Alpher, former Mossad officer and head of the Jaffe Center for Strategic Studies. See Orly Halpern, "Experts Question Wisdom of Boycotting Hamas," *The Forward*, February 9, 2007, www .forward.com/articles/10055; Mazal Mualem, "Mofaz Supporters: Poll Shows Israelis Willing to Talk with Hamas," *Ha'aretz*, November 15, 2009, www.haaretz.com/print-edition/news /mofaz-supporters-poll-shows-israelis-willing -to-talk-with-hamas-1.4166; Barak Ravid, "Ami Ayalon to Call for Cease-Fire Talks with Hamas," *Ha'aretz*, March 3, 2008, www.haaretz.com/print -edition/news/ami-ayalon-to-call-for-cease- fire-talks-with-Hamas-1.240526; Yigal Hai and Mijal Grinberg, "Sderot Mayor Denies Calling for Cease-Fire Talks with Hamas," *Ha'aretz*, February 22, 2008, www.haaretz.com/news/sderot -mayor-denies-calling-for-cease-fire-talks-with -Hamas-1.239935; Steven Erlanger, "For Israel, Gaza Offers a Range of Risky Choices," *New York Times*, February 17, 2008,www.nytimes .com/2008/02/17/world/middleeast/17assess .html?ex=1361336400&en=428d41ec4fc72ec7& ei=5088&partner=rssnyt&emc=rss; Americans for Peace Now, "Readings re: Israeli Public Opinion and Hamas, Israel's Security Brass Weigh In, & Commentary," March 5, 2008, http://peacenow.org/entries/archive4667; Yossi Alpher, "Hard Questions, Tough Answers," Americans for Peace Now, May 2, 2011, http: //peacenow.org/entries/alpher_may_2_2011.

44. Ahmad Khalidi, "The West Bank Anachronism," *The Guardian*, April 19, 2011; Joel Greenberg, "Palestinians Plan New Marches on Border," *Washington Post*, June 4, 2011.

45. Hussein Ibish, *What's Wrong with the One-State Agenda?* (Washington, DC: American Task Force on Palestine, 2009), p. 136.

46. Robert Danin, "A Third Way to Palestine: Fayyadism and Its Discontents," *Foreign Affairs* 90, no. 1 (January/February 2011): 108.

47. Though the agreement to reconcile Hamas and Fatah has thus far maintained the current division of labor, with the Palestinian Authority's

newly trained security forces remaining solely in control of security in the West Bank, there is a reasonable concern regarding their continued efforts to rein in potential Hamas terrorist cells. This concern will become particularly acute in the event that there is no tangible progress toward negotiating and implementing a viable and contiguous Palestinian state in the West Bank.

48. Danin, "A Third Way to Palestine," p. 109.

49. There is another, countervailing assessment that is skeptical of a revived Arab Peace Initiative, particularly vis-à-vis the Saudi regime. First, the Saudi leadership is frail and aging, pre-occupied by revolts directed, in part, against the Arab world's authoritarian gerontocracies. Second, their attention is increasingly drawn away from the Palestinian-Israeli conflict, toward the Persian Gulf. The Saudis are preoccupied by a military intervention aimed at saving the regime of the al-Khalifa family across the causeway in Bahrain. All the while, the specter of Iranian-Shiite encroachment looms large. For an elaboration upon this analysis, see Madawi al-Rasheed, "Saudi Dilemmas and the Arab Peace Initiative," Bitterlemons-api, April 6, 2011, www.bitterlemons-api.org/previous.php?opt=1&id=12.

Bibliography

Books

Albright, Madeleine. *Madam Secretary: A Memoir.* New York: Miramax Books, 2003.

Allison, Graham. *Nuclear Terrorism: The Ultimate Preventable Catastrophe.* New York: Times Books, 2004.

American Jewish Yearbook (annual).

Auerbach, Jerold S. *Hebron Jews.* Lanham, MD: Rowman & Littlefield, 2008.

Aumann, Moshe. *Conflict & Connection: The Jewish-Christian-Israel Triangle.* Jerusalem: Geffen Books, 2003.

Banki, Judith H. *The UN's Anti-Zionism Resolution: Christian Responses.* Washington, DC: American Jewish Committee, 1976.

Bass, Warren. *Support Any Friend: Kennedy's Middle East Policy and the Making of the US-Israel Alliance.* New York: Oxford University Press, 2003.

Bayme, Steven. *Jewish Arguments and Counterarguments.* Hoboken, NH: Ktav and AJC, 2002.

Beilin, Yossi. *The Path to Geneva: The Quest for a Permanent Agreement, 1996–2004.* New York: RDV Books, 2004.

Ben-Zvi, Avraham. *Decade of Transition: Eisenhower, Kennedy, and the Origins of the American-Israeli Alliance.* New York: Columbia University Press, 1998.

———. *Lyndon B. Johnson and the Politics of Arms Sales to Israel: In the Shadow of the Hawk.* London: Cass, 2004.

Bernstein, Louis. *Challenge and Mission.* New York: Shengold Publishers, n.d.

Biddle, Stephen D., and Jeffrey A. Friedman. *The 2006 Lebanon Campaign and the Future of Warfare: Implications for Army and Defense Policy.* Carlisle, PA: SSI Publications, US Army War College, 2008.

Boykin, Willliam G. *Never Surrender.* New York: Faith Words, 2008.

Brog, David. *Standing with Israel: Why Christians Support the Jewish State.* Lake Mary, FL: Frontline Publishers, 2006.

Bush, George W. *Decision Points.* New York: Random House, 2010.

Carothers, Thomas, and Marina Ottoway, eds. *Uncharted Journey: Promoting Democracy in the Middle East.* Washington, DC: Carnegie Endowment, 2005.

Chafets, Zev. *A Match Made in Heaven.* New York: Harper, 2007.

Clark, Clifford. *Counsel to the President: A Memoir.* New York: Random House, 1991.

Clark, Victoria. *Allies for Armageddon: The Rise of Christian Zionism.* New Haven, CT: Yale University Press, 2007.

Cohen, Avi. *History of the Air Force in the War of Independence.* Tel Aviv: Ministry of Defense Publications, 2004, vol. 3. In Hebrew.

Cohen, Avner. *Israel and the Bomb.* New York: Columbia University Press, 1998.

Cohen, Steven M., and Ari Kelman. *Beyond Distancing: Young Adult American Jews and Their Alienation from Israel.* New York: Bronfman Philanthropies, 2008.

Cohen, Stuart A. *Israel and Its Army: From Cohesion to Confusion.* London: Routledge, 2009.

Curtiss, Richard. *Stealth PACs: How Israel's American Lobby Took Control of US Middle East Policy*. Washington, DC: American Educational Trust, 1990.

Dayan, Moshe. *Vietnam Diary*. Tel Aviv: Dvir, 1977. In Hebrew.

Eilam, Uzi. *Keshet Eilam*. "Eilam's Arc." Miskal: Tel Aviv, 2009.

Eldar, Akiva. *Lords of the Land*. New York: Nation Books, 2007.

Farber, Seth. *An American Orthodox Dreamer*. Hanover, NH: University Press of New England, 2004.

Farquhar, Scott C., ed. *Back to Basics: A Study of the 2nd Lebanon War and Operation CAST LEAD*. Fort Leavenworth, KS: US Army Combined Arms Center, 2009.

Findley, Paul. *They Dare to Speak Out: People and Institutions Confront Israel's Lobby*. Westport, CT: Lawrence Hill, 1985.

Fleshler, Dan. *Transforming America's Israel Lobby—The Limits of Its Power and the Potential for Change*. Washington, DC: Potomac Books, 2009.

Foyle, Douglas C. *Counting the Public In: Presidents, Public Opinion, and Foreign Policy*. New York: Columbia University Press, 1999.

Freedman, Robert O. *Moscow and the Middle East: Soviet Policy Since the Invasion of Afghanistan*. Cambridge: Cambridge University Press, 1991.

———. *Russia, Iran, and the Nuclear Question: The Putin Record*. Carlisle, PA: Strategic Studies Institute of the US Army War College, 2006.

———. *Contemporary Israel: Domestic Politics, Foreign Policy, and Security Challenges*. Boulder, CO: Westview Press, 2009.

Freedman, Sam. *Jew vs. Jew*. New York: Simon & Schuster, 2000.

Friedman, Robert I. *The False Prophet*. Brooklyn, NY: Lawrence Hill Books, 1990.

Frum, David. *The Right Man: The Surprise Presidency of George W. Bush*. New York: Random House, 2003.

Ganchrow, Mendy. *Journey Through the Minefield*. Silver Spring, MD: Eshel Books, 2004.

Gilboa, Eytan. *American Public Opinion Toward Israel and the Arab-Israeli Conflict*. Lanham, MD: Lexington Books, 1987.

Gilboa, Eytan, and Efraim Inbar, eds. *US-Israeli Relations in a New Era*. London: Routledge, 2009.

Gold, Dore. *Israel as an American Non-NATO Ally*. Tel Aviv: Jaffee Center, 1992.

Goldberg, J. J. *Jewish Power: Inside the American Jewish Establishment*. Reading, MA: Addison-Wesley, 1996.

Gorenberg, Gershom. *The End of Days: Fundamentalism and the Struggle for the Temple Mount*. Oxford: Oxford University Press, 2000.

———. *The Accidental Empire*. New York: Henry Holt, 2006.

Greenberg, Yitzchak. *The Israeli Reserve Army: Laying Down the Foundations, 1949–1950*. Sdeh Boker: Ben-Gurion Research Center, 2001. In Hebrew.

Grose, Peter. *Israel in the Mind of America*. New York: Knopf, 1983.

Gurock, Jeffrey S. *American Jewish Orthodoxy*. Hoboken, NJ: Ktav, 1996.

Hagee, John. *Beginning of the End, Final Dawn over Jerusalem, Day of Deception*. Nashville, TN: Thomas Nelson Publishers, 2000.

Hahn, Peter L. *Caught in the Middle East: US Policy Toward the Arab-Israeli Conflict, 1945–1961*. Chapel Hill: University of North Carolina Press, 2004.

Harris, Ron, et al. *The History of Law in a Multi-Cultural Society: Israel, 1917–1967*. Hants, UK: Ashgate Publishing, 2002.

Heilman, Sam. *Sliding to the Right*. Berkeley: University of California Press, 2006.

Helmreich, William. *The World of the Yeshiva*. New York: Free Press, 1982.

Holsti, Ole R. *Public Opinion and American Foreign Policy*, rev. ed. Ann Arbor: University of Michigan Press, 1996.

Ibish, Hussein. *What's Wrong with the One-State Agenda?* Washington, DC: American Task Force on Palestine, 2009.

Kaplan, Robert D. *The Romance of an American Elite*. New York: Free Press, 1993.

Kitfield, James. *Prodigal Soldiers*. New York: Simon & Schuster, 1995.

Korn, Eugene. *Meeting the Challenge: Church Attitudes Toward the Israeli-Palestinian Conflict*. New York: Anti-Defamation League, 2002.

Kurtzer, Daniel, and Scott Lasensky. *Negotiating Arab-Israeli Peace: American Leadership in the Middle East*. Washington, DC: US Institute of Peace Press, 2007.

Lahav, Pnina. *Press Law in Modern Democracies: A Comparative Study.* New York: Longman Publishing Group, 1985.

———. *Judgment in Jerusalem: Chief Justice Simon Agranat and the Zionist Century.* Berkeley: University of California Press, 1997.

Laqueur, Walter, and Barry Rubin, eds. *The Israel-Arab Reader.* New York: Penguin Books, 2008.

Levey, Zach. *Israel and the Western Powers.* Chapel Hill: University of North Carolina Press, 1997.

Likhovski, Assaf. *Law and Identity in Mandate Palestine.* Chapel Hill: University of North Carolina Press, 2006.

Lindsey, Hal. *The Late Great Planet Earth.* Grand Rapids, MI: Zondervan, 1970.

Lustick, Ian. *For the Land and the Lord.* New York: Council on Foreign Relations, 1988.

Luttwak, Edward, and Dan Horowitz. *The Israeli Army.* London: Allen Lane, 1976.

Makovsky, David. *Engagement Through Disengagement: Gaza and the Potential for Renewed Israeli-Palestinian Peacemaking.* Washington, DC: Washington Institute for Near East Policy, 2005.

Malachy, Yona. *American Fundamentalism and Israel: The Relation of Fundamentalist Churches to Zionism and the State of Israel.* Jerusalem: Hebrew University, 1978.

Marsden, George M. *Fundamentalism and American Culture.* Oxford: Oxford University Press, 2006.

Mearsheimer, John J., and Stephen M. Walt. *The Israel Lobby and US Foreign Policy.* New York: Farrar, Straus & Giroux, 2007.

Medoff, Rafael. *Jewish Americans and Political Participation.* Santa Barbara, CA: ABC-CLIO, 2002.

Merkley, Paul Charles. *American Presidents, Religion, and Israel: The Heirs of Cyrus.* Westport, CT: Praeger Publishers, 2004.

Miller, Aaron David. *The Much Too Promised Land: America's Elusive Search for Arab-Israeli Peace.* New York: Bantam, 2008.

Moore, Deborah Dash, and I. S. Troen. *Divergent Jewish Cultures: Israel and America.* New Haven, CT: Yale University Press, 2001.

Morris, Benny. *Righteous Victims: A History of the Zionist-Arab Conflict, 1881–2001.* New York: Vintage Books, 2001.

———. *1948: A History of the First Arab-Israeli War.* New Haven, CT: Yale University Press, 2008.

Oldfield, Duane Murray. *The Right and the Righteous: The Christian Right Confronts the Republican Party.* Lanham, MD: Rowman & Littlefield, 1996.

Oren, Michael B. *Power, Faith, and Fantasy: America in the Middle East, 1776 to the Present.* New York: W. W. Norton, 2007.

Organski, A. F. K. *The $36 Billion Bargain: Strategy and Politics in US Aid to Israel.* New York: Columbia University Press, 1990.

Page, Benjamin I., and Marshall M. Bouton. *The Foreign Policy Disconnect: What Americans Want from Our Leaders but Don't Get.* Chicago: University of Chicago Press, 2006.

Page, Benjamin I., and Robert Y. Shapiro. *The Rational Public: Fifty Years of Trends in America's Public Preferences.* Chicago: University of Chicago Press, 1992.

Pollack, Kenneth M. *Arabs at War: Military Effectiveness, 1948–1991.* Lincoln: University of Nebraska Press, 2002.

Poupko, Yehiel. *Looking at Them Looking at Us: A Jewish Understanding of Christian Responses to Israel.* New York: Jewish Council for Public Affairs, 2008.

Puschel, Karen L. *US-Israel Strategic Cooperation in the Post–Cold War Era.* Boulder, CO: Westview Press, 1992.

Quandt, William B. *Peace Process: American Diplomacy and the Arab-Israeli Conflict Since 1967,* 3rd ed. Los Angeles: University of California Press, 2005.

Rabinovich, Itamar. *The Brink of Peace: The Israeli-Syrian Negotiations.* Princeton, NJ: Princeton University Press, 1998.

Rabinovich, Itamar, and Yehuda Reinharz, eds. *Israel in the Middle East: Documents and Readings on Society, Politics, and Foreign Relations, 1948–Present.* Oxford: Oxford University Press, 1984.

Rackman, Emanuel. *A Modern Orthodox Life.* Jersey City, NJ: Ktav, 2008.

Romjue, John L. *From Active Defense to Air Land Battle: The Development of Army Doctrine, 1973–1982.* Fort Monroe, VA: TRADOC, 1984.

Rosenthal, Stephen. *Irreconcilable Differences? The Waning of the American Jewish Love Affair with Israel.* Hanover, NH: Brandeis University Press/University of New England Press, 2001.

Ross, Dennis. *The Missing Peace: The Inside Story of the Fight for Middle East Peace*. New York: Farrar, Straus & Giroux, 2005.

Rubinstein, A., and B. Medina. *The Constitutional Law of the State of Israel*. Tel Aviv: Shocken, 2008.

Rudin, James. *The Baptizing of America: The Religious Right's Plans for the Rest of Us*. New York: Thunder's Mouth Press, 2006.

Rumsfeld, Donald. *Known and Unknown: A Memoir*. New York: Sentinel, 2011.

Sagan, Scott D., and Kenneth N. Waltz. *The Spread of Nuclear Weapons: A Debate Renewed*. New York: W. W. Norton, 2003.

Said, Edward. *The Question of Palestine*. New York: Times Books, 1979.

Sasson, Theodore, Charles Kadushin, and Leonard Saxe. *American Jewish Attachment to Israel: An Assessment of the "Distancing" Hypothesis*. Waltham, MA: Steinhardt Social Research Institute, Brandeis University, February 2008.

Schelling, Thomas C. *Arms and Influence*. New Haven, CT: Yale University Press, 1969.

Schiff, Alvin. *Beyond the Melting Pot*. New York: Devora Publishing, 2009.

Schubert, Frank. *Building Air Bases in the Negev: The US Army Corps of Engineers in Israel, 1979–1982*. Washington, DC: Office of History, US Army, 1992.

Segal, Z. *Freedom of the Press: Between Myth and Reality*. Tel Aviv: Papyrus, 1996.

Seliktar, Ofira. *Divided We Stand: American Jews, Israel, and the Peace Process*. New York: Praeger, 2002.

Sharansky, Natan. *The Case for Democracy: The Power of Freedom to Overcome Tyranny and Terror*. New York: PublicAffairs, 2004.

Sharp, Jeremy M. *US Foreign Aid to Israel*. CRS Report for Congress no. RL 33222. Washington, DC, December 2009.

Sheleg, Yair. *The North American Impact on Israeli Orthodoxy*. New York: AJC and Argov Center of Bar Ilan University, 1999.

Shipler, David. *Arab and Jew: Wounded Spirits in a Promised Land*. New York: Random House, 1986.

Simon, Merrill. *Jerry Falwell and the Jews*. Middle Village, NY: Jonathan David Publishers, 1984.

Sobel, Richard. *The Impact of Public Opinion on US Foreign Policy Since Vietnam*. New York: Oxford University Press, 2001.

Soloveitchik, Joseph B. *Kol Dodi Dofek (My Beloved Knocketh)*. Translated by David Z. Gordon. New York: Yeshiva University Press, 2006.

Spector, Stephen. *Evangelicals and Israel: The Story of American Christian Zionism*. New York: Oxford University Press, 2009.

Spiegel, Steven. *The Other Arab-Israeli Conflict: Making America's Middle East Policy from Truman to Reagan*. Chicago: University of Chicago Press, 1985.

Sprinzak, Ehud. *The Ascendance of the Israeli Radical Right*. New York: Oxford University Press, 1991.

Staub, Michael. *Torn at the Roots: The Crisis of Jewish Liberalism in Postwar America*. New York: Columbia University Press, 2004.

Steigman, Yitzchak. *From the War of Independence to Kadesh: The IAF, 1949–1956*. Tel Aviv: Ministry of Defense Publications, 1990. In Hebrew.

Tenet, George. *At the Heart of the Storm: My Years at the CIA*. New York: HarperCollins, 2007.

Tira, Ron. *The Limitations of Standoff Firepower-Based Operations*. INSS Memorandum no. 89. Tel Aviv, 2007.

Van Creveld, Martin. *The Sword and the Olive: A Critical History of the IDF*. New York: PublicAffairs, 1998.

Vatikiotis, P. J. *Nasser and His Generation*. New York: St. Martin's Press, 1978.

Waxman, Chaim. *American Aliyah*. Detroit: Wayne State University Press, 1989.

Weber, Timothy P. *On the Road to Armageddon: How Evangelicals Became Israel's Best Friend*. Grand Rapids, MI: Baker Academic, 2004.

Weizmann, Ezer. *On Eagles' Wings*. Tel Aviv: Maariv, 1975. In Hebrew.

Winograd Commission Israel. *Final Report*. January 2008.

Woodward, Bob. *Bush at War*. New York: Simon & Schuster, 2002.

Zaller, John R. *The Nature and Origins of Mass Opinion*. New York: Cambridge University Press, 1992.

Articles and Chapters in Books

Adler, Emanuel, and Michael Barnett. "A Framework for the Study of Security Communities." In *Security Communities,* edited by Emanuel Adler and Michael Barnett. Cambridge: Cambridge University Press, 1998.

Ben-Mosheh, Tuviah. "Liddell Hart and the IDF—A Reappraisal." *Journal of Contemporary History* 16 (1981).

Bronfeld, Saul. "Fighting Outnumbered: The Impact of the Yom Kippur War on the US Army." *Journal of Military History* (April 2007).

Bruck, Connie. "Back Roads: How Serious Is the Bush Administration About Creating a Palestinian State?" *New Yorker,* December 15, 2003.

Cohen, Steven M., and Charles S. Liebman. "Israel and American Jewry in the Twenty-First Century." In *Beyond Survival and Philanthropy,* edited by Allon Gal and Alfred Gottschalk. Cincinnati, OH: Hebrew Union College Press, 2000.

Cohen, Stuart A. "Restructuring the Militia Framework of the IDF." *Journal of Strategic Studies* 18 (December 1995).

Danin, Robert. "A Third Way to Palestine: Fayyadism and Its Discontents." *Foreign Affairs* 90, no. 1 (January/February 2011).

Ehrenkrantz, Gil. "How the United States Has Benefited from Its Alliance with Israel." *Middle East Review of International Affairs* 14, no. 2 2010).

Feaver, Peter D. "Command and Control in Emerging Nuclear Nations." *International Security* 17, no. 3 (Winter 1992–1993).

Freedman, Robert O. "The Religious-Secular Divide in Israeli Politics." *Middle East Policy* 6, no. 4 (June 1999).

———. "Sharon: The Evolution of a Security Hawk." *Midstream* 48, nos. 6–7 (May–June 2004).

———. "Israel and the United States." In *Contemporary Israel,* edited by Robert O. Freedman. Boulder, CO: Westview Press, 2009.

———. "The Bush Administration and the Arab-Israeli Conflict: The First Term and Beyond." In *The Middle East and the United States,* 4th ed., edited by David W. Lesch. Boulder, CO: Westview Press, 2009.

Ghanem, As'ad, and Mohamad Mustafa. "Coping with the Nakba: The Palestinians in Israel and the 'Future Vision' as a Collective Agenda." *Israel Studies Forum* 24, no. 2 (2009).

Gur-Ze'ev, Isaac. "Total Quality Management and Power/Knowledge Dialectics in the Israeli Army." *Journal of Thought* 32 (1971).

Gutenmacher, Daniel. "Agudath Israel of America and the State of Israel." In *Israel and Diaspora Jewry,* edited by Eliezer Don-Yehiya. Ramat Gan: Bar-Ilan University Press, 1991.

Inbar, Efraim. "The Need to Block a Nuclear Iran." *Middle East Review of International Affairs* 10, no. 2 (2006).

Ivry, David. "United in Vision, Strategic Partnership & Friendship." In *Peace—Dream or Vision: A Decade Since the Assassination of Prime Minister Yitzhak Rabin,* edited by Aviva Palter. Netanya: S. Daniel Avraham Center for Strategic Dialogue, 2007.

Kamrava, Mehran. "Iranian National Security Debates: Factionalism and Lost Opportunities." *Middle East Policy* 14, no. 2 (Summer 2007).

Kretzmer, David. "Freedom of Speech and Racism." *Cardozo Law Review* 8 (1987).

Lahav, Pnina. "American Influence on Israel's Jurisprudence of Free Speech." *Hastings Constitutional Law Quarterly* 9 (1981).

Lieberman, Elli. "Israel's 2006 War with Hizbollah: The Failure of Deterrence." In *Contemporary Israel,* edited by Robert O. Freedman. Boulder, CO: Westview Press 2009.

Lindsay, James, and Ray Takeyh. "After Iran Gets the Bomb." *Foreign Affairs* 89, no. 2 (March–April 2010).

Lizza, Ryan. "The Consequentialist: How the Arab Spring Remade Obama's Foreign Policy." *New Yorker,* May 2, 2011.

Massing, Michael. "The Storm over the Israel Lobby." *New York Review of Books,* June 8, 2006.

Medoff, Rafael. "Rav Chesed: The Life and Times of Rabbi Haskell Lookstein." In *Rav Chesed,* vol. 2, edited by Rafael Medoff. Jersey City, NJ: Ktav, 2009.

Miller, Jack C. "Black Viewpoints on the Middle East Conflict." *Journal of Palestinian Studies* 10, no. 1 (Winter 1981).

Miller, Steven E. "Assistance to Newly Proliferating Nations." In *New Nuclear Nations: Consequences for US Policy,* edited by Robert D. Blackwill and Albert Carnesale. New York: Council on Foreign Relations, 1993.

Mobley, Richard A. "US Joint Military Contributions to Countering Syria's 1970 Invasion of Jordan." *Joint Force Quarterly* 55 (2009).

Oren, Michael B. "Orde Wingate: Friend Under Fire." *Azure* 10 (2000).

"The Palestine Papers: Chronicling the US Abandonment of the Road Map." *Journal of Palestine Studies* 40, no. 3 (Spring 2011).

Peters, Joel. "Europe and the Arab-Israeli Peace Process: The Declaration of the European Council of Berlin and Beyond." In *Bound to Cooperate: Europe and the Middle East,* edited by Sven Behrendt and Christian-Peter Hanelt. Gutersloh, Germany: Bertelsmann Foundation, 2001.

Raffel, Martin J. "History of Israel Advocacy." In *Jewish Polity and American Civil Society,* edited by Alan Mittleman, Jonathan Sarna, and Robert Licht. Lanham, MD: Rowman & Littlefield, 2002.

Reich, Bernard. "The United States and Israel: A Special Relationship." In *The Middle East and the United States,* 4th ed., edited by David W. Lesch. Boulder, CO: Westview Press, 2007.

Rosenblum, Mark. "After Rabin: The Malaise of the Israeli Zionist Left." In *Contemporary Israel: Domestic Politics, Foreign Policy, and Security Challenges,* edited by Robert O. Freedman. Boulder, CO: Westview Press, 2009.

Sadr, Ehsaneh I. "The Impact of Iran's Nuclearization on Israel." *Middle East Policy* 12, no. 2 (Summer 2005).

Sagan, Scott, Kenneth Waltz, and Richard K. Betts. "A Nuclear Iran: Promoting Stability or Courting Disaster?" *Journal of International Affairs* 60, no. 2 (Spring/Summer 2007).

Sanders, Ralph. "UAVs: An Israeli Military Innovation." *Joint Force Quarterly* 48 (2003).

Sasson, Theodore. "Mass Mobilization to Direct Engagement: American Jews' Changing Relationship to Israel." *Israel Studies* 15, no. 2 (Summer 2010).

Satloff, Robert. "Shifting Sands: The US's Disturbing New Israel Policy." *New Republic,* June 1, 1998.

Schulzinger, Robert. "The Impact of Suez on US Middle Eastern Policy." In *The Suez-Sinai Crisis, 1956,* edited by Selwyn Troen and Moshe Shemesh. New York: Columbia University Press, 1990.

Siperco, Ian. "Shield of David: The Promise of Israeli National Missile Defense." *Middle East Policy* 17, no. 2 (Summer 2010).

Slonim, Shlomo. "The 1948 Embargo on Arms to Palestine." *Political Science Quarterly* 94 (1979).

Spiegel, Steven L. "US Relations with Israel: The Military Benefits." *Orbis* 30, no. 3 (Fall 1986).

Van Creveld, Martin. "Why Israel Doesn't Send Women into Combat." *Parameters* (Spring 1993).

Wagner, Donald. "Evangelicals and Israel: Theological Roots of a Political Alliance." *Christian Century,* November 1998.

Wall, John. "Managing Construction of Israeli Air Bases in Negev." *Journal of Management in Engineering* 1 (1985).

Waltz, Kenneth N. "More May Be Better." In *The Spread of Nuclear Weapons: A Debate Renewed,* edited by Scott D. Sagan and Kenneth N. Waltz. New York: W. W. Norton, 2003.

Waxman, Dov. "From Controversy to Consensus: Cultural Conflict and the Israeli Debate over Territorial Withdrawal." *Israel Studies* 13, no. 2 (2008).

———. "From Jerusalem to Baghdad? Israel and the War in Iraq." *International Studies Perspectives* 10, no. 1 (February 2009).

Weiss, Leonard. "Israel's Future and Iran's Nuclear Program." *Middle East Policy* 16, no. 3 (Fall 2009).

Index

Abbas, Mahmoud (Abu Mazen), 49–50, 66, 71,
    273
    Hamas-Fatah agreement, 41, 66–67
    Israeli-Palestinian peace process and, 45,
        46, 54, 55–56, 59, 60, 63
    UN resolution on Palestinian state and, 66,
        275
    weakness of/attempts to strengthen, 37, 54,
        56, 59
Abdel-Shafi, Haider, 266
Abdullah II, 40, 65
Abdullah (Saudi Crown Prince), 40
Abraham, S. Daniel, 270
Ackerman, Gary, 274
Actual malice rule, 196
Age, American public attitudes toward Israel,
    112, 113
Agranat, Simon, 18, 206
    investigation of Yom Kippur War mistakes,
        195–196
    Kol Ha'am v. Minister of the Interior and,
        190–192
    Yeredor v. Central Elections Committee,
        193–194
Agreement on Trade in Agricultural Products,
    134
Agudath Israel of America, 216
Ahmadinejad, Mahmoud, 52, 58, 64, 167,
    172–173, 175
AIPAC. *See* American Israel Public Affairs
    Committee (AIPAC)
AJC. *See* American Jewish Committee (AJC)
al-Aqsa Intifada (second Intifada), 8, 12,
    13–14, 38, 39, 40–41, 71, 90–91, 154,
    248, 271
al-Aqsa Martyrs Brigade, 46
Albright, Madeleine, 8–9, 269–270
Aliyah, among American Jewish day school
    students, 219–220, 221, 223
Allen, Leslie C., 243
Alliance for Peace and Justice, 91

Alliance of Baptists, 247
Alon, Yigal, 150
Alpha Plan, 2
al-Qaeda, 1, 39, 167
American Emergency Committee for Zionist
    Affairs, 83
American Friends of Ariel, 223
American Friends of Likud, 93
American Friends Service Committee, 260
American Institute of Holy Land Studies, 246
American Israel Public Affairs Committee
    (AIPAC), 16
    American Jewish peace movement *vs.*, 272
    as centrist group, 92
    Christian evangelicals and, 236–237
    creation/growth of, 85, 87–88
    Johnson administration and, 87
    mission of, 86
    Netanyahu and, 9
    Obama speech to, 69–70
    Olmert speech to, 54–55
    Oslo Accords and, 89–90
    Powell speech to, 38
    power of, 94–95, 96
    Rice speech to, 49
American Jewish Committee (AJC), 82, 90, 92,
    246, 248, 249
American Jewish community
    contributions to Israel, 126
    George W. Bush and, 43, 48–49
    pro-Israel lobby and, 96
    response to support of evangelical
        Christians for Israel, 246–250
    split over Israeli-Palestinian peace process,
        9
American Jewish Congress, 85, 247, 260
American Jewish peace movement, 19, 257–278
    Americans for Peace Now, 257, 261–268
    Breira, 257, 259–261
    characteristics necessary for success of,
        258–259

289

American Jewish peace movement *(continued)*
  Israel Policy Forum, 257, 268–272
  J Street, 257, 272–274
  at present moment, 274–278
American Jewish Yearbook (1998), 270
American military journals, 155–156
American Orthodox Jews and Israel, 18–19,
    215–229
  assassination of Rabin and, 225, 227
  defining who is Jew, 218, 225–226
  divisions within, 216
  evangelical Christians and, 249–250
  extremism within American Orthodoxy,
    220, 224–225
  Gaza disengagement and, 227–228
  growth of Orthodoxy in US, 216, 228
  Hebron massacre and, 227
  Israeli foreign policy and, 226
  Jewish settlements on West Bank and, 223–
    224
  Non-Orthodox Jews and, 220, 229
  Oslo process and, 226–227
  rabbinate and, 217–218
  religious nationalism and, 228–229
  residence in /visits to Israel, 218–223
  Zionism and, 215–216, 222
American Palestine Committee, 84
American public attitudes toward Israel, 16,
    100–123
  group differences, 111–119
  by political party identification, 117–119,
    120
  public support, 103–106
  by religious groups, 114–117
  sympathies in Middle East conflict, 101–102,
    103, 109–111
  view of Israel as friendly country or US ally,
    106–109
Americans for Peace Now (APN), 16, 19, 89,
    93, 261–270, 271
American Zionist Bureau, 83
American Zionist Committee for Public
    Affairs, 86
American Zionist Council, 86
American Zionist Emergency Council
    (AZEC), 83–84
American Zionist Left. *See* American Jewish
    peace movement
Amir, Yigal, 227
Amona, 227–228
Anat Kam affair, 207–208
Anglican Church, 243
Annapolis Peace Conference, 242, 272

Anti-Defamation League, 85, 87, 92, 248, 249
Anti-Semitism, evangelical Christians and,
    239, 247–248, 251
APN. *See* Americans for Peace Now (APN)
Arab boycott, 138
Arab-Israeli conflict, United States and, 22–35
  2001–2011, 36–74
  Bush administration (George W.), 37–57,
    70–74
  converging interests of Israel and Arab
    states, 33–34
  Eisenhower administration and, 26–27
  Johnson administration and, 27–29
  Obama administration, 57–74
  post-Cold War, post-9/11, 32–33
  public sympathies in, 101–102, 103,
    109–111
  Roosevelt administration and, 23–25
  Truman administration and, 25–26
  Yom Kippur War and, 29–32
Arabists, 28, 35
  U.S.-Israeli relationship and, 23, 24–25, 26
  Yom Kippur War and, 29, 30–31
  See also Arab-Israeli conflict, United States
    and
Arab League, 29, 55–56, 60, 63, 67, 138, 278
Arab Peace Initiative, 55–56, 278
Arab Spring, 65–66, 68, 74, 276
Arab states
  American sympathy for, 110–111
  converging interests with Israel, 33–34
  democratization of, 37, 47, 49, 68, 74
  Iran and, 33, 34
  nuclear programs in, 167
  Obama's outreach to, 58
  reaction to Hizbollah's war against Israel,
    33–34
  relations with Soviet Union, 104–105,
    106–107
  request that US dissociate itself from
    Zionism/Israel, 24–25
Arafat, Yasser, 6, 13, 265
  death of, 37, 49
  Diplomatic Quartet and, 44–45
  George W. Bush and, 38, 39, 41, 43–44, 49
  Israeli-Palestinian peace process and, 10,
    14–15, 32, 40–41, 89, 240, 266, 268, 270,
    271
  Netanyahu and, 7–8
  pressure on to enact cease-fire, 38, 39,
    40–41
  terrorism and, 43
Armed Forces Quarterly (journal), 155, 156

Armey, Dick, 117
Armor (journal), 155
Arms + cash template, 145–146
Arms embargo against Israel and Arab states, 2, 26, 104
Arms sales to Israel, US, 3, 30, 87, 128, 132, 145, 150–151
Arquilla, John, 158
Arrow anti-missile system, 144, 181
Ashkenazi, Gabi, 153
Assad, Bashar, 55
al-Assad, Hafiz, 12
Atoms for Peace Program, 168
Ayalon, Daniel, 47
AZEC. *See* American Zionist Emergency Council (AZEC)

Baghdad Pact, 2
Baker, James, 6, 267
Bakri, Muhammad, 205
Balancing of interests test, 199, 203
Balfour Declaration, 83, 216, 239
Bank Hamizrahi v. Migdal, 201
Barak, Aharon, 196, 200, 201, 203, 204
Barak, Ehud, 8, 11–15, 59, 151, 236, 271
BARD. *See* Binational Agricultural Research and Development Fund (BARD)
Bar-Ilan, David, 246
Bar-Ilan University, 218, 220
Bar-On, Mordechai, 265
Basic laws, 188, 198, 201–204
Basiji, 172
Bayme, Steven, 18
Beckett, Ted, 241
Begin, Menachem, 5, 6, 89, 261–262, 265
    relationship with evangelical Christians, 232–233, 240, 245–246
Beilin, Yossi, 47, 91
Beinisch, Dorit, 204–205, 207
Ben, Aluf, 200
Ben-Ali, Zine el-Abidine, 40, 65
Ben-Ami, Jeremy, 91
Ben-Artzi, Efraim, 146
Bendheim, Jack, 269, 270
Ben-Gurion, David, 2, 3, 84, 146–147, 148, 150, 191
    Christian Zionists and, 232, 239, 245
Ben-Meir, Yehudah, 224
Ben-Zvi, Avraham, 151
Ber, Yisrael, 150
Bernstein, Louis, 227
Besser, James, 274
Biden, Joe, 60, 70, 72, 73

Biltmore Program, 84
Binational Agricultural Research and Development Fund (BARD), 134–135
Binational Industrial Research and Development Foundation (BIRD), 134, 135
Binational Science Foundation (BSF), 134, 135
bin Laden, Osama, 39, 67–68
BIRD. *See* Binational Industrial Research and Development Foundation (BIRD)
Blackstone, William Eugene, 238
Blackstone Memorials, 238–239
Blair, Tony, 45, 53, 277
Blau, Ury, 207–208
B'nai B'rith, 85, 260
Boycott, divestment, and sanctions efforts (BDS movement), 243–244
Boykin, William, 154
Brandeis, Louis, 82, 83, 191, 203, 206, 207, 208
Breira, 19, 89, 257, 259–261
Brennan, William, 197, 203
Breslau, Isadore, 83
Brickner, Balfour, 259
Bridges for Peace, 244
Bright Star exercises, 144
Briley, Gaylord, 232
Britain
    influence on Israeli army, 146–147, 149
    influence on Israeli legal system, 188
    as Israeli ally, 2, 3
    public sympathies in Middle East conflict, 101, 103
Brit Tzedek v'Shalom (Alliance for Peace and Justice), 91, 272–273
Brock, William, 132
Brog, David, 240–241
Brown, Gordon, 169
BSF. *See* Binational Science Foundation (BSF)
Bubis, Gerald, 263–264
Burns, Nicholas, 38, 130
Burns, William, 40
Bush, George H. W., 15, 70, 137
Bush, George W., 15
    Arafat and, 38, 39, 41, 43–44, 49
    evangelical Christians and, 233, 242, 248
    Jewish vote in 2004 election, 48–49
    nuclear weapons and, 173
    Republican commitment to Israel and election of, 117
    Sharon and, 38, 47–48
    support for Israel, 15–16, 37
    worldview, 70–71

Bush administration (George H.W.), Arab-Israeli conflict and, 6, 267–268
Bush administration (George W.), Arab-Israeli conflict and, 37–57
  from Arafat's death to Hamas election victory, 49–51
  from Hamas seizure of power to end of Bush administration, 55–57
  from Hamas victory to seizure of Gaza, 51–55
  from inauguration to 9/11, 37–38
  from June 2002 to November 2004, 44–49
  Middle East peace process and, 271–272
  military aid to Israel, 130–131
  from 9/11 to June 2002, 39–44
Byroade, Henry, 85

California, trade and investment office in Israel, 134
CAMERA. See Committee for Accuracy in Middle East Reporting in America (CAMERA)
Camp David Accords, 5, 13, 31, 124, 129–130
Carter, Jimmy, 5, 177, 233
Case for Democracy, The (Sharansky), 47
Catastrophe Zionism, 208
Catholics, attitudes toward Israel, 115–116
Cavari, Amnon, 16
Censorship
  in context of war against terrorism and, 204–207
  film, 199–200, 205–206, 208
  of Israeli press, 190–192, 195–197, 199–200
Center for Israeli Peace and Security, 263
Centrist Orthodoxy, 223
Centrist pro-Israel lobby, 92–93
Chabad-Lubavitch, 226
Chafets, Zev, 236
Chamberlain, Neville, 83
Cheney, Dick, 42, 54–55
Cheshin, Mishael, 204
Chief Rabbinate, as halachic decider, 218, 225
Chomsky, Noam, 260
Christian Coalition, 236
Christian Council on Palestine, 84
Christian Friends of Israel, 244
Christian Friends of Israeli Communities, 241
Christian groups, American public attitudes toward Israel and, 114–117. See also Evangelical Christians and Israel
Christianity Today (journal), 240
Christian Right, 117, 248
Christians United for Israel (CUFI), 96, 236, 249, 250

Christian Zionism, 114–117, 232–235, 240–241, 244. See also Evangelical Christians and Israel
Chronicle of Philanthropy (journal), 250
Church, Frank, 138
Churchill, Winston, 24, 185
Clinton, Bill
  Barak and, 12–15
  Intifadas and, 8, 14
  Israeli-Palestinian peace process and, 6–7, 8, 9–11, 32, 268, 269, 271
  Netanyahu and, 246
Clinton, Hillary, 62, 64, 65, 68, 69, 73
Clinton Parameters, 14, 54
Cohen, Eliot, 157
Cohen, Steven M., 224
Cohen, Stuart A., 17
Cohen v. California, 206
Cold War
  Arab-Israeli relations post-, 32–33
  US-Israeli relations and, 4, 5, 22–23, 104–105, 106–107
Combat Forces Journal, 155
Committee for Accuracy in Middle East Reporting in America (CAMERA), 81
Committee on New Alternatives in the Middle East, 260
Conference of Presidents of Major American Jewish Organizations, 85, 87, 92, 96, 264, 270
"Constitutional Revolution, The" (Barak), 201
Cranston Amendment, 130
CUFI. See Christians United for Israel (CUFI)

Dagan, Meir, 64–65
Danin, Robert, 277–278
Danon, Dani, 274
Darby, John Nelson, 237–238
David, Steven, 17–18
Dayan, Moshe, 146, 149, 155, 259
Dayton, Keith, 50
Declaration of Independence (Israeli), 192, 193, 239
Defamation, Israeli law of, 196–197
DeLay, Tom, 43, 117
Democratic Party, attitudes toward Israel, 118–119
Democratization of Arab states, 37, 47, 49, 68, 74
Demographic factors, American public opinion on Israel and, 112–119, 120
Dennis v. United States, 191, 192
DePuy, William, 154, 156
Dershowitz, Alan, 206–207

Deterrence, nuclear weapons and, 170–172, 174, 176
Dimona nuclear installation, 150
Dine, Thomas, 87
Diplomacy
  as means to halt Iranian nuclear threat, 178–179
  Track Two, 266
Diplomatic Quartet, 44–46, 52, 55, 277
Dispensationalism, 115, 234, 237–238, 239, 251
Dorner, Dalia, 205, 206
Douglas, William O., 206
Druckman Chaim, 226
Dulles, John Foster, 2, 27, 85

East Jerusalem, 14, 60, 61, 62, 63
Eban, Abba, 85
Eckstein, Yechiel, 250
Economic relations between US and Israel
  economic aid to Israel, 139–140
  US foreign aid to Israel, 17, 70, 80, 108, 124–131, 136–137, 139–140
  See also Trade between US and Israel
Economic sanctions, as means to halt Iranian nuclear threat, 179–180
Economic Stabilization Plan, 130
Economic Support Funds (ESF), 125–126, 130, 131
Edelman, Peter, 264, 267
Educational level, American public attitudes toward Israel and, 112, 113
Egypt
  American public opinion on, 101, 103, 106, 107
  Arab Spring and, 65–66
  Israeli qualifying industrial zones in, 133
  Six-Day War, 28–29
  Suez War, 2, 3, 26–27
  ties to US, 31–32, 129–130, 144
  Yom Kippur War, 29–32
Egyptian-Israeli peace process, 4–5
Ehrman, Sara, 264, 270
Eichmann, Adolf, 202
Eisenhower administration, Arab-Israeli conflict and, 1, 2–3, 26–27
Eitan, Raful, 262
El Ard, 193
Elon, Benny, 245
Emergency Wartime Supplemental Appropriations Act, 137
Energy Independence and Security Act, 135
Ephraim Goes to the Army (Laor), 199
Episcopal Church, 243

ESF. *See* Economic Support Funds (ESF)
European Union, Diplomatic Quartet and, 44–46, 52, 55, 277
Evangelical Christians and Israel, 16, 19, 115, 116–117, 232–251
  American Jewish response, 246–250
  criticism of Bush for pressuring Israel on peace process, 43
  evangelical splits on Israel, 242–243
  evangelical splits with other Christians, 243–244
  evangelical theology and political activity, 233–235
  future of relationship, 250–251
  history of evangelical views on Jewish state, 237–241
  how evangelicals entered political mainstream, 235–237
  Israeli government and evangelicals, 244–246
  pro-Israel lobby and, 96–97
Evangelical tourism, 245

Falwell, Jerry, 9, 19, 115, 117, 232, 233, 235, 236, 240, 241, 246, 249, 250
Fatah-controlled government, 66–67, 273
Fatuna, David, 157–158
Fayaadism, 277–278
Fayyad, Salam, 59, 272, 273, 277
FAZ. *See* Federation of American Zionists (FAZ)
Feaver, Peter, 175
Federation of American Zionists (FAZ), 82–83
Film, censorship of Israeli, 199–200, 205–206, 208
Findley, Paul, 88
Fleischer, Ari, 39
Fleshler, Dan, 19, 92, 262
FMF. *See* Foreign Military Financing (FMF)
Ford administration, relations with Israel, 4
Foreign Affairs (journal), 155
Foreign Military Financing (FMF), 125, 127, 130–131, 145
Forrestal, James, 2, 25, 26
Foxman, Abraham H., 87, 248, 249
France
  public sympathies in Middle East conflict, 101, 103
  relations with Israel, 3, 128, 149
Frankfurter, Felix, 203
Freedman, Robert O., 15, 264
Freedman, Samuel, 262
Freedom of expression, in Israeli law, 189–192, 201, 203–204, 208

Free Trade Agreement (FTA), between US and
    Israel, 17, 124, 132–134
Friends of Peace Now, 263
FTA. *See* Free Trade Agreement (FTA)
Fuller, Melville, 238
"Fundamental Truths," 239
Furman, Gloria, 265

Gadhafi, Muammar, 67
Ganchrow, Mendy, 227
Gap year programs in Israeli yeshivot, 220–221
Gates, Robert, 64, 66
Gaulle, Charles de, 128
Gaza Strip, 3, 5, 37, 47, 227–228, 241
Gazit, Shlomo, 265
Gender, American public attitudes toward
    Israel and, 114, 115
Genesis 12:30, Christian Zionists and, 234–235
Geneva Accord, 91
Gesher, 220
Gilboa, Eytan, 103
Glazer, Nathan, 259
Goldberg, J. J., 87, 262
Goldmann, Nahum, 85
Goldstein, Baruch, 227
Gorbachev, Mikhail, 5
Gorenberg, Gershom, 246
Graham, Billy, 235–236
Gronich, Fred, 148
Grunis, Asher, 205
Gulf War, 6, 32, 267
Gunther, Richard, 264
Gush Emunim, 224, 225, 259, 260

Ha'aretz (newspaper), 200, 207, 250
Ha'aretz v. Electric Company, 196–197, 204
Haetzni, Elyakim, 224
Hagee, John, 19, 96, 234, 236–237, 241, 248,
    249
Haggard, Ted, 242
Ha'ir (magazine), 200
Halutz, Dan, 159
Hamas, 1, 17, 39
    Abbas and, 50–51
    attacks on/war with Israel, 7, 41, 52–53, 54,
        56–57, 58, 66
    electoral victory, 37, 51–52
    Iran and, 33, 34
    Israeli-Palestinian peace process and, 7, 46,
        54, 55
    nuclear weapons and, 170, 173, 174, 177,
        183
    Palestinian civil war and, 50

seizure of power in Gaza, 55, 72
    Syria and, 71
    unity pact with Palestinian Authority,
        275–276
Hamas-controlled government, 37, 51–52, 273
Haniyeh, Ismail, 51
Haredi Orthodoxy, 216, 223
Har Homa, 8
Hariri, Rafik, 71
Harkabi, Yehoshafat, 260, 265
Harlan, John, 206
Harris, David, 249
Harris, Fred (**Fred Gronich**), 148
Hart, Basil Liddell, 149
Hasmonean tunnel, secret opening of, 8, 269
Hawk missile sale to Israel, 150–151
Hebron, 7, 8, 60, 227, 269, 270
Herzl, Theodor, 216
Hidden Imam, 172–173
Hikin, Dov, 241
Hizbollah, 1, 12, 17, 39, 71
    nuclear weapons and, 170, 171, 173, 174,
        177, 183
    war with Israel, 33–34, 37, 53, 58
Holmes, Oliver Wendell, 191, 206
House, Edward, 83
Howe, Irving, 259
Hudna, 46
Hussein, Saddam, 32, 178, 182
Husseini, Faisal, 266

IAEA. *See* International Atomic Energy
    Agency (IAEA)
Ibish, Hussein, 276–277
Ibn Saud, Abdul Aziz, 24, 26
IDF. *See* Israeli Defense Forces (IDF)
IFCJ. *See* International Fellowship of
    Christians and Jews (IFCJ)
Independents, attitudes toward Israel, 118–119
Infantry School Quarterly (journal), 155
Inhofe, Jim, 117
Intellectual property rights, Israel and, 133,
    135–136
International Atomic Energy Agency (IAEA),
    63, 168, 170, 179
International Christian Embassy in Jerusalem,
    244, 245
International Fellowship of Christians and
    Jews (IFCJ), 250
Intifada, 8, 89, 105, 154, 266
    second, 8, 12, 13–14, 38, 39, 40–41, 71, 154,
        248, 271
IPF. *See* Israel Policy Forum (IPF)

Iran
    Arab states and, 33, 53
    disagreement between Israel and US over
        actions against, 58, 63–65, 70, 71
    Obama and, 58, 60
    support for terrorist groups, 33, 34
Iranian nuclear threat against Israel, 17–18,
    165–185
    appropriate response to, 183–185
    how threatens Israel's existence, 170–178
    Iran as suicide nation, 172–173
    Iranian behavior since 1973 revolution,
        173–174
    Iranian leaders in control of, 175–176
    Iranian nuclear program, 64–65, 167–170
    responding to Iranian threat, 64, 178–183
    vulnerability of Israel, 166–167
Iraq, 6, 32, 44, 108, 138, 157, 267
Iraq War, US relationship with Israel and,
    117–118
Iron Dome anti-rocket system, 70, 131, 144
Islamic Action Front, 33
Islamic Conference, 55
Islamic Jihad, 7, 39, 41, 46, 50, 66
Islamic Revolutionary Guard Corps, 173, 175,
    177
Israel
    American Orthodox Jews and (see
        American Orthodox Jews and Israel)
    American public attitudes toward (see
        American public attitudes toward Israel)
    challenges to existence of, 165
    converging interests with Arab states,
        33–34
    economic relations with U.S. (see Trade
        between US and Israel)
    evangelical Christians and (see Evangelical
        Christians and Israel)
    immigrants to, 137
    Iranian nuclear threat against (see Iranian
        nuclear threat against Israel)
    as liability to U.S., 22–23
    military strikes against nuclear facilities,
        182–183, 184, 185, 240
    military ties with US (see Military ties,
        US-Israeli)
    move to right politically, 59–70
    nuclear capability of, 3, 62–63, 71, 150,
        171–172, 180–181
    qualifying industrial zones in Jordan and
        Egypt, 133
    qualitative military edge, 128, 144
    relations with Hamas-led government, 51–52

    US foreign aid to, 17, 70, 80, 108, 124–131,
        136–137, 139–140
    war with Hamas, 52–53, 54, 56–57, 58
    war with Hizbollah, 37, 53, 58
    See also Arab-Israeli conflict
Israel Advocacy Initiative, 248
Israeli Arabs, Yeredor v. Central Elections
        Committee and, 192–194
Israeli Defense Forces (IDF)
    American influence on, 148, 158–159
    American observation of, 154–156
    American volunteers in, 148
    British influence on, 146–147, 149
    military facilities, 151–152
    military journals, 155
    military training, 152–153
    poor performance in Second Lebanon War,
        158–159
    topics for inquiry, 156–158
Israeli defense industry, US aid and, 131
Israeli-Jordanian peace treaty, 32
Israeli law, American influence on, 18,
        187–208
    Basic Law: Human Dignity and Freedom,
        201–204
    censorship, 190–192, 195–197, 199–200,
        204–207
    contemporary issues, 204–209
    differences between US and Israeli systems,
        188–189, 193–194
    Kol Ha'am v. Minister of the Interior,
        190–192
    law of defamation, 196–197
    racist speech, 197–199
    Yeredor v. Central Elections Committee,
        192–194
    Yom Kippur War and, 194–196
Israeli-Palestinian peace process, 7–11, 13,
        14–15
    George W. Bush administration and, 38–51,
        54–57, 70–74
    Madrid peace conference, 6, 32, 105, 266,
        267
    Obama administration and, 59–74
    pro-Israel lobby and, 81
    Wye Accords, 10–11, 226, 270–271
    See also Oslo Accords
Israeli Policy Forum, 19
Israeli-Syrian peace process, 12
Israel Policy Forum (IPF), 89, 268–272, 270

Jabotinsky, Ze'ev, 262
Jafari, Mohammad-Ali, 175

Jaryis, Sabri, 260
Jefferson, Thomas, 208
Jenin Jenin (film) case, 205–206, 208
Jenkins, Jerry B., 237
"Jerusalem Declaration on Christian Zionism,
    The," 244
Jerusalem Post (newspaper), 241
Jesus Is Coming (Blackstone), 238
Jewish Agency, 136
Jewish Brigade, 146–147
Jewish Council for Public Affairs, 87, 90, 92,
    248
Jewish day schools, 216, 219, 220, 221
Jewish Defense League, 197, 261
Jewish Institute for National Security Affairs,
    81, 93
Jewish lobby. *See* Pro-Israel lobby
Jewish Observer (journal), 216
Jewish Peace Fellowship, 260
Jewish settlements, 8, 12, 66, 69, 95, 223–224,
    267
    criticism over, 6, 59, 60, 70, 263, 269–270,
        273
    evangelical Christian support for, 241
Johnson, Lyndon B., arms sales to Israel, 128,
    151
Johnson administration, relations with Israel,
    1, 3, 27–29
Joint Force Quarterly (journal), 156
"Jointness," 157–158
Jones, A. Jase, 240
Jones, James L., 91
Jordan, 28
    American public opinion on favorability of,
        101, 103, 106, 107
    Israeli qualifying industrial zones in, 133
    peace treaty with Israel, 7, 32
    US and Israeli support for, 1, 4
J Street, 16, 19, 72, 91, 93, 257, 272–274
JStreetPAC, 91, 273
J Street University, 273
Judicial activism/judicial restraint, 202
Judicial review, 201
Juniper Cobra, 144

Kahane, Meir, 197–198, 220, 224
Karine A (ship), 41
Kasztner, Rudolf, 202
Keaney, Thomas, 157
Kenen, Isaiah "Si," 86
Kennedy, Anthony, 203
Kennedy, John F., 150
Kennedy administration, relations with Israel,
    1, 3

Kerry, John, 48
Khalidi, Ahmed, 266
Khamenei, Ali, 64, 173, 175–176
Khatib, Ghassan, 266
Khomeini, Ayatollah, 168
King Hussein, 4, 8, 10, 28
Kissinger, Henry, 4, 5, 30, 87, 129
Klein, Morton, 89
Klutznick, Philip, 85
Knesset Christian Allies Caucus, 245
Kol Ha'am v. Minister of the Interior, 190–192

Lahav, Pnina, 18
LaHaye, Tim, 237
Lamm, Norman, 18–19, 224, 225, 226, 227
Landau, Moshe, 195, 197
Land for peace approach, 28, 241
Laor, Yitzhak, 199–200
Laor v. Film and Censorship Board, 199–200,
    208
Laskov, Haim, 146
Late Great Planet Earth, The (Lindsey), 237
Law of defamation, 196–197
Law of incitement, 202
Law of Return, 218, 225–226
Lebanon, 5–6, 53, 154, 158–159
Left Behind (LaHaye & Jenkins), 237
Left-wing pro-Israel lobby, 91, 92, 93
Lender, Marvin, 268–269
Lerner, Motty, 202
Levinger, Avraham, 224
Levinger, Miriam, 224
Lewis, Bernard, 173
Liability school, 22–23, 34, 35
Liberty University, 236, 250
Libya, 67, 138
Lichtenstein, Rav Aharon, 224, 227
Lieberman, Avigdor, 59, 273
Liebman, Charles S., 259–260
Lifton, Robert K., 268
Lincoln, Abraham, 192, 194
Lindsey, Hal, 237
Linkage argument, 23–25, 29
Livni, Tsippy, 56, 263
Loan guarantees, 88, 136–137, 267–268
Lookstein, Haskell, 226–227
Lovett, Robert, 25
Lubavitcher Rebbe, 224, 226

Ma'archot (journal), 155, 158
Macgregor, Douglas, 157
Madison, James, 201, 208
Madrid peace conference, 6, 32, 105, 266, 267
Makvosky, David, 15

Malachy, Yona, 244–245
Mandelbaum, Ron, 17
Manichaeanism, Bush administration and, 272
Mann, Theodore, 267
Marbury, William, 201
Marbury v. Madison, 201–202
Marcus, Mickey, 148
Margolies, Moses, 215
Marshall, George, 2, 25, 26
Marshall, John, 201
Massachusetts, trade and investment office in
    Israel, 134
McKinley, William, 238
Mearsheimer, John, 15, 22, 28, 32
Media watchdogs, pro-Israel, 81–82
Meimad, 220
Meir, Golda, 27, 145, 194, 232, 259
Meretz USA, 93
Mesbah-Yazdi, Mohammad-Taqi, 172
Messianism, 224, 272
Militarism, Bush administration and, 272
Military aid to Israel, 125, 126–128, 130–131,
    139–140
    American public opinion on, 108–109
    Foreign Military Financing (FMF), 125,
        127, 130–131, 145
Military censorship, 195–196, 200
Military journals, 155–156
Military Review (journal), 155, 156
Military strikes, against Iranian nuclear
    facilities, 182–183, 184, 185
Military ties, US-Israeli, 17, 143–159
    1948–1962, 146–150
    arms sales, 3, 30, 87, 128, 132, 145, 150–151
    effect on Israeli military effectiveness,
        158–159
    flow of ideas, 153–158
    memoranda of understanding, 153
    modes of inquiry, 154–156
    person-to-person influence, 151–153
    topics of inquiry, 156–158
Military training, Israeli, 152–153
Millennarians, 233
Miller, Aaron David, 271
Mitchell, George, 14, 57, 60, 68, 72, 273, 275
Mitchell Report, 38
Mizrahi, 83
Modern Orthodox Rabbinical Council of
    America, 217, 218
Modern Orthodoxy. *See* American Orthodox
    Jews and Israel
Mohammed VI, 40
Moody Monthly (journal), 239
Moral Majority, 236, 247

Morgan, J. P., 238
Mossad, *Shnitzer v. the Military Censor* and, 200
Mubarak, Hosni, 31–32, 40, 65
Mullen, Michael, 153
Muslim Brotherhood, 33, 66
Muslims, Obama's outreach to, 58, 72

Nachman, Ron, 223
Nakba Law, 208
Narkis, Uzi, 149
Nasser, Gamal Abdel, 26–27, 28, 105, 149, 181
Nathanson, Roby, 17
National Association of Evangelicals, 233,
    239–240, 242
National Community Relations Advisory
    Committee, 87, 88
National Conference of Evangelical Christians
    and Jews, 246
National Council of Young Israel, 226, 227
National Defense University, 17, 152
National Jewish Post & Opinion (newspaper),
    260
National Opinion Research Center, 101
Nat PAC, 88
Naval Vessel Transfer Act of 2008, 144
Naveh, Shimon, 157
Naylor, Sean, 157
Neoconservatives, criticism of Bush for
    pressuring Israel on peace process, 43
Netanyahu, Benjamin
    Bush and, 71
    Falwell and, 9, 246
    Hamas-Fatah agreement and, 67
    Jewish housing construction in East
        Jerusalem and, 60, 61, 62, 63
    J Street and, 273
    Obama and, 57, 58, 61, 62, 63, 71, 73
    Palestinian UN membership bid and, 275
    peace process and, 10, 59–60, 73, 269, 270–
        271
    as prime minister, 7–12
    Republicans and, 68, 69
Neusner, Jacob, 260
New York Times (newspaper), 42, 61, 73, 167,
    200, 237, 242, 260
New York Times v. Sullivan, 196, 197, 203
Niagara Bible Conference, 238
Niles, David, 25
9/11, Arab-Israeli conflict post-, 32–33, 39–44
Nixon, Richard, 30, 87, 129, 130, 145, 195
Nixon administration, support for Israel, 1, 4
Not a Good Day to Die (Naylor), 157
Nuclear Non-Proliferation Treaty, 62, 169, 180,
    184

Nuclear weapons
    Arab states and, 167
    as deterrent, 170–172, 174, 176
    Iran and (*see* Iranian nuclear threat against
        Israel)
    Israel and, 3, 62–63, 71, 150, 171–172,
        180–181
    unique destructiveness of, 166–167
Nusseibah, Sari, 266

Obama, Barack
    approach to world affairs, 57–58, 71
    on Arab Spring, 65–66, 68–70
    Iran and, 169
    Israeli-Palestinian peace process and,
        61–62, 72–74, 275
    J Street and, 273
    Libya and, 67
    mission against bin Laden and, 67–68
    Netanyahu and, 57, 58, 61, 62, 63, 71, 73
    outreach to Muslim world, 72
    relations with Israel, 15–16, 36, 59–60
    Syria and, 71
Obama administration, Arab-Israeli conflict
    and, 57–74, 250
Oil, US access to Mideast, 23, 25, 26, 32
Olim (immigrants to Israel), 218–219
Olmert, Ehud, 52, 54–55, 56, 66, 81, 228, 241
Olson, Arnold T., 240
Operational shock, 157
Operation Cast Lead, 66, 154, 204, 207, 274
Operation Defensive Shield, 42, 204, 205, 233
Operation Desert Storm, 108, 157
Oren, Michael, 91, 215
Orthodox Union, 93, 226, 227–228
Oslo Accords, 7, 9, 18, 32
    American Jewish peace movement and,
        268–272
    American Orthodox Jews and, 226–227
    pro-Israel lobby and, 81, 88–90

PA. *See* Palestinian Authority (PA)
PACs. *See* Political action committees (PACs)
Palestine, two-state solution for, 42, 47–48, 59,
    72–73, 242, 265, 276–277
Palestine Liberation Organization (PLO), 4, 7
Palestinian Authority (PA), 7
    acceptance of Road Map, 46
    converging interests with Israel, 34
    Hamas-led, 51–55
    relations with U.S., 11, 50
    unity pact with Hamas, 275–276
Palestinian civil war, 50, 55

Palestinian-Israeli peace process. *See* Israeli-
    Palestinian peace process
Palestinians
    American Jewish peace movement and,
        260–261, 264, 265–267, 273, 275–278
    American public attitudes toward, 100–102,
        103, 110–111
    evangelical Christians and, 242–243
    Palestinian terrorism, 7, 8, 10–11, 40–42, 43,
        46, 66. *See also* Hamas; Hizbollah;
        Islamic Jihad
Palileaks, 66
Parameters (journal), 155, 156
Pardes Institute of Jewish Studies, 220
Passion of the Christ, The (film), 249, 251
Peace movement. *See* American Jewish peace
    movement
Peace Now movement, 260, 261–268
Peace processes
    Egyptian-Israeli, 4–5
    Israeli-Palestinian (*see* Israeli-Palestinian
        peace process)
    Israeli-Syrian, 12
Pelosi, Nancy, 54
Percy, Charles, 88
Peres, Shimon, 7, 39, 130
Peretz, Yair, 245
Petraeus, David, 61
PLO. *See* Palestine Liberation Organization
    (PLO)
PLO Covenant, 260–261
Poalei Zion, 83
Pogrebin, Letty Cottin, 264
Political action committees (PACs), 82, 88, 91,
    273
Political activity, of American evangelical
    Christians, 235–237
Political parties, banning in Israel, 192–194
Pollard, Jonathan, 144
Powell, Colin, 38, 39–40, 42, 49, 117–118
Presbyterian Church (USA), 243
"President George W. Bush—A Friend of the
    American Jewish Community," 48–49
Press, regulation/censorship of Israeli,
    190–191, 190–192, 195–197
Prinz, Joachim, 259
Probable danger test, 191–192, 199, 200
Procaccia, Ayala, 205, 206, 207
Pro-Israel lobby, 79–97
    activities of, 81–82
    defining, 80–82
    divisions within, 89–95
    evangelical Christians and, 96–97

future of, 95–97
history of, 82–91
partisan makeup of, 119
present, 92–95
Project Nishma, 267, 269
Proselytizing of Jews, evangelical Christians
and, 247
Protestants, attitudes toward Israel, 115–117,
243–244. *See also* Evangelical Christians
and Israel
Publisher's Weekly (journal), 237

Qualitative military edge (QME), Israeli, 128, 144

Rabbinical Council of America, 225, 227
Rabbo, Yasser Abed, 91
Rabin, Yitzhak, 11, 196, 265
assassination of, 7, 18, 202, 225, 227, 269
military training, 149
peace process and, 4, 7, 32, 240, 268
settlement building and, 6
Race, American public attitudes toward Israel
and, 114
Racist speech, in Israel, 197–199
Rackman, Emanuel, 218
Raffel, Martin, 90
Rafsanjani, Akbar Hashem, 167, 168
Rapaport, Era, 224
Ratner, Yochanan, 146
Reagan, Ronald, 5–6, 132, 233
Reagan administration, AIPAC and, 87, 88
Realist school, 22–23, 184–185
Regent University, 236, 250
Regime change, as means to halt Iranian
nuclear threat, 181–182
Religious groups, American public attitudes
toward Israel and, 114–117
Republican Party
American Jewish peace movement and, 274
evangelical Christians and, 234, 250
Netanyahu and, 9, 68, 69
support for Israel in, 16, 117–119, 120
Research and development, cooperation
between Israel and US in, 134–135
Revolution in military affairs (RMA), 157, 158
Rice, Condoleezza, 39, 45, 49, 51, 52, 53–54, 56
Right-wing pro-Israel lobby, 92, 93–94
RMA. *See* Revolution in military affairs
(RMA)
Road Map for Middle East Peace, 37, 44–46,
48, 71, 272
Robertson, Pat, 19, 117, 235, 236, 241, 250
Rockefeller, John D., 238

Rodman, Peter, 27
Rogers, William, 4
Ronfeldt, David, 158
Roosevelt, Franklin D., 24, 83
Roosevelt administration (Franklin D.), Arab-
Israeli conflict and, 23–25
Rosenblum, Mark, 19
Rosenthal, Steven, 261
Ross, Dennis, 8, 14, 37
Rubin, James P., 11
Rubin, Neil R., 19, 115
Rudin, James, 247
Rumsfeld, Donald, 49
Ruskay, John, 260
Russia, Hamas and, 52. *See also* Diplomatic
Quartet; Soviet Union

Sadat, Anwar
peace process and, 5, 31, 128, 261–262, 265
Yom Kippur War and, 29, 30, 31
Said, Edward, 265
Said, Nuri, 27
Saleh, Ali Abdullah, 65
Saperstein, David, 259, 267
Sarkozy, Nicolas, 67, 169
Sartawi, Issam, 260
Satmar Hassidism, 216
Saudi Arabia, Arab-Israeli peace plan and, 42,
54
Sayeret Matkal, 264
Scalia, Antonin, 203
Schelling, Thomas, 166
Schiff, Jacob, 82
Schneller, Otniel, 274
School of Advanced Military Studies, 157
Scofield, C. I., 238
Scofield Study Bible, 238
Second Lebanon War, 53, 154, 158–159
Security fence, 47, 48
Senesh, Giora, 202–203
Senesh, Hannah, 202–203, 204
Seniora, Hanna, 266
Shalom Achshav (Peace Now), 258, 261–268
Shamgar, Meir, 196–197
Shamir, Yitzhak, 6, 88, 137, 267
Shanah bet, 221, 223
Shapiro, Andrew, 131
Sharansky, Natan, 47
Sharm al-Shaykh, 14
Sharon, Ariel, 8, 12, 129, 202
Abbas and, 50
Bush and, 38, 47–48, 71
effect of stroke on, 52, 72, 241

Sharon, Ariel *(continued)*
  Hamas's participation in elections and, 51
  Israeli forces and, 42, 43, 149
  loan guarantees and, 137
  Peace Now and, 262–263
  peace process and, 39, 46
  visit to Temple Mount/Haram, 13, 14
Shira Hadasha minyan, 220
Shnitzer v. the Military Censor, 200
Shtern, Yuri, 245
Shultz, George, 94
Shvil Ha-Zahav (Golden Mean), 226–227
Silver, Hillel, 83
Sinai Peninsula, 3, 28
Siniora, Fouad, 53
Six-Day War (1967), 3, 16, 28–29, 86, 105, 194,
  239
*Society of Foreign Journalists v. Minister of
  Defense,* 207
Sojourners (journal), 243
Solender, Sanford, 264
Soloveitchik, Joseph B., 217–218, 219, 222, 224
Sonneborn Circle, 148
Soviet Union, as ally of Arab states, 28, 30,
  104–105, 106–107. *See also* Cold War
Specter-Shelby Amendment, 89
Stalin, Joseph, 24
Stand for Israel, 235
Starry, Donn, 154, 156
Stassen, Glen, 243
Staub, Michael, 259, 260
Straits of Tiran, 3, 27, 28
Strict scrutiny test, 199
Stuxnet, 64
Suez War, 2, 26–27
Supercessionism, 238, 247
Syria
  Arab boycott of Israel and, 138
  invasion of Jordan, 1, 4
  Israeli bombing of nuclear reactor in, 33
  Obama and, 71
  peace process with Israel, 12
  support for Hamas and Hizbollah, 53, 60,
    67, 71
Szold, Henrietta, 82

Tamir, Avraham, 265
Tanzim, 46
Temple Mount/Haram, 8, 13, 14
Tenet, George, 38
Terminiello v. Chicago, 206
Terrorism, 1
  Arab-Israeli relations and, 32–33
  censorship in context of war against,
    204–207

  Palestinian, 7, 8, 10–11, 40–42, 43, 46, 66
  pro-Israel lobby and, 91
Terrorist groups, nuclear weapons and, 167,
  174, 177. *See also* Hamas; Hizbollah;
  Islamic Jihad
Think tanks, pro-Israel, 81
Ticktin, Max, 260
Time (magazine), 60, 73
Track Two diplomacy, 266
Trade between US and Israel, 17, 124–125,
  138–139
  Free Trade Agreement, 124, 132–134
  intellectual property rights, 135–136
  Israeli exports to U.S., 124, 133
  R&D cooperation, 134–135
  Training and Doctrine Command
    (TRADOC), 154, 156
Transformation Under Fire (Macgregor), 157
Truman, Harry S, Israel and, 2, 26, 103–104
Truman administration, Arab-Israeli conflict
  and, 1, 25–26, 85
Two-state solution, 42, 47–48, 59, 72–73, 242,
  265, 276–277
Tziklon (journal), 155

Union of Orthodox Rabbis, 216
Union of Progressive Zionists, 273
United Church of Christ, 243
United Israel Appeal, 136
United Methodist Church, 243–244
United Nations, request that Palestine be
  admitted as member state, 66, 275. *See
  also* Diplomatic Quartet
UN General Assembly Resolution No. 181, 101
UN General Assembly Resolution No. 3379, 240
UN Security Council Resolution No. 242, 3, 4,
  6, 28
UN Security Council Resolution No. 1397, 42
UN Security Council Resolution No. 1701, 53
United States
  Agreement on Trade in Agricultural
    Products, 134
  economic aid to Israel, 17, 70, 80, 108,
    124–131, 136–137, 139–140 (*see also*
    Trade between US and Israel)
  immigration of Jews to, 187–188
  military ties with Israel (*see* Military ties,
    US-Israeli)
  as peace mediator in Middle East, 35
  protection of free speech in, 189, 191–192,
    194, 198
  relationship with Israel (1948–2000), 2–15,
    22–35
  See also Arab-Israeli conflict, United States
    and

US Army War College, 17, 152
US foreign aid
    to Egypt, 32
    to Israel, 17, 70, 80, 108, 124–131, 136–137,
        139–140
US-Islamic World Forum, 68, 69
US-Israeli Energy Cooperation Act, 135
USS *Liberty,* attack on, 3, 144
Utopian Zionism, 208

van der Hoeven, Jan Willem, 245
Vilan, Abu, 264
Vineyard, James, 241
Vladimir Jabotinsky Medal, 246

Wagner, Donald, 243
Waldheim, Kurt, 240
Walker, Peter, 243
Wall Street Journal (newspaper), 237
Walt, Stephen, 15, 22, 28, 32
Waltz, Kenneth, 170
Walvoord, John F., 239
Ward, William, 50
War of Independence (Israeli), 2, 106, 165
Washington Institute for Near East Policy, 81
Washington Jewish Week (newspaper), 260
Washington Post (newspaper), 61, 73, 200, 270
Washington Times (newspaper), 49
Waskow, Arthur, 260
Waxman, Chaim, 223
Waxman, Dov, 16
Wedemeyer, Albert, 148
Weinberger, Caspar, 129, 154
Weizmann, Chaim, 84
West Bank
    development of state infrastructure in,
        277–278
    Israeli occupation of, 5, 9, 10, 28
    See also Jewish settlements
Whitney v. California, 203

"Why Evangelical Support for Israel Is a Good
        Thing" (Foxman), 249
Wikileaks, 63
Wilson, Woodrow, 83, 238–239
Wingate, Orde Charles, 146
Winograd Commission, 159
Wise, Stephen, 82, 83
Wolfensohn, James, 50
Women in Green, 220
World Intellectual Property Organizations
        Copyright Internet Treaties, 136
World War I, pro-Israel lobby and, 82–83
World War II, pro-Israel lobby and, 83–84
World Without Zionism Conference, 167
World Zionist Organization, 84
Wye Accords, 10–11, 226, 270–271

Yedidya synagogue, 220
Yeredor v. Central Elections Committee, 192–
        194
Yeshivat Har Etzion, 224
Yeshivat Shaalvim, 221
Yeshiva University, 215, 218, 221, 222, 223,
        224, 227
Yisrael Beiteinu Party, 59
Yoffie, Eric, 248–249, 274
Yom Kippur War (1973), 4, 29–32, 86, 129,
        194–196, 259
Young Israel movement, 220

Zayyad, Ziad Abu, 266
Zell, Rachel, 242
Zinni, Anthony, 40–41, 42
Zionism, 187–188
    American Orthodox Jews and, 215–216, 222
    Christian, 114–117, 232–235, 240–241, 244
    Utopian *vs.* Catastrophe, 208
Zionist lobby. *See* Pro-Israel lobby
Zionist Organization of America (ZOA), 16,
        83, 89, 93

About the Contributors

Steven Bayme is the national director of the William Petschek Contemporary Jewish Life Department of the American Jewish Committee and is also a visiting professor at the Jewish Theological Seminary. Among his publications are *American Jewry's Comfort Level* (coauthored with Manfred Gerstenfeld) and *Continuity and Change: A Festschrift in Honor of Irving Greenberg's 75th Birthday* (coauthored with Steven T. Katz).

Amnon Cavari, who recently received his PhD from the University of Wisconsin, is a lecturer in the Government Department of the Interdisciplinary Center, Herzliya, Israel. The title of his dissertation, which is now being considered for publication, is "The Party Politics of Presidential Rhetoric." The dissertation won the American Political Science Association's George C. Edwards Award for the best dissertation on the US presidency in 2009 or 2010.

Stuart A. Cohen is professor of political studies at Bar-Ilan University. Among his recent publications on Israeli security issues are *Israel and Her Army: From Collusion to Confusion,* and *Israel's National Security Law: Development and Dynamics, 1948–2011* (coauthored with Amichai Cohen).

Steven R. David is professor of political science and vice dean for undergraduate education at Johns Hopkins University. Among his recent publications are *Choosing Sides: Alignment and Realignment in the Third World* and *Catastrophic Consequences: Civil Wars and American Interests.*

Dan Fleshler, a media and public affairs consultant, is the author of *Transforming America's Israel Lobby—The Limits of Its Power and the Potential for Change.* He is also a longtime board member of Americans for Peace Now and is a member of J Street's Advisory Council.

Robert O. Freedman is the Peggy Meyerhoff Pearlstone professor of political science emeritus at Baltimore Hebrew University and is visiting professor of political science at Johns Hopkins University, where he teaches courses on the Arab-Israeli conflict and on Russian foreign policy. Among his recent publications are *Contemporary Israel: Domestic Politics, Foreign Policy, and Security Challenges* and *Russia, Iran, and the Nuclear Question: The Putin Record*.

Pnina Lahav is professor of law and law alumni scholar at Boston University. Among her recent publications are *Judgment in Jerusalem: Chief Justice Agranat* and *The Zionist Century*. She is working on a monograph on the 1956 Suez War and its significance in the history of foreign affairs.

David Makovsky is the Ziegler distinguished fellow and director of the Washington Institute for Near East Policy's project on the Middle East peace process. An adjunct professor of the School of Advanced International Studies of Johns Hopkins University, he is the author of numerous books on the Middle East, including most recently *Myths, Illusions, and Peace: Finding a New Direction for America in the Middle East* (coauthored with Dennis Ross).

Ron Mandelbaum is a researcher in the Macro Center for Political Economics in Tel Aviv. He is also a teaching assistant in the Department of Political Science of Tel Aviv University.

Roby Nathanson is director general of the Macro Center for Political Economics in Tel Aviv. He has served as director of the Histadrut's Institute for Economic and Social Research and headed Israel's Office for Economic and Social Planning During Peace at the prime minister's office in 1995.

Mark Rosenblum is professor of history at Queens College of the City University of New York, where he is director of the Center for Jewish Studies, the Michael Harrington Center, and the Center for Ethnic, Racial, and Religious Understanding. Among his recent publications is *The Jewish Condition: Challenges and Responses—1938–2008* (cowritten with William B. Helmreich and David Schimel).

Neil Rubin is editor of the *Baltimore Jewish Times* and is visiting assistant professor at the University of Maryland-Baltimore County. His recently completed doctoral dissertation, "American Jews and the Oslo Years," has been accepted for publication by Palgrave MacMillan.

Dov Waxman is associate professor of political science at Baruch College and the Graduate Center of the City University of New York. Among his publications are *The Pursuit of Peace and the Crisis of Israeli Identity: Defending/ Defining the Nation* and *Israel's Palestinians: The Conflict Within* (coauthored with Ilan Peleg).